THE EPISTLE TO THE ROMANS.

THE EPISTLE TO THE ROMANS

WITH NOTES CRITICAL AND PRACTICAL

BY THE REV. M. F. SADLER
LATE RECTOR OF HONITON AND PREBENDARY OF WELLS

WIPF & STOCK · Eugene, Oregon

Wipf and Stock Publishers
199 W 8th Ave, Suite 3
Eugene, OR 97401

The Epistle to the Romans
With Notes Critical and Practical
By Sadler, M. F.
ISBN 13: 978-1-62564-969-0
Publication date 6/18/2014
Previously published by G. Bell & Sons, 1888

INTRODUCTION.

THE GENERAL RECEPTION OF THE EPISTLE TO THE ROMANS BY THE CHURCH.

AS it has always been the province of the Church to decide upon what books are to be accounted Holy Scripture, and what books are not, we must first glance over the testimony of the Church to the place of this Epistle in the Canon.

Tracing the citations or references upwards, we find that Eusebius, born at the conclusion of the reign of Gallienus, writes: "The Epistles of Paul are fourteen, all well known and beyond doubt" (E. H. iii. c. 3); and a little further on he mentions that "the same Apostle in the addresses at the close of the Epistle to the Romans, has, among others, made mention also of Hermes," &c.

Origen wrote a commentary on this Epistle, "which is preserved entire only in a loose Latin translation by Rufinus."

Of the three great writers flourishing at the close of the second century—Irenæus, Clement of Alexandria, and Tertullian—I find that, in an index of quotations I have now before me, Irenæus quotes this Epistle alone above 70 times, Clement of Alexandria 114 times, and Tertullian 142 (and this in an index to only a part of his works).

This Epistle is also cited in the letter of the Churches of Lyons and Vienne, in the words (quoting from the letter as given in Eusebius), "These coming in close conflict endured every species of reproach and torture. Esteeming what was deemed great but little, they hastened to Christ, showing in reality that the sufferings of this time are not worthy to be compared with the glory that shall be revealed in us."

It is included amongst the Pauline Epistles in the Canon of Muratori (about A.D. 170). The notice is exceedingly interesting: "Epistolæ autem Pauli, quæ, a quo loco, vel quâ ex causâ directæ sint, volentibus intelligere ipsæ declarant. Primum omnium Corinthiis schisma hæresis interdicens, deinceps Galatis circumcisionem, Romanis autem ordine Scripturarum, sed et principium earum esse Christum intimans," &c. Upon which Professor Westcott has this note: "*Ordine Scripturarum*, according to the general tenour of the Scriptures. Compare Tregelles, p. 48, who points out that there are more quotations from the Old Testament in the Epistle to the Romans than in all the other Epistles of St. Paul together."

We next come to Justin Martyr, in the middle of the second century. He quotes or alludes to the Epistle twelve or fourteen times. Most of his quotations are worth reproduction. I will give eight.

1. "For when Abraham himself was in circumcision he was justified, and blessed by reason of the faith which he reposed in God, as the Scripture tells. Moreover, the Scripture and the facts themselves compel us to admit that he received circumcision for a sign, and not for righteousness." (Dial. ch. xxiii.)

2. "But now, by means of the contents of these Scriptures, esteemed holy and prophetic among you, I attempt to prove all (that I have adduced), in the hope that some one of you may be found to be of that remnant which has been left by the grace of the Lord of Sabaoth for the Eternal Salvation." (Dial. xxxii.)

3. "No one, not even of them (the fleshly seed of Abraham), has anything to look for, but only those who in mind are assimilated to the faith of Abraham." (Dial. xliv.)

4. "Because of your wickedness God has withheld from you the ability to discern the wisdom of His Scriptures. Yet there are some exceptions, to whom, according to the grace of His long suffering, as Isaiah said, He has left a seed for salvation, lest your race be utterly destroyed as Sodom and Gomorrah." (Dial. lv.)

5. "For Abraham was declared by God to be righteous, not on account of circumcision, but on account of faith, for, before he was circumcised, the following statement was made regarding him: 'Abraham believed God, and it was accounted to him for righteousness.' And we, therefore, in the uncircumcision of our flesh, believing God through Christ, and having that circumcision which is of advantage to us who have acquired it—namely, that of the heart—we hope to appear righteous before, and well-pleasing to, God." (Dial. xcii.)

INTRODUCTION. vii

6. "For God sets before every race of mankind that which is always and universally just, as well as all righteousness; and every race knows that adultery, and fornication, and homicide, and such like are sinful: and though they all commit such practices, yet they do not escape from the knowledge that they act unrighteously whenever they so do, with the exception of those who are possessed with an unclean spirit, and who have been debased by education, by wicked customs, and by sinful institutions, and who have lost, or rather quenched, or put under, their natural ideas." (Dial. xciii.)

7. "For as he (Abraham) believed the voice of God, and it was imputed unto him for righteousness, in like manner we, having believed God's voice spoken by the Apostles of Christ, and promulgated to us by the prophets, have renounced even to death all the things of the world." (Dial. cxix.)

8. "That (circumcision) was given for a sign, and not for a work of righteousness, as the Scriptures compel you to admit." (Dial. cxxxvii.)

I have given the above citations somewhat in full, inasmuch as they seem to show what an invaluable store of controversial argument this Epistle contains to enable the Christians to deal with the Jews, ever their bitterest and most formidable opponents. Justin was well acquainted with the letter, and permeated with the spirit of St. Paul's Epistles; and, if he thus used them in controversy, no doubt multitudes of others did the same, so that we cannot over-estimate their importance in the Early Church.

In the Epistles of Ignatius to the Smyrneans (shorter form) there is one very clear reference to Rom. i. 3; and one in the Epistle to Polycarp, and a reference to xiv. 10-12 in the Epistle of Polycarp.

There are also two or three very distinct references to this Epistle in the first Epistle of Clement, the contemporary of St. Paul, particularly to Rom. iv., "Abraham as justified by faith;" and xii. 5, "Every one members one of another."

THE ORIGIN OR FIRST PLANTING OF THE ROMAN CHURCH.

Nothing whatsoever is told us in Scripture respecting the origin of the Roman Church. Late traditions ascribe it to St. Peter, who is supposed to have commenced there an Episcopate of twenty-five years in the year 42. But it is impossible to believe that if he had been residing in Rome as its Bishop, St. Paul would have sent to him no loving greeting. St. Paul writes to the Christians of Rome as if they required no organization, and had been so long established in the truth of the Gospel that "their faith was spoken of throughout the whole world." It seems most probable from the mention of " strangers of Rome, both Jews and proselytes," who evidently, from their mention here, joined with the rest in the exclamation, "We do hear them speak in our tongues the wonderful works of God,"—that such, being devout men, would speak when they returned to Rome of what they had heard and seen; and so a Church principally of Jews or Israelites would be formed in the Imperial city very soon after Pentecost. Such a Church so composed would be reckoned under the Apostles of the circumcision; but, as time went on, Rome being the centre of the world, and having intercourse with all Greece and the shores of the Mediterranean, many Greeks and inhabitants of Asia and Syria, who had been converted by St. Paul or his disciples, or those who worked in concert with him, would settle in Rome, and so a Church, which was originally Jewish, would, as to its members, become more and more Gentile, and so would come more and more under the Apostolate of St. Paul. St. Paul evidently considered that, having had the Gentiles committed to him by the Lord, the Church of Rome was under him. On this account he wrote his Epistle to them with authority (xii. 3), and speaks to them as if they were part of that offering of the Gentile world which he was ordained to make to God through the preaching of the Gospel (xv. 16).

But now the question arises, Was he the first Apostle or person with apostolic or quasi-apostolic powers who visited them? It is generally assumed that he was, on two grounds: 1st, That he says he desired to see them, in order that he might impart to them some spiritual gift, that is, one which only an Apostle could impart; and 2ndly, That as his rule was not to build upon another man's foundation, he would not have gone to Rome to impart to them such gifts if another Apostle had done so before him: but I believe that both these assertions are made under a great misconception. It seems certain that, in what he writes in Rom. xii., the Apostle implies that the Roman Church possessed spiritual gifts—for prophecy, ministry, teaching, and ruling, are all reckoned in 1 Corinth. xii. and xiv. as spiritual gifts. I cannot believe that all the gifts of

Rom. xii. 6, 7, were natural gifts, sanctified by faith or grace. They seem, though not so many in number, to be (some at least), of the same supernatural character as those mentioned in other Epistles.

And then, with respect to the Apostle not preaching or otherwise exercising ministerial functions in Churches founded by others, this is fully answered by the very probable assumption that there was, as time went on, a considerable change in the nationality of the Roman Church. If a Church, originally Jewish, became mainly Gentile, it would, according to the compact, come under the supervision of the Apostle of the Gentiles, even if St. Peter himself had founded it, or visited it after it was founded.

And now let us look a little more closely into this alleged neglect of the Church of Rome by the Apostolic College.

Though we have no record of its foundation, all the circumstances of the case point to a very early establishment of a Church in Rome.

Its faith was, thirty-five years or so after its founding, spoken of throughout the whole world. Long before his wish was gratified, St. Paul himself earnestly desired to see it. Now are we to suppose that for, in all probability, twenty-five years, the existence of this Church was ignored by the Apostles of the Circumcision? Supposing that Peter and John could not find time to visit it, was there no quasi-Apostle, such as Barnabas, whom they could send to organize, and confirm, and supply such needful gifts as prophecy, and teaching, and Church rule? If the Church of Jerusalem sent Barnabas to Antioch, surely someone with equal powers might be sent to the Church of the world's metropolis, notwithstanding its distance. But to this it is answered that we have no record of such a visit in the Acts of the Apostles, which we should have if the Apostles, or any one of them, had noticed the Church of Rome. But the people who allege this seem, one would say, never to have read with any attention the Book of the Acts. For, if they had, they must have known that of the original twelve Apostles ten are never mentioned from the middle of the first chapter to the end of the book. Of the two who are mentioned one, St. John, altogether drops out of sight after his visit to Samaria in the company of St. Peter, to the close of the history, a period, according to Usher, of thirty-two years, and Simon Peter himself is only once mentioned from the death of Herod in A.D. 44 to the close (the single mention being that of his presence in the council), a period of twenty-one years. Common sense tells us that such a Church could not have remained unvisited either in person or by a sufficiently empowered representative, by men who had any respect for the Apostolic function which Christ had commissioned them to exercise; and that someone must have conferred upon the Roman Christians the gifts alluded to in Rom. xii. 6, is plain.

The early settlement of the Roman Church is by many ancient writers associated with St. Peter in conjunction with St. Paul. Three times by Eusebius; first in the following: "But the holy Apostles and disciples of our Saviour being scattered over the whole world, Thomas, according to tradition, received Parthia as his allotted region; Andrew received Scythia, and John, Asia, where, after continuing for some time, he died at Ephesus. Peter appears to have preached through Pontus, Galatia, Bithynia, Cappadocia, and Asia, to the Jews which were scattered abroad, who also, finally coming to Rome, was crucified with his head downwards, having requested of himself to suffer in this way. Why should we speak of Paul spreading the Gospel of Christ from Jerusalem to Illyricum, and finally suffering martyrdom at Rome under Nero? This account is given by Origen in the third book of his Exposition of Genesis. After the martyrdom of Paul and Peter, Linus was the first that received the Episcopate at Rome. Paul makes mention of him in his Epistle from Rome to Timothy, in the address at the close of the Epistle, saying, 'Eubulus and Pudens, and Linus, and Claudia, salute thee.'" (Bk. iii. ch. i. 2.)

The second: "During this time (Trajan's reign) Clement was yet Bishop of the Romans, who was also the third that held the Episcopate there after Paul and Peter, Linus being the first, and Anenclitus next in order." (Book iii. c. 21.)

The third is a quotation by Eusebius from Irenæus: "The blessed Apostles having founded and established the Church of Rome, transmitted the office of the Episcopate to Linus. Of this Linus Paul makes mention in his Epistles to Timothy. He was succeeded by Anenclitus, and after him Clement held the Episcopate, the third from the Apostles." (Irenæus "Against Heresies," Book iii. ch. 3, quoted in Eusebius, B. v. ch. 6.)

Now the reader should remember that Eusebius was an ecclesiastical historian who was born within two hundred years of St. Paul's imprisonment in Rome, and that Irenæus, in his youth, could have conversed with men who had seen both Apostles.

I cannot but think that it is very probable, then, that St. Peter

INTRODUCTION.

visited Rome some time during that long period of his active ministerial life, of which no mention is made by St. Luke, very probably during the six years between his deliverance from prison on the death of Herod and his presence at the council. If any Church, from its situation, natural influence, and piety, demanded his presence, this Church of Rome did. People who write as if they believed that St. Peter could not visit Rome except to organize a papacy, and that his presence in the city would have sanctioned all the extravagances of the Bishops of Rome during the last thousand years, seem to me to play into the hands of Romanists. A man who had been a disciple of the Baptist, who had been chosen by the Lord Himself from amongst those disciples, who had seen the whole life of the Lord during His entire ministerial career, in whose house the Lord had constantly lodged, who had heard all His discourses and His parables and seen all His miracles, who, though not the Prince of the Apostles, was undoubtedly their leader and spokesman —to whom first of the Apostles the Lord appeared on the day of His Resurrection, and who had received such a commission as that given by the lake of Galilee, who was commissioned by the Lord to open the door of faith—first to the Jews, then to the Gentiles—surely the presence of such an one would be most edifying to any Church, even though he had nothing like the controversial ability of St. Paul, and was perhaps his inferior in decisiveness of action.

TIME AND PLACE OF WRITING.

All expositors are of one mind, that this Epistle was written during the three months of the Apostle's stay in Greece, at Corinth, mentioned in Acts xx. 3.

That it was written from Corinth appears from the fact that it was conveyed to the Roman Church by Phœbe, a deaconess of the Church at Cenchrea, the port of Corinth, on the east side of the isthmus. Gaius, in whose house St. Paul was lodged at the time (xvi. 23), is probably the person mentioned as one of the chief members of the Corinthian Church in 1 Cor. 1, 14., though the name was very common. Erastus, here designated the treasurer of the city ($οἰκονόμος$, xvi. 23, E. V. "chamberlain"), is elsewhere mentioned in connection with Corinth (2 Tim. iv. 20); see also Acts xix. 22.

Secondly, having thus determined the place of writing to be

xii INTRODUCTION.

Corinth, we have no hesitation in fixing upon the visit recorded in Acts xx. 3 during the winter and spring following the Apostle's long residence at Ephesus, as the time during which the Epistle was written. For St. Paul, when he wrote the letter, was on the point of carrying the contributions of Macedonia and Achaia to Jerusalem (xv. 25, 27). And a comparison with Acts xx. 22, xxiv. 17 and also with 1 Cor. xvi. 4, 2 Cor. viii. 1, 2, ix. *sq.*, shows that he was so engaged at this period of his life (see Paley's "Horæ Paulinæ," ch. ii. 1). Moreover, in this Epistle he declares his intention of visiting the Romans after he has been at Jerusalem (xv. 23-25), and that such was his design at this particular time appears from a casual notice in Acts xix. 21.

"The Epistle then was written from Corinth during St. Paul's third missionary journey, on the occasion of the second of the two visits recorded in the Acts. On this occasion he remained three months in Greece (Acts xx. 3). When he left the sea was already navigable, for he was on the point of sailing for Jerusalem when he was obliged to change his plans. On the other hand it cannot have been late in the spring, because, after passing through Macedonia, and visiting several places on the coast of Asia Minor, he still hoped to reach Jerusalem by Pentecost (xx. 16). It was, therefore, in the winter or early spring of the year that the Epistle to the Romans was written. According to the most probable system of chronology adopted by Anger and Wieseler this would be the year A.D. 58."— Smith's "Dictionary of the Bible," article by Dr. Lightfoot.

THE PURPOSE FOR WHICH THE EPISTLE WAS WRITTEN.

The purpose for which St. Paul was directed by God to write this Epistle was intimately connected with the great controversy or struggle then going on respecting the Church, whether it was to be a Catholic body, on its inner or spiritual side the mystical body of Christ, inheriting all the privileges of the Sion of the Prophets, or whether it was to be an appanage of Judaism. On the settlement of this controvery hung all the future of the Church, as One, Catholic, and Apostolic. The purpose of the Epistle, it seems to me, was to assure the Gentiles that being justified by faith they possessed the only true Justification, and having accepted Christ

INTRODUCTION. xiii

and been grafted into Him as the True Vine, and Divine Olive-tree of grace, they were the true elect people of God.

Very few writers seem to me to write with any idea of the difficulty of the questions of Justification and Election in the infancy of the Church from the power of the Judaizing faction everywhere; for I think it is very plain that few Jews, even when thoroughly converted, and sincerely Christian, could rise completely above their prejudices as St. Paul did, and welcome unreservedly every converted Gentile as a trophy to the power of Christ.

One of the strongholds of the Judaizer seems to have been the letter of the Old Testament, coupled with the absence for at least half a century of anything but a mere fragment of our New Testament. For instance, it must have been many years after the death of St. Paul before all his Epistles were collected and distributed amongst the Churches: St. John's Gospel was not generally received before the close of the century, and the Apocalypse and Epistles of Peter and John certainly not till the same time. Now during the whole of this period the Scriptures would be the Old Testament—the Prophets and other books of the Old Testament would form by far the greater part of the reading of Scripture in the Churches (Justin Martyr), the Psalms would form the leading feature in the daily service. During this time the definite instruction about the person and work of Christ would be from one Gospel, which in the Churches of Jewish origin would be, I believe, St. Matthew, in the Churches founded by St. Paul it would be (latterly, of course) St. Luke. I find that many write as if they imagined that immediately on the publication of a book of the New Testament it must be assumed to be known everywhere; but this seems a great mistake. It would take many years before the Pauline Epistles would be received *ex animo* by Churches in which the Jewish element prevailed to any considerable extent.

Now let us see how this bears on the retention of circumcision under the New Covenant and on Justification by Faith. In the roll of the Scriptures in every Church would be read (Gen. xvii. 7-13): "I will establish my covenant between me and thee, and thy seed after thee in their generations for an everlasting covenant, to be a God unto thee, and to thy seed after thee. This is my covenant . . . . Every man child among you shall be circumcised . . . . And my covenant shall be in your flesh for an everlasting covenant."
How could this be met? It is generally supposed that St. Paul

xiv INTRODUCTION.

meets it sufficiently when he cites Abraham as an example of one who was justified before he was circumcised, "He received the sign of circumcision, a seal of the righteousness of the faith which he had, being yet uncircumcised." But see how the Judaizer would rejoin. He would say, "It is all very well to cite Abraham as a solitary instance of justification before circumcision, but this can be no rule for any of his descendants, whether fleshly or spiritual, because God, in commanding him to be circumcised, commanded all his descendants. 'I will establish my covenant between me and thee and thy seed after thee in their generations.'"

Now the full and effectual answer to the Judaizer is not in a solitary text, or an inference from such text, but in the Catholic faith. St. Paul's opening words of this Epistle settle everything to a real believer in his Gospel: "The gospel of God, concerning his Son Jesus Christ our Lord, which was made of the seed of David according to the flesh; and declared to be the Son of God with power, according to the spirit of holiness, by the resurrection from the dead." Now if such an One came into the world to establish a covenant of salvation, as He assuredly did, it is clear that His covenant must supersede all others. Moses was esteemed by the Jews the greatest man that God had ever raised up; but if St. Paul's Gospel be true he was a mere servant; whereas He Whose faith or Gospel St. Paul preached was the Son, the only Son, a Son over His own house—the own Son of God—the Eternal Son, Who was in the bosom of the Father, and had come down to be the Light and Life of men. His covenant then must supersede every preceding one, and if He ordained a sign or sacrament to initiate men into it such sign or seal must render every other one obsolete. For a Gentile to receive circumcision after he had received baptism, was not only unbelief, but impertinent folly.

So far for circumcision, and now about Justification. Nothing can be clearer than that very much in the Old Testament is on the side of Justification by the works of the law; thus "ye shall keep my statutes and my judgments which, if a man do, he shall live in them" (Levit. xviii. 5, and Deut iv. i.; vi. 1, 2; Psalm i., xv., cxix. *passim;* Ezekiel xviii. *passim*). Now how did the Apostle meet this? Not, as is usual in these latter days, by citing passages which show the unsatisfactoriness of all human works—far less by telling them, as Luther did, that when God demanded works He spoke ironically, or that works done before Justification are splendid sins; but by

INTRODUCTION. xv

showing them that by the coming of the Son of God amongst us in our nature, by His having assumed a Body for us, and by having in this passible Body offered Himself as a Sacrifice for sin, and having been raised again in this Body, but in an exalted and glorified state, He has put us in possession, if we will but receive it, of an infinitely higher and better righteousness, even the righteousness of God, which, if we accept it, will enable us to fulfil the law, not in the letter, but in the spirit. The words by which St. Paul really sets aside justification by the law, or by any law, are an embodiment of the Catholic faith, and are, "What the law could not do, in that it was weak through the flesh, God sending his own Son in the likeness of sinful flesh, and for sin, condemned sin in the flesh; that the righteousness of the law might be fulfilled in us, who walk not after the flesh, but after the Spirit." It is clear that if, for purposes of Justification, we can be made partakers of the righteousness of a Person in the Trinity, all reliance on any other method is a virtual refusal of the grace of God in its highest possible manifestation.

Such is the procedure of the Apostle with respect to Judaism and Judaizing. He meets it with *the* faith—not faith, but *the* faith. Faith in the own Son of God, the Eternal Son, to be apprehended by our faith, and when apprehended, to be in us the power of the highest imaginable righteousness—the righteousness of God. Now it is because of all this that the Apostle lays such stress in his preaching upon the Lord's Resurrection. It is God's seal to the truth of all that His Son assumed to be and to do. It is the proof of His Incarnation, Atonement, and future Judgment. It is also the means by which the grace of Justification reaches us.

But, notwithstanding all this, the difficulty in the matter of Judaism was not fully met. There was another very formidable question, that of Apostolic authority. The Judaizers everywhere disparaged the Apostleship of St. Paul. He was inferior to the twelve, especially to their leader, and to the Bishop of Jerusalem, the Lord's brother. He had not seen the Lord, as the others had. Now it was of vital importance that this should be met, and it could only be met in one way, and that is, by the evidence of miracles. And in this way St. Paul meets it. "In nothing am I behind the very chiefest apostles, though I be nothing. Truly the signs of an apostle were wrought among you in all patience, in signs, and wonders, and mighty deeds " (2 Cor. xii. 12), and again in this Epistle, "Througn mighty signs and wonders, by the power of the Spirit of God; so that from Jerusalem, and round about unto Illyricum, I have fully preached the gospel of Christ" (xv. 19).

Now this is what he appealed to in the matter of Justification by faith in his Epistle to the Galatians: "He therefore that ministereth to you the Spirit, and worketh miracles among you, doeth he it by the works of the law, or by the hearing of faith?" (Gal. iii. 5.)

And no doubt this was what lay at the root of his desiring to see them, "*that he might impart unto them some spiritual gift, to the end that they might be established.*" It is to be remembered that at this early time no Church which contained any Jewish element could be thoroughly *established* unless a final decision had been come to respecting this Judaical question, and one of the first elements in this decision was the Apostolate of St. Paul, and there was but one absolute and incontrovertible seal to his Apostleship, and that was the power of doing the same mighty works which SS. Peter and John did.

The full and free acknowledgment of his Apostleship, then, was essential to the unity, purity, and Catholicity of the Church. It was in no spirit of self-assertion, no matter how lawful, that he insisted upon his Apostleship, but because "a dispensation had been committed to him." It would have been treason to his Master if he had been behindhand in this matter.

And now again we see how it is that he gave such prominence to the preaching of the Resurrection. It is not only because through His Resurrection the life-giving Nature of the Lord is made over to us, to be in us a new power to do the will of God; but it is also because the Lord's Resurrection is that article of the faith which sets its seal to the truth of all the rest. How do we know that Jesus is the very Son of God—His Only Son—that His Death is all-atoning, His Body and Blood capable of being received by all His people for their Spiritual food and sustenance, and that at the last day He will raise all men from the dead, and judge them for the deeds done in the body? Simply and solely because of His Resurrection. If He be dead then the Apostolic witness and preaching is vain, we are yet in our sins. If He lives we shall live also.

Such, then, is the purpose of the Epistle to the Romans. It was

INTRODUCTION.

written for the assurance of the Church of Christ, that its children were the true children of Abraham, and that it possessed the true election—that the Church itself and every member of it might claim a part in the words, "Israel mine elect." "Mine elect shall inherit it." "Jacob, whom I have chosen." "Fear not Jacob, my servant, and thou Jeshurun whom I have chosen." "The Lord hath chosen Zion to be an habitation for himself—he hath longed for her. This shall be my rest for ever, here will I dwell, for I have a delight therein."

And it has not failed. It has established the Church in its right to be the inheritrix of all the ancient promises. Now take as one illustration of this the universal, the Catholic use of the book of Psalms. Anyone unacquainted with the Church in its final development in the New Testament as Catholic and Apostolic, would, if he looked over the Book of Psalms, pronounce it to be the book of devotion of a local religious community. He would ask, What right have Christians all over the world to claim the promises made to Zion and to Jerusalem, and to use the book as if they had an interest in it all? And yet it would be the gravest loss to us if we could not, for no words, if spiritually used, can bring us so near to God. Let the reader turn to two Psalms—the sixty-second and sixty-third—and say how can anyone imagine sweeter intercourse with God? Now the use of this book, with all the promises of it, and of all the other books, such as Isaiah, we can claim to be absolutely ours. They belong to us far more than they can possibly belong to any earthly city of God. And under God, the man who claimed them for us, and by his determination and courage won them for us, was St. Paul—not, of course, apart from other inspired teachers. but still he was foremost among them to claim for the Catholic Church its full rights in the Word of God.

We do not sufficiently realize this because we tacitly assume that we enter into all the promises of God to Israel as a matter of course; but God in the New Testament teaches us that this is by no means a matter of course. In the earliest stage of the Church it was fiercely disputed, and even St. Paul himself tells us that we are not a tree of God in our own right, but come in to fill a blank place in the original one, where some of its branches had been broken off. (Rom. xi.)

Perhaps we are tempted to think that when God introduced a New Dispensation, He should have discarded the use of the terms of the Old—that there should have been an entirely new nomenclature of love and grace—but it is not so; God judged otherwise. The Head and Minister is Joshua, the Messiah. He is our Passover, our sin-offering, our Melchizedec, our David. His Church is the Israel of God—the Jerusalem from above—the Mount Zion. His people are not only the good, the virtuous, the devout, but the elect, the called, the flock, the bride, the children of Abraham.

MANUSCRIPTS AND ANCIENT VERSIONS OF ST. PAUL'S EPISTLES.

A. Codex Alexandrinus. See Scrivener's Introduction, pp. 93-101. 2 Cor. iv. 13—xii. 6 wanting.

א. Codex Sinaiticus. Scrivener, pp. 86-93.

B. Codex Vaticanus. Scrivener, pp. 101-117. Wants the whole of the two Epistles to Timothy, and those to Titus and Philemon; also Hebrews ix. 14 to end.

C. Codex Ephræmi rescriptus. Scrivener, p. 119.

D. Codex Claromontanus. Scrivener, pp. 163-166. In Royal Library at Paris (not D. Codex Bezæ). Middle of sixth century, Greek and Latin.

E. Codex Sangermanensis now Petropolitanus. Scrivener, p. 166. Ninth century, a Greek Latin MS. Defective in Rom. viii. 21-23, xi. 15-25, nearly all of first Epistle to Timothy, Hebr. xii. 8-xiii. 25.

F. Codex Augiensis. Scrivener, p. 167. Greek and Latin. End of ninth century.

G. Codex Boernerianus. At Dresden. End of ninth century. Scrivener, pp. 169-172.

H. Codex Coislinianus. Only a few fragments, in all 56 verses. Scrivener, p. 172.

I. Only fragments.

K. Codex Mosquensis. Ninth century. Scrivener, p. 162.

L. Codex Angelicus. At Rome. Ninth century. Scrivener, p. 162.

M. N. O. Q. Fragments.

P. Codex Porphyrianus. A Palimpsest, beginning of ninth century. Scrivener, p. 162.

Of Cursives Scrivener enumerates 295.

Latin Versions.
- *d.* Latin of Codex Claramontanus.
- *e.* Latin of Codex Sangermanensis.
- *f.* Latin of Codex Augiensis.
- *g.* Latin of Boernerianus.

Vulg. Amiatinus, Fuldensis, &c.

A COMMENTARY.

THE EPISTLE TO THE ROMANS.

CHAP I.

PAUL, a servant of Jesus Christ, [a] called *to be*

Anno
DOMINI
60.

a Acts xxii. 21.
1 Cor. i. 1.
Gal. i. 1.
1 Tim. i. 11.
& ii. 7. 2 Tim.
i. 11.

1. "Paul, a servant of Jesus Christ," &c. A servant, literally, a bondman, a slave. He was not a hired servant who sold his services to a master for wages, whilst retaining the liberty of leaving his household when it suited him; but a slave, the property of his master. Now it was he whom we especially look upon as the Apostle of Christian liberty who thus described himself, and if any man ever served Jesus in the spirit of freedom it was this man; so that the word "slave," by which he here calls himself, does not look to the spirit of his service, but to the fact that as a slave he was the absolute property of his Divine Master. He held that he was bought with that Master's Blood, and that besides this he was under the greatest conceivable obligations to Him, for in redeeming him Jesus Christ had restored to Paul his true self, so that from the time when Christ claimed him, his soul was restored to union with the Father of spirits, and he had a place in His family for ever as His son.

"A servant of Jesus Christ." Here we have the Lord's Godhead asserted by implication. How could Paul call himself the slave or property of anyone in the unseen and eternal world, except of God? We have only to conceive of the Apostle calling himself the servant of some angel, or archangel, or principality, or power, to see how utterly impossible such a thing could be, and that no one can say that he serves any being in heaven except the God of heaven.

CALLED TO BE AN APOSTLE. [ROMANS.

^b Acts ix. 15. & xiii. 2. Gal. i. 15.   an apostle, ^b separated unto the gospel of God.

"Called to be an apostle." St. Paul here asserts that "blasphemer and injurious" though he had once been. Christ had seen fit to call him to exercise that unique ministry to which He had designated the twelve. To him, as much as to them, belonged the words "As my Father sent me, so send I you;" "He that heareth you heareth me;" and to him there belonged more particularly and personally the commission, "Go ye and teach all nations;" "Go ye to all the world;" for he was the Apostle of the Gentiles, not of any particular tribe, or race, or nation, but "of the Gentiles."

St. Paul was called at his conversion, for then the Lord said of him to Ananias, "Go thy way; for he is a chosen vessel unto me, to bear my name before the Gentiles, and kings, and the children of Israel" (Acts ix. 15).

"Separated unto the gospel of God." He says of himself (Gal. i. 15) that God had separated him from his mother's womb. He was separated both secretly and openly—secretly, in God's election, as Jeremiah had been (Jerem. i. 5), but God openly manifested the fact of this election when the Holy Ghost said, "Separate me Barnabas and Saul to the work whereunto I have called them." There may be also a reference to St. Paul's nurture and education, his preservation from actual defilement by gross sin, his education so that he should be brought up in the knowledge of Rabbinical traditions at the foot of Gamaliel, and yet be acquainted with Greek literature and philosophy. All this, coming to pass by God's all-ruling providence, set him apart, long before he was conscious of it, as a fitting instrument for the accomplishment of God's purposes of grace.

"The gospel of God." The gospel here is opposed to the law; and means not only the verbal message respecting Christ, and the proclamation of that message by word of mouth, but the whole system of means of grace, ministries of reconciliation, bonds of union, and accounts of the life and works of Jesus, which is called sometimes the Gospel dispensation, sometimes the kingdom of God.

2. "Which he had promised afore by his prophets in the holy scriptures." It is one of the great anxieties of the Apostle to show

CHAP. I.] CONCERNING HIS SON. 3

2 (^c Which he had promised afore ^d by his prophets in the holy scriptures,)

3 Concerning his Son Jesus Christ our Lord, ^e which was ^f made of the seed of David according to the flesh ;

c See on Acts xxvi. 6. Tit. i. 2.
d ch. iii. 21. & xvi. 26. Gal. iii. 8.
e Matt. i. 6, 16. Luke i. 32. Acts ii. 30. 2 Tim. ii. 8.
f John i. 14. Gal. iv. 4.

3. "Jesus Christ our Lord." These words in the Revised Version are placed at the end of the fourth verse. This is the order of the words in the Greek.
"Which was made." "Which was born."

that the Gospel was not a new thing, an invention of his time, but foretold by the Spirit through the utterances of all the prophets, from Moses to the seer whose short prophecy was the last added to the roll. The very form which the propagation of the Gospel took—that of preaching—was predicted: thus Isaiah, "How beautiful upon the mountains are the feet of him that bringeth good tidings" (Is. lii. 7), and "Who hath believed our report?" (liii. 1) In this matter of preaching consisted the great contrast between the old and the new dispensations: Aaron and his successors were never commanded to preach, the prophets who were sent to comfort or reprove the chosen people were never commanded to disciple the heathen ; but the inauguration of the new state of things was in the words "Go ye and disciple all nations;" "Go ye into all the world, and preach the gospel to every creature."

And now the Apostle comes to lay down the contents of the message. It is all

3. " Concerning his Son Jesus Christ our Lord, which was made of the seed," &c. "Which was made," rather, which was "born" of the seed of David. Inasmuch as Mary and not Joseph was His parent, St. Paul here asserts that she was of the house and lineage of David, as well as her husband.

"According to the flesh." The flesh here signifies the whole and perfect human nature; as the Creed words it, "Perfect man, of a reasonable soul and human flesh subsisting." Thus the Apostle enunciates the Incarnation, the Son of God was made man; and now he proceeds to set forth, as the counterpart to this, not so much the Godhead or Natural Sonship, which he had already done in calling Him the Son of God, as the declaration and demonstration of that Sonship.

† Gr. *determined*.
g Acts xiii. 33.

4 And †ᵍ declared *to be* the Son of God with

4. "And declared to be the Son of God with power, according to the Spirit of holiness," &c. This word "declared" is the translation of ὁρίζειν, to define, separate, limit, and may be translated "and was separated" from all other beings to be the Son of God, and so was defined or marked to be the Son of God. And thus we come to the rendering of the two Greek Fathers Chrysostom and Theodoret. Chrysostom, "What, then, is the being 'declared?' It is being shown, being manifested, being judged, being confessed, by the feelings and suffrage of all, by Prophets, by the marvellous Birth after the flesh, by the power which was in the miracles, by the Spirit through which He gave Sanctification, by the Resurrection through which He put an end to the tyranny of death."

Theodoret's exposition seems to me admirable. "Before His Cross and Passion the Lord Christ, not only to the other Jews, but to the Apostles themselves, did not seem to be God. For they stumbled at His human weaknesses when they saw Him eating and drinking, and sleeping, and weary, and not even the very miracles led them on to the opinion that He was God. And so when they had seen the miracle wrought on the sea of Galilee they said, 'What manner of *man* is this that even the winds and the sea obey him?' and so also the Lord said to them, 'I have many things to say unto you, but ye cannot bear them now. Howbeit, when he the Spirit of truth shall come, he will guide you into all the truth.' And again, 'Abide here in this city until ye be endued with power from on high, when the Holy Ghost shall come upon you.' Before His Passion, then, their opinions respecting Him were of such a sort as those. But after His Resurrection and Ascension into heaven, and the coming of the Spirit, and the miracles of every kind which they performed by the invocation of His Adorable Name, all they who believed acknowledged that He was God, and the only begotten Son of God. This, then, the Divine Apostle taught, that He Who was named the Son of David according to the flesh, was defined and demonstrated to be the Son of God, through the power which they exercised by the Holy Spirit after the Resurrection of our Lord Jesus Christ from the dead."

"With power." Various significations are given to these words: some hold that there is an implied contrast between the weakness of the nature according to the flesh and the power of the

CHAP. I.] BY THE RESURRECTION. 5

power, according ^h to the Spirit of holiness, by the resurrection from the dead: ^h Heb. ix. 14.

Divine Sonship; others that "with power" signifies that He was manifested in impressive fashion, powerfully, strikingly; but there is little real difference between these.

"According to the Spirit of holiness." This seems to signify that it was by the Holy Spirit, Who was the immediate Agent in His Resurrection, that He was declared to be the Son of God. It would then signify "according to the witness of the Holy Spirit." Many, on the contrary, consider that there is an implied contrast between "according to the flesh" and "according to the Spirit;" and that as the first undoubtedly means according to His human or lower nature, so the second signifies according to His higher or Divine nature; and John iv. 24 is cited, where He says that "God is a spirit." The objection to this latter view seems to be that the Divine Nature in our Lord is never called the "Spirit of Holiness," though, of course, His Spirit is divinely holy. Christ has, as man, a perfectly holy human spirit, but the Resurrection was not intended to demonstrate this, but that He was the Son of God in deed and in truth, God's own proper begotten Son. Now Christ had prophesied that the third Person in the Godhead, the Comforter, the Holy Spirit, should "glorify him" (John xvi. 14); and if the Holy Spirit be the immediate Agent in the Resurrection of Christ, as He undoubtedly will be in our resurrection (Rom. viii. 11), then, with all deference to the good and learned men who have held the contrary, we must believe that the Spirit of Holiness here means the Holy Spirit.[1]

"By the Resurrection from the dead." Christ, if we may so speak, had rested the truth of all His claims, especially His claims to be the Son of God, and the Christ, on His Resurrection; so that, however we take the intermediate words "with power," and

---

[1] There is another objection which seems to me very weighty against understanding the Spirit of Holiness to be the Divine Nature of the Lord. If we take "according to the flesh" to be according to His human nature, and "according to the Spirit of holiness" to be according to His spiritual Divine existence, do we not seem to deny that, according to his whole manhood, He is the Son of God? God and man is one Son of God—one Christ—and thus in St. Luke (St. Paul's Gospel) we read, "the Holy Ghost shall come upon thee, and the power of the highest shall overshadow thee, therefore also that Holy Thing which shall be born of thee, shall be called the Son of God."

5 By whom [1] we have received grace and apostle-

[1] ch. xii. 3. & xv. 15. 1 Cor. xv. 10. Gal. i. 15. & ii. 9. Eph. iii. 8.

"according to the Spirit of holiness," Jesus Christ is defined or determined to be the Son of God by His Resurrection from the dead.[1]

Such is the Gospel of St. Paul. It may be asked, Why does he make no mention of the atoning Death? Because both the Incarnation and the Resurrection imply the atoning Death. He took upon Him a nature of flesh and blood which could be separated in death, and being the flesh and blood which was assumed by the Eternal Son, that Death could be no ordinary death, but its virtues must be as far reaching as the effects of the sin for which God ordained it to be the remedy; and the Resurrection implies the previous Death, and stamps it with God's seal of all-sufficiency. But, undoubtedly, we learn from this stress laid upon the Resurrection, that St. Paul held it to be the leading feature of his Gospel in its aspect of being good tidings. The proclamation of the Crucifixion by itself could be no good tidings, because death was the common lot of all men; but if it was followed by the Resurrection, it was the best of all possible good tidings to a sinful race, for it assured them that the Son of God had on the cross effected that for which He had been nailed to it, even reconciliation with God.

I have dwelt thus at large upon this declaration of the Gospel on the part of St. Paul, because in it he sets forth his Gospel as consisting primarily of outward objective facts, and not of abstract doctrines, much less of inward experiences. The Gospel, according to St. Paul, was not justification by faith, though that was a direct and necessary deduction from his doctrine, neither was it a sense of assurance, but what he says that it was when he categorically describes it in his First Epistle to the Corinthians as the evidence of the Resurrection (1 Cor. xv. 1-11). The fullest conceivable embodiment of it is the creed of the Catholic Church.

5. "By whom we have received grace and apostleship," &c. By whom, *i.e.*, through Christ as the Mediator and Head of the Church.

---

[1] Some take the resurrection from the dead here to be not our Lord's Resurrection, but the resurrection of all men in Him; but this seems impossible, for St. Paul is speaking of the manifestation of Christ as the Son of God in the preached Gospel. Now He will not be manifested as *the* Resurrection of all men, till the last day: at present His own Resurrection is taken as the pledge of it.

ship, ‖ for ^k obedience to the faith among all nations, ¹ for his name:

6 Among whom are ye also the called of Jesus Christ:

‖ Or, *to the obedience of faith.*
k Acts vi. 7.
ch. xvi. 26.
l Acts ix. 15.

The ultimate source of grace is God the Father, " Thine they were, and thou gavest them me " (John xvii. 6).

" Grace and apostleship." Some, as Augustine, take this to mean that he first received grace—the common grace of the dispensation, as forgiveness, membership in the Body of Christ and the Holy Spirit for his personal sanctification, and then also apostleship, which was an unique gift, in which, so far as the Roman Christians were concerned, he stood alone. He asserts this apostleship as a reason why he wrote to persons whom he had never seen, with the authority which he assumes throughout his Epistle. Some think that the words describe one thing, " the grace of apostleship;" thus Theodoret: " For he himself has appointed us to be preachers, committing to us the salvation of all the Gentiles, and bestowing grace analogous to the preaching."

" For obedience to the faith among all nations." Some suppose that only the reception of the faith is here meant; for when men receive and believe the preaching, they obey God, their faith itself being an act of obedience to a Divine command; but must we not rather interpret it by the similar expression in chap. xv. 18, " to make the Gentiles obedient by word and deed "? Each particular of the Gospel has not only to be received but to be obeyed. The Death of Christ is to make us each personally die to sin, the Crucifixion is that they who are Christ's should crucify the flesh with its affections and lusts; the Resurrection of Christ should oblige us to walk in newness of life; the abiding of Christ in heaven is that we should set our affections on things above.

" For his name," *i.e.*, that the name of Christ may be glorified. This is a proof of the Lord's Godhead, that as the Name of God is dishonoured or honoured by the wickedness or holiness of those who name it (Rom. ii. 24), so it is with the Lord's Name.

" Among whom are ye also the called of Jesus Christ." " Among numberless other Gentiles who have received the faith are ye also who through the preaching of the word have received the calling of Jesus Christ." This he says in order to include them under his commission.

BELOVED OF GOD. [ROMANS.

<small>m ch. ix. 24.
1 Cor. i. 2.
1 Thes. iv. 7.
n 1 Cor. i. 3.
2 Cor. i. 2.
Gal. i. 3.
o 1 Cor. i. 4.
Phil. i. 3. Col.
i. 3, 4. 1 Thes.
i. 2. Philem. 4.</small>

7 To all that be in Rome, beloved of God, ᵐ called *to be* saints: ⁿ Grace to you and peace from God our Father, and the Lord Jesus Christ.

8 First, ᵒ I thank my God through Jesus Christ

---

7. "To all that be in Rome, beloved of God, called to be saints." If anyone had in such a city as Rome separated himself from the heathenism and wickedness around him, and embraced the Gospel, it was a sure sign of God's grace working in him, and that he was "beloved of God," and must "abide in His Love."

"Called to be saints." "Saints" is here used, not in its modern sense of very holy and devout persons, but as signifying Christians, who by their profession and their baptism are assumed to be separated from the world. Thus the Jews were to God "a kingdom of saints and an holy people," and throughout the book of the Acts "Saints" is the common appellation of Christians (Acts ix. 32, 41). By their calling of God, and their acceptance of the call, they were saints dedicated to God and partakers of all the privileges of the Gospel, for they were part of the Holy Catholic Church.

"Grace to you and peace from God our Father," &c. Here the Apostle invokes grace and peace upon them equally from God and from Christ, as if they came from both alike. Thus Chrysostom: "See in this passage the 'from' is common to the Father and the Son. For he did not say, 'Grace be unto you and peace from God the Father through our Lord Jesus Christ,' but 'from God the Father, and our Lord Jesus Christ.'"

But why is not the Holy Spirit also mentioned? Because He is the gift here invoked from God and Christ. He is the power proceeding from the Father and the Son, Who comes into the Christian to fill him with grace and peace.

8. "First, I thank my God through Jesus Christ for you all." An exordium worthy of this blessed spirit, and able to teach all men to offer unto God the firstlings of their good deeds and words, and to render thanks, not only for their own, but also for others' well-doing (inasmuch as the Romans had not been evangelized by St. Paul); which also maketh the soul pure from envy, and grudging, and draweth God in a greater measure toward the loving spirit of them that so render thanks (Chrysostom).

"Through Jesus Christ." That is, through Him as the One

CHAP. I.] GOD IS MY WITNESS. 9

for you all, that ᵖ your faith is spoken of through- ᵖ ch. xvi. 19.
out the whole world. 1 Thes. i. 8.

9 For ᑫ God is my witness, ʳ whom I serve   ᑫ ch. ix. 1.
2 Cor. i. 23.
Phil. i. 8.
1 Thes. ii. 5.
ʳ Acts xxvii.
23. 2 Tim. i. 3.

8. "Is spoken of." Rather, "proclaimed, announced." Vulg., *annunciatur*.

Mediator: all intercourse with God, whether prayer, intercession, praise, thanksgiving, or eucharists, must be offered in His Name to God, inasmuch as all grace comes from God through Him.

"That your faith is spoken of throughout the whole world." Many treat this world-wide fame of the Christians of Rome as if it was natural, because of Rome being the centre and metropolis of the world; but there seem to be many indications of the fact that the Roman Christians were pre-eminent amongst Gentile Churches for faith and holiness; and what wonder? If there was any place upon earth of which it might be said that Satan's seat was there, surely it would be Rome, and so *that* would be the very place where God would raise up a special witness to the power of His truth. We can scarcely account for the Apostle's earnest desire to see Rome, except there was something very exceptional in the faith of the Church there. This is one of those places from which we learn that the progress of Christianity attracted far more attention than the infrequency of the notices of it in heathen writers would lead us to believe.

9. "For God is my witness, whom I serve with my spirit in the gospel of his Son, that," &c. It has been surmised that St. Paul here calls God to witness to the truth of a comparatively unimportant fact; but nothing can be unimportant which brings out the spiritual unity of the Church, and the care which its members have for one another's advancement in the Divine life. Chrysostom asks: "Will, then, any one of us be able to boast that he remembers, when praying at his house, the entire body of the Church? I think not. But Paul drew near to God in behalf, not of one city only, but of the whole world, and this not once, or twice, or thrice, but continually." It is worthy of notice that St. Paul, in several of his Epistles to particular Churches, mentions what he prays for on behalf of each Church, and each prayer is different, showing that he did not pray for them in general terms, but according to his knowledge of their particular wants.

with my spirit in the gospel of his Son, that *without ceasing I make mention of you always in my prayers;

10 ᵗMaking request, if by any means now at length I might have a prosperous journey ᵘby the will of God to come unto you.

| Or, *in my spirit*, John iv. 23, 24. Phil. iii. 3.
* 1 Thes. iii. 10.
ᵗ ch. xv. 23, 32. 1 Thes. iii. 10.
ᵘ James iv. 15.

---

9. "Always in my prayers." The Revisers of 1881 take this with beginning of next verse, "Always in my prayers making request."

"Whom I serve with my spirit in the gospel of his Son." This is not said as bringing the vain worship of the heathen or empty forms of the Pharisaic Jew into contrast with his purer spiritual worship, but as strongly asserting his own sincerity in his prayers for them. He worshipped God in the spirit, in that part of his nature which God had expressly fitted to have communion with the Father of spirits.

"In the gospel." This, of course, means not only in preaching, but in building men up, and in uniting them to the Christ Who was preached. Preaching is not mere proclamation or heralding, but proclamation for an end, the gathering together of souls, and uniting them to Christ.

10. "Making request, if by any means now at length." Here he specifies one of the desires which he prayed to have accomplished, but which seems to have been constantly thwarted ("by any means," "now," "at length"). The first recorded expression of this desire is in Acts xix. 21, when he was in Ephesus. It was his intention to go to Rome as soon as he had paid his next visit to Jerusalem, but such was not God's will. There must intervene the two years at Jerusalem, and the, to all appearance, most disastrous voyage in which he was shipwrecked; but was this voyage really disastrous? Not a hair of his head, or of those that were with him, perished. God gave him, we believe, not the bodies only, but the souls of all that sailed with him; and we know not how different his reception at Rome might have been if he had not come under the protection and patronage of Julius, whose friendship he made in this voyage. His prayers were answered in a way he little thought, but so that the "things which happened unto him fell out rather unto the furtherance of the Gospel" (Phil. i. 12).

CHAP. I.] OFTENTIMES I PURPOSED. 11

11 For I long to see you, that ˣI may impart unto you some spiritual gift, to the end ye may be estab- lished; ˣ ch. xv. 29.

12 That is, that I may be comforted together ‖ with you by ʸ the mutual faith both of you and me. ‖ Or, *in you.* ʸ Tit. i. 4.

13 Now I would not have you ignorant, brethren, that ᶻ oftentimes I purposed to come unto you, (but ᵃ was let hitherto,) that I might have some ᵇ fruit ‖ among you also, even as among other Gentiles. 2 Pet. i. 1. ᶻ ch. xv. 23. ᵃ See Acts xvi. 7. 1 Thes. ii. 18. ᵇ Phil. iv. 17. ‖ Or, *in you.*

12. "Mutual faith." Rather, "common faith."
13. "Let hitherto," "hindered hitherto."

11. "For I long to see you, that I may impart unto you some spiritual gift." The German commentators warn us that we are not to take "spiritual gift" in its natural acceptation of "miraculous gift," which only Apostles could impart, but simply of the mutual comfort which any ordinary Christian could give to, and take from, those with whom he was holding converse. But why is this? The Apostle would not come to them as an Apostle if he did not impart to them something special; and he evidently intended to come to them as an Apostle, and not as an ordinary minister. And surely the imparting to them some such spiritual gift as those which he imparted to other Churches would not hinder him from enjoying mutual comfort with them through their mutual faith. If he enabled some of them to prophesy and others to heal the sick, their faith in Him Who sent him could not fail to be increased, and his comfort in seeing that Christ acknowledged him as their Apostle would be increased also ; which comfort would be the fruit of the faith common to them and to himself, which faith, even in an Apostle, admitted of some increase. I do not think then that the Apostle spoke words of mere Christian courtesy in reminding them that the benefit would not be wholly on their side, but words of truth, if, as we must suppose, the grace of faith in all imperfect human beings is capable of increase.

13. "Now I would not have you ignorant, brethren, that oftentimes I purposed," &c. He throws this in as a vindication of himself; he said he had longed to see them; why, then, had he not visited them long before this? The answer is, he had hitherto been

14 ᵉ I am debtor both to the Greeks, and to the Barbarians; both to the wise, and to the unwise.

ᵉ 1 Cor. ix. 16.

15 So, as much as in me is, I am ready to preach the gospel to you that are at Rome also.

16 For ᵈ I am not ashamed of the gospel of Christ: for ᵉ it is the power of God unto salvation

ᵈ Ps. xl. 9, 10. Mark viii. 38. 2 Tim. i. 8.
ᵉ 1 Cor. i. 18. & xv. 2.

16. *"Of Christ"* omitted by אּ, A., B., C., D., E., G., 5, 17, 67, 137, 171, 178, d, e, g, Vulg., Syriac, Copt., Arm.; retained by K., L., P., and most Cursives.

hindered, for he greatly desired to have, as the Apostle of the Gentiles, some fruit among them. He trusted, if he preached in Rome, to win some more souls to Christ, who should be his hope, his joy, his crown of rejoicing, in the day of the Lord (1 Thess. ii. 19).

14. "I am debtor both to the Greeks, and to the Barbarians; both to the wise," &c. The Greeks called all those who spoke any other language than Greek barbarians; so here the Apostle divides the whole Gentile world into two divisions, and there is no doubt that he repeats the idea in the latter clause. The Greeks assumed to be the wise of the earth. Philosophy seemed to be exclusively theirs. The Romans sent their youth to Greek schools or universities, so the Apostle for the time honoured their claim. It may be asked, however, seeing that he is writing to Rome, why he does not mention the Romans: and the answer is very interesting: for very many years the Roman Church was Greek in its language, and probably recruited itself mainly from the Greek-speaking population. It used, for instance, a Greek liturgy, and the Roman-speaking Church was African.

15. "So, as much as in me is, I am ready to preach the gospel to you that are at Rome also." The strict grammatical rendering of this verse is difficult: the sense, however, is plain, and is that which is given in our Authorized, to which the Revisers have suggested no alteration. "I have no control over the circumstances of my life, I must leave all to the providence of God, but as far as I myself personally am concerned, I am ready to preach the gospel to you at Rome."

16. "For I am not ashamed of the gospel of Christ," &c. It may be asked, how came he to write this, seeing that he wrote, "God forbid that I should glory save in the cross of our Lord Jesus Christ," &c.

CHAP. I.] THE JEW FIRST. 13

to every one that believeth; ᶠ to the Jew first, and also to the Greek.

17 For ᵍ therein is the righteousness of God re-

ᶠ Luke ii. 30, 31, 32. & xxiv. 47. Acts iii. 26. & xiii. 26, 46. ch. ii. 9.
ᵍ ch. iii. 21.

16. "To the Jew first." "First" omitted by B. and G. only.

We shall see if we remember what the Gospel was. It was the proclamation that a crucified Jew, one of a despised and hated race, had reconciled all men to God by His Death, and the proof of this reconciliation was His Resurrection. The unbelieving Jew received this announcement with unbounded hatred and scorn, the Greek with all possible superciliousness and contempt. And so one who did not fully believe the Gospel would be ashamed of proclaiming such a salvation. St. Paul believed that this seeming weakness—this foolishness—of the Gospel of a crucified and risen Jesus, was power, and not human power but the power of God—the power of God to save the human race from all its evils, even from sin and death.

"To the Jew first and also to the Greek." This was the rule ever observed by the Apostle. He first sought out the synagogue, and preached to his countrymen or to the religious proselytes, hoping that through their conversion a freer course might be given to the word of God. In the beginning of this Epistle, in which he will have to say so much to humble the pride of the Jews, he asserts this principle of God's dealings, in order to show that he desired to keep for the Jew the pre-eminence which God had assigned to him.

17. "For therein is the righteousness of God revealed from faith to faith," &c. The words "the righteousness of God" taken by themselves, without any reference to any context, or the known opinions of the writer or utterer of them, can have but one meaning, which is, the good, holy, and just character of Almighty God, but throughout this Epistle the Apostle seems to connect two other ideas with this righteousness; that it can be imputed or at least that, as it exists in Jesus Christ, it can; and that it can be imparted; but no matter what shades of meaning the term may bear, its root is always in the perfectly just and holy character of God.

There can, I think, be no doubt that the Apostle here does not mean merely that the righteousness of God is revealed in the Gospel (which no doubt it is, and in all its perfection), but that it

vealed from faith to faith: as it is written, [h] The

<small>[h] Hab. ii. 4.
John iii. 36.
Gal. iii. 11.
Phil. iii. 9.
Heb. x. 38.</small>

is revealed so as, in some sense, to be made ours, to be brought within our reach, so that we should possess it within ourselves. Calvin has an admirable note upon this: "This is an explanation and a confirmation of the preceding clause, that 'the Gospel is the power of God unto salvation.' For if we seek salvation, that is, life with God, righteousness must be first sought, by which being reconciled to Him, we may through Him being propitious to us, obtain that life which consists only in His favour; for in order to be loved by God we must first become righteous, since He regards unrighteousness with hatred," and in order that his readers might not think that he considers this bestowal of righteousness as a matter of mere imputation, he adds, "this righteousness does not only consist in the free remission of sins, but also, in part, includes the grace of regeneration." Calvin may not adhere to this: he may, as is probable, somewhere afterwards nullify his own words, but he has here written an axiom which is absolutely true in itself when he says, "In order to be loved by God we must first become righteous, since He regards unrighteousness with hatred." This does not for a moment affect the glorious truth that "we love Him because He first loved us," and that all good proceeds originally and directly from Him, but it asserts the plain palpable truth that "the righteous Lord loveth righteousness;" "The Lord loveth the righteous;" "The eyes of the Lord are over the righteous, and his ears are open to their prayers."

"From faith to faith." This, I think, is best explained by the "from glory to glory" of 2 Corinth. iii. 18—"from one degree of faith to another." God's revelation of his righteousness to man's soul begins with something comparatively feeble, and goes on from strength to strength, as our faith makes progress, and as it advances in knowledge, so the righteousness of God increases in us at the same time, and the possession of it is in a manner confirmed. There is another explanation of the words, however, which seems to me very good, which is that of Augustine: "From the faith of those who preach to the faith of those who hear and believe." The prophets were men of faith, and the Apostles were men of faith, and the evident fire of their faith kindled the faith of those who heard them.

"As it is written, The just shall live by faith." This is the text

just shall live by faith.

---

of all the rest of the Epistle. With these words the great argument respecting sin and righteousness, faith and works, the law and faith, the being in Adam and the being in Christ, commences (i.-vii.), and from it the discussion respecting the older election and the election according to grace branches out (viii.-xi.), and it concludes with the accounts of the fruits of faith in the daily life which are produced by him who lives by faith (xii.-xiv.).

The words are taken from the prophecy of Habakkuk. During his time the iniquity of the Jews and their kings had provoked God to cast them away for a time by the Babylonish captivity, but He consoled the righteous among them by the promise that they should live by faith. What the Lord meant by this, so far as concerns the righteous Jews of the times of Habakkuk, whether He meant that they should be providentially preserved alive during the invasion and desolation by the " bitter and hasty nation ; " or that, no matter what their outward calamities, they should have a life of God in their souls by which they should enjoy peace and tranquillity, we cannot say ; but the meaning of St. Paul, or rather of God speaking by him, admits of not the smallest doubt. It is that the root, and the continuance, and the perfection of the life of God in the soul of the just man is by faith, *i.e.*, not by education or by mere precept, or by any system of outward law, but by the operation of that faculty which God has given to men whereby they are enabled to lay hold of and realize whatever God reveals to them respecting Himself, and His nature, and His designs.

The just then means the " justified " person spoken of throughout the rest of the Epistle.

The living (" shall live ") means living with the life of God, and consequently living soberly, righteously, and godly.

" Faith " means believing, (not primarily trusting, relying on, hoping, loving, obeying ; all these come afterwards in their course,) but believing in the ordinary sense of the word, as when we say to a person, " I believe that what you say is true ; " " I do not believe that what you say is true."

Now faith or belief, by its very nature, must have something to rest itself upon or lay hold of. You say, " I believe." " Believe what ? " I rejoin ; " what do you believe ? " This faith, this belief by which the just man lives is the Gospel, or rather the Lord

18. ¹ For the wrath of God is revealed from heaven against all ungodliness and unrighteousness of men, who hold the truth in unrighteousness;

¹ Acts xvii. 30.
Eph. v. 6.
Col. iii. 6.

Jesus, about Whom is the Gospel as it is set forth in verses 3 and 4 of this Epistle; which account of the Gospel, as the object of faith, we shall see the Apostle has before him and recurs to, all through the Epistle.

I shall take up the fuller consideration of justification in a note or excursus further on; but before leaving this verse shall ask the reader to notice that in this prophecy, cited no less than three times in the New Testament, Justification is set forth as a matter of life—not of imputation merely, or of pardon, or of acceptance, or of acquittal, but of life.

18. "For the wrath of God is revealed from heaven against all ungodliness," &c. The "for" no doubt refers to the revelation of righteousness in the last verse. There is a revelation of the righteousness of God, because there has been a revelation of the just anger of God, as revealed from heaven against those who wilfully sin. When was it thus revealed? We answer, in every way and on every occasion on which the God of heaven made His will known against sin. Did God speak *from heaven* when He gave the law? It was to declare His anger against sin. Did God speak in the prophets by the Spirit which He sent down *from heaven?* It was to warn them of the fast-coming punishment of sin. Did God send His Son *from heaven?* It was before He saved men to declare to them the wrath of God in far more awful terms than He had ever set it forth by any angel or prophet; and the day in which Christ will come *from heaven* to judge is called in this Epistle "the day of wrath and revelation of the righteous judgment of God."

"Who hold the truth in unrighteousness." Most commentators translate "hold" in the sense of holding back, detaining, even imprisoning the truth, *i.e.*, not allowing it to have its natural effect; but in several places it simply means to possess or retain, as in 1 Cor. vii. 30, "they that buy, as though they possessed not."

What follows to the middle of the third chapter seems to me to be written not merely to bring the Gentiles, and then the Jews under sin, but to show the weakness and insufficiency to produce righteousness of any mere law, whether it be the original law given

CHAP. I.] GOD HATH SHEWED IT. 17

19 Because ᵏ that which may be known of God is manifest ‖ in them; for ¹ God hath shewed *it* unto them.

20 For ᵐ the invisible things of him from the creation of the world are clearly seen, being under-

ᵏ Acts xiv. 17.
‖ Or, *to them.*
¹ John i. 9.
ᵐ Ps. xix. 1, &c. Acts xiv. 17. & xvii. 27.

---

20. "From the creation." Since creation, but still they are known by the marks of design and goodness in the creation.

to all men at the beginning, the knowledge of God manifest in them; or whether it be a law given through Revelation, as the Jewish Revelation—it was weak through the flesh, and shut men up to the righteousness which was afterwards to be revealed.

19, 20. "Because that which may be known of God is manifest in them .... so that they are without excuse." "That which may be known of God," does not mean, of course, the knowledge of all God's attributes and perfections. It required Revelation to teach all this, but it means the two attributes, or rather three, ascribed to Him at the end of the 20th verse, His Eternal Power and Godhead, that is, His Eternity, Power, and Divinity. These the Apostle declares to be so set forth by His works of creation, that all men can, if they will, read them there. To this Aristotle, for instance, bears witness when he writes: "God, Who is invisible, becomes visible from His very works to every mortal nature" ("De Mundo," ch. vi.). Socrates: "Learn, therefore, not to despise those things which you cannot see; judge of the greatness of the power by the effects which are produced, and reverence the Deity" ("Memorabilia," iv. 3). Thales: "God is the oldest of existences, for He is unbegotten; the world is the most beautiful, for it is the work of God" (Thales, in "Diog. Laertius," quoted in "Pearson on the Creed," 20, notes). It may be said that these are the words of great philosophers, but I think that they rather represent the common sense of mankind. Men, unless their minds are utterly perverted by atheistical sophistry, can plainly see that a house must be builded by someone, and that a machine, whether of iron or of flesh, must be devised by some inventive mind, and that life cannot come from dead matter, and that laws which regulate all visible things so as to make them act together in some sort of system, must be imposed from without; and that if we require some intelligence to understand design, and to appreciate beauty, design and beauty must exist by the will of

C

stood by the things that are made, *even* his eternal power and
Godhead; ‖ so that they are without excuse:

¶ Or, that they may be.

21 Because that, when they knew God, they

---

some infinitely more wise and powerful intelligence than ourselves.

The question arises whether St. Paul means to bring in here the moral sense or original light respecting good and evil, right and wrong, which God at the first gave to man. I can only say that these two verses do not express this. They only express that witness of the outward creation to the perfections of God, which, if duly considered, would have kept men from the idolatry which the Apostle proceeds to stigmatize as the root of such frightful moral evil.

"So that they are without excuse." "What will the Greeks say in that day? That we were ignorant of thee? Did ye, then, not hear the heavens sending forth a voice by the sight, while the well-ordered harmony of all things spake out more clearly than a trumpet? Did ye not see the hours of night and day abiding unmoved continually, the goodly order of winter, spring, and the other seasons, which is both sure and unmoved, the tractableness of the sea amid all its turbulence and waves. All things abiding in order, and by their beauty and their grandeur preaching aloud of the Creator."
—Chrysostom.

"So that they are without excuse." The margin reads, "that they may be without excuse." A difficulty has been made of this, and it has been asked, Did God make men see or apprehend His power and divinity simply that they might be inexcusable, and so that He might condemn them? Assuredly not. The place is easy enough if we understand, "if they did not believe and obey." But even supposing that one great design of God was to bring man in guilty before Him, we must remember that this was for a most merciful purpose, to prepare them to receive a fuller revelation in Redemption.

21. "Because that, when they knew God, they glorified him not as God," &c. Could it be ever said that the Gentiles knew God? St. Paul here assumes that they could, and the oldest forms of idolatry seem to be but perversions of the truth. God was first one and above nature; then this idea being too spiritual for carnal minds, was perverted, and He was identified with nature; then the divinity

CHAP. I.]   VAIN IN THEIR IMAGINATIONS.   19

glorified *him* not as God, neither were thankful; but ⁿ be- |
came vain in their imaginations, and their foolish | ⁿ 2 Kings xvii.
heart was darkened. | 15. Jer. ii. 5.
 | Eph. iv. 17, 18.

was parted, as it were, amongst the forces of nature, and the mind of man, continuing in its downward course, invested these deities with the worst vices of mankind.[1]

Thus they glorified Him not as God. If they believed Him, however dimly, to have brought all things into being, it was clearly wrong to represent Him under any form, for how could One Who possessed such virtual omnipresence and infinity as to be able to create the universe, be represented under the form of any of the creatures which He had made? It was clearly, then, their duty to glorify Him under the highest conception which they could form of Him, and this would be a divine and spiritual conception.

"Neither were thankful." If they acknowledged a supreme Being at Whose will all living creatures existed, such a Being, if He could receive them, was worthy of thanks and praise. It was only due to Him for men to acknowledge that they received all blessings from His hands. "As therefore amongst men we best make trial of the affection and gratitude of our neighbour by showing him kindness, and discover his wisdom by consulting him in distress, do thou, in like manner, behave towards the gods; and if

---

[1] My friend Canon Cook, in his "Origin of Languages and Religion," has clearly shown that some of the earliest Vedic hymns representing the primitive worship of the Aryan race were addressed to one Deity, Varuna, who seems to have been possessed of the highest moral attributes. His worship, however, gradually gave way to that of such gross impersonations of what is lowest in man, as we have in Vishnu and Siva. The following is a Vedic Hymn to Varuna, translated by Monier Williams:—

> "The mighty Varuna, who rules above, looks down
> Upon these worlds, his kingdom, as if close at hand.
> When men imagine they do ought by stealth, he knows it,
> No one can stand or walk or softly glide along,
> Or hide in dark recess, or lurk in secret cell,
> But Varuna detects him, and his movements spies.
> Two persons may devise some plot, together sitting,
> And think themselves alone; but he, the king, is there—
> A third—and sees it all. His messengers descend
> Countless from his abode, for ever traversing
> And scanning with a thousand eyes its inmates.
> Whoever exists within this earth, and all within the sky
> Yea, all that is beyond, King Varuna perceives.
> The winking of men's eyes are numbered all by him."

22 ᵒ Professing themselves to be wise, they became fools,

23 And changed the glory of the uncorruptible ᵖ God into an image made like to corruptible man, and to birds, and fourfooted beasts, and creeping things.

o Jer. x. 14.
p Deut. iv. 16, &c. Ps. cvi. 20. Isa. xl. 18, 25. Jer. ii. 11. Ezek. viii. 10. Acts xvii. 29.

---

thou wouldst experience what their wisdom and what their love, render thyself deserving the communication of some of those divine secrets which may not be penetrated by man, and are imparted to those alone who consult, who adore, who obey the Deity. Then shalt thou, my Aristodemus, understand there is a Being whose eye pierceth throughout all nature, and whose ear is open to every sound; extended to all places, extending through all time; and whose bounty and care can know no other bounds than those fixed by his own creation." (Socrates in "Memorabilia," i. 4.)

21. "But became vain in their imaginations, and their foolish heart was darkened." The words "vanity," "became vain," &c., are Old Testament expressions, denoting the worthlessness and the nothingness of the false gods and idols for whom the Israelites so constantly forsook Jehovah, and in this sense of nothingness and so worthlessness and emptiness St. Paul used it here, as in 1 Corinth. viii. 4, "We know that an idol is nothing in the world." They became empty and windy in their conceits,

"And their foolish heart was darkened," because, of course, they determinedly shut out the light.

22. "Professing themselves to be wise, they became fools." This seems to mean that, whilst boasting or proclaiming their natural wisdom, and considering themselves too wise to honour the "unknown and unknowable," God gave them up to their vanity, and they became fools, and their folly culminated in this,

23. "And changed the glory of the uncorruptible God into an image," &c. No folly seems so great as this, that men should change the highest spiritual, or at least immaterial, conception to a low material one; but it is in accordance with that evil principle within us which is wearied with contemplating what is lofty and unapproachable, and seeks refuge in that which is in our sphere, and, as it were, more on our own level.

In providing against this we see the Divine Wisdom of Christianity, which, in the life and character of Jesus Christ, sets before

24 ᵠ Wherefore God also gave them up to un- q Ps. lxxxi. 12.
Acts vii. 42.
Eph. iv. 18, 19.
2 Thes. ii. 11, 12.

24. "Wherefore God also." "Also" [καὶ] omitted by ℵ, A., B., C., a few Cursives, Vulg., Copt., Syriac, Arm.; but retained by D., E., G., K., L., P., and most Cursives, and d, e, g.

us a worthy and fitting image of the invisible God. The Incarnate Son has revealed Him Whom no man hath seen, nor can see.

The heathen to whom St. Paul alludes had not this unspeakable advantage, and so they did what was in accordance with corrupt and fallen human nature. This place clearly shows us that polytheism and idolatry were not the original form of the religious worship of the Gentiles, but a corruption. They must have had to some extent an idea of the glory of the incorruptible God before they could change it. Godet well remarks: "Futility of thought had reached the height of folly. What, in fact, is polytheism except a sort of permanent hallucination, a collective delirium, or, as is so well said by M. Nicolas, a possession on a great scale? and this mental disorder rose to a kind of perfection among the very peoples who, more than others, laid claim to the glory of wisdom. When he says, *professing to be wise*, Paul does not mean to stigmatize ancient philosophy absolutely; he only means that all that labour of the sages did not prevent the most civilized nations, Egyptians, Greeks, Romans, from being at the same time the most idolatrous of antiquity. The popular imagination, agreeably served by priests and poets, did not allow the efforts of the wise to dissipate this delirium."

"Corruptible"—"uncorruptible." There seems to be something more in this contrast than the idea of mere bodily decay or corruption. "Paul sets not the immortality of God in opposition to the mortality of man, but that glory which is subject to no defects he contrasts with the most wretched condition of man" (Calvin), and certainly the image of corruptible man, which the Greeks worshipped, embodied his worst moral corruptions.

"And to birds, and fourfooted beasts, and creeping things." Here, no doubt, the Apostle had in his mind the Egyptian idolatry, which made images of the bull Apis, the hawk, the ibis, and the scarabæus.

24. "Wherefore God also gave them up to uncleanness through the lusts," &c. St. Paul here asserts the punishment to which God

cleanness through the lusts of their own hearts,' to

<small>ʳ 1 Cor. vi. 18.
1 Thes. iv. 4.
1 Pet. iv. 3.</small>

gave them over. He surrendered them, He gave them over to themselves. He did, that is, to the Gentiles, what He had done to His people Israel. "My people would not hear my voice, and Israel would none of me. So I gave them up unto their own hearts' lusts, and they walked in their own counsels." (Ps. lxxxi. 12.)

In the case of the heathen the punishment was analogous to the sin. They dishonoured God by debasing Him to the level of His creatures, and God gave them over to the most debasing lusts. They had dishonoured Him, the Eternal Spirit, by worshipping bodily forms, and God suffered them to dishonour their own bodies. They became more and more unclean and polluted in their worship, and God gave them over to their own inherent uncleanness.

Now in examining this terrible passage I desire the reader to give due weight to the following:—

1. The seeds of this uncleanness were already in themselves. It was not that God permitted Satan to tempt them to the commission of new sins. He simply gave them up to that which was already within them. Hitherto He had restrained their innate lusts from breaking out into these horrid forms: now, in just punishment for their having so wickedly dishonoured Him, He no longer restrained them. In this He did what we ourselves constantly do. We know and have an interest in someone who will take his own bad course: we remonstrate, we threaten, we use what punishment is in our power, but it is to no purpose, and we leave him to himself. Some commentator notices that this was exactly the conduct of the father in the parable of the Prodigal Son. It stands to reason that the Prodigal could not have become at once such a libertine. He very probably showed many signs of wilfulness and selfishness long before he asked for his portion of goods; and it was given to him, knowing that he would squander all in vice and prodigality, and that the want which would naturally ensue would be the only way of bringing him to himself. With respect to these particular forms of sin or punishment we must remember that the innate propensity implied in "the lusts of their own hearts" will, unless restrained by Divine grace, or by self-respect, or strong Christian public opinion, constantly break out into what is unnatural. Instances of this in the midst of Christian society perpetually come to light, and those who receive confessions

dishonour their own bodies ᵇ between them- ᵇ Lev. xviii. 22
selves:

know too well what a multitude do not come to light in this world. In writing this, let it not be supposed for a moment that I ignore the change made by Christianity. It can scarcely be overrated; but what I do assert is, that the deep-seated uncleanness of human nature would, if God was to withdraw His grace, be manifested in the same crimes. At least, it always has been, and it is so to this day.

2. Then we are to remember that God thus left the heathen to themselves in a certain way of mercy, as regards their final doom. The worst case conceivable is not that of a wicked man, but of one who goes on in his wickedness in spite of the misgivings of conscience, or in spite of the remonstrances of the Spirit of God. When God has withdrawn His Spirit, the man or the community thus left to themselves have clearly not the continued resistance to the Holy Spirit to answer for. And we are also to remember that St. Paul, in these verses, seems to lose sight of the sin of individuals in that of a community. Now, a man born and bred in a community steeped in moral pollution is in a very different case to a man who has been born and bred in a community permeated with Christian teaching which takes as its standard the life and character of Christ.

Again the Apostle represents the withdrawal of God's Spirit so that men should be abandoned to these sins as itself a fearful punishment. Now the spurious liberality of this our day—the oft-repeated excuse that religion is wholly a matter between each man and God—that we must respect the convictions of each man's conscience, and so on, has a tendency to make us invest the Deity Himself with these lax feelings, so that we secretly think He is indifferent to the manner of men's worship, provided they worship at all.

Now the Scriptures teach us that in this matter of worship God is a jealous God, and is offended and angry, and most reasonably so, when men change the glory of the incorruptible into some form of corruption. It is, I say it with all reverence, a personal insult to Him, and He resents it as such.

These and other considerations, which I cannot now dwell upon, are to be taken into account if we would form some judgment of the righteousness of God's dealings in this fearful matter. And we

25 Who changed ᵗthe truth of God ᵘinto a lie, and worshipped and served the creature || more than the Creator, who is blessed for ever. Amen.

ᵗ 1 Thes. i. 9.
1 John v. 20.
ᵘ Isa. xliv. 20.
Jer. x. 14. &
xiii. 25. Amos
ii. 4.
|| Or, *rather*.

must form some judgment on it, for it is the Reprobation of Scripture. It comes before us here in the matter of God's dealings with the Gentiles in, perhaps, prehistoric times, and it reappears in the book of Exodus in God's dealings with Pharaoh, and St. Stephen recognized it when he told the Jews that God turned and gave them up to worship the host of heaven (Acts vii. 42), and Isaiah recognized it in the hardening of the hearts of the Israelites, that they might suffer the full punishment due to their idolatry.[1] There is nothing strange or abnormal, then, in St. Paul recognizing it in the fast approaching rejection of his countrymen and co-religionists, because of their unbelief in the Son of God.

I humbly ask the forgiveness of our Heavenly Father if I am in any way misrepresenting His truth in this matter when I say that this reprobation, or giving men up to themselves, never contemplates the everlasting punishment in Gehenna of individuals. In almost all the cases referred to in Scripture it has to do with communities, and the common life or mind of communities by which they, as one man, at times embrace certain sins, is a very dark mystery indeed.[2]

25. "Who changed the truth of God into a lie." God is an eternal, all-perfect, all-wise Intelligence, and any representation of Him, either as a human being or an animal, is a lie, because a most abominable misrepresentation.

"Who is blessed for ever." Two reasons have been given why St. Paul here interjects this short doxology. One as a sort of act of amends to God and relief to his own spirit, in that he was forced to write such things in connection with God's Name: the other, that he desired to show that God's blessedness was in no real way injured or even lowered by this changing of God's truth into a lie.

---

[1] See my notes on Matth. xiii. 14, 15.

[2] It has not been sufficiently noticed that God not only hardened the heart of Pharaoh, but that of his servants, and that of his people. Thus Exod. x. 1, "I have hardened his heart, and the heart of his servants." Again, xiv. 17, "And I, behold, I will harden the hearts of the Egyptians." And to this the book of Samuel witnesses: "Wherefore then harden ye your hearts, as the Egyptians and Pharaoh hardened their hearts?" &c. (1 Sam. vi. 6.)

CHAP. I.]   GOD GAVE THEM UP.   25

26 For this cause God gave them up unto ˣ vile affections: for even their women did change the natural use into that which is against nature: ˣ Lev. xviii. 22, 23. Eph. v. 12. Jude 10.

27 And likewise also the men, leaving the natural use of the woman, burned in their lust one toward another; men with men working that which is unseemly, and receiving in themselves that recompence of their error which was meet.

28 And even as they did not like ‖ to retain God in *their* knowledge, God gave them over to ‖ a ‖ Or, *to acknowledge*. ‖ Or, *a mind void of judgment*.

Though men so grievously dishonoured Him, He abode in eternal blessedness. Similarly with regard to God's truth, the Apostle writes: "If we believe not (*i.e.*, are unfaithful), yet he abideth faithful, he cannot deny himself." (2 Tim. ii. 13.)

26, 27. "For this cause God gave them up . . . . their error which was meet." Upon these verses it will be sufficient to remark that heathen writers, both Greek and Latin, abundantly confirm what is here asserted by the Apostle. I have also heard from one who travelled in Egypt that there are delineations of these sins on the walls of their temples and tombs. And education and culture, and even philosophy, could not save men from this fearful gulf of sin. Cornelius à Lapide gives (principally from Diogenes Laertius), notices of philosophers of eminence who thus dishonoured their bodies.

The word error is much too mild a term. "The original πλάνη expresses in Scripture that sort of delusion which is at once wilful, immoral, and corrupting" (Dean Vaughan, who quotes 1 Thess. ii. 3, where πλάνη is associated with δόλος and ἀκαθαρσία): and in Jude 11 the word is applied to the extreme wickedness of Balaam.

28. "And even as they did not like to retain God in their knowledge, God gave them over to a reprobate mind." The Apostle here enters upon a new count against the Gentiles. His withdrawal of grace, His leaving of them to themselves, not only brought out the wickedness of the natural man in that he delighted to wallow in filthy lusts, but also in that he surrendered himself to every other sort of evil. There is the same parallel drawn by the Apostle here in the original between the forsaking of God by men, and His forsaking them, but it is not observable in our English translations.

reprobate mind, to do those things ʸ which are not con-
ʸ Eph. v. 4.   venient;

29 Being filled with all unrighteousness, fornication, wickedness, covetousness, maliciousness; full of envy, murder, debate, deceit, malignity; whisperers,

30 Backbiters, haters of God, despiteful, proud, boasters, inventors of evil things, disobedient to parents,

---

29. "Fornication" omitted by ℵ, A., B., C., K., 17, 23, 26, 67**, 73, 117, Copt., Æth.; retained by L. and most Cursives, and placed after "wickedness" by D., E., G., a few Cursives, d, e, g, Vulg.
30. "Haters of God." See below.

We might render it, "as they did not approve to retain God in their knowledge, God gave them over to an unapproved mind," only the word "unapproved" is far too weak to express God's utter disapproval, His abhorrence of their state of heart.

"To do those things which are not convenient." "Convenient," according to our use of the word, has a meaning so inadequate as to be almost absurd. Disgraceful, or unsuited to a reasonable creature, formed in the image of God, more correctly expresses the idea.

29. "Being filled with all unrighteousness [*i.e.*, injustice], fornication." This reading is doubtful, as the reader will see by referring to the critical notes. "Debate," *i.e.*, contention or strife. "Haters of God," this word is also of doubtful meaning; it may mean, haters of God, or hated of God. We are told that it has always a passive sense, hated of God, and yet a contemporary of St. Paul, Clement of Rome, in his Epistle to the Corinthians, ch. xxxv., undoubtedly understands it actively, "casting away from us all hatred of God;" and also Theodoret, "who are of a hostile mind towards God." It has its place in a black list of sins committed by man, and so would seem to be a sin committed by him rather than the effect of his sin upon the mind of God. "Despiteful" is usually translated insolent or injurious. "Disobedient to parents." This must be no small sin, though lightly thought of in these days, if it is found in such a catalogue. "Without understanding." Used not of dulness of comprehension, but in a moral sense, as it is often found in the book of Proverbs, and in Wisdom, i. 5.

31 Without understanding, covenantbreakers, || without natural affection, implacable, unmerciful:

|| Or, *unsociable*.

32 Who ˣ knowing the judgment of God, that they which commit such things ᵃ are worthy of death, not only do the same, but || ᵇ have pleasure in them that do them.

ˣ ch. ii. 2.
ᵃ ch. vi. 21.
|| Or, *consent with them*.
ᵇ Ps. l. 18. Hos. vii. 3.

---

31. "Implacable" omitted by ℵ, A., B., D., E., G., d, e, g, Copt., Syriac; but retained by C., K., L., P., most Cursives, Vulg., &c.

32. "Them that do them." "Practise them," Revisers.

32. "Who knowing the judgment of God, that they which do such things are worthy of death," &c. How can the heathen be said to know this judgment of God?

Probably the Apostle here refers to the universal belief in a Hades of punishment, as well as of reward; a Tartarus in which fierce retribution will be exacted of those who have escaped punishment here. "What appeals to God's justice do we find in the writings of Gentile historians and philosophers! What a description of the punishments inflicted on malefactors in Tartarus! . . . Death here denotes death as God only can inflict it," &c.—Godet.

"Not only do the same, but have pleasure in them that do them." This is the climax of evil. They are not only led by the flesh to do the works of the flesh, but their mind or spirit is so perverted that they have pleasure in contemplating the practising of these evil things by others. Such a mind is like that of Satan, whom the poet represents as saying "Evil, be thou my good." To approve of—to applaud evil for its own sake above and beyond our own gratification in the commission of it, seems the death of the moral sense within us, and the lowest depth to which any human being can descend.

CHAP. II.

THEREFORE thou art ^ainexcusable, O man, whosoever thou art that judgest: ^bfor wherein thou judgest another, thou condemnest thyself; for thou that judgest doest the same things.

^a ch. i. 20.
^b 2 Sam. xii. 5, 6, 7. Matt. vii. 1, 2. John viii. 9.

---

1. "Therefore thou art inexcusable, O man, whosoever .... doest the same things." The Apostle has now finished his count against the Gentiles, and he turns to the Jews, but instead of treating them as a *community* which had fallen from God, he individualizes. He singles out a particular Jew whom he supposes to be standing by him, and brings to bear upon him the judgment he passes on others, as his own condemnation. It seems to me a mistake to suppose that the Apostle treats the Jew as a hypocrite: he rather considers him to be a proud, overweening, censorious, self-righteous person who supposed that his election, his knowledge of Scripture, his circumcision, his Sabbath observance entitled him to consider any Gentile he might meet as unholy and unclean, a sinner to whom he was fully entitled to say, "Stand by thyself, come not near to me, for I am holier than thou." This judging, this censoriousness seems to have been in the Lord's time a special characteristic of all strict Judaism. They judged the Lord Himself, they judged His Apostles. They were ever on the watch to assert their superiority and to find fault. Were there then no humble-minded religious Jews who were "Jews inwardly," and were "circumcised in heart"? Very few, I believe, and for this reason, that all who were led by the Spirit had become or were fast becoming Christians, and the typical, the normal, the Pharisaic Jew was, we may say, invariably a judge. St. James, supposed to be of all others the one who would be lenient with his co-religionists, and do them justice, warns even the converted Jews against this national sin. "He that speaketh evil of his brother, and judgeth his brother, speaketh evil of the law, and judgeth the law: but if thou judge the law, thou art not a doer of the law but a judge ... who art thou that judgeth another?" (iv. 11, 12). But could it be said that the

THINKEST THOU THIS?

2 But we are sure that the judgment of God is according to truth against them which commit such things.

3 And thinkest thou this, O man, that judgest them which do such things, and doest the same, that thou shalt escape the judgment of God?

---

2. "But we are sure." So A., B., D., E., G., K., L., P., most Cursives; but ℵ, C., some Cursives, 7, 17, 26, 37, 62, 80, 122, 179, d, e, m, Vulg., Copt., Arm., read, "for"—"for we are sure."

Jews had so forsaken the true worship of God as to be given up by Him to unnatural lust? No, it may not have been so, but nevertheless the Lord, Who seeth the heart, when He sojourned among them, brought them in guilty of the state of mind and heart set forth in the 29th, 30th, and 31st verse of the last chapter, full of unrighteousness, wickedness, covetousness, maliciousness, full of envy, deceit, despiteful, proud, disobedient to parents, so that they made void the law in order to excuse themselves when they withheld from their parents needful sustenance.

"Wherein thou judgest another, thou condemnest thyself . . . same things." It is not likely that any Jew whom St. Paul might cite as a type of his countrymen would have within him the whole of this evil mind: but he would assuredly have sufficient to bring him in guilty before God on the principle "Whosoever shall keep the whole law, and yet offend in one point, he is guilty of all." (James ii. 10.)

2. "But we are sure that the judgment of God is according," &c. That is, it will be perfect and impartial, not allowing any sinner to escape because of religious privileges, or religious ancestry, but rather holding him the more guilty for having sinned against so much clearer light.

3. "And thinkest thou this, O man, that judgest . . . escape the judgment of God?" This is what the Jew actually did think. It was rooted in his belief that Israelites, as such, in virtue of their descent from Abraham, would never suffer the punishment of Gehenna.[1] This was the very crown of their election, and this

---

[1] No principle was more fully established in the popular conviction than that all Israel had part in the world to come (Sanh. x. 1), and this specifically, because of their connection with Abraham. This appears not only from the New Testament, from Philo and Josephus, but from many Rabbinical passages. "The merits of the Fathers" is one of the

4 Or despisest thou ᶜthe riches of his goodness and ᵈ forbearance and ᵉlongsuffering; ᶠnot knowing that the goodness of God leadeth thee to repentance?

ᶜ ch. ix. 23.
Eph. i. 7. &
ii. 4, 7.
ᵈ ch. iii. 25.
ᵉ Ex. xxxiv. 6.
ᶠ Is. xxx. 18.
ᵍ Pet. iii. 9, 15.

must be ever borne in mind in all the subsequent parts of this Epistle which bear on Election, that the Apostle, so far from asserting an absolute decree of Election irrespective of falling from God, was combating the idea of such a doctrine extensively, if not universally, held by his countrymen.

With respect to the principle, the common sense of the Jew, we should think, would have taught him that his judgment of what was right and wrong in others, would at least have made him surmise, that God would deal with him as he dealt with them.

4. "Or despisest thou the riches of his goodness?" &c. Despisest thou? dost thou make light of—dost thou take no notice of, the riches of His goodness? "The riches of his goodness." This is a phrase peculiar to St. Paul; thus Ephes. i. 7, 18, "The riches of his grace," "the riches of the glory of his inheritance."

"Goodness and forbearance and long-suffering." This may mean that God keeps them in life in order that they may be brought to hear and accept the Gospel, or that He yet mercifully delays His vengeance on the guilty nation in order that a still greater number may be induced to "save themselves from this untoward generation."

"Not knowing that the goodness of God leadeth thee to repentance." Thus 2 Peter, iii. 9, "Account that the long-suffering of our Lord is salvation." "Not willing that any should perish, but that all should come to repentance." The wilful sinner does not understand this. He in his secret heart attributes the long-suffering of God which has not, as yet, called him to account, to God's indifference to sin. "This is the notion that goes about, that God doth not exact justice, because He is good and long-suffering. But, in saying this, he would answer, You do but mention what will make the vengeance intenser. For God showeth this goodness

---

commonest phrases in the mouth of the Rabbins. Abraham was represented as sitting at the Gate of Gehenna, to deliver any Israelite who otherwise might have been consigned to its terrors. (Edersheim, "Life and Times of Jesus the Messiah," book ii. ch. xi. p. 271.)

CHAP. II.]   TREASURING WRATH.   31

5 But after thy hardness and impenitent heart ᵍ treasurest up unto thyself wrath against the day of wrath and revelation of the righteous judgment of God;

6 ʰ Who will render to every man according to his deeds:

ᵍ Deut. xxxii. 34. James v. 3.
ʰ Job xxxiv. 11.
Ps. lxii. 12.
Prov. xxiv. 12.
Jer. xvii. 10.
& xxxii. 19.
Matt. xvi. 27.
ch. xiv. 12.
1 Cor. iii. 8.
2 Cor. v. 10.
Rev. ii. 23.
& xx. 12. &
xxii. 12.

that you may get free from your sins, not that you may add to them."—Chrysostom.

5. "But after thy hardness and impenitent heart treasurest up unto thyself," &c. "What," asks St. Bernard, "is a hard heart? It is that heart which is neither broken by compunction, nor softened by pity, nor is it moved by prayers, nor does it yield to threats, it is hardened by stripes, ungrateful for kindnesses." As treasures of reward can be laid up in heaven, so can treasures of wrath, and as surely as God will repay the one in full so also He will the other. Every day of hardness and impenitence lays up its evil account, so every day of devotion and prayer and Christian duty lays up its good. And not only does the record of wilful sins and unrestrained evil passions add to this fearful treasure, but covetousness and selfishness do also. St. James on this matter illustrates the teaching of his brother Apostle: "Your riches are corrupted, and your garments are motheaten. Your gold and silver is cankered: and the rust of them shall be a witness against you, and shall eat your flesh as it were fire. Ye have heaped treasure together for the last days" (v. 2, 3).

6. "Who will render to every man according to his deeds." The doctrine here stated of a judgment strictly according to works is Pauline—not that it is not recognized by SS. James, Peter, and John in their respective Epistles, but that Christ's teaching respecting it seems far more clearly and categorically reproduced by St. Paul than by any other New Testament writer. The following are some instances: "Every man shall receive his own reward according to his own labour" (1 Cor. iii. 8); "We must all appear before the judgment-seat of Christ, that every one may receive the things done in his body, according to that he hath done, whether it be good or bad" (2 Cor. v. 10). "He that judgeth me is the Lord; therefore, judge nothing before the time, until the Lord come, who will bring to light the hidden things of darkness, and will make manifest the

7 To them who by patient continuance in well doing seek for glory and honour and immortality, eternal life:

---

counsels of the hearts, and then shall every man have praise of God" (1 Cor. iv. 5). Again, "Knowing that whatsoever good thing any man doeth the same shall he receive of the Lord" (Ephes. vi. 8). Again, "Whatsoever ye do, do it heartily, as to the Lord, and not unto men. Knowing that of the Lord ye shall receive the reward of the inheritance: for ye serve the Lord Christ" (Col. iii. 23). "Be not deceived, God is not mocked, for whatsoever a man soweth, that shall he also reap. For he that soweth to the flesh shall of the flesh reap corruption; but he that soweth to the Spirit shall of the Spirit reap life everlasting" (Gal. vi. 7, 8). I could have given twice as many, but I will add one more assertion from this Epistle: "We shall all stand before the judgment-seat of Christ. For it is written, As I live, saith the Lord, Every knee shall bow to me, and every tongue shall confess to God. So then every one of us shall give account of himself to God" (xiv. 10, 11).

I have given these passages in full as corroborating from his own writings the assertion of the Apostle in verse 6, because this verse, with the four verses which follow, are of unspeakable importance in settling the relations of the doctrine of St. Paul with that of his Master and with that of his brother Apostle. If we take them as we find them, and understand them according to their seemingly plain meaning, they are, if we except the sayings of the Lord Himself, the strongest words in the New Testament on the side of good works, and the necessity of a holy life if we are to be saved at the last great day. They are much stronger on the side of a final justification by works than the single assertion of St. James, "Ye see then how that by works a man is justified, and not by faith only." The slightest acquaintance with them, connected, of course, with what we find in the rest of the Pauline Epistles, ought to have saved many estimable Church writers from hazarding such teaching as that St. Paul's doctrine of Justification needs to be corrected or supplemented by that of St. James—that if taken by itself it leads to Antinomianism, and so forth. I myself have heard such statements, and I have been told that it was no uncommon thing to hear such absurdities in the University pulpits. It makes one think that men who could say such things could never have once carefully read the Pauline Epistles—certainly never seriously

INDIGNATION AND WRATH.

8 But unto them that are contentious, and [1] do not obey the truth, but obey unrighteousness, indignation and wrath,

[1] Job xxiv. 13. ch. i. 18.
[2] 2 Thes. i. 8.

compared them with themselves, and with the rest of Scripture, but taken their ideas of the Apostle's doctrine at second-hand, from the assertions of Antinomians and Solifidians.

But some of the foremost German Lutherans have treated this place as if it did not represent St. Paul's real sentiments. He speaks here, they think, not as a Christian from the Christian standpoint, but as a Jew: but if this be so, then the Apostle unequivocally declares that men can be justified and attain eternal life by the law, and that too after Pentecost—after the promulgation of faith in Christ as the one thing needful. Now, if it be really needful to reconcile the Apostle to himself, we have only to ask, why did St. Paul preach Christ? Evidently that men might live Christian lives—not merely that they might be washed from sin or pardoned, but that they might partake of His power and grace and so "live soberly, righteously, and godly in this present world." This is what the Apostle declares in the very centre of this Epistle: "What the law could not do, in that it was weak through the flesh, God, sending his own Son in the likeness of sinful flesh, and for sin [or as a sin-offering] condemned sin in the flesh: that the righteousness of the law might be fulfilled in us, who walk not after the flesh, but after the Spirit" (Rom. viii. 1-4).

When then St. Paul says that "God will render eternal life to them who, by patient continuance in well-doing, seek glory, honour, and immortality" (or incorruption), he means those who by repentance, and faith, and prayer, and careful continuance in the Body of Christ, and endeavours to keep the unity of the Spirit in the bond of peace, and constant watchfulness lest they fall, and diligent use of the means of grace, seek for glory and immortality. All these things are included under that "law of the Spirit of life in Christ Jesus," which "makes us free from the law of sin and death." St. Paul here unequivocally declares that patient continuance in well-doing is what God will reward; but it is impossible to imagine that he meant to teach that this might take place independently of the grace of Christ.

8, 9. "But unto them that are contentious . . . of the Gentile." "Contentious" here signifies dividing into factions and being ani-

9 Tribulation and anguish, upon every soul of man that doeth evil, of the Jew ᵏfirst, and also of the †Gentile;

ᵏ Amos iii. 2. Luke xii. 47, 48. 1 Pet. iv. 17.
† Gr. *Greek*.

mated by party spirit. It is very noteworthy that a sin which very many professing Christians account to be no sin at all, is singled out from all others as one that will be punished by God at the last; but so it is, and this is in accordance with very much that is in the writings of this Apostle; as, for instance, he writes to the Corinthians: "Ye are yet carnal; for whereas there is among you envying, and strife, and divisions, are ye not carnal and walk as men?" (1 Cor. iii. 3) and he includes strife (ἐριθεῖαι, same word) as among the works of the flesh which will prevent men from inheriting the kingdom of God (Gal. v. 20). According to this men require to be converted from a factious, caballing, schismatical spirit as much as they require to be converted from covetousness or fornication, and indeed it was when the Apostles exhibited this spirit in seeking the highest places that the Lord laid down the need of their conversion: "Except ye be converted and become as little children ye shall not enter into the kingdom of God" (Matth. xviii. 3).

"And do not obey the truth." The truth of God has not only to be believed in, held, pondered over, but obeyed. Do we hold, for instance, the great truth of God that He sent His Son to redeem us from sin? we only obey this truth—we only let it rule supreme in our hearts, when we renounce and fight against that sin from the dominion of which He died to save us.

9. "Tribulation and anguish." The indignation and wrath is in the mind of the Judge—the tribulation and anguish is that which He inflicts as a punishment.

"Upon every soul of man that doeth evil." So that no one shall escape. unless, that is, he has repented of and forsaken his sin, and come to God for remission and grace. "To the Jew first," *i.e.*, because he has sinned against the clearer light and the greater love of God manifested in the election of the seed of Abraham to be the people of God.

"And also to the Gentile." As the knowledge of the Jew will not for a moment be accepted instead of love and obedience, so the ignorance of the Gentile, his non-election, his vain conversation received from his forefathers, will be no excuse, because by faith, followed by Baptism, he can become as fully as the Jew a member of the mystical body of Christ.

CHAP. II.] NO RESPECT OF PERSONS. 35

10 ¹But glory, honour, and peace, to every man that worketh good, to the Jew first, and also to the †Gentile:

11 For ᵐthere is no respect of persons with God.

12 For as many as have sinned without law

¹ 1 Pet. i. 7.
† Gr. *Greek*.
ᵐ Deut. x. 17.
2 Chron. xix. 7.
Job xxxiv. 19.
Acts x. 34.
Gal. ii. 6.
Eph. vi. 9.
Col. iii. 25.
1 Pet. i. 17.

10. "But glory, honour, and peace." The Apostle will not allow vengeance to have the last word; so he returns again to the brighter side of judgment, that which judges and rewards rather than judges and punishes.

11. "For there is no respect of persons with God." God will deal impartially with all. In pronouncing judgment He will take everything into account, whether as enhancing or extenuating. This truth appears for the first time in Deut. x. 17, where God is said to "regard not persons, nor take reward." Again St. Peter repeats it to himself when he perceived that God was about to open the door of faith to the Gentiles (Acts x. 34). Again (Gal. ii. 6) with respect to the very Apostles themselves, St. Paul says, "God accepteth no man's person." Amongst many applications of it two require notice. It must be taken into account at every step of the argument in this Epistle, and elsewhere, respecting Election. God elects to nothing so absolutely, that His election should not require to be "continued in" (Rom. xi. 22), or "made sure" (2 Pet. i. 10). This is what the Jews never could realize. In spite of all warning they clung tenaciously to the delusion that God was bound to deal with them differently to the way in which He would deal with the Gentiles.

But, secondly, there is an innate persuasion in the hearts of most of us that God will deal strictly with our neighbours, but leniently with ourselves. We freely judge others and condemn them, but we console ourselves in thinking that He will not thus judge and condemn us. We have need constantly to remind ourselves that in the matter of the sins of our daily life—in the secret sins of our own souls, God is no respecter of persons. It is safest to be severe with ourselves. If we are to escape the severity of His judgment, it must be by judging ourselves and condemning ourselves.

12. "For as many as have sinned without law shall also perish without law." The being "without law" does not mean that they have no inward law written on their hearts by which they will be

shall also perish without law: and as many as have sinned in the law shall be judged by the law;

13 (For ⁿ not the hearers of the law *are* just before God, but the doers of the law shall be justified.

ⁿ Matt. vii. 21. James i. 22, 23, 25. 1 John iii. 7.

---

judged, but that they have no revealed law as the Jews had. The meaning of the Apostle seems to be that the Gentiles, because of their being without the pale of the law, will have no unfair advantage. If they have sinned against conscience and internal light, they will be punished in just proportion to their sin; but this we must leave entirely to God. The "perish" cannot possibly mean in every case everlasting destruction in Gehenna. In by far the greater part of cases where the word is used it means simply perishing by death, and the nearest approach which we can make to an explanation is that they will "die in their sins," and be subject to such punishment as God in His combined justice and mercy will award. This seems saying little, but it is all that we have any business to say. To say that they will not be punished at all, is to stultify the Apostle for having written the sentence: and yet virtually to say that God has put it out of His power to inflict any but the extremest punishment of everlasting torture leads to the denial of the existence of God.

"And as many as have sinned in the law shall be judged by the law." "In the law," evidently means in or under the dispensation of the written law of Moses. For instance, in the matter of confessing but one true God and of idolatry, the Jew who has had the first and second commandments, and has had the long experience of his race and nation, will be in a very much worse position than the Gentile who has known no other religion except polytheism and idolatry. The Jew also will be judged according to the letter and spirit of the law of the Sabbath, which was utterly unknown to the Gentile. The increased sanction also given by the revelation on Sinai to the natural duties of the Second Table must increase the guilt of the Jew who has broken them.

13. "For not the hearers of the law are just before God, but the doers of the law shall be justified." St. Paul here is laying down not so much a theological as a general truth, that, not they who merely hear any law, but they who do it, are right, *quoad* the

A LAW UNTO THEMSELVES.

14 For when the Gentiles, which have not the law, do by nature the things contained in the law, these, having not the law, are a law unto themselves:

particular law. It is quite clear that a law is given not to be heard only, but to be obeyed, and that those hearers only who obey fulfil the purpose of the Giver of the law.

It has been asked whether it is not a paradox that the Apostle should say here "the doers of the law shall be justified" when we find him laying down in the next chapter, "By the deeds of the law shall no flesh be justified." But the Apostle does not say absolutely the doers of the law shall be justified, as if it was an independent truth. He says it with reference to "hearing" without "doing." It is quite conceivable that a law might be given by God which a man could do in his natural strength. If a man obeyed such a law he would be justified so far as that law was concerned. How this justification would bear upon his eternal interests is another matter altogether. But an unprejudiced Christian, who understands the whole argument of the Apostle, need not entertain the question. By doers of the law he understands those who do what is good and right in the sight of God by the power of Christ's risen Life and the grace of the Holy Spirit, according to the words of the Apostle I have quoted above, "God sent His own Son in the likeness of sinful flesh . . . . that the righteousness of the law may be fulfilled in us who walk not after the flesh, but after the Spirit" (Rom. viii. 4).

14, 15. "For when the Gentiles, which have not the law, do by nature the things . . . . accusing or else excusing one another." These words are put in by way of parenthesis. In verse 13 the Apostle had laid down that not hearers of the law, but doers, shall be justified. It may be asked, then, whether the Gentiles can be judged, seeing they have no revealed law. St. Paul says that they have a law, and that the conduct of some of them—how many we know not—shows that this law, though not given in letters on stone, or written on parchment, is written on their hearts; "their conscience also bears witness," for, however it may be now utterly hardened in some of them, yet, in a general way, it witnesses to the goodness of virtue and to the evil of sin; and there is also a sort of court within them in which their actions are tried, and in this court their thoughts or reasonings are advocates, taking one

15 Which shew the work of the law written in their hearts,
their conscience also bearing witness, and *their* thoughts the mean while accusing or else excusing one another;)

¶ Or, *the conscience witnessing with them.*
¶ Or, *between themselves.*

---

side or another. This is most graphically described by Godet: "The soul of the Gentile is also an arena of discussions. The thoughts (λογισμοί) denote the judgments of a moral nature which are passed by the Gentiles on their own acts, either, as is most usually the case, acknowledging their guilt, or also sometimes pronouncing them innocent. Most commonly the voice within said: That was bad! Sometimes, also, this voice becomes that of defence, and says: No, it was good! Then before this inner court the different thoughts accuse or justify, make replies and rejoinders, exactly as advocates before a seat of judgment handle the text of the law. And all this forensic debating proves to a demonstration, not only that the code is there, but that it is read and understood since its application is thus discussed."

It has been asked, Do not the words "do by nature the things contained in the law," "these, having not the law, are a law unto themselves, which shew the work of the law written in their hearts"—do not these words seem to mean that natural religion, or natural virtuous principles, or the light of conscience, apart from revelation, is sufficient? No, certainly not. The light of nature, though given by God at the first, was like the Jewish law, only preparatory. It was to convince men of sin, and to lead them to desire more light to understand the will of the Supreme Being, and more power to fulfil it, both of which were given only in Christ. But though it did not cover the whole ground of human life, it was good, so far as it reached, for it was light from God Himself. And not only was it light from God, but it was light from Christ. It was the light of the Indwelling Word, the pre-existent Word or Son.

We must acknowledge this if we give its due weight to the statement of St. John that "the life" which was in Christ "was the light of men," and that Christ in His pre-existent state was the light which "lighteth every man that cometh into the world" (John i. 4, 8). This is acknowledged by one of the earliest of Christian writers, a philosophical believer in the best sense. "Whatever," he writes, "either lawgivers or philosophers uttered

16 °In the day when God shall judge the   °Eccles. xii.
14. Matt. xxv.
31. John xii.
48. ch. iii. 6.
1 Cor. iv. 5.
Rev. xx. 12.

well, they elaborated by finding and contemplating some part of the Word. But since they did not know the whole of the Word, which is Christ, they often contradicted themselves." And again, "No one trusted in Socrates so as to die for this doctrine, but in Christ, who was partially known even by Socrates, for he was and is the Word Who is in every man," &c. "For each man [he has particularly named Plato] spoke well in proportion to the share he had of the Spermatic Word;" and again, "For all the writers were able to see realities darkly through the sowing of the implanted Word that was in them" (Justin Martyr, Apol. ii. ch. 10, 13). This seems to be a reproduction of what we find in the book of Proverbs, where the Divine Wisdom is represented as saying, "Then was I by him, as one brought up with him; and I was daily his delight, rejoicing always before him; Rejoicing in the habitable part of his earth; and my delights were with the sons of men" (Prov. viii. 31). When, then, we are told that it is impossible to suppose that the Apostle here means that these good and virtuous persons among the heathen were saved or justified by doing "by nature the things contained in the law," because men can only be saved by Christ, we answer that we can never know in the case of any heathen man whether his goodness may not be from Christ, and that "by nature" does not mean by unaided nature, but by such aid as God the Father of Lights may see fit to give, though He may not see fit to reveal it to us. If it be rejoined that they certainly had not the conscious knowledge of Christ, we reply, No more have Christian infants, whom yet we believe to be in a state of salvation.

One correction which has an important bearing on the meaning of the latter part of the 15th verse requires notice. The word "the meanwhile" [μεταξὺ] should rather be rendered "one with another," or "between themselves:" perhaps we might say, mutually. It has no reference to the "day" when God shall judge, in the next verse. Their thoughts accuse or condemn them among themselves, now in this present time.

16. "In the day when God shall judge the secrets of men, by Jesus Christ," &c. A difficulty has been made respecting the connection of this verse with what precedes. It has been supposed to

secrets of men ^p by Jesus Christ ^q according to my gospel.

^p John v. 22. Acts x. 42. & xvii. 31. 2 Tim. iv. 1, 8. 1 Pet. iv. 5.
^q ch. xvi. 25. 1 Tim. i. 11. 2 Tim. ii. 8.

depend upon "shew" in the 15th verse—God will shew in the day of judgment that the work of the law has been written on the hearts of the Gentiles, which thing cannot be shown before; but though I believe that this verse is not without reference to what is contained in verses 14 and 15, yet that it really carries on and completes the meaning of verse 13. "The doers of the law shall be justified." When? No doubt "in the day when God shall judge the secrets of men." Justification is not *here* in this life awarded to those who have been "doers of the law," or else all penitent sinners would be shut out from justification: but at the last day works will be the test whether men have rightly used the grace of God given to them, whatever it be: and this judgment will be of the Gentiles, because they, too, have had some grace from God in the law written on their hearts, and the witness of their consciences.

"The secrets of men." God will then "bring to light the hidden things of darkness, and make manifest the counsels of the hearts" (1 Cor. iv. 5). "Now let each man enter into his own conscience, and reckon up his transgressions, let him call himself to a strict account that he be not condemned with the world. For fearful is that court, awful the tribunal, full of trembling the accounts, a river of fire rolls along. A brother doth not redeem, shall man redeem? Call then to mind what is said in the Gospel of the angels running to and fro, of the bridechamber being opened, of the lamps which are extinguished, of the powers which drag to the flames. And consider this, that if a secret deed of any one of us were brought forth into the midst, to-day, before the Church only, how would the doer pray to perish, and would he not offer to have the earth gape upon him, rather than to have so many witnesses of his wickedness? How then shall we feel, when, before the whole world, all things are brought into the midst, in such a theatre, so bright and open, with both those known and those unknown to us seeing into everything" (Chrysostom).

"According to my Gospel." St. Paul's Gospel is, as I have noticed, the Gospel of the Resurrection of Christ. This is its

CHAP. II.] THOU ART CALLED A JEW. 41

17 Behold, ʳthou art called a Jew, and ˢrestest in the law, ᵗand makest thy boast of God,

ʳ Matt. iii. 9.
John viii. 33.
ch. ix. 6, 7.
2 Cor. xi. 22.
ˢ Mic. iii. 11.
ch. ix. 4.
ᵗ Is. xlv. 25.
& xlviii. 2.
John viii. 41.

17. "Behold thou art called." Only Dᶜ, L., and a few Cursives read this (ἴδε); but ℵ, A., B., D*, E., K., most Cursives, d, e, g, Vulg., Syriac, Copt., Arm., read, "now if" (εἰ δὲ).

---

leading feature: but this Resurrection of the Lord assures us of two things—perfect forgiveness through His Blood (Acts xiii. 37, 38), and a perfect judgment to be exercised by Him at the last. Thus at Athens St. Paul preaches that "God hath appointed a day in the which he will judge the world in righteousness by that man whom he hath ordained, whereof he hath given assurance unto all men in that he hath raised him from the dead" (Acts xvii. 31).

Notice here that St. Paul's Gospel is not merely one of grace and forgiveness, but of strict judgment of every man at the last. The certainty of judgment to be exercised on believers and unbelievers alike has, to a great extent, dropped out of the popular teaching of the day, and yet there can be no true conception of Almighty God without it.

17. "Behold [or, Now if] thou art called a Jew, and restest in the law," &c. It was before the coming of Christ the most honourable thing to be called a Jew. He belonged to the one elect race. His very name, Jehodah, is "the praised one." "He whom his brethren shall praise" is a title significant of his high position.

"And restest upon (or in) the law." This denotes the confidence which the Jews had in the fact that the law was given to their ancestors. Now this confidence or "resting in," might not be evil at all, though as a rule, the stiff-necked part of the nation used it for an evil purpose. If they used the fact of their having had the gift from God as a sign of God's favour, without respect to their keeping the law, then they used it to their destruction; but if they considered that God gave them the law as a sign that He desired to bring them nearer to Himself, and did their best to submit themselves to this expressed will of God, then this was a natural source of confidence to them. They might rest in it till God revealed Himself more fully.

"And makest thy boast of God." It was quite right that they should make their boast of God, the one true God, as their God, if this boast of the exclusive knowledge of God made them humble

18 And ᵘknowest *his* will, and ||ˣapprovest the things that are more excellent, being instructed out of the law;

19 And ʸart confident that thou thyself art a guide of the blind, a light of them which are in darkness,

20 An instructor of the foolish, a teacher of babes, ᶻwhich hast the form of knowledge and of the truth in the law.

ᵘ Deut. iv. 8. Ps. cxlvii. 19, 20.
| Or, *triest the things that differ*.
ˣ Phil. i. 10.
ʸ Matt. xv. 14. & xxiii. 16, 17, 19, 24. John ix. 34, 40, 41.
ᶻ ch. vi. 17. 2 Tim. i. 13. & iii. 5.

---

and God-fearing, and merciful in their judgment of those to whom God had not as yet given so inestimable a privilege.

18. "And knowest his will." There could be no doing of His will with the conscious endeavour to please Him except they knew it.

"And approvest the things that are more excellent." This seems to mean that their knowledge of the law was a Divine sense within them leading them not only to make distinctions between right and wrong; but also, if two ways of serving God were presented to them, to choose the more excellent, or, if two commands seemed to clash, to know which was really the most important.

19. "And art confident that thou thyself art a guide of the blind, a light," &c. This confidence would not have been wrong in a Jew who acted upon it in a right spirit, for God most assuredly had given him that pure light of revealed truth which He had not given to the Gentiles. His duty, then, was to instruct the idolaters who came in his way, in a spirit of meekness, remembering that this want of a Divine revelation such as he had, was their misfortune rather than their fault. Compared to those who had the teaching of the Old Testament the Gentiles were "in darkness," "foolish," "babes;" but this was no reason why the Jew should pride himself, but rather humble himself; because his exhibition of pride and exclusiveness would repel the Gentile world, whereas his humility and charity would attract it.

20. "Which hast the form of knowledge and of the truth in the law." This does not mean that he has the form as opposed to the reality, but that he has the reality, as it were, in an outward tangible form in the books of Moses and the rest of the Old Testa-

CHAP. II.]   TEACHEST THOU NOT THYSELF?   43

21 ª Thou therefore which teachest another, teachest thou not thyself? thou that preachest a man should not steal, dost thou steal?

22 Thou that sayest a man should not commit adultery, dost thou commit adultery? thou that abhorrest idols, ᵇ dost thou commit sacrilege?

ª Ps. l. 16, &c.
Matt. xxiii. 3, &c.

ᵇ Mal. iii. 8.

---

ment. The light vouchsafed to the Gentiles being scattered, as it were, in different breasts, could not have the distinct form which the Jews possessed in the Scriptures.

21. "Thou therefore which teachest another, teachest thou not thyself? thou that preachest," &c. The Apostle in writing this must have had in his mind Psalm l. 16. "But unto the wicked God saith, What hast thou to do to declare my statutes, or that thou shouldest take my covenant in thy mouth? Seeing thou hatest instruction and castest my words behind thee. When thou sawest a thief then thou consentedst with him, and hast been partaker with adulterers." St. Paul would not have said this if his countrymen could with any show of reason have objected to the covert accusation of theft, or adultery, or sacrilege, which he brings against them. With respect to the second of these charges, adultery, they were literally an adulterous generation.

When they brought the woman accused of adultery before the Lord and He said, "He that is without sin among you, let him cast the first stone at her," and they all, convicted by their own consciences, went out, there can be no doubt but that their consciences convicted them of the same crime as that of which they accused the woman. Godet tells us that adultery is a crime which the Talmud brings home to the three most illustrious Rabbis, Akiba, Mehir, and Eleazar.

"Thou that abhorrest idols, dost thou commit sacrilege?" We should have rather supposed that the Apostle would have written "Thou that professest to abhor idols, dost thou worship an idol?" But whatever sins the Jews fell into in St. Paul's time, idolatry had certainly no place among them; the Babylonian captivity seemed to have altogether purged them from the sin of open idolatry. Some have supposed that as the word sacrilege here means the robbing of sacred shrines or temples, allusion is made to the sins of which the last of the prophets accuses them, of robbing

44 DISHONOUREST THOU GOD? [ROMANS.

23 Thou that ^c makest thy boast of the law, through breaking the law dishonourest thou God?

24 For the name of God is blasphemed among the Gentiles through you, as it is ^d written.

^c ver. 17.

^d 2 Sam. xii. 14. Is. lii. 5. Ezek. xxxvi. 20, 23.

God by withholding the tithes and offerings due to Him, and that they in the persons of the heads of their religion had made sacrilegious gain of part of the area of the Temple courts by letting it out to those who sold sheep, oxen, and doves; but most probably the Jews were at this time given to assist in the actual robbery of temples. Such is implied in the words of the town clerk of Ephesus: " Ye have brought hither these men, who are neither robbers of churches," (Acts xix. 37), where the same word is used as here. If they had not been known to take part in such robbery the official would not have thought of making such a denial. Godet seems to give the meaning in his exposition: "Thy horror of idolatry does not go the length of preventing thee from hailing as a good prize the precious objects which have been used in idolatrous worship, when thou canst make them thine own." The Jews probably did not pillage the Gentile temples themselves, but they filled the place of receivers of the things stolen.

23. " Thou that makest thy boast of the law, through breaking the law," &c. It is strange that men should boast of that which they disobeyed—of that which condemned them because of their disobedience to it; but in this very day the whole matter is re-enacted. The Gospel requires as much to be obeyed in the life as the law did, and yet men now are extensively given to boast in the possession of the pure Gospel, as they call it, whilst they cheat, lie, slander, and commit fornication.

24. " For the name of God is blasphemed among the Gentiles through you," &c. As far as I remember, all the references to the Jews and their religion in classical writers are contemptuous, which could not have been if they had set forth the purer morality of the law in their lives.

The law of the Jews was so identified with the Revelation of the One true God, that disobedience to it was accounted as if the God of the Jews was indifferent to His own expressed will. There are several places where this is "written," particularly Ezekiel xxxvi. 20: "When they entered unto the heathen, whither they went, they

CIRCUMCISION PROFITETH.

25 *For circumcision verily profiteth, if thou keep the law: but if thou be a breaker of the law, thy circum-   * Gal. v. 3. cision is made uncircumcision.

26 Therefore ⨍if the uncircumcision keep the   ⨍ Acts x. 34, 35. righteousness of the law, shall not his uncircumcision be counted for circumcision?

---

26. "Keep the righteousness." Revisers, "keep the ordinances;" but this is clearly a misleading translation, for "ordinances" now only mean "outward ceremonies," or are almost universally understood to have this meaning. If the word must be altered, let us have "requirements."

profaned my holy name, when they said to them, These are the people of the Lord, and are gone forth out of his land."

25. "For circumcision verily profiteth, if thou keep the law: but if thou be," &c. As long as thou observest the law, circumcision assures thee that thou art one of the elect of God. Thou art included under the covenant of Abraham and art the son of God by adoption, so far as the Old Testament dispensation is concerned. Thou hast an interest in all the promises of God, especially the promise that if thou seekest it God will circumcise thine heart.

"But if thou be a breaker of the law, thy circumcision is made," &c. Evidently this must be so, for circumcision made a man a debtor to keep the whole law. If then a Jew wilfully disobeyed the law and continued to do so, he belied his circumcision; so far from profiting him, it witnessed against him.

There seems to have been a popular opinion among the Jews that no circumcised man could suffer the torments of Gehenna; but a place from the Schemoth Rabba is quoted by Schoettgen which seems intended to correct this. "Dixit R. Barechias: Ne hæretici et apostatæ et impii ex Israelitis dicant: quemadmodum circumcisi sumus in infernum non descendemus. Quid aget Deus Sanctus Benedictus? Mittet angelum, et præputia ipsorum attrahet, ita ut ipsi in infernum descendant." (Quoted in Godet.)

26. "Therefore if the uncircumcision keep the righteousness," &c. This, in St. Paul's view, was not an impossible thing. The Apostle does not mean that he could keep the law perfectly, so as not to need pardon and redemption, but that he could be like Cornelius, like Socrates, like many earnest and devout feelers after the unknown God.

"Shall not his uncircumcision be counted for circumcision?"

27 And shall not uncircumcision which is by nature, if it fulfil the law, ^g judge thee, who by the letter and circumcision dost transgress the law?

^g Matt. xii. 41, 42.

28 For ^h he is not a Jew, which is one outwardly; neither *is that* circumcision, which is outward in the flesh:

^h Matt. iii. 9. John viii. 39. ch. ix. 6. 7. Gal. vi. 15. Rev. ii. 9.

The uncircumcised Gentile who lived, though imperfectly, up to the light which God had vouchsafed to him, fulfilled, though unconsciously, the purpose which God had in giving the law and imposing circumcision; and so it seems in accordance with the character of a righteous God, that such an one should be, in His sight, as if he were in covenant with Him.

27. "And shall not uncircumcision which is by nature," &c. The circumcision of the Jew was not natural—that is, not belonging to the natural order of things, but was part of a system introduced by God into the world, and so, in its origin at least, supernatural.

Those who are thus in their purely natural state, and yet have obeyed the law written in their hearts, will rise up in the judgment against those who, having the written law and circumcision, transgress the law.

The letter and circumcision were turned against such, and made their sin the more sinful. Thus the Lord says, "Many shall come from the east and west, and shall sit down with Abraham, and Isaac, and Jacob, in the kingdom of heaven," &c. (Matth. viii. 11.)

28. "For he is not a Jew, which is one outwardly; neither is that circumcision," &c. Though he may be a Jew by nationality, he is not a true Jew unless he answers to the purpose of God in separating the Jews from all other nations, that they should be holy, both in body and soul, before God.

"Neither is that circumcision, which is outward in the flesh." Circumcision, though not a sacrament, was yet a rite which had a spiritual and moral significance. It had a spiritual significance in that it signified that the descendant of Abraham, when he received circumcision, was in covenant with God, and could claim all His promises. It had a moral significance in that it signified to the person circumcised that he must cut off and cast away all evil lusts. The mere outward circumcision, then, when held in unrighteousness, was nothing; rather, it was worse than nothing—it

29 But he *is* a Jew, ¹which is one inwardly; and ᵏcircumcision *is that* of the heart, ¹ in the spirit, *and* not in the letter; ᵐ whose praise *is* not of men, but of God.

l 1 Pet. iii. 4.
k Phil. iii. 3.
Col. ii. 11.
1 ch. vii. 6.
2 Cor. iii. 6.
m 1 Cor. iv. 5.
2 Cor. x. 18.
1 Thes. ii. 4.

was a witness against the man who, though a professing Jew, lived the life of a heathen.

But in all this we must take care that we do not give to the words of the Apostle a meaning which he himself would have been the first to repudiate. Supposing that St. Paul had heard of a Jew who, before the time of Christ, or the preaching of the Gospel, had refused to circumcise his child, or to receive circumcision himself, if in his case it had been neglected, on the ground that circumcision was that of the heart, and the circumcision of the flesh was needless, or obsolete, or unspiritual, what would he have said? He would have said that such a temper of mind which could say this was utterly Godless and profane. He would have said: By such a refusal you exalt yourself against God, and proudly reject the covenant of His love towards you. For He has solemnly affirmed, "My covenant shall be in your flesh for an everlasting covenant."

29. "But he is a Jew, which is one inwardly; and circumcision is that of the heart," &c. Thus to the Philippians he writes, "We are the circumcision, who worship God in the Spirit, and rejoice in Christ Jesus, and have no confidence in the flesh" (iii. 3).

"Circumcision is that of the heart, in the spirit, and not in the letter." This was the promise of God to the Israelites in the last times: "The Lord thy God will circumcise thine heart, and the heart of thy seed to love the Lord thy God with all thine heart, and with all thy soul, that thou mayest live" (Deut. xxx. 6.)

"In the spirit, and not in the letter." "In the spirit," of course, means in the inmost soul or spirit, and not the mere compliance with the letter. The words, however, are taken by many to signify in the Holy Spirit, and of course no change like that of spiritual circumcision can be made in any man except by the Holy Spirit.

"Whose praise is not of men, but of God." Here, again, there seems a reference to the name of Jew as meaning one who is praised, but it is God Who knows the secrets of the heart Who praises him, and not his brethren after the flesh (Gen. xlix. 8).

CHAP. III.

WHAT advantage then hath the Jew? or what profit *is there* of circumcision?

2 Much every way: chiefly, because that [a] unto them were committed the oracles of God.

3 For what if [b] some did not believe? [c] shall their unbelief make the faith of God without effect?

[a] Deut. iv. 7, 8. Ps. cxlvii. 19, 20. ch. ii. 18. & ix. 4.
[b] ch. x. 16. Heb. iv. 2.
[c] Numb. xxiii. 19. ch. ix. 6. & xi. 29. 2 Tim. ii. 13.

1. "What advantage then hath the Jew? or what profit is there of circumcision?" The Apostle now meets an objection which we may say naturally suggests itself. If the uncircumcision so keep the righteousness of the law that his uncircumcision can be counted for circumcision, and the true circumcision be that of the heart, which the Gentile can have as well as the Jew, what advantage has the nation of the Jews, the circumcision? for I take it that the two questions, what advantage hath the Jew, and what profit of circumcision are the same, "the circumcision" being a name for the circumcised nation.

The Apostle answers, "Much every way," and this because God gave them His Revelation. This Revelation was, of course, above all, the written Word; but besides this they had other means of ascertaining the will of God, as the inquiry through the priests by the Urim and Thummim, and also the inspired voices of the prophets, all through the dispensation, the greater part of whose utterances have not been embodied in the sacred volume. So that it was not merely a book, but other means of guidance and counsel subsidiary to it which God committed to them.

3. "For what if some did not believe? shall their unbelief make the faith," &c. But another question arises upon this. The lively oracles, whether the law or the voices of the prophets, were only really accepted and followed by a part of the nation, sometimes by only a small remnant. Does this destroy the benefit? Verse 3 might properly be rendered: What if some were unfaithful, shall

CHAP. III.] LET GOD BE TRUE. 49

4 ^d God forbid: yea, let ^e God be true, but ^f every man a liar; as it is written, ^g That thou mightest be justified in thy sayings, and mightest overcome when thou art judged.

d Job xl. 8.
e John iii. 33.
f Ps. lxii. 9.
& cxvi. 11.
g Ps. li. 4.

---

their unfaithfulness invalidate the faithfulness of God? Far be it from us, he answers, to imagine such a thing.

4. "Let God be true, but every man a liar." I take this to mean, Though all men disbelieved God and discredited His Revelation, and so showed their innate falseness and crookedness of heart, yet still there were the oracles, there were the voices of the God-inspired prophets, and if any one single man among them, though he were alone, would but turn from sin and turn to God, and embrace some promise of His word, God would meet that man, and show to him His faithfulness and truth. So that the most wide-spread declension could not undo the fact that God had given to them His word and its promises, and that this word, these oracles, were theirs whenever they chose to turn to God.

"As it is written, That thou mightest be justified in thy sayings, and mightest overcome when thou art judged." The simplest way of taking this place, and the most consonant to the argument, or rather discussion, in these verses, is that the Holy Ghost here utters a truth of the most general application. Whenever God's sayings are canvassed as regards their truth, He will show that He is justified in having uttered them. Whenever God's words or doings are brought into judgment, He will overcome in that judgment, and convince His adversaries that He is right and they are wrong. David's confession that his sin was committed principally against God, so that by his confession of it he also confessed the justice of God, whatever sentence He passed upon him, is only a particular instance in which God is justified in His sayings. But now what are the sayings of God which the Apostle here supposes that men, though wrongly, may arraign? Evidently those which seem to upset the permanence of all God's promises to Israel, such promises as those in Deut. xxx. 1-6, where God engages that if the Jews—no matter where they may be carried captive for their sins—will return to Him, He will return to them. The seeming non-performance, or holding in abeyance of such promises, is what would make the captious or desponding Jew declare that the unbelief of some invalidated the faithfulness of God.

50 WHY AM I JUDGED AS A SINNER? [ROMANS.

5 But if our unrighteousness commend the righteousness of God, what shall we say? *Is* God unrighteous who taketh vengeance? (^h I speak as a man)

6 God forbid: for then ⁱ how shall God judge the world?

7 For if the truth of God hath more abounded through my lie unto his glory; why yet am I also judged as a sinner?

^h ch. vi. 19. Gal. iii. 15.
ⁱ Gen. xviii. 25. Job viii. 3. & xxxiv. 17.

---

7. "For if the truth." So B., D., E., G., K., L., P., most Cursives, Vulg., Syr.; but א, A., 5, 23, 57, 74, 124, Cop. read, "but if."

5, 6. "But if our unrighteousness commend the righteousness of God . . . God judge the world?" The Apostle now anticipates another objection, which seems to arise out of the use which he had made of his citation from the 51st Psalm. If sin and unfaithfulness on the part of man always bring out into stronger relief the righteousness of God, *i.e.*, His faithfulness, is it right that God should punish sin, seeing that sin is the means of establishing the righteousness of God? Now it might have been said that the sinner is justly punished for his sin, because it was the furthest from his thought to establish the righteousness of God by his wrong-doing; he only thought of his own gratification. But St. Paul does not meet the objection in this way. He falls back upon a far higher principle, the judgment of God as the great moral Governor of the universe. It is the first idea of God as the Governor of all intelligences that He will judge all those who are capable of being judged, and who ought to be judged, as the children of men, all of them, assuredly, ought to be: but if we hold that God cannot judge and punish evil actions, because they ultimately commend His righteousness, then He can no longer act as the Supreme Judge. His highest honour is taken away, for His righteousness depends upon His judging all men righteously.

7, 8. "For if the truth of God hath more abounded . . . whose damnation is just." Here St. Paul anticipates not so much another objection, as one springing out of the evil thought that, because sin ultimately brings out His righteousness, therefore God ought not to punish it. "If," he says, "the truth," *i.e.*, the whole righteous character of God, "hath more abounded," *i.e.*, hath been more abundantly manifested, "through my lie," *i.e.*, through my whole false unfaithful life, "unto his glory, why yet am I also judged as a sinner?"

ALL UNDER SIN. 51

8 And not *rather*, (as we be slanderously reported, and as some affirm that we say,) ᵏ Let us do evil, that good may come? whose damnation is just.

9 What then? are we better *than they?* No, in no wise: for we have before † proved both Jews and Gentiles, that ˡ they are all under sin;

ᵏ ch. v. 20. &
vi. 1, 15.

† Gr. *charged*.
ch. i. 28, &c.
& ii. 1, &c.
ˡ ver. 23. Gal.
iii. 22.

9. "Are we better than they?" The word probably is passive, "are we excelled, are we surpassed?" but the sense is the same.

My sin has glorified God—it has, so far as a creature can benefit his Creator, benefited Him—for a sinner can only benefit his Creator by advancing His glory: Why, then, am I judged and punished as a sinner, as one who has dishonoured God: and, besides this, if my false evil life hath brought out so great a good as the greater glory of God, why may I not always do so? Why may not this be the rule with me, to do evil that the greater glory of God may ensue? To this the Apostle deigns only to answer that persons who have got themselves to say such things are reprobate, and deserve to be damned.

I have not noticed as yet the sentence interjected parenthetically, "As we be slanderously reported, and as some affirm that we say, Let us do," &c. It is of great importance. It shows that in St. Paul's own time his preaching, because he taught that the law could not justify, was put down as Antinomianism. Here he repudiates any such an idea in very strong, indignant language. " He is blasphemed," he says, " by such an imputation reported of him." (καθὼς βλασφημούμεθα. To be slanderously reported is much too weak an expression.) "Blaspheme" is usually applied to speaking wilfully against God, and we could not with propriety say that a man "spread slanderous reports of God." It is applied to God's Name in the last chapter, verse 24, "For the name of God is blasphemed among the Gentiles," &c.

9. " What then? are we better than they? No, in no wise: for we have," &c. There is much difficulty amongst translators respecting the proper rendering of προεχόμεθα. The Vulgate translates it as our Authorized—" do we excel them? " So Wordsworth and Alford—"have we (the Jews) any pre-eminence?" We have the outward and visible advantage of the possession of the oracles of God, but inasmuch as we have not as a nation lived up to this know-

10 As it is written, ᵐ There is none righteous, no, not one:
11 There is none that understandeth, there is none that seeketh after God.

ᵐ Ps. xiv. 1, 2, 3. & liii. 1.

12 They are all gone out of the way, they are together become unprofitable; there is none that doeth good, no, not one.

13 ⁿ Their throat *is* an open sepulchre; with their tongues they have used deceit; ᵒ the poison of asps *is* under their lips:

ⁿ Ps. v. 9.
Jer. v. 16.
ᵒ Ps. cxl. 3.

---

ledge, we are equally with them under sin, as we have before proved (ch. i. and ii., 1-10, 21-24).

10. "As it is written, There is none righteous, no, not one," &c. The Apostle now cites against the Jews certain very sweeping assertions of the universality of their guilt. The following words are general assertions, and are not to be taken as if there were no pious God-fearing Jews in the darkest times of their history; just as in the very midst of the horrible depravity of the Gentile races there were many seekers after God, and witnesses to the truths which He had written on their hearts.

10-12. "There is none righteous . . . none that doeth good, no, not one." The first clause, "There is none righteous," seems to be an inference from the whole of the 14th and 53rd Psalms. The clause, "There is none that understandeth, there is none that seeketh," &c., seems to be an inference from verses 2 and 3 of Psalm 14. The Lord looked down from heaven upon the sons of men to see if there were any that understood or sought after God, but there were none, for "They are all gone out of the way, they are together become unprofitable; there is none that doeth good, no, not one."

13. "Their throat is an open sepulchre; with their tongues they have used deceit; the poison of asps is under their lips." The first clause is from the 5th Psalm, 9th verse, and may either signify a tomb yawning to receive its dead, or a tomb casting forth from its mouth putrid, life-destroying vapours. "With their tongues they have used deceit" seems a reproduction of the next clause (in our Bible version "They flatter with their tongue").

The last clause, "the poison of asps is under their lips," is taken

FULL OF CURSING.

14 ᵖ Whose mouth *is* full of cursing and bitterness:
15 ᵠ Their feet *are* swift to shed blood:

p Ps. x. 7.
q Prov. i. 16.
Is. lix. 7, 8.

from Psalm cxl. 3: "They have sharpened their tongues like a serpent; adders' poison is under their lips."

14, 15. "Whose mouth is full of cursing and bitterness: Their feet are swift to shed blood." The fourteenth verse is the reproduction of Psalm x. 7. In the Psalm it is in the singular number, as it may be rendered here, and runs, "His mouth is full of cursing, deceit, and fraud." The fifteenth verse, "Their feet are swift to shed blood," is almost verbatim from Proverbs i. 16: "Their feet run to evil, and make haste to shed blood." But it may be suggested by the eighth verse of Psalm x., "He sitteth in the lurking places of the villages, in the secret places doth he murder the innocent."

16, 17. "Destruction and misery are in their ways. And the way of peace have they not known." These verses are only to be found in the Septuagint version of Psalm xiv. [xiii.] They are to be found almost verbatim in Isaiah lix. 7, 8.

18. "There is no fear of God before their eyes." This is taken from Psalm xiv., and also from Ps. xxxvi., verse 1: "The transgression of the wicked saith within my heart, that there is no fear of God before his eyes."

Such are the places from their own Scriptures quoted by the Apostle with the view of bringing his countrymen, as a nation (or a church), guilty before God. In the Hebrew Scriptures they are not found together, but are scattered about, principally in the Psalms. One (verse 15) is to be found only in the book of Proverbs, another in Isaiah. But in the Septuagint version of Psalm xiv., they are all collected together as a part of one Psalm.¹

We learn from this that the Jews to whom the Apostle wrote must have acknowledged the authority of the Septuagint. St. Paul, in bringing them all under sin, must have done so by means of scriptures which they acknowledged. Whether the Septuagint version differed from the Hebrew in giving the sense of the latter rather than a literal translation is of no consequence. The fact is clear that if these allegations were true of the people of God in general, they

---

1 Some have supposed that St. Paul first collected together this series of passages, and that they were afterwards inserted into the margin of the Septuagint of Psalm xiv., and partially into the margin of Psalm liii.

16 Destruction and misery *are* in their ways:
17 And the way of peace have they not known:

---

needed a redemption which would bring down to them and put within their reach a far higher righteousness.

Another and a deeper question, however, requires to be taken notice of. Certain words of Psalm xiv. are, along with other words not found in the Hebrew version of that Psalm, cited by the Apostles as bringing all men universally under sin, and not only under sin, but if we take verses 13, 14, 15, 16 into account, as alike guilty of very grievous crimes indeed, "the poison of asps under their lips," "their feet swift to shed blood." Now is this count absolutely universal in its application? The second and third verses certainly seem to put this beyond doubt. If we take them literally righteousness must have been absolutely extinct; but the Psalm itself forbids us to do this, for in the fourth verse there is the usual distinction made between the workers of iniquity and the true people of God. Then in the fifth verse the existence of a "generation of the righteous," in which God dwells, is recognized; then in the sixth verse the poor are said to have made God their refuge. So great is this contrast that some have supposed that the former part is written of the heathen, but the wording of verse 4, which pre-supposes that the wicked must have had knowledge, and that they knew God, so as to be able to call upon Him if they would, renders this impossible. No: the Apostle's argument does not depend upon every man (for instance, such contemporaries of David as Samuel or Jonathan) being proved to be absolutely devoid of righteousness, but upon the people of Israel in general—perhaps the great majority of them—having become as the Gentiles—not, perhaps, given over to unnatural lusts, but still in such a state of sin that they could not boast themselves against the Gentiles, for they required redemption just as much as did the Gentiles. Now this is St. Paul's mode of bringing all men, Jews and Gentiles alike, under sin. It is exceedingly noteworthy, for it is altogether contrary to the mode adopted by Evangelical divines since the Reformation, in this country at least. The mode adopted to bring all men guilty before God has been, not to set forth the wickedness of the wicked, but the wickedness of the righteous—to show that the seeming righteousness of so-called unconverted men is all hollow—not only imperfect, but unreal—in fact, displeasing to God. They almost go to the

18 ʳ There is no fear of God before their eyes. ᶠ Ps. xxxvi. 1.

---

extent of saying that a man might as well commit a gross sin as live a moral life in his so-called natural state. Now I do not here wish to show the wrongness of all this, I merely desire that the reader should mark its utter contrariety to the teaching of the God-inspired Apostle. I do not remember that the Apostle ever attempts to show the worthlessness of what men are pleased to call natural righteousness: if he did so he would contradict himself, for in two places of this Epistle, ii. 14, 15, 26, he shows its worth, for it turns the uncircumcision of the Gentile into circumcision. If, then, the Apostle had desired to bring in all men guilty before God by showing the unrighteousness of seeming righteousness, he would have taken another line altogether, he would have laid himself out to show the imperfection of the righteousness of such men as Samuel and Jonathan and Zadok, and other pious, God-fearing contemporaries of the Psalmist. If it were urged against the Apostle that, by allowing the righteousness of such God-fearing people, he was undoing the effect of his own preaching of grace, he would have answered, No, not for a moment: whether a man be in the pale of God's covenant or out of it, he cannot be even imperfectly righteous without the inspiration and help of God, which help and grace He vouchsafes to every man as He will. If it were further objected that such men might rest satisfied without accepting Christ, if He were preached to them, the Apostle would answer: If men, before the Gospel, act under the guidance of the law, then He Who has given to them the law, and the good will to endeavour to obey it, will assuredly bring it about that the law shall be the schoolmaster of such persons, to lead them to Christ (Gal. iii. 24). If it be further objected that the most righteous commit sin and obey the law imperfectly, and have need of Christ, he would at once say: " I grant it most fully, but how is this sense of the need of Christ to be brought about? I cannot do it. God must give them repentance unto life. He has not given to me to say that any degree of righteousness is unrighteous; on the contrary, He has given to me to say what I have said, that the Gentiles, who certainly never have had Christ preached unto them, can do what is in some degree pleasing to Him. I can only deal with men in general—with classes, with religions, with churches—God alone can bring each man's sin, or his latent insincerity, or the deficiency of his best doings, home to him."

19 Now we know that what things soever *the law saith, it saith to them who are under the law: that ᵗ every mouth may be stopped, and ᵘ all the world may become ‖ guilty before God.

20 Therefore ˣ by the deeds of the law there

* John x. 34. & xv. 25.
ᵗ Job v. 16. Ps. cvii. 42. Ezek. xvi. 63. ch. i. 20. & ii. 1.
ᵘ v. 9, 23. ch. ii. 2.
‖ Or, *subject to the judgment of God.*
ˣ Ps. cxliii. 2. Acts xiii. 39. Gal. ii. 16. & iii. 11. Ephes. ii. 8, 9. Tit. iii. 5.

19. "Now we know that what things soever the law saith, it saith," &c. The Apostle had, in the first chapter, easily, if one may so say, convicted the Gentiles of sin. The prevalence of the worst form of idolatry, and of unnatural crimes, the universal diffusion of the sins of unrighteousness, wickedness, maliciousness, covetousness, had made this no difficult task, at least in the eyes of the Jew. But how was the Jew—the Jewish race—the seed of Abraham, to be brought under sin? Their own law—for the law means here, not only the law of Moses, but the enforcement of that law in the Psalms and Prophets [1]—could do this. The passages respecting the sins of Israel were, of course, said to those who received the law, and so were *under* it. These passages (and thousands more might have been cited) showed that the Jews, in whose Scriptures these were contained, were as much under sin as the Gentiles. So that every mouth which vaunted of its own righteousness might be stopped, and all the world, Jew and Gentile alike, might become guilty, or rather subject to the judgment of God.

20. "Therefore by the deeds of the law there shall no flesh be justified in his sight," &c. The first word, διότι, means rather, "because." It does not introduce a sequence to what has been said, but a reason for it. All the world may become guilty before God. Why? Because, by the deeds of the law, there shall no flesh be justified in His sight. And why do not the deeds of the law

---

[1] The Psalms are called the Law by our Lord Himself in John x. 34, xii. 34, and xv. 25, and Isaiah by St. Paul in 1 Cor. xiv. 21. I confess I cannot understand the difficulty which has been made about this phrase, owing to the first νόμος meaning citations from the Psalms, and the second the law of Moses. God spake in the law, and He also spake in the Psalms. They are all in one book, the whole of which is given by inspiration of God. A man who is under, and spoken to in, the law of Moses, is also under, and spoken to by, and bound to obey, any utterance of God in the Psalms. So Chrysostom, "For what reason did he not say, we know that what things soever the prophet saith, but what things soever the Law saith? It is because St. Paul uses to call the whole Old Testament the Law."

shall no flesh be justified in his sight: for ʸ by the law *is* the
knowledge of sin.   ʸ ch. vii. 7.

---

justify? We shall see afterwards, when we come to consider the Justification of Life of chap. v. Suffice it now to say, because of their insufficiency. They could not be accepted as making atonement for sins, and they could not make men partakers of the higher life of the Gospel, which comes to us through the Incarnation of the Lord. Because of the weakness of the flesh (Rom. viii. 3), the law never could do what it was seemingly designed to do. It declared the will of God, but it did not renew the will of man, so that it never could justify, but it prepared for Justification through Christ.

"For by the law is the knowledge of sin." "By the law," or rather by "law"—any law—whether by that originally written in the heart, or by the revealed law, men know what is wrong, and so they know that they must not commit that which the law coming from God has bid them avoid. But the law has no power in itself to make them do what it commands, or leave undone what it forbids. The law addresses itself to the will, but the strength or the weakness is in the will. The law tells men what is right, but it gives no power to do it. As the Apostle tells the Galatian Christians (iii. 21), it could not give righteousness because it could not give life. Of course there would be, both among Jews and heathen, men in whom God had implanted strong wills on the side of righteousness, but these would be very few, and the great mass would, by the law, be brought under sin rather than delivered from it.

But now a question of infinite importance meets us. Seeing that the law cannot justify by the deeds which are done in obedience to it, did God when He gave men the law intend them to keep it? This has been formally denied, especially by Luther and his followers, and by the Revival preachers of our own day. But a moment's consideration ought to show us, first of all, that if we say that God gives us commands which He does not in reality desire us to obey, we destroy His moral character. How can such a view of Him be compatible either with His truth or His holiness? and, secondly, we can only practically know sin, that is, its sinfulness, the depth to which it has struck its roots into our nature, our secret love of it, and so the power of our indwelling corruption, by our endeavouring, with all our might, to fulfil the law. Are we then to attempt to fulfil it in our own strength? Certainly, if God has not

58 THE RIGHTEOUSNESS OF GOD. [ROMANS.

a Acts xv. 11. ch. i. 17. Phil. iii. 9. Heb. xi. 4, &c.
a John v. 46. Acts xxvi. 22.
b ch. i. 2. 1 Pet. i. 10.

21 But now *a* the righteousness of God without the law is manifested, *a* being witnessed by the law *b* and the prophets;

---

revealed to us His strength, for unless we endeavour to fulfil it as we are, we never can practically know our own weakness—our inability in our own strength, and without Christ, to do what God requires. Whensoever the commandment comes to us, whether we are heathen or converted, or unconverted, we are bound to receive it as the will of God, and set ourselves to work to do it without delay. If we attempt this with any sincerity—with any desire to please God, we shall then soon find that "by the law is the knowledge of sin," we shall realize our innate sinfulness, and if we are heathen, and hear the Gospel of Christ, we shall accept it as a means of deliverance and strength, and if we are but nominal Christians, unconscious of the work and claims of Christ, we shall come to Him or to God through Him, for grace and life.

21. "But now the righteousness of God without the law is manifested," &c. Now, *i.e.*, in the present time—the time succeeding the Incarnation and Manifestation of the Son of God.

"The righteousness of God," *i.e.*, the original uncreated righteousness ever existing in the Persons of the Ever-blessed Trinity.

"Without the law," *i.e.*, apart from it—independent of it. The Gospel is not a part of the law given to supplement it, but a new and original production which, though ever in the mind of God, has been introduced amongst us only in these latter days.

"Is manifested," has been, and yet continues to be manifested. Manifested in the coming amongst us of the Son of God—in the account of His all-holy Character, in His Death, His Resurrection, in the coming of the Spirit, in the preaching of the Word, in the witness of the Church, particularly in the character of its members. All these things manifest to us the righteousness of God in every way in which it can be conceived of as righteousness.

"Being witnessed by the law and the prophets." That a righteousness at some future time would be given by God is clear from Deut. xxx. 6: "And the Lord thy God will circumcise thine heart, and the heart of thy seed to love the Lord thy God, with all thine heart and with all thy soul, that thou mayest live." In the Prophets, the same is declared in closer connection with the

CHAP. III.] BY FAITH. 59

22 Even the righteousness of God *which is* [c] by faith of Jesus Christ unto all and upon all them that believe: for [d] there is no difference:

[c] ch. 4, throughout.
[d] ch. x. 12. Gal. iii. 28. Col. iii. 11.

22. "And upon all." Omitted by ℵ, A., B., C., P., Cop., Arm., Æth.; but retained by D., E., F., G., K., L., most Cursives. Theodoret comments on both. With respect to the omission of the words, "and upon all," it has been justly remarked that it would be impossible to account for their interpolation, as there was nothing in the clause, *for all them*, to demand this explanatory addition. It is easy to understand, on the contrary, how these words were omitted, either through a confusion of the two πάντας by the copyists—the Sinaitic abounds in such omissions—or because this clause seemed to be a pleonasm after the preceding. It is quite in keeping with Paul's manner thus to accumulate subordinate clauses to express by a change of preposition the different aspects of the moral fact which he means to describe. (Godet.)

coming Messiah in the prophecy of Jeremiah respecting "the Lord our Righteousness" (xxiii. 6), and that faith is to be the instrument by which individuals compass this righteousness is shown by the law in the account of Abraham believing in the Lord and it being accounted unto him for righteousness; and in the Prophets by the declaration of Habakkuk, "The just shall live by faith."

22. "Even the righteousness of God which is by faith of Jesus Christ," &c. This is an emphasizing repetition, but with a difference; in the last verse it was "the righteousness of God, without the law," which is manifested. Now it is the righteousness of God which is (which comes to us) by faith of Jesus Christ. It is not merely manifested, but it comes to us, and the mean is faith.

"By faith." What is faith? It is belief, but belief in what? Not in God as *a* Father, but in God as the Father of His Only-Begotten, Whom, out of His Supreme love, He gave for us. It is belief in Jesus Christ as the Only-Begotten Son—in all that is said of Him in Scripture as Incarnate, Crucified, Risen and Ascended—not that it embraces the whole revelation respecting Jesus at the first, but it has that in it which will refuse nothing, but will proceed to embrace and realize all.

"Unto all and upon all them that believe [εἰς πάντας καὶ ἐπὶ πάντας]. "Unto all." What is the signification of this "unto"? Surely it cannot mean that the righteousness of God moves towards a man, and stops short of entering into him—that would do him no good. He only receives a benefit when the righteousness enters into him, and subdues him according to the special prophecy respecting the New Covenant "I will put my law in their hearts and

23 For ᵉall have sinned, and come short of the glory of God:

ᵉ ver. 9. ch. xi. 32. Gal. iii. 22.

---

write it in their minds." Why, then, should not this preposition be here rendered "into"? In a very, very large number of places it must be rendered "into:" and so in this Epistle: "We have access by faith into this grace," "Sin entered into the world." There is a peculiar reason why in this place it should be rendered "into:" for how comes the righteousness of faith into us? does it not come in with, and only with, the Author of faith? Does not Christ, "The Lord our Righteousness," so come into us that the Apostle could say to the Corinthians: "Know ye not how that Jesus Christ is in you except ye be reprobates?"

"And upon all them that believe." As Philippi says: "It comes unto [into] all, and pours itself upon all like a stream." If both words are retained, "unto all" marks the destination, and "upon all," or "over all" the extension which the righteousness of God is to have. "Tò vero *super omnes*, significat sublimitatem justitiæ, quod scilicet illa supra naturæ vires et merita, desuper e cælo homini infundatur" (Anselm).

"For there is no difference." No difference amongst those who believe. Belief unites us to Him "in Whom is neither Jew nor Greek, Barbarian, Scythian, bond nor free, but Christ is all and in all" (Coloss. iii. 11).

23. "For all have sinned, and come short of the glory of God." The glory of God seems to mean here the glory which God will at last put upon the righteous: "Then shall the righteous shine forth as the sun in the glory of their Father." "Glory, honour, and peace to every man that worketh good."

The translation "coming short" of our Authorized seems exactly to express the idea of the original. None of themselves, or in their own strength, come up to the mark.

"In thy sight," the Psalmist says, "shall no man living be justified." "When ye have done all, say, We are unprofitable servants." "In many things we offend all," &c.

24. "Being justified freely by his grace through the redemption," &c. This, of course, does not mean that all are justified, but that all who are justified are so justified freely by God's grace.

CHAP. III.] JUSTIFIED FREELY. 61

24 Being justified freely ᶠ by his grace ᵍ through the redemption that is in Christ Jesus:

25 Whom God hath ‖ set forth ʰ *to be* a pro-

ᶠ ch. iv. 16.
Ephes. ii. 8.
Tit. iii. 5, 7.
ᵍ Matt. xx. 28. Ephes i. 7. Col. i. 14.
1 Tim. ii. 6.
Heb. ix. 12.
1 Pet. i. 18, 19.
‖ Or, *fore-ordained.*
ʰ Lev. xvi. 15.
1 John ii. 2.
& iv. 10.

"Freely," that is, without merits of their own. No matter how deeply they have offended God, if they turn from sin and turn to God, believing in Jesus Christ, they shall be justified. This word freely also anticipates what is coming respecting the redemption of captives. They are justified freely in that they are required to pay nothing themselves. It is impossible to suppose that anything can be added to that "Blood of God," that Blood of the Eternal Son by which the Church has been purchased.

"By his grace." The grace is not only the goodwill and loving purpose of God, whereby He graciously regards us, but the going forth of that goodwill in our actual justification.

"Through the redemption." Redemption means the buying again of captives. In Wickliffe it is translated the "agenbiynge." We were as a race sold to evil—the early Fathers said, sold to Satan —and God, by the Death and Blood-shedding of His Son, in some sense paid what was due from us in the way of punishment; for, after all, it comes to this, that we are ransomed from sin, from death, from the grave, from the hell of punishment. The theory, as it were, of Redemption, in the Divine Mind may be infinitely above comprehension; but the declaration of it in human language can only be by the expression of our being bought again from the dominion of sin and the obligation to be punished, in order that we may become the sons of God and heirs of Eternal Life.

"In Christ Jesus," that is, in His Death upon the Cross, the efficacy of which depends upon His Divinity and Incarnation, and the proof and assurance of it on His Resurrection.

25. "Whom God hath set forth to be a propitiation through faith in his blood." In this verse, which seems to contain the whole pith and marrow of the Gospel in its redemptive and propitiatory aspect, the initiative is given to the First Person in the Ever Blessed Trinity—God the Father, as it is in the words of Christ, "God so loved the world that he gave his only begotten Son." (John iii. 16.)

"God set forth." This may mean, God foreordained or decreed Him to be the propitiation or mercy seat; or it may mean, put

pitiation through faith [1] in his blood, to declare

[1] Col. i. 20.

Him before men, manifested Him in His Incarnation, Sufferings, and Exaltation. (Alford.)

"To be a propitiation." The only other place in which the Greek word (ἱλαστήριον) is used in the New Testament, is in Hebrews ix. 5: "Over it the cherubims of glory overshadowing the mercy seat." The mercy seat of the Jewish Tabernacle or Temple was the throne of God as peculiarly the God of mercy, where He engaged to meet His people and commune with them, thus, Exod. xxv. 21: "And thou shalt put the mercy seat above upon the ark ... And there will I meet with thee and I will commune with thee from above the mercy seat, from between the two cherubims which are upon the ark of the testimony, of all things which," &c. The mercy seat, therefore, taken in connection with this promise, was the most perfect type of God reconciling men to Himself and taking them into communion with Himself, of all the Old Testament types. It was also an abiding type. The propitiatory sacrifices and burnt offerings all passed away in the offering of them, whereas the mercy seat remained. And so, though the Bloody Sacrifice of the Eternal Son is not repeated, He ever abides as the Hilasterion, the place of meeting in terms of amity between God and His people, which is the effect of the Sacrifice. It is impossible to suppose that St. Paul could write the word Hilasterion or mercy seat without having in his mind the one thing which was actually called by the name. All the associations of that most holy thing were those of atonement, propitiation, continued access and communion. It is true that the mercy seat was for centuries behind a veil; but this veil was rent, and there is now access to the holiest through the Blood of Jesus.

This agrees with the words "set forth." Christ is now set forth, not under a veil, but plainly.

"Mercy seat" is the interpretation given by Theodoret and the Syriac. Most moderns, however, content themselves with a propitiation, or a propitiatory sacrifice.[1]

---

[1] Philippi, however, is very strong about the interpretation "mercy seat." He quotes Hengstenberg as saying, "To the Kapporeth, mercy-seat, all sin and trespass offerings stood in the closest relation. It formed their objective base, a summons and obligation to present them. What took place outwardly but once a year in the great sacrifice on the day of

CHAP. III.] THE FORBEARANCE OF GOD. 63

his righteousness ^k for the ‖ remission of ^l sins that are past, through the forbearance of God;

^k Acts xiii. 38, 39. 1 Tim. i. 15.
‖ Or, *passing over*.
^l Acts xvii. 30. Heb. ix. 15.

"Through faith in his blood." Nowhere else is the Blood of Christ said to be the object of faith, but it is surely a perfectly true and legitimate expression, if we understand it as faith in the efficacy of His Blood, faith in His Blood as atoning and propitiatory. Others, who do not seem desirous to accept a phrase not used in the rest of Scripture, render it a propitiation *in* or *by* His Blood, through faith, *i.e.*, given to those who have faith—faith is the medium through which the propitiating virtue comes to us.

"To declare his righteousness for the remission [or passing over, see Acts xvii. 30] of sins that are past." This place, difficult though it be in some respects, can have, as far as I can see, but one meaning—that the righteousness of God must be vindicated in that He passed over or remitted past sins (probably the sins of the ages before the coming of Christ) without exacting a penalty. Sin deserves punishment, and a just God must inflict it, and the only way of deliverance for the sinner from the effect of his past sins, is that "Christ himself bare our sins in his own body on the tree, that we being dead to sin should live to righteousness." But the Scripture idea of satisfaction is not the forensic idea of an angry judge, requiring an exact amount of penalty, but of a God graciously accepting a sacrifice. It is a great mystery, is that of atonement, but the mystery is hidden in the sacrifices of a temple, not in the proceedings of a law court. It is also connected with the fact that God has ordained that men should live as nations, and tribes, and families, each springing from one head, and taking their character in a great degree from that head. This, however, by the way. God had constantly, in every prophet, declared His displeasure against sin, and that it deserved punishment: and yet He had not punished it: now this His conduct towards sinners was not the forgiveness or ἄφεσις of their sins, but the πάρεσις, a word only used here in the New Testament. Godet translates it, the tolerance shown towards sins that were past. St. Paul here seems to

atonement, *i.e.*, the sprinkling of blood before the Kapporeth, took place spiritually on all sacrifices. Hence, according to Hebrews iv. 16, it is the type of the heavenly θρόνος τῆς χάριτος."

26 To declare, *I say*, at this time his righteousness: that

assert that the atoning work of Christ was the vindication of God's forbearance. He had not wholly remitted the sins of His people. He had for the time passed them over, anticipating through His foreknowledge that the time was coming when He should lay on the Messiah the iniquity of all. But why is the forbearance through which God passed over past sins specially mentioned? We answer, Because in the next verse St. Paul declares the present justification of believers through faith, and so he naturally puts in a word for those who "before faith came" (Gal. iii. 23), could not believe as men could after Christ was preached. These ages were not without some benefit from the Infinite Atonement, but their full forgiveness was suspended till the consummation of the Sacrifice, when the veil was rent, which by its existence in the Sanctuary to hide the mercy seat, betokened that perfect reconciliation was not till then effected.

26. "To declare, I say, at this time his righteousness: that he might be just," &c., *i.e.*, "for declaration of his righteousness." The declaration of the righteousness mentioned in the former verse was for a further purpose. It was to prepare the way for the fuller showing forth of His righteousness at the present time; not merely with reference to vindicating His righteousness in dealing forbearingly with the past sins of the world, but with their present and future sins. "It was partly owing to the long suffering of God that He "winked at" past sins, but there was likewise a further object, that He should set forth His Righteousness at the time appointed. He hid Himself that He might be revealed. The manifestation of His righteousness was the counterpart of His neglect [to punish] and His longsuffering. When the declaring ($\check{\epsilon}\nu\delta\epsilon\iota\xi\iota\varsigma$) was first mentioned this point of view was not touched upon, it is now indicated by the article ($\pi\rho\grave{o}\varsigma$ $\tau\grave{\eta}\nu$ $\check{\epsilon}\nu\delta\epsilon\iota\xi\iota\nu$). Compare for a similar mode of connecting the two halves of the dispensation, chap. v. verse 20, 'The law came in that sin might abound, but where sin abounded grace did much more abound.'" (Jowett.)

Alford translates, "with a view to the manifestation of His righteousness, in the present time"; similarly, Archdeacon Gifford in Speaker's Commentary.

"At this time," *i.e.*, when Christ is fully revealed.

"His righteousness: that he might be just, and the justifier of

CHAP. III.]   JUST AND THE JUSTIFIER.   65

he might be just, and the justifier of him which believeth in Jesus.

27 ᵐ Where *is* boasting then? It is excluded. By what law? of works? Nay: but by the law of faith.

ᵐ ch. ii. 17, 23. & iv. 2. 1 Cor. i. 29, 31. Ephes. ii. 9.

him," &c. His righteousness is now declared that men may see Him to be just, in that He does not pass over sins as if He cared not for them, but that in the very way by which He ordained that forgiveness should reach us—*i.e.*, the way of the Death of Christ, He should magnify the guilt of sin, which requires, in the way of atonement and propitiation, such a Sacrifice.

"The justifier of him which believeth in Jesus," or of him that is of the faith of Jesus. A repetition in other words of the idea in verse 22—" the righteousness of God which is by faith of Jesus Christ unto (into) all and upon all them that believe." He causes His righteousness to come into men as well as to envelop them. By an act of His sovereign grace acting through His Spirit He makes Christ to be unto us " wisdom and righteousness, and sanctification, and redemption."

"To declare . . . his righteousness." "What is declaring of righteousness? It is like the declaring of His riches, not only so as to show Himself as rich Himself, but so also as to make others rich, or declaring of life, not that He only is Himself living, but also that He makes the dead to live; and of His power, not that He only is powerful, but also that He makes the feeble powerful. So also is the declaring of His righteousness, not only that He is Himself righteous, but that He also maketh them that are filled with the putrefying sores of sin suddenly righteous . . . doubt not then, for it is not of works, but of faith; and shun not the righteousness of God, for it is a blessing in two ways: it is easy and also open to all men." (Chrysostom.)

27. "Where is boasting then? It is excluded. By what law? of works? Nay: but," &c. Why does the Apostle thus suddenly bring in "boasting"? Because boasting is the fruit of pride and self-sufficiency; and the Apostle experienced in his inmost soul that the doctrine of Salvation by grace through faith was a humbling doctrine, and he also saw and felt, from his own experience in his Jewish state, that the doctrine which he was opposing, that men were justified or saved by their own deeds, done in their own

F

n Acts xiii. 38, 39. ver. 20, 21, 22. ch. viii. 3. Gal. ii. 16.

28 Therefore we conclude ⁿ that a man is justi-

28. "Therefore we conclude." So B., C., K., L., P., most Cursives, Syriac; but ℵ, A., D., E., F., G., several Cursives (5, 9, 33, 38, 39, and d, e, f, g), Vulg., Copt., Arm., read, "for we conclude."

strength, apart from the strength of Christ, was a self-asserting principle irreconcilable with His Divine Master's first beatitude, "Blessed are the poor in spirit, for theirs is the kingdom of heaven." Boasting was the most prominent feature of the Jewish character. It was most painfully conspicuous in the strictest professors. And it was of all evil things within them (except covetousness) the most contrary to the realization of God's grace as *given* to His creatures. The whole evil, and indeed absurdity of boasting, is contained in the Apostolic question, "Who maketh thee to differ from another, and what hast thou that thou didst not receive? Now, if thou didst receive it, why dost thou glory as if thou hadst not received it?" *i.e.*, "as if it was properly and strictly thine own." (1 Cor. iv. 7.)

"By what law? of works? Nay, but by the law of faith." The law of faith excludes boasting or self-sufficiency, for its first function is to bring in all men guilty before God. All are in this respect on a level. None who apprehend it in the least degree will expect more from God on the ground that they have done more or are more holy; just as little will they presume that they have more faith, more spiritual perception, clearer views, and so are entitled to more consideration from God. The latter is the worst danger to some in these days.

"Nothing in my hand I bring,
Simply to thy Cross I cling."

28. "Therefore, we conclude that a man is justified by faith without the deeds of the law." There is a difference of reading, as will be seen by the critical note, some MSS. reading "therefore" others "for." Boasting is excluded by the law of faith, *for* we reckon that there is no room for it, because a man is justified by faith apart from the deeds of the law, or

"Therefore," from all that we have been saying, "we conclude that a man is justified," &c.

"Justified by faith without the deeds of the law." Or rather apart from, independent of, the deeds of the law.

fied by faith without the deeds of the law.

From the constant reference to the pretentiousness and boasting of the Jews in the preceding verses, and from the question in the succeeding verse (29), we have no doubt that the Apostle by "the works of the law" means the works of the Jewish law, moral as well as ceremonial.

In commencing our remarks upon this most momentous verse, we shall first have to ask whether "by faith without the works of the law" St. Paul means faith *alone*, irrespective of anything else in the man who is, or desires to be justified, *i.e.*, irrespective of the state of his soul.

It is impossible to believe such a thing for a moment, for a man's faith, as good or bad, moral or immoral, depends upon the state of the man's soul, whether penitent or impenitent, desirous to be rid of all sin, or hoping that being justified he may continue in the sin which he loves.

The faith of Mahometans, for instance, is in many respects stronger, in appearance at least, than the faith of most Christians; but then it is a faith which in no respect purifies the heart. On the contrary, it is the product of an impure heart looking to a god who has no love for holiness, that the man may enjoy after death the carnal delights of a sensual paradise. Now the faith of St. Paul is the opposite of this. It is the faith of one to whom God has given such a sense of sin that he earnestly desires to be delivered from its guilt and power, and so he comes to God through Him Whom God has set forth to be a propitiation, and through Him Whom God has set forth to be within us the origin of a new life of real goodness and holiness.[1] The relation of faith to a previous repentance is set forth in the parable of the Pharisee and the Publican.

The man who is not justified is the man who looks at himself and his works with satisfaction, and asserts them even before God; the man who says "I am no adulterer or fornicator, I keep myself chaste, I am honest and never take advantage of another in my dealings, I never backbite or slander: give me the reward of my just dealing,"—this man continues unjustified. Whereas the man who comes feeling and confessing, and deploring the sin of his past

---

[1] For a full examination of the relations of faith to the state of the soul, see my work on "Justification of Life," chap. iii.

life, and throwing himself upon God's promises declared unto mankind in Christ Jesus, coming consciously by faith to God through Christ, for pardon through His Blood, and grace and power to serve God through Christ's strength worked in Him, this man is justified.

I put out of sight here the means of grace, for the means of grace in the Christian Church—notably, the two great Sacraments—are not works, but acts of grace and faith. They are acts of grace on God's part, proffering to us membership with Christ, and His Body and Blood to be our spiritual food and sustenance; and we submit ourselves to this will of God, to give us His grace under such veils, through faith, steadfastly believing the promises of God made to us in the particular Sacrament which we receive. Again, it is quite obvious that we cannot be justified without prayer; and yet no one that I ever heard of has said that we are justified, either partly or wholly, by prayer.

Again, and lastly, St. Paul says that the only thing which availeth before God is "faith which worketh by love" (Gal. v. 6); and he very distinctly asserts that if a man have faith, so that he could remove mountains (and he evidently means by this the highest faith conceivable), and have not love, he is nothing. Now men have asked, and disputed with, and anathematized one another in their disputes on questions such as these. Does the love which is united to the faith, or is mixed with it, or inherent in it, contribute to the justification, or not? Surely it is, to say the least, beyond measure impertinent to entertain the question. Whether there be justifying faith, there is certainly no availing faith, no faith worth anything, without love. We have nothing to do with such analyzations, such dividings asunder of what is known only to God or to His Word—quick, powerful, sharper than any two-edged sword —Who alone discerns the thoughts and intents of the heart. What we have to do is to see to it, that we remember, with respect to forgiveness, that the great Dispenser of forgiveness has said: If ye forgive men their trespasses, your heavenly Father will also forgive your trespasses. But if ye forgive not men their trespasses, neither will your heavenly Father forgive you your trespasses.

"When the expression, 'without the deeds of the law,' is used, does this mean without the deeds of the ceremonial or the moral law, or without the fruits of faith, or without love, or without holiness? Or, when the Apostle says 'justified,' does he mean thereby to distinguish 'justified' from 'sanctified,' or a first

CHAP. III.]   ONE GOD WHO JUSTIFIES.   **69**

29 *Is he* the God of the Jews only? *is he* not also of the Gentiles? Yes, of the Gentiles also:

30 Seeing °*it is* one God, which shall justify the   ° ch. x. 12, 13.
                                                                                                                                               Gal. iii. 8, 20,
                                                                                                                                               28.

30. "Seeing [ἐπείπερ] it is one God." So D., E., F., G., K., L., P., most Cursives; but א, A., B., C., 5, 6, 47ᵗˣᵗ, 80, 137, &c., read, "If at least," (εἴπερ) "surely," as implying no doubt.

from a second justification, or to identify Justification with Baptism, or with Conversion? On such questions, in past times, have hung the fates of nations and of Churches. May we venture to supply the Apostle's answer to them? He might have replied that he meant only that men were justified from within, not from without; from above, not from below; by the grace of God, and not of themselves; by Christ, not by the law; not by the burden of ordinances, but by the power of an endless life." (Jowett.)

29. "Is he the God of the Jews only? is he not also of the Gentiles?" If He be the God of the Gentiles, then He must desire the moral well-being and salvation of the Gentiles. But this would not be consistent with men being justified by the deeds of the law, seeing that the Jews alone had as a body or nation that which could be called "Law," whereas faith was the common faculty of all, and when Jesus Christ was preached unto men, could be exercised by all to their present regeneration and final salvation.

30. "Seeing it is one God which shall justify," &c. One God; and so His method is one, *i.e.*, justifying men, whether Jews or Gentiles, by faith.

"Which shall justify the circumcision by faith and uncircumcision through (the) faith"—literally, who shall justify the circumcision of faith (or, out of faith) and uncircumcision through *the* faith. What is the reason for this difference, for reason there must be? The Apostle in part of one short verse speaks of the justification of Jews as "of" or "from" faith, and that of the Gentiles as "by *the* faith." The ancient commentators, Chrysostom and Theodoret, take no notice of the difference; most moderns also say that we are to lay no stress upon the difference, and in some way or other consider the terms as in reality synonymous. Origen, however, cited by Dr. Gifford, says: "It is not to be supposed that St. Paul has varied his use of prepositions at random;" and, as Dr. Gifford proceeds to say: "His use of the article is equally free from caprice."

circumcision by faith, and uncircumcision through faith.

I believe that the key to the meaning of the passage is in the use of the article before the second πίστεως. Διὰ τῆς πίστεως means "through the faith," not faith, not their faith, but *the* faith—the faith once delivered to the saints, the faith which was not revealed till the coming of Christ, when it first "came" (Gal. iii. 23, 25). *The* faith was the truth of Jesus Christ, which in its fulness could be more readily apprehended by the Gentiles than by the Jews, simply because the mind of the Gentile was not preoccupied; it was as a *tabula rasa*—any belief which might have remained in his mind respecting the old Gentile deities had vanished utterly; and the Christian conceptions respecting the Trinity and the creation of the world by the Son, and His absolute equality in nature with the Father, and the Divine Headship of Christ over the Church, the people of God, could easily take its place; but it was by no means so with the Jew. He had been brought up in, as he supposed, a system of strict Monotheism, and though there are intimations that this Monotheism might be consistent with a Second Person being included in this Unity, they are not very clear, and so God dealt very tenderly with his ancient people. As He permitted the Jewish converts to retain their sacrifices, their Jewish purifications, their Temple service, so apparently He did not impose on them at once and at the first the Catholic faith in all its fulness, especially that part of it which sets forth the equality of Christ with God, and His pre-existent state of glory in which He had created all things. Now all this is clear from the comparison of such books of Scripture as the Gospel of St. Matthew and the Epistle of St. James, on the one side, with the Gospel of St. John and the Epistle to the Colossians on the other. The Gospel of St. Matthew contains no absolute explicit statement respecting the Deity and pre-existence of Christ, and His creation of all things, such as that with which St. John's Gospel begins. The Epistle of St. James contains nothing like the theological doctrine respecting the person and works of the Eternal Son which we have in the Epistle to the Colossians.

But let me not be misunderstood. All the Divine glory of the Redeemer is contained by implication in the Gospel of Matthew and the Epistle of James; but it is certainly not on the surface of these books—not on their front, so to speak—as it is with the others

31 Do we then make void the law through faith? God

I have named. Could, then, the Christian Jews rest in a somewhat imperfect realization of the Saviour? Certainly not; and they did not. If they followed on to know the Lord, and when Judaism as a system was ready to vanish away, then they could take in and assimilate such meat as the Epistle to the Hebrews. So that, compared with them, the Gentiles were justified διὰ τῆς πίστεως—the whole system of the Gospel considered as the independent "law of the Spirit of Life in Christ Jesus;" whereas, in the case of the Jews, ἡ πίστις was not so pronounced and prominent. It was rather πίστις which for some time had not its full complement in the Catholic faith—the faith once for all delivered to the Saints.[1]

31. "Do we then make void the law through faith? God forbid," &c. This question seems to come in abruptly; but that would not be altogether contrary to the usage of St. Paul. Some have thought that what follows in the next chapter, respecting Abraham, taken from the first book of the law, was an instance of that establishing of the law by faith which is here asserted. And, if so, it would be parallel to what we find in close connection with this subject in Gal. iv.: "Tell me, ye that desire to be under the law, do ye not hear the law?" And then he proceeds to unfold the instruction respecting the bondage of the law, and the freedom of the Gospel, contained in the history of Abraham's household; but I think that we should rather take the question as one which naturally occurred to the Apostle's mind. He was profoundly alive to the accusation of Antinomianism brought against the Gospel. He alludes to it here but for a moment, and then sets it aside with his emphatic Μὴ γένοιτο; and then returns to it again in chap. vi. and the beginning of chap. viii. And in chap. xiii. we find him applying the law of the Second Table to all Christians, through the summary of it in the law of love: "Thou shalt love thy neighbour as thyself."

---

[1] Of modern expositors Dr. Vaughan seems to come nearest to the truth. "ἐκ πίστεως, of (as the outgrowth of) faith. διὰ τῆς πίστεως, through (by means of) the Faith. The two terms are equivalent and convertible, but they differ in form. The one is (1) faith, the act of believing; the other is (2) the faith, the object of belief in the Gospel. For an illustration of the distinction see Gal. iii. 22-26, ἵνα ἡ ἐπαγγελία ἐκ πίστεως(1)'Ιησοῦ Χριστοῦ δοθῇ . . . . πρὸ τοῦ δὲ ἐλθεῖν τὴν πίστιν (2) . . . . εἰς τὴν μέλλουσαν πίστιν (2) ἀποκαλυφθῆναι . . . . ἵνα ἐκ πίστεως (1) δικαιωθῶμεν . . . . ἐλθούσης δὲ τῆς πίστεως (2) . . . . υἱοὶ Θεοῦ ἐστε διὰ τῆς πίστεως (2)."

forbid: yea, we establish the law.

How then did the preachers of Justification by faith, apart from the works of the law, establish the law? They established the law because they put it on a firmer and higher basis as a spiritual law. They established it as a rule of outward and, at the same time, inward life. They extended its application to the most secret thoughts and intents of the heart; above all, they established it because they preached that men had through Christ a power of fulfilling it, and that, at the bar of Christ the Judge, they would be examined as to whether they had spiritually, as well as literally, lived in conformity with it, because of the new power and grace—indeed, the new life—which they had received under the Gospel.

CHAP. IV.

ᵃ Is. li. 2.
Matt. iii. 9.
John viii. 33, 39. 2 Cor. xi. 22.

WHAT shall we say then that ᵃAbraham our father, as pertaining to the flesh, hath found?

---

1. "Our father, as pertaining," &c. So D., E., F., G., K., L., P., most Cursives, Vulg., d, e, f, g, &c.; but ℵ, A., B., C., 5, 10, 21, 137, Syr., Cop., Arm., read "forefather." Respecting order of words, see below.

1. "What shall we say then that Abraham our father, as pertaining to the flesh, hath found?" Some take the words "as pertaining to the flesh" with "hath found"—what shall we say that Abraham hath found "as pertaining to the flesh," opposing "the flesh" as meaning his unrenewed nature, to "the spirit" as meaning faith; but the Apostle has not mentioned hitherto the opposition between flesh and spirit; nor does he, till the seventh chapter, so that the anticipation of it would be quite out of place.

"Hath found," *i.e.*, hath attained to, *i.e.*, what righteousness or justification, or acceptance with God hath he received, and how?

The Apostle now proceeds to cite and argue upon the strongest case conceivable in the eyes of the Jew. Abraham's righteousness

2 For if Abraham were ^b justified by works, he hath *whereof* to glory; but not before God.

3 For what saith the scripture? ^c Abraham believed God, and it was counted unto him for righteousness.

^b ch. iii. 20, 27, 28.
^c Gen. xv. 6. Gal. iii. 6. James ii. 23.

---

was considered by the Jew as thrown round and enveloping, or imputed to all his descendants (*i.e.*, through Isaac and Jacob), so that in the way of imputed righteousness he was to them as Christ is to us. How stands the matter respecting Abraham's justification? Cannot Abraham, at least, boast? Has he not something to boast of in himself, apart from the help or grace of God?

2. " For if Abraham were justified by works, he hath whereof to glory." By works, of course, are here meant works done before justification or the reception of the Spirit of God—works done in his own strength.

"But not before God." Even he cannot of himself stand before God, much less boast before Him.

3. "For what saith the scripture? Abraham believed God, and it was counted," &c. This account of Abraham's faith is found in Gen. xv. 6. He had had the promise that he should be the father of many nations, and that his seed should possess the land of Canaan, and that in his seed all the families of the earth should be blessed, and yet the fulfilment of this had been delayed so long, that, as regards the begetting of children, his body was now dead, and so was the womb of Sarah. It was after he had generously rescued Lot and the people of the cities of the plain from their invaders, and had received the solemn blessing of Melchisedech the priest of the most high God, the type of the Son of God in His Sacerdotal and Kingly office, that the word of the Lord came unto him in a vision: "Fear not, Abraham: I am thy shield, and thy exceeding great reward," and to this Abraham replied, "Lord God, what wilt thou give me, seeing I go childless, and the steward of my house is this Eliezer of Damascus? Behold, to me thou hast given no seed, and lo one born in my house is mine heir. And behold the word of the Lord came unto him, saying, This shall not be thine heir; but he that shall come forth out of thine own bowels shall be thine heir. And God brought him forth abroad [*i.e.*, to the door of his tent] and said, Look now toward heaven, and tell the stars, if

TO HIM THAT WORKETH NOT. [ROMANS.

4 Now ^d to him that worketh is the reward not reckoned of grace, but of debt.

^d ch. xi. 6.

5 But to him that worketh not, but believeth on him that justifieth ^e the ungodly, his faith is counted for righteousness.

^e Josh. xxiv. 2.

---

thou be able to number them: and God said to Abraham, So shall thy seed be. And Abraham believed in the Lord, and he counted it to him for righteousness."

This the Apostle takes as meaning that he was justified by faith, and not by works, and it is the one single place where the justification of Abraham, or righteousness being imputed to him, is mentioned: the extraordinary significance of this we shall soon see.

4. "Now to him that worketh is the reward not reckoned of grace, but of debt." The workman who works for hire receives his reward, *i.e.*, his hire, not as a thing given to him out of benevolence or charity, but as a debt due to him. St. Paul by saying this here, very emphatically separates Abraham from the number of those who served God for rewards of any sort.

5. "But to him that worketh not, but believeth on him that justifieth the ungodly," &c. The solemn accounting of Abraham's faith for righteousness, *i.e.*, his justification by faith, took place (and designedly so on God's part) when Abraham did nothing in the way of work, but only came out at God's bidding to the door of his tent, and believed in the promise of God that his seed should be as the stars of heaven for multitude. Considered with regard to external circumstances, it was as bare an act of faith as could well be imagined: considered, however, with respect to what took place in Abraham's soul, it was indeed a faith which removed mountains; but on this we shall find opportunity to say something when we come to verses 19, 21. Now the significance of this reckoning of Abraham's faith to him for righteousness will be apparent when we consider that there are three instances of Abraham's faith recorded—the first and third of these, accompanied by marvellous acts of self-denial and self-surrender; the second, on the contrary, without any work accompanying it, was when he took God at His word. The first of these works was when he left his country and his kindred and father's house and lived as a stranger in a strange land, the third when in intention he offered up his son Isaac on the altar;

CHAP. IV.] GOD IMPUTETH. 75

6 Even as David also describeth the blessedness of the man, unto whom God imputeth righteousness without works,

7 *Saying,* ⁱBlessed *are* they whose iniquities are forgiven, and whose sins are covered.

ⁱ Ps. xxxii. 1, 2.

8 Blessed *is* the man to whom the Lord will not impute sin.

---

but no word is said by St. Paul of his justification in connection with either of these; whereas, in connection with the second, when he simply believed that his seed should be as the stars of heaven for multitude, an expression is used, unique in the Old Testament, "He believed in the Lord, and he counted it to him for righteousness." So unique, I say, is the expression that it startles us. It seems a verse of the New Testament interpolated into the Old. And in point of fact this is not far from the truth, when we remember that St. Paul writes a little farther on, "It was not written for his sake alone, that it was imputed to him, but for us also." There is but one place in the Old Testament which, as regards the efficacy of faith, can come near to it, "The just shall live by faith," and this has been already cited by the Apostle (Rom. i. 17).

6-8. "Even as David also describeth the blessedness of the man, unto whom God imputeth righteousness .... will not impute sin." The second case which the Apostle cites as teaching the same lesson is that of David in Psalm xxxii.

There is no direct mention in this quotation of God imputing faith as righteousness to David, but the imputation takes a negative form. The man who wrote the Psalm had evidently sinned most grievously (verses 5, 6), and yet the Lord had not imputed sin to him, because He had treated him as if he had not sinned, *i.e.*, He had wiped away or blotted out his sin, and having done this, God treated the man as if he were righteous. Now, why had the Lord so passed over the man's sin? Evidently because he had acknowledged and confessed it, as we are told in so many words in verses 5 and 6. But as evidently the whole Psalm bears testimony that God imputed the Psalmist's faith to him as righteousness, because there is no Psalm which in so short a space expresses such deep— one may say such Evangelical—faith in God. The Psalmist from beginning to end makes no mention of any works of his own, but simply and merely expresses his faith in God, and throws himself upon His mercy.

9 *Cometh* this blessedness then upon the circumcision *only,* or upon the uncircumcision also? for we say that faith was reckoned to Abraham for righteousness.

10 How was it then reckoned? when he was in circumcision, or in uncircumcision? Not in circumcision, but in uncircumcision.

" I said, I will confess my sins unto the Lord, and so thou forgavest the iniquity of my sin. . . . Thou art a place to hide me in, thou shalt compass me about with songs of deliverance," and above all, verse 10, "Whoso putteth his trust in the Lord, mercy embraceth him on every side."

There is one passage in the Psalm to be noted: I said that justification, though in no respect depending upon works, depends upon the state of a man's soul in God's sight, and this is acknowledged by the Psalmist in the latter clause of the verse quoted by the Apostle in the words, " and in whose spirit there is no guile." Now this undoubtedly means that the justified man whom the utterer of the Psalm represents, was sincere in his profession both of a sense of sin and of trust in God, and in fact that God should justify a man dishonest and insincere, or hypocritical either in profession or practice, is a thing not to be named.

9, 10. " Cometh this blessedness then upon the circumcision . . . not in circumcision but in uncircumcision." This blessedness means this declaration of blessing, this beatification, as some render it.

The Apostle here anticipates an objection which a Jew was sure to make. The Jew would say, was not Abraham circumcised? and so was he not under the law? and though that law might not have been given in full till some four hundred years after, still, being circumcised, was he not under the dispensation of the law? was he not at any rate under a covenant of works? The Jew, in order that he might exalt the sign and seal of the Mosaic covenant ignored all the life of Abraham till his circumcision; his blessedness, his covenant with God only dating really, in the Jew's eyes, from the moment of his circumcision. Now St. Paul does not allow this for a moment. He reminds the Jew that God imputed righteousness to Abraham, *i.e.*, He justified him, long before he was circumcised, certainly thirteen years before, perhaps more: for Abraham was

THE SIGN OF CIRCUMCISION.

11 And ^g he received the sign of circumcision, a seal of the righteousness of the faith which *he had yet being uncircumcised*: that ^h he might be the father of all them that believe, though they be not circumcised; that righteousness might be imputed unto them also:

g Gen. xvii. 10.
h Luke xix. 9. ver. xii. 16. Gal. iii. 7.

---

justified on his believing the word of God respecting the number of his seed, and then there intervened the birth of Ishmael, and when Ishmael was thirteen years old Abraham circumcised him along with himself (Gen. xvii. 25). What then was circumcision to Abraham? The Apostle answers,

11. "And he received the sign of circumcision, a seal of the righteousness," &c. So then not only was Abraham justified before he was circumcised, but his very circumcision witnessed to the value of his previous righteousness, for God would not make a solemn religious covenant with an unrighteous man, that is, a man living wilfully and determinedly in unrighteousness. But what was Abraham's righteousness previous to his circumcision? It was a righteousness of faith, not of the law, *i.e.*, it was a righteousness whose root was an acceptance of the promises of God, which raised up Abraham's soul to God and united him to God, and when the need came it appeared in fruits of outward righteousness utterly beyond the power of any mere law to produce, as, for instance, his offering of his son. His circumcision then was the seal of the approval with which God regarded his faith and its fruits, which were the fruits of a higher principle by far than that of the normal Jew, or of the servant who works for hire, or of the slave who works through fear.

But there was a further reason for God's action in justifying Abraham before his circumcision. The principle of justification by faith was for some time to be somewhat in abeyance, when God brought in the law (Rom. v. 20, Gal. iii. 19, 23), but this was only for a time. As soon as God had reconciled the world to Himself, and Christ His Son had sent His Apostles to preach the Gospel to all, then the old principle of righteousness through faith was restored, and God had prepared for its restoration by causing that the great Father of His chosen people should receive justification before he received circumcision; by this enabling Abraham to be the father

12 And the father of circumcision to them who are not of the circumcision only, but who also walk in the steps of that faith of our father Abraham, which *he had* being *yet* uncircumcised.

13 For the promise, that he should be the [i] heir of the world, *was* not to Abraham, or to his seed, through the law, but through the righteousness of faith.

[i] Gen. xvii. 4, &c. Gal. iii. 29.

---

of all them that believe, in order that, apart from the law, they might receive justification through faith as Abraham had.

12. "And the father of circumcision to them who are not of the circumcision only," &c. There is a doubt respecting the exact meaning of this verse. It may mean, "And the father of circumcision to them who are not of the circumcision only, but to those also who walk in the footsteps of that faith of our father Abraham which he had when he was justified in the state of uncircumcision." In this case the latter clause would refer to the faithful Gentiles, whose uncircumcision would then be counted for circumcision, so as to make them the children of Abraham, so that then Abraham would be the father of all the faithful.

Or the verse may mean, The father of circumcision not to them who are of the circumcision only, *i.e.*, who have the bare rite and nothing more, but have also the circumcision of the heart, who "walk in the steps of that faith," &c. In the former case the fatherhood of Abraham is extended to all the faithful uncircumcised. In the latter, the fatherhood of Abraham is restricted to those Jews who walked in the steps of Abraham's faith, according to our Lord's words (John viii. 39), "If ye were Abraham's children ye would do the works of Abraham." The latter meaning seems most in accordance with strict grammatical accuracy.

Both meanings are true. Abraham is the spiritual father of all the faithful, but only of the faithful. It is an absolutely Catholic principle, one of the most general application, that faith, which is the faculty of the soul which recognizes God and Christ, and the unseen and eternal world, is the only ground of acceptance with God.

13. "For the promise, that he should be the heir of the world, was," &c. The promise to Abraham that he should be the heir of the world can only be the promise that the Messiah, Who should

14 For ᵏ if they which are of the law *be* heirs, faith is made void, and the promise made of none effect: ᵏ Gal. iii. 18.

---

have universal dominion, and in Whom all families of the earth should be blessed, should be his seed; but this promise was given to him long before he was circumcised, and long (400 years) before the promulgation of the law; so that whatever righteousness he had then was not through circumcision, which might be taken to be a sort of anticipation of the covenant of Sinai, much less through the covenant of Sinai itself, but through faith. It was a free, loving, filial laying hold of the promises of God, a realization of His holy character, and a determination to live with a view to His approval.

14. "For if they which are of the law be heirs, faith is made void, and the promise," &c. It seems impossible to suppose that by the law, or rather "law," St. Paul means anything else than the law of Moses. Some suppose that he means law in the abstract, but St. Paul never opposes law, taken abstractedly, to the Gospel. The law written on the heart—the natural law—is never, as far as I can remember, set by him against the Gospel as the law of Moses always is. We must then take this to mean what in ninety-nine cases out of a hundred law means, the law of the Ten Commandments. If they which are under the dispensation of the law, pure and simple, are heirs, faith is made void. What is faith which is here made void? The word in the Greek has the article just as "promise" has, and the sentence should be translated "The faith is made void, and the promise made of none effect." In this case faith would have the same meaning as it has in Gal. iii. 23, 25; and would signify the dispensation of faith—the dispensation of the Gospel—the faith once for all delivered to the saints; this would be made void, if the law made men heirs of glory, for in that case there would be no reason for the setting aside of the law and the introduction of the Gospel. A further consideration will make plain the opposition of *the* faith to the law in which the Apostle insists. Under the law faith (taken subjectively) was never made void, for it was that disposition of soul which made the keeping of the law, even in an imperfect way, acceptable to God. For instance, what use would the keeping of the first commandment be if the man who professed to keep it merely abstained from recognizing any other gods, but did not believe Jehovah to be

THE LAW WORKETH WRATH. [ROMANS,

ⁱ ch. iii. 20. &
v. 13, 20. & vii.
8. 10. 11. 1
Cor. xv. 56.
2 Cor. iii. 7, 9.
Gal. iii. 10, 19.
1 John iii. 4.

15 Because ¹the law worketh wrath: for where no law is, *there is* no transgression.

---

15. " For (γὰρ) where no law is." So D., E., F., G., K., L., P., most Cursives, d, e, f, g, Vulg., Syriac; but ℵ, A., B., C., 10, 31, 80, 124, Copt., read, " but." " But where no law is," &c.

the one living and true God? Faith then, to a certain extent, existed all through the older dispensation, but *the* faith did not. It *came* only when Christ was preached. It consisted in the proclamation of the Gospel—that the Son of God was, for our Salvation, Incarnate, Crucified, Risen, and Ascended. This was proposed to men that they should accept it, and be regenerated and renewed by it. The acceptance of it made them enter into all the redeeming love of God. Now if the law had been able to do all that "the faith" did, why should God set it aside as a means of justification? If the law then justified men, and made them heirs of the kingdom, the faith was useless. Christ came and died and rose again in vain.

"The promise made of none effect." This probably means that if only those under the law, *i.e.*, Israelites after the flesh, were the seed of Abraham, then the promise that he should be the heir of the world came to nothing, or it may mean that if all mankind were to be saved through the law, then there was no need of any promise. The Apostle opposes the law and the promise in Galatians iii. 18, " If the inheritance be of the law it is no more of promise, but God gave it to Abraham by promise." Abraham was justified by faith, and received the promise of the inheritance long before the law came in; and so both his justification and his inheritance of the world through his seed must be independent of the law.

15. "Because the law worketh wrath; for where no law is, there is no transgression." Why does the law work wrath? Because it calls down punishment upon offenders. This effect of the law is not in the law itself, but in the evil nature of those who come under it. It convinces them of sin, but has no offers of mercy in itself whereby their sins may be pardoned and the power of evil habits broken. These offers of mercy belong to another system, that of grace, or of the Gospel, which, in some respects, was anticipated, though very imperfectly, in the atoning sacrifices of the law. In another way also the law works wrath, for owing to the rebellion

CHAP. IV.]   OF FAITH—BY GRACE.   **81**

16 Therefore *it is* of faith, that *it might be* ^m by grace; ⁿ to the end the promise might be sure to all the

^m ch. iii. 24.
ⁿ Gal. iii. 22.

against God inherent in our fallen nature, it irritates us into disobedience. This, however, I shall have many opportunities of considering further on in this Epistle.

"Where no law is, there is no transgression." Children, idiots, and the inferior creatures not being able to apprehend any law, are not held to be responsible for their actions. The heathen also having no direct revelation respecting the Unity of the Divine Essence, could not be held to be so sinful as the Jews if they worshipped the gods which their fathers worshipped.

16. "Therefore it is of faith, that it might be by grace; to the end the promise might be sure to all the seed," &c. "Therefore," *i.e.*, from all the preceding argument. All that the Apostle has hitherto written culminates in this, that the law being mere command to do right without imparting grace to obey to creatures whose nature was weakened through sin, could not justify, and besides this it could not justify because it was the means of convicting those to whom it came of sin, and was further the means of calling out the sinfulness of their nature. This law, good and holy though it was, as coming from God, must be superseded if all men were to be justified before God and inherit Eternal Life. But what could supersede it? Evidently something which satisfied these two conditions: first, that it could be attainable by all; and secondly, that it could impart perfect reconciliation and forgiveness to those who had sinned, and grace and power to those who are weak. Now all this was in the Gospel of the Son of God. It is the good news of the Eternal Son coming amongst us, clothing Himself with our nature, in His life amongst us manifesting the righteousness of God, dying for us as our Sacrifice for sin, rising again to assure us that He had fully atoned for all sin, and could also impart to us the virtue and power of His risen life, and all this to be given to us at once, on our believing it. So that it is "of grace" in this way, that a circumcised Jew and an uncircumcised Gentile are at once put on the same level. If they believe and are baptized they are made members of Christ, and they cannot be made anything greater; and, besides this, they have not to wait for one, or two, or three years, or even months, whilst they are doing good works which may entitle them to be made members of Christ, but

G

seed; not to that only which is of the law, but to that also which is of the faith of Abraham; °who is the father of us all,

<small>° Isai. li. 2.
ch. ix. 8.</small>

---

they are without further delay entitled to be grafted into His mystical Body in order that they may bring forth fruit unto God. Now God has ordained that for the salvation of every soul this should be apprehended by faith, that faith which God has given to all human beings as the means by which they apprehend the things of the eternal world when they are duly presented to them, and this for a further reason, that it may be "by grace," that is, that they may receive all from God's hands as a free gift; for it makes the very greatest difference in our conception of God whether we look upon Him as an open-handed, generous God, or as one Who gives the gifts pertaining to salvation tardily, sparingly, almost grudgingly, demanding something first before He bestows even His first gifts.

In such wise are the words, "it is of faith that it might be by grace," to be understood. But the Apostle proceeds further, "that the promise might be sure to all the seed, not to that only which is of the law, but to that also which is of the faith of Abraham." What is the faith of Abraham? At first we should suppose that it was his faith in God as fulfilling His promise, "so shalt thy seed be," and we know also that the true fulfilment of this promise was bound up in the coming of the Messiah out of his loins, because it was only through the Messiah that he became the father of all the faithful, a family infinitely more numerous than the legal or Israelitish family: but must we not look to the next verse, or rather the following verses, for the true interpretation? What did Abraham really believe, if he believed in the promise that the seed of his own body should be as numerous as the stars? Evidently in God as the Quickener of the dead, and having in His mind the whole temporal and spiritual seed which should result through that restoration to life of what was dead in Abraham's body. Now if there be one thing in the dealings of God with man upon which the Apostle would fix the eye of our faith, it is upon God quickening the dead Body of the Lord Jesus, and through His power quickening first the dead souls, and then the dead bodies of those in Jesus. The same faith in God as the Quickener of the dead which enabled Abraham to embrace God's promise, enables the Christian now to

17 (As it is written, ᵖ I have made thee a father of many nations,) ‖ before him whom he believed, *even* God, ᑫ who quickeneth the dead, and calleth those ʳ things which be not as though they were.

18 Who against hope believed in hope, that he might become the father of many nations, according to that which was spoken, ˢ So shall thy seed be.

ᵖ Gen. xvii. 5.
‖ Or, *like unto him.*
ᑫ ch. viii. 11.
Ephes. ii. 1, 5.
ʳ ch. ix. 26.
1 Cor. i. 28.
1 Pet. ii. 10.
ˢ Gen. xv. 5.

---

embrace the infinitely greater promises of which the Lord's quickened Body is the assurance. And so Abraham, because his belief rested in God as the Quickener of the dead, is the father of us all. An examination of verses 16, 17, 20-24, will show the truth of this.

17. "As it is written, I have made thee a father of many nations." This is thrown in by the way, as it were, and is valuable as showing that the many nations were not the fleshly descendants of different tribes, as Ishmaelites and Edomites, but the children of God scattered throughout all the world.

"Before him whom he believed." This follows upon "The father of many nations." In the sight of God, Who knows all who through faith will belong to Him, though Abraham was then childless, he was yet, in the eyes of God, the father of the whole family of the faithful.

"Whom he believed, even God, who quickeneth the dead, and calleth those things," &c. Godet well remarks: "The two divine attributes on which the faith of Abraham fastened at this decisive moment were the power to quicken, and the power to create. It was, indeed, in this twofold character that God presented Himself when He addressed to him the words quoted: ' I have made thee '—here is the assurance of a Resurrection—'father of many nations,' here is the promise of a creation . . . . It is in the Patriarch's own person, already a centenarian, and his wife almost as old as he, that a resurrection must take place if the Divine promise is to be fulfilled."

18. "Who against hope believed in hope, that he might become the father," &c. "Against hope," *i.e.*, against all earthly human hope, all natural hope, all human probability.

"Believed in hope." Believed in God's words, and so his hope rested in his belief in God's faithfulness and power.

19 And being not weak in faith, [t] he considered not his own body now dead, when he was about an hundred years old, neither yet the deadness of Sarah's womb:

[t] Gen. xvii. 17. & xviii. 11. Heb. xi. 11, 12.

---

19. "He considered not." So D., E., F., A., K., L., P., most Cursives (d, e, f, g); but אּ, A., B., C., 67**, 93, 137, Vulg. (Cod. Amiat.), Syriac, Copt., omit "not."

Notice how in this first and greatest act of faith the true nature of faith shines forth in the father of the faithful. It is the evidence of things not seen. According to nature—according to all the sequences, or so-called laws of nature—Abraham could have no son, but Abraham believed in God, Who being the Author of nature could order it as He pleased; above all he believed that He could quicken that which was dead. Now all nature with one voice proclaims the absolutely universal and irreversible law that life cannot be restored to the dead, whereas the first truth which the faith of Abraham grasps, is that God quickens the dead.

"That he might become the father of many nations," &c. "That he might become" should be rendered "in order that he might become." The exercise of his faith on his part was the condition on which so infinite an honour was bestowed upon him by God.

If God can set aside or reverse this sequence—this so-called "law of nature"—He can reverse or set aside all. Nothing can be impossible which He promises.

19, 20. "And being not weak in faith, he considered not his own body," &c. "He considered not," that is, "he took no account of"— his own deadness as regards the begetting of children presented no difficulty. Such seems the only possible meaning in accordance with what has gone before, especially in verses 17, 18; but here we have to face the fact that the principal Uncial MSS. omit the "not," and read, "he considered (or took into account) the deadness of his own body, and the deadness of Sarah's womb." So that in this case we should paraphrase it: "Being not weak in faith, he realized his deadness in the matter of procreation; and yet, notwithstanding this, he was not moved from his faith, believing that nothing is impossible with God."

In the former case, retaining the negative "not," reference is made to Genesis xv. 6, where there is no hesitation on the part of Abra-

GIVING GLORY TO GOD.

20 He staggered not at the promise of God through unbelief; but was strong in faith, giving glory to God:
21 And being fully persuaded that, what he had promised, ^u he was able also to perform.

u Ps. cxv. 3.
Luke i. 37, 45.
Heb. xi. 19.

---

ham expressed or implied; but if the negative is to be omitted, then it is supposed that the Apostle has in his mind Genesis xvii., where after God had promised that the seed should come from Sarah, Abraham fell upon his face, and laughed, and said in his heart, Shall a child be born unto him that is an hundred years old, and shall Sarah that is ninety years old bear? So that here we have a slight staggering at the promise, not as it was originally delivered, "so shall thy seed be," but that this seed should proceed from Sarah. Abraham did not for a moment doubt respecting the original promise of Genesis xv. 6; but he evidently thought that it might come to pass through Ishmael, for he prayed, "O that Ishmael might live before thee!" St. Paul then must, I think, have written, "He considered not," which would be perfectly true of the original promise at the tent door, but not so absolutely true of the promise of Gen. xvii., which limited the performance to the child of Sarah.

"But was strong in faith, giving glory to God." "Was strong in faith." "See the pertinacity of Paul. For since the discourse was about those that work and those that believe, he shows that the believer works more than the other, and requires more power [from God], and great strength, and sustains no common degree of labour. For they (the Jews) counted faith worthless, as having no labour in it. Insisting, then, upon this (that the believer requires more power) he shows that it is not only he that succeeds in temperance, or any other virtue of this sort, but he who displays faith also who requires even greater power. For as the one requires strength to break off the reasonings of intemperance, so hath the faithful also need of a soul endued with power that he may thrust aside the suggestions of unbelief. How, then, did he become strong? By trusting the matter (he replies) to faith, and not to reasonings: else he had fallen." (Chrysostom.)

"Giving glory to God:"

21. "And being fully persuaded that, what he had promised, he was able," &c. Nothing so glorifies God as belief in His Divine

22 And therefore it was imputed to him for righteousness.

Attributes. Now by this act of faith Abraham believed in God's truth, His power, His fore-knowledge, His all-ruling providence, and His goodness.

"And being fully persuaded that what he had promised," &c. What was it that impressed Abraham with this belief in God? Evidently constant intercourse with Him. We do not know the nature of God's revelations of Himself to Abraham, but when God chose him at the first He chose a noble soul, fitted to receive all that God taught him respecting Himself, desirous of rising up to the greatness of the revelations vouchsafed to him. See how Abraham realized God as a God Who hears and answers prayer in his intercession for Sodom. See how Abraham realized the justice of God's character when he exclaimed, "Shall not the judge of all the earth do right?" Quesnel says of his faith : "A faith ready with respect to the most difficult things ; undisturbed amidst all the contradictions of human reason ; obedient, so far as to sacrifice everything, persevering under the severest trials ; and constant and faithful amidst the infidelity of the rest of the world : this is the fulness of Abraham's faith : let us study to imitate it that we may be the true children of God." (Quesnel.)

22. "And therefore it was imputed to him for righteousness." We must now carefully consider in what sense faith could be accounted, or reckoned, or imputed unto him for righteousness.

Now, first of all, it is quite clear that neither faith nor anything else could be reckoned by a righteous God to Abraham in lieu of, or instead of, his ultimately possessing any branch or sort of righteousness which an intelligent creature of God ought to possess ; take, for instance, one thing, which shall be the righteous bringing up of, or ruling of, or instructing a family—God, long after He had counted Abraham's faith to him as righteousness, said of Abraham, "I know him that he will command his children and his household after him, and they shall keep the way of the Lord, to do justice and judgment, that the Lord may bring upon Abraham that which he hath spoken of him" (Gen. xviii. 19). And, again, if anything could be imputed to any intelligent creature of God which should be instead of his possessing some department of righteousness, that creature would be irremediably injured by it, because it is to the infinite advantage of any intelligent being that he should be morally perfect, because being so he is in accord with the great governing Spirit of the universe. How, for instance, can the righteousness of Christ be imputed to us so that He should be our righteousness, in the sense of honesty or uprightness, whilst we are rogues? He our purity, whilst we are filthy in heart or life? He our love or charity, whilst we bite and devour one another? The idea cannot be entertained for a moment. And yet in one shape or another it is practically entertained by vast numbers of professing Christians.

Again, if faith is imputed to Abraham, or any other person, for righteousness, that faith must be on the side of righteousness, or calculated, if persevered in, to produce righteousness, or to end in righteousness. The faith which can be imputed for righteousness cannot be indifferent to righteousness. On the contrary, it must proceed from a soul in its very depths renouncing sin and desirous of righteousness, and in the case of the Christian it must be directed to, and be fastened upon, a Saviour Whose mission is to implant and perfect righteousness in His people. Consequently that faith cannot be imputed for righteousness, which merely or mainly looks upon Christ as a substitute, so that He should be righteous for us whilst we wilfully or knowingly continue unrighteous; but *that* faith only can be imputed for righteousness which regards Him as come to make good in each man's case His own beatitude, " Blessed are they which do hunger and thirst after righteousness, for they shall be filled."

Now the faith which could be imputed unto Abraham for righteousness was one which could be imputed in no arbitrary, or forensic, or unreal way, but which could naturally be so imputed by One Who was able to discern it in all its issues—in all its capacities for good. If we in our poor way can impute to a seed which we know to have the germ of life in it the beauty and fruitfulness of the future plant, and so impute life to it as to treat it as if it had the capacities of a living organism latent within it, much more could God, looking into the capacities for good of Abraham's faith, impute it to him for righteousness: and God, if one may so speak, was justified in so doing, for in due time this faith which could believe in God's multiplying the seed of a childless man, so that it should be as the stars of heaven, moved Abraham to surrender at God's bidding his son, his only son, whom he loved, accounting that God was able to raise him from the dead.

23 Now ˣ it was not written for his sake alone, that it was imputed to him;

24 But for us also, to whom it shall be imputed, if we believe ʸ on him that raised up Jesus our Lord from the dead;

ˣ ch. xv. 4.
1 Cor. x. 6, 11.

ʸ Acts ii. 24.
& xiii. 30.

---

23. "Now it was not written for his sake alone, that it was imputed," &c. It was not written merely for Abraham's honour, or the credit of his faith.

24. "But for us also, to whom it shall be imputed, if we believe on him," &c. This means not only that he should be an example of faith, that, imitating his faith, we should be justified, but rather that it was recorded as a precedent, that, as so eminent a servant of God was justified by his faith, so should we be—that as one so loved of God had not whereof to glory, so should we lay aside all reliance on self and supposed merit, and plead only the merits of the Son of God.

"If we believe on him that raised up Jesus our Lord from the dead."

25. "Who was delivered for our offences, and was raised again," &c. There is a certain parallel hinted at between the justification of Abraham and ours, in that in each case belief rested on restoration of life. In Abraham's case it was God Who restored to life the virtual deadness, as regards procreation, of the bodies of Abraham and Sarah—in ours it is God Who restored the Body of Jesus to life.

But why is not our faith directed to the Death of the Son of God, seeing that by it we are redeemed? Because faith in the death of a man would be no faith at all. Death is natural to every human being. It is appointed unto all men once to die; so that faith in so natural a thing as a man's death would be nothing, whereas faith in the Lord's Resurrection as brought about by the express will and power of God, is faith in what is not only unseen and supernatural, but in the highest imaginable sphere of the unseen and supernatural. It is faith in the highest action of God in a matter which most deeply concerns His faithfulness and truth. God had promised a Redeemer from sin and death; Jesus Christ in His holy teaching and mighty works exhibited all that could be expected of such a Redeemer, but He succumbed to death. How then could He redeem from sin and the grave? The answer is, God

CHAP. IV.] DELIVERED FOR OUR OFFENCES. 89

25 *Who was delivered for our offences, and

*Is. liii. 5, 6.
ch. iii. 25. &
v. 6. & viii. 32.
2 Cor. v. 21.
Gal. i. 4. Heb.
ix. 28. 1 Pet.
ii. 24. & iii. 18.

rais⋅ˇ Him from the dead. He had staked the truth of His claims as th ∶on of God, and the Ransom for Sin, and the Imparter of Life on God's raising Him from the dead. God did so raise Him, and thereby acknowledged Him to be His own and very Son—the Ransom from Sin and the Imparter of Life. And so our faith is fixed not only on the Son but on the Father, according to the Lord's words, "He that heareth my word, and believeth on him that sent me hath everlasting life " (John v. 24). And again, "He that believeth on me, believeth not on me, but on him that sent me " (John xii. 44).

It seems to me a grave misfortune that the belief in Jesus has been so often practically separated from that in God the Father. The belief in Jesus, as man, and so capable of receiving human affections, has too often degenerated into fanaticism, fastening upon what is human in the Lord to the exclusion of what is Divine in His relations to His Father, whereas it would not have been so if the ultimate object of faith had been the Eternal Father. Deep-seated awe and reverence would have rendered fanaticism and irreverent familiarity impossible. The *ultimate* Object of all intelligent faith must be God the Father—God the Father sending His Son, laying our sins on His Son, raising Him from the dead, exalting Him to His Right Hand, and committing all judgment to Him.

25. " Who was delivered for our offences, and was raised again for our justification." Here, in this most important conclusion of St. Paul's argument, as elsewhere, the functions of the Death and Resurrection are distinguished. He died for, or on account of, our sins—to make atonement for them. He rose again for our justification, *i.e.*, to make us partakers of Justification of Life.

This is the only possible meaning of the passage. It has been explained (by Bishop Horsley in the last century and Godet in this) that He died for our offences, *i.e.*, because we had sinned, and He rose again for our justification, because He had justified the world or the Elect. But this is impossible if we adhere to Scripture; for all for whom He died are not justified—if, that is, justification is of life—and apparently immense numbers pass out of the world in a

^a 1 Cor. xv. 17. 1 Pet. i. 21.

^a was raised again for our justification.

state of sin which cannot possibly be a state of justification. So that the only meaning is that which both Scripture and facts demand. He died for our sins to atone for them and procure our pardon. He rose again for our justification, *i.e.*, to enable us to be justified by the communication to us of His Life.[1]

CHAP. V.

^a Is. xxxii. 17. John xvi. 33. ch. iii. 28, 30.
^b Ephes. ii. 24. Col. i. 20.

THEREFORE ^a being justified by faith, we have ^b peace with God through our Lord Jesus Christ:

1. "We have peace" (ἔχομεν). So corrections of MSS., ℵ, and B., Greek of F. and G. and P. (Cent. ix.), and most Cursives; but "Let us have peace" (ἔχωμεν), in ℵ, A., B., C., D., E., K., L., thirty Cursives, d, e, f, g, Vulg., Syriac, Copt., Arm., Æth.

1. "Therefore being justified by faith, we have peace with God, through," &c. By faith, that is by the faith just mentioned; certainly the Apostle does not mean justified by *any* faith, but by faith in or believing on "Him Who raised up Jesus our Lord from the dead." Whatever be the teaching respecting faith current now, the faith just before described is what the Apostle set forth for purposes of justification.

"We have peace with God," or "Let us have peace with God." It is impossible not to take into very full account the difference of reading. According to our Authorized we have an assertion re-

---

[1] I append some translations by modern scholars:—

διὰ τὰ ... διὰ τήν. "For the sake of." In either case the sense suggests the necessary modifications: for the sake of (to take away) our offences; for the sake of (to secure) our justification.—DEAN VAUGHAN.

On account of our sins, *i.e.* to expiate and atone for them; on account of our justification, *i.e.* to effect it, to convey to us the righteousness of God.—PHILIPPI.

But this glorification of Christ consisted of two main parts—His Death and His Resurrection. In the former of these He was made a sacrifice for sin; in the latter He elevated our humanity into the participation of that Resurrection life, which is also by union with Him the life of every justified believer.—ALFORD.

specting those who, like St. Paul, are justified, "We have peace." According to a vast preponderance of ancient authorities we have an exhortation, "Let us have peace." But in addition to this we must take into account the different meanings which may properly be given to the word "peace." (1) Does it mean, for instance, a state opposite to warfare or enmity? Thus in this very chapter, "if when we were enemies we were reconciled to God by the death of his Son." Again (Coloss. i. 21), "You that were sometime alienated and enemies in your mind by wicked works, yet now hath he reconciled." In this case it is a state of reconciliation. (2) Or it may mean an internal feeling of peace, answering to the peace of a good conscience. Such a peace is that alluded to in Phil. iv. 6, " Be careful for nothing; but in every thing by prayer and supplication with thanksgiving let your requests be made known unto God. And the peace of God, which passeth all understanding, shall keep your hearts and minds through Christ Jesus."

In the first case, taking "peace" to mean a state of peace or reconciliation, God reconciled to us, and we continuing in the unity of His Son's Church or Mystical Body, then it is clear that we must read "we have peace," because we have not to enter into, but are already in, such a state of acceptance.

But if peace means an internal feeling of peace, a sense of God's love filling our minds with holy tranquillity, or, as St. John expresses it, " perfect love casting out fear," *i.e.*, all slavish tormenting fear, then it is very needful that we should be exhorted to have such a calm, heavenly state of mind, and so inasmuch as so many have, through their own fault, not attained to this, we must read "let us have peace." And how is this to be brought about? Not by merely resting in justification by faith, but by building upon it (2 Pet. i. 5). The blessing which St. Paul invokes on the Philippian Christians that " the peace of God, which passeth all understanding, may keep their hearts," follows upon the exhortation, " Be careful for nothing; but in every thing by prayer and supplication with thanksgiving let your requests be made known unto God." Such constant intercourse with God, such casting all our care respecting everything temporal or spiritual, upon Him, would naturally, one may say, cause peace to flow into us.

This place is often used as supplying a test whether we are justified, but, in many cases, most wrongly. I have, myself, during the course of my ministry, known many persons who lived in all good

ACCESS BY FAITH. [ROMANS.

2 °By whom also we have access by faith into this grace ^dwherein we stand, and ^erejoice in hope of the glory of God.

^c John x. 9. & xiv. 6. Ephes. ii. 18. & iii. 12. Heb. x. 19.
^d 1 Cor. xv. 1.
^e Heb. iii. 6.

2. "Access by faith." So ℵ, A. (ἐν τῇ πίστει), C., K., I., P., most Cursives, Vulg., Syriac, Copt., Arm. "By faith" omitted by B., D., E., F., G., d, e, f, g.

conscience towards God, who believed thoroughly all the truth respecting Jesus, and who were rich in good works, who perhaps from bodily constitution, perhaps from mental disease, seemed unable to enjoy the comforts of religion; and I have known others who professed to enjoy them, in whose case, from their manifest living in sin, such a profession was an undoubted delusion.

I think it is well then to treat the reading as doubtful, particularly as many assert that all internal evidence is against the reading "let us have," and to show that whether we read "we have" or "let us have," there is a good and useful meaning.

2. "By whom also we have access by faith into this grace wherein we stand." "We have," rather "we have had access," i.e., entrance; compare Ephes. ii., "Through him we both have access by one Spirit unto the Father."

"Unto this grace." Unto this state of grace, of justification, of peace with God.

"Wherein we stand"—stand accepted before God in Christ. Chrysostom speaks of this state as one of knowledge as well as of nearness. "What grace is this? Tell me. It is the being counted worthy of the knowledge of God, the being forced from error, the coming to a knowledge of the truth, the obtaining of all the blessings which come through Baptism."

"And rejoice in hope of the glory of God." Of the glory that shall be revealed at the last day. It was, in the nature of things, given to those who were converts from heathenism, to realize this more vividly than we who have been brought up in an ancestral Christianity. For the prospect of eternal life and glory was new to them. They once had no hope of the future worth speaking of, and now they were by the Resurrection of Jesus Christ from the dead, "born again to a lively hope." They naturally gloried in the assured prospect of such an eternity, and the same hope ought to be ours, and would be if the world was as unfriendly to us as it was to them. *They* can best rejoice in hope of future happiness to whom

3 And not only so, but ᶠwe glory in tribulations also: ᵍknowing that tribulation worketh patience;

ᶠ Matt. v. 11, 12. Acts v. 41. 2 Cor. xii. 10. Phil. ii. 17. Jam. i. 2, 12. 1 Pet. iii. 14.
ᵍ Jam. i. 3.

3. "We glory in." So ℵ, A., D., E., F., G., K., L., P., forty-two Cursives, Vulg., Copt., Arm., Æth.; but B. and C. read, "glorying in."

this world is a weariness, and they also to whom God has given to feel and to say, "O wretched man that I am, who shall deliver me from the body of this death?" and to go on to realize the truth: "If the Spirit of Him that raised Jesus from the dead dwell in you, He that raised up Christ from the dead shall also quicken your mortal bodies by His Spirit that dwelleth in you."

3. "And not only so, but we glory in tribulations also: knowing that tribulation," &c. The true Christian who by God's illumination has been led to see all things in their right light, knows that everything which we call tribulation is or may be turned by us into a blessing from God. It, to say the least, reminds us that our heaven is not here. The Church brings this very closely home to us in the Office for the Visitation of the Sick: "There should be no greater comfort to Christian persons than to be made like unto Christ, by suffering patiently adversities, troubles, and sicknesses. For He Himself went not up to joy, but first He suffered pain, He entered not into His glory before He was crucified. So truly our way to eternal life is to suffer here with Christ; and our door to enter eternal life is gladly to die with Christ," &c. And much more is this true if the suffering, as so frequently in the Apostolic times, is directly for the sake of Christ. St. Paul in another Epistle treats this as a great gift of God. "To you it is given in the behalf of Christ, not only to believe on him, but also to suffer for his sake" (Phil. i. 29). And again, St. Paul's brother Apostle writes: "Rejoice, inasmuch as ye are partakers of Christ's sufferings; that when His glory shall be revealed, ye may be glad also with exceeding joy" (1 Pet. iv. 13).

"Knowing that tribulation worketh patience," *i.e.*, endurance. Tribulation, if received as sent by God, and submitted to as part of the discipline of a Father that loves us, works endurance, or constancy, and indeed perseverance. "He that endureth (ὑπομείνας) to the end the same shall be saved." Again, remember the Lord's message to the Church of Thyatira, "I know thy works, and

4 ʰ And patience, experience; and experience, hope:

5 ⁱ And hope maketh not ashamed; ᵏ because the love of God is shed abroad in our hearts by the Holy Ghost which is given unto us.

ʰ Jam. i. 12.
ⁱ Phil. i. 20.
ᵏ 2 Cor. i. 22.
Gal. iv. 6.
Eph. i. 13, 14.

---

charity, and service, and faith, and thy patience," endurance in Christian graces being the crown of all (Rev. ii. 19).

4. "And patience, experience," or rather approval, or approvedness. We may translate "trial well borne." Confidence in self after trial (Jowett). This is the state of a force or virtue which has stood trials (Godet). The radical meaning of δοκιμή is testing (1 Cor. xi. 28, 2 Cor. viii. 2), then the word denotes the testing well borne = tried with approval (Philippi). It can hardly mean experience—certainly not experience in its modern religious signification.

And "trial well borne," hope. The first entrance into the state of grace was accompanied by rejoicing in hope of the glory of God; but this hope must be tested, for it is possible not to hold fast the confidence of the hope firm unto the end, or we should not be so earnestly exhorted so to do. It is tested or tried by tribulations; if we receive these tribulations as coming from God and submit to them, then we have the confidence of "trial borne well," and this doubles our hope. We hope not only because of the general promises of the Gospel, but because we are sure from God's having given us such grace to sustain trials and persecutions, that He intends us to partake of the future glory, according to the words of the Apostle, "if we be dead with him we shall also live with him— if we suffer we shall also reign with him" (2 Tim. ii. 11, 12).

5. "And hope maketh not ashamed; because the love of God is shed abroad," &c. There has been a singular difference of opinion about this verse, or rather about the meaning of the words " the love of God."

The natural meaning appears to me to be somewhat of this sort. The hope which we not only had at the first, but which has been since strengthened and confirmed by the trials which God has enabled us to bear, never makes ashamed, because, through God's grace, the Spirit of God has diffused in our hearts the love of God. We are conscious that, notwithstanding all mistakes and imperfections, we love God, and this could not possibly be unless God has first loved us.

6 For when we were yet without strength, ‖ in due time ¹ Christ died for the ungodly.

‖ Or, *according to the time*, Gal. iv. 4.
¹ ver. 8. **ch.** iv. 25.

6. "For when we were." B. alone reads "if."

It has, however, been asserted, and great names are quoted as bearing out the assertion, that the love of God which is said to be shed abroad in our hearts, and by the Holy Spirit, too, is God's love to us, and not ours to God; but it seems to me that the thing is inconceivable.

Supposing that God by His Spirit diffuses His love into our hearts, surely it cannot be a diffusion of God's love without a sense of His love, and if God thus diffuses a sense of His love into a sinner's heart, and the sinner's heart does in no way respond to it, then I contend that the man in whom this takes place is *ipso facto* reprobate.

This love cannot be shed abroad in the heart without some sensible effect upon the heart, and what can such effect be except the exciting of a counter love, a love to meet the love of God? If such be the effect, then the soul in which this takes place will be prepared for the glory for which it hopes, and its hope will not be ashamed; but if not, then the soul will not be prepared for the glory to be revealed, because its faith does not work by love. Christ would say, if such a thing were possible, to such souls, "I know you that ye have not the love of God in you."

One question more respecting this verse has to be considered. Are those and those only justified by faith of whom these verses 3, 4, and 5 are true? Certainly not. In these verses we have not justifying faith, *per se*, but the faith which justifies working by love. These three verses show what justifying faith ought to work up to; but to say that they describe justifying faith so that as soon as a man is justified he at once necessarily glories in tribulation, is without warrant from Scripture. A soul may produce the fruits of mature faith at the moment of justification, but we have no right to demand it.

6. "For when we were yet without strength, in due time Christ died for the ungodly." "When we were yet without strength," *i.e.*, before the strengthening power of the Incarnation was applied and made over to us by the Spirit.

There seems to be a reminiscence of Ezekiel xvi. 4, " As for thy

7 For scarcely for a righteous man will one die: yet peradventure for a good man some would even dare to die.

8 But ^m God commendeth his love toward us, in that, while we were yet sinners, Christ died for us.

^m John xv. 13.
1 Pet. iii. 18.
1 John iii. 16.
& iv. 9, 10.

---

nativity ... neither wast thou washed in water to supple thee ... None eye pitied thee, to do any of these things unto thee, to have compassion upon thee; but thou wast cast out in the open field," &c.

"In due time." This may mean either at the time appointed, or when iniquity was at its height, and the long-suffering of God well nigh exhausted.

"Christ died for the ungodly." Not so much in the place of the ungodly, as on their behalf, to reconcile them to God by the sacrifice of Himself.

7. "For scarcely for a righteous man will one die: yet peradventure for a good man," &c. The righteous man here signifies the just, who, however, may be severe, stern, and unyielding, one whom we only respect and may not love; the good man signifies one who in addition to righteous qualities has amiable ones, so that we not only respect, but love him. Some, however, as Jowett, think that we must lay no stress upon the difference, but why then should the Apostle make it?

8. "But God commendeth his love towards us, in that, while we were," &c. God manifests, or commends, or establishes His love towards us, in that, while we were yet sinners, and so enemies to God, and turning away from Him, and rejecting Him, Christ died for us.

I cannot help thinking that there is some contrast implied between *the* good man (ὁ ἀγαθὸς), for whom his one friend would *perhaps* die, and the multitude of sinners for whom Christ died. In the case of the man dying for his good friend there was friendship, but there could be no such distinguishing friendship in Christ dying for a whole world, lying in wickedness. In Him it would be pure philanthropy. First, the love of God to His fallen creatures, because of their destitution, then the love to the race whose nature He had assumed.

Notice also how God commends His love in giving His Son. This can only be feebly entered into by those who contemplate

CHAP. V.] JUSTIFIED BY HIS BLOOD. 97

9 Much more then, being now justified ⁿ by his blood, we shall be saved ᵒ from wrath through him.

ⁿ ch. iii. 25.
Eph. ii. 13.
Heb. ix. 14.
1 John i. 7.
ᵒ ch. i. 18.
1 Thes. i. 10.

the love which the Persons of the Godhead have to one another. "The Father loveth the Son" (John iii. 35). Again, "The Father loveth the Son, and sheweth him all things," &c. (v. 20). Again, "Therefore doth my Father love me, because I lay down my life, that I might take it again" (x. 17).

"While we were yet sinners." He who would estimate the force of this sentence must know something of the wickedness of the time in which the Lord came amongst us. The "iniquity of the Amorites" was then full indeed. The first chapter of this Epistle tells us the kind of sinners they were for whom Christ died. The pages of Josephus tell us something of the state of degradation into which the Jews had fallen. The satires of Horace and Juvenal and the histories of Tacitus and Suetonius witness to the state of the heathen world.

9. "Much more then, being now justified by his blood, we shall be saved from wrath," &c. "Being now justified." How is it that here the Blood of Christ is said to have justified us, whereas in the last chapter it is His Life which is set forth as justifying? To which we answer, the power of His Life to justify depends upon His Sacrifice, which was the shedding of His Blood. His Sacrifice was the meritorious cause which won for His Resurrection His renewed Life that It should justify. We may be said to be justified by His Blood, but through His Resurrection. He died to rise again with a justifying Life. He rose again because not two whole days before He had died an all-atoning Death. But if the Apostle speaks of justification, why does he not bring in faith? Because he had said enough about it to satisfy any reasonable person. He mentions only the Blood, *i.e.*, the Sacrifice, because in the Sacrifice was involved the Resurrection, and its consequent Life on the one side, and this Life being made over to us by way of grace on the other.

"We shall be saved from wrath." From *the* wrath, *i.e.*, from the wrath of the judgment day—from the wrath of the world to come.

If God has given His Son to die for us, He will see to it that He shall receive the full reward of such sufferings. "He shall see of the travail of His soul and be satisfied." And that reward of His

H

10 For ^p if, when we were enemies, ^q we were reconciled to God by the death of his Son, much

<small>p ch. viii. 32.
q 2 Cor. v. 18, 19. Eph. ii. 16. Col. i. 20, 21.</small>

Sufferings, that satisfaction of His Soul, is the present holiness and future blessedness of those who repent and believe. Compare viii. 34, "Who is he that condemneth? It is Christ that died, yea rather, that is risen again, Who is even at the right hand of God, Who also maketh intercession for us." God having done so much to make a way for His mercy to reach us, will not allow what He has done to be frustrated, and certainly not in the case of those who, through His grace, have been led to plead His Son's Blood.

10. "For if, when we were enemies, we were reconciled to God by the death," &c. "We were reconciled to God." Does this mean that the enmity or anger of God to man is pacified, or that our enmity to God which all have, more or less, who are living in sin, is done away through that result of our Lord's Death which consists in our being turned from sin and turned to God? We are constantly told that nowhere in Scripture is it said that God is reconciled to us. But then what is the meaning of such a phrase as "children of wrath"? Of whose wrath are we children, if it be not that of God? But it appears to me that all difficulty is removed if we take an illustration from the conduct of earthly fathers to earthly sons. A wayward son may be under the serious displeasure of his father, and yet intensely loved by that father. The father may be so displeased with the son as not to admit him into his house, or into his presence, and yet may be supporting him, and using all sorts of means to bring his son to a better mind. And so though in one sense we are all children of wrath, yet, in another, "the Lord is loving unto every man," and still more we are so under the love of God that "God sent not his Son into the world to condemn the world, but that the world through him might be saved" (John iii. 17).

The Death of Christ opened the way for God's mercy to reach us, and the same Death of Christ opened the way for our return in heart and soul to God.

"Much more, being reconciled, we shall be saved by his life." Here we have a return to the distinction which the Apostle had made in iv. 25 respecting the different effects of the Death and Resurrection of Christ. "He was delivered for our offences" answers to "We were reconciled to God by the death of his Son."

more, being reconciled, we shall be saved ʳ by his life.

_{ʳ John v. 26. & xiv. 19. 2 Cor. iv. 10, 11.}

"He was raised again for our justification" answers to "We shall be saved by his life." Justification, as we shall soon see more clearly (on verse 18), is Justification of Life. It is here called, or implied to be, salvation, because, if the Life of Christ be communicated to us, we cannot but be saved. His Life is the Life of reconciliation and holiness in our souls, and the Life of Resurrection in our bodies.

This verse is of unspeakable importance as distinguishing between Reconciliation and Justification. It is the root—it is the warrant and vindication of the Catholic view of Justification—that it is a matter of Life rather than of mere imputation. The law could not justify, because it could not give life, for St. Paul expressly says that the law would have justified if it could have given life (Gal. iii. 21). But what the law could not do, God did by the gift of His Son—not surely in His Death only, for death cannot give life, a living thing only can communicate life ("Because I live ye shall live also"), but in His Resurrection, and God has brought about by His power that His Son's risen Body should give life. And so St. Paul here introduces in effect what forms the theme of the remainder of this chapter, that there are two Adams set opposite to one another; one by the communication of his nature diffusing sin and death, the other by the supernatural communication of His nature diffusing righteousness and Life. The means for the communication of this Life we shall consider shortly; suffice it, before leaving this verse, to draw attention to the expression "much more." The Death of Christ was that which, reverently speaking, was attended on God's part with infinite cost. The gift of His Son to suffer and die was ten thousandfold more than the gift of the whole universe, whereas the present communication of His Life costs Him nothing in the way of humiliation, pain, or distress, but is simply the putting forth of His power.

It is clear, I think, that those commentators are wrong who explain this Life of His Life of Glory in heaven, *i.e.*, His ruling over all things and His Intercession on behalf of His Church. If the Apostle had meant this he would have said it, and the Life, with which the remainder of this chapter is occupied, is that of the Second Adam, communicated to us to counteract the evil nature

THE ATONEMENT.

^a ch. ii. 17. &
iii. 29, 30.
Gal. iv. 9.
‖ Or, *reconciliation*, ver. 10. 2 Cor. v. 18, 19.

11 And not only *so*, but we also ^ajoy in God through our Lord Jesus Christ, by whom we have now received the ‖ atonement.

---

of the first Adam's life which we received on our coming into the world.

11. "And not only so, but we also joy in God," &c. We have not only peace with God—we not only rejoice in the prospect of His glory being revealed, but we rejoice in the thought of God Himself. God, though an object of the utmost reverence, is no longer an object of terror; on the contrary our sin, even if we hate it and desire to be rid of it, does not prevent us from rejoicing in God—but not in a God known only by reason—not in the God of the Law of Sinai, but the God revealed in Jesus Christ, according to the Apostle's expression, "the light of the knowledge of the glory of God in the face of Jesus Christ." (2 Cor. iv. 6.)

"By whom we have now received the atonement." This is the only place where this remarkable word is used. The reader, of course, knows that it is two words in one: the at-one-ment. To atone is a very old word, signifying to make at one, *i.e.*, to reconcile. Thus in Shakespeare, Richard III. i. 3:—

> "He desires to make atonement
> Between the Duke of Gloucester and your brothers."

The word is now only used theologically, to express the reconciliation brought about by the Death of Christ. As thus restricted it is a most suggestive word, signifying that there is not only an external, but the closest internal reconciliation. "God was in Christ reconciling the world to himself" on the one side, and "ye in me and I in you" on the other.

12-21. We have now to enter upon by far the most important and the most difficult place in the Epistle.

The most important, for it gives the reason why St. Paul was able to write respecting our Saviour: "All have sinned and come short of the glory of God. Being justified freely by his grace . . ." "Whom God hath set forth to be a propitiation through faith in his blood," and "in due time Christ died for the ungodly," "While we were yet sinners Christ died for the ungodly." It was not because the Death of Christ was the Death of the best and wisest of men, neither was it because He was the Eternal Son in our Nature, but because God in His all-wise counsels had appointed Him to be the Second Head of the human race, so that " as in Adam all die, even so in Him should all be made alive."

Being the new Head of the race He was able to be their surety or ransom, so that His Life, Sufferings, and Death should be accepted on their account to deliver them from sin and to endow them with immortality.

But this is not all or nearly all; for if Adam and Christ be counterparts of one another, as the respective heads of the race, or of those who are "in" the one, and "in" the other, then there must be in Christ that principle of the transmission of His nature which there was in Adam. For Adam transmitted his nature—his sinful and mortal nature—to all in him, *i.e.*, to all his descendants. Now he, the first Adam, did this in what we call the course of nature. He was the natural physical fountain and source of the nature of flesh and blood of all his family, that is, of all mankind; but how was the action of the Second Adam on the human race to be analogous to this, seeing He had no descendants after the flesh? It could not be in the way of nature, but it was very likely to be so in the way of grace. For if the Second Adam be the Son of God, His only Son, manifest in the flesh, if He be the Lord of Glory, and if in Him dwells all the fulness of the Godhead bodily, then it is only likely that there should be in Him the capacity of diffusing this better and holier nature of His; indeed, it is difficult to see how He could be properly an Adam if He does not so diffuse His nature. For the characteristic feature of Adam's relation to us is that we should partake of his flesh and blood; and so of his weak and sinful and mortal life. Now the Lord Himself, in the most mysterious discourse in all Scripture, lays it upon us that we are to eat His Flesh and drink His Blood, or we have not His Life in us, and again in His equally mysterious parable of the "Vine and the Branches," He lays it upon us that we are to be in Him, and united to Him, not as disciples by merely receiving knowledge, nor as individual sinners by merely receiving atonement, nor even as subjects by being under Him as a King, or sheep, by being led and pastured by Him as our Shepherd, but we are to be in Him as parts of one living thing, which has one life in all its parts—which life flows from one centre to the remotest part of the organism.

The Second Adam then is the source of life to all in Him, by

† Gen. iii. 6.
1 Cor. xv. 21.

12 Wherefore, as † by one man sin entered into

communicating to them His holy and immortal Life, just as the first Adam is the source of death to all in him by communicating to them his unholy and mortal life.

Now this analogy between Adam and Christ as transmitters of nature is to be realized, if we would in the least degree enter into something of the meaning of what is coming. It seems to me to be a passage which rises above criticism, and requires something of the Apostle's inspiration. *Sursum corda.*

I said at the outset that this passage is not only exceedingly important, but also exceedingly difficult, and well it may be, for it deals with the most mysterious problem that can be treated of by man's intellect—the problem of human nature—how whilst all other creatures in the world live according to the perfection of their nature, man lives contrary to the perfection of his, and how a being who by his Divine intelligence and moral faculties seems destined to live for ever is invariably cut off in the midst of his days. If then such a multitude of insoluble questions crop up, as it were, in every sentence of what is coming, we must neither marvel nor complain: the issue is clear, and that is, that, "as sin hath reigned unto death, so might grace reign through righteousness unto eternal life through Jesus Christ our Lord."

12. "Wherefore, as by one man sin entered into the world, and death by sin," &c. "Wherefore," *i.e.*, on this account, as a deduction from what has been laid down in the Apostle's words: "If when we were enemies we were reconciled to God by the death of His Son, much more, being reconciled, we shall be saved by His life."

"As by one man sin entered into the world." This is the reason why we were enemies. It was because of the unity of mankind in having one father, by whose one transgression sin entered into him, and in him into all his descendants, and this sin is the root of all enmity to God.

In this way St. Paul, in accordance with the teaching of the Old Testament, accounts for the sinfulness of the human race. Now the sinfulness of man must be accounted for, for it is by far the most mysterious phenomenon which presents itself to us. It is no other than this: that whilst all other creatures in the world live according to the type or perfection of their nature, man alone, the reason-

CHAP. V.]   DEATH PASSED UPON ALL MEN.   **103**

the world, and ᵘ death by sin; and so death passed upon all men, ‖ for that all have sinned:

u Gen. ii. 17.
ch. vi. 23.
1 Cor. xv. 21.
‖ Or, *in whom.*

---

ing, the governing creature, violates the supreme law of his nature. For reason and conscience and the moral sense are in human beings what their instincts are to the inferior creatures, and whilst all the inferior creatures live according to their instincts, man alone does not live according to his. In writing this I am, of course, not writing for Atheists or Agnostics—such have nothing to do with the Epistle to the Romans—but I am writing for those who believe in God and the obligation of the moral law and the supremacy of conscience and the certainty of a judgment. Such persons will readily acknowledge that the great problem of human nature is the prevalence of sin in a race of reasonable beings who acknowledge the obligations of morality. St. Paul, following the Old Testament, sets forth that the principle through which evil has infected the whole race is that of heredity, the principle of inheritance through which races derive from their progenitor their physical and moral peculiarities.

This, I need hardly tell the reader, is in accord with the most advanced science of the day.

But then the Apostle proceeds.

"And death by sin." Now, the unreasoning and irresponsible animals are subject to death: how is it that man is not similarly subject, but that his death is treated as a punishment? In answer to this, we say that a being endowed with reason and conscience, and having the moral law written in his heart, could not but have a very different destiny to the unreasoning part of the creation. How man would have increased and multiplied on the earth, unchecked by death, we do not know; but the things in which man differs from the brutes pertain to a higher, because a spiritual state of things, and so savour of immortality. The entrance of death through sin is not in itself so great a mystery as would have been the decrepitude, disease, and death of sinless beings created in God's image. It is a matter of revelation, but is in accordance with reason, that moral and spiritual death go together.

"And so death passed upon all men, for that all have sinned." The universality of death is ascribed by the Apostle to the universality of sin.

13 (For until the law sin was in the world: but ˣ sin is not imputed when there is no law.

14 Nevertheless death reigned from Adam to Moses, even over them that had not sinned after the similitude of Adam's transgression, ʸ who is the figure of him that was to come.

ˣ ch. iv. 15.
1 John iii. 4.

ʸ 1 Cor. xv.
21, 22, 45.

13, 14. "For until the law sin was in the world . . . figure of him that was to come." And now here the Apostle does not finish the reasoning with which he began, for in such a case the verse would have ended with, "so by one man righteousness entered into the world, and eternal life by his righteousness;" but he turns aside in his argument, as he very frequently does (see Eph. iii. 1), and asserts the reign of death because of the reign of sin. And then he goes on to assert that this reign of sin and death was prior to the giving of the law, and so could not have been occasioned by transgressions of the law of Moses. If then sin, as he says, was not imputed where there is no law, how came all men to die? For death, the consequence of sin, reigned from Adam to Moses, and reigned not only over wilful sinners, but over infants, who must be meant by "those that had not sinned after the similitude of Adam's transgression." There can be but one answer: Death reigned not only by reason of actual, but by reason of original sin. The life of the race was poisoned at its fountain-head. The seeds of sin and its companion, death, were in every human being coming into the world. Now this does not mean that Adam's sin was imputed to infants, but that the poison of Adam's nature passed into infants, rendering them mortal in their bodies, and liable to sin in their souls.

Now why does St. Paul in such sweeping terms assert the universality of sin in the race which God had created in their forefather in His image after His likeness? Simply and for no other purpose than to enhance the universality of the remedy, *i.e.*, of redemption, for he finishes with "Adam, who is the figure of Him which was to come."

In what sense, then, was Adam the figure of Him that was to come? Principally, if not entirely, in this—that as Adam was the transmitter of sin, so Christ is the transmitter of righteousness; but Adam was the transmitter of sin because he was the transmitter of

CHAP. V.] THE OFFENCE . . . THE FREE GIFT. 105

15 But not as the offence, so also *is* the free gift. For if through the offence of one many be dead, much more the

---

15. "Many be dead ; " rather, " the many."

his own nature, and so, if the parallel is to hold good, Christ must be the transmitter of righteousness because the transmitter of His Nature. Adam transmitted sin not by example, but by generation; and Christ, if He is an Adam, must transmit righteousness in some way analogous, though Spiritual.

But there must be, I think, a further analogy. Adam transmitted an evil nature to those who had never sinned consciously; and if the Second Adam be in this as in other respects superior to the first, He, too, must be able to transmit His grace and righteousness to those in a like state of unconsciousness—to those who have not sinned wilfully, *i.e.*, to infants.

15. "But not as the offence, so also is the free gift . . . abounded unto many." Offence should rather be translated trespass, or transgression.

The offence of one is the one sin of Adam. The free gift is the gift of Christ, and the wisdom, righteousness, sanctification, and redemption which He is made unto us (1 Corinth. i. 30).

" For if through the offence of one many be dead." The many [οἱ πολλοί], for all have died or die.

" Much more the grace of God and the gift by grace, which is by one man, Jesus Christ, hath abounded unto the many." Not " unto many," as if without the article, but unto "the many " [εἰς τοὺς πολλούς], " the many " in the first clause corresponding to, and apparently being the same as " the many " in the second. Chrysostom's exposition should be reproduced here :—" If sin had so extensive effects, and the sin of one man, too, how can grace, and that the grace of God—not the Father only, but also the Son—do otherwise than be the more abundant of the two ? for the latter is far the more reasonable supposition. For that one man should be punished on account of another does not seem to be much in accordance with reason; but for one to be saved on account of another is at once more suitable and more reasonable. If, then, the former took place, much more may the latter."

As this verse is the text, as it were, of the succeeding verses, we had better now consider it more closely; and there is, at the very

grace of God, and the gift by grace, *which is* by one man,

---

outset, this very great difficulty—that the sin of Adam and its effects are matters of sight, whereas the grace of God in Christ and its effects are matters of faith. We see disease, decrepitude, death, but we do not see the glory of the righteous, the astonishing power of their risen bodies, made like unto the angels; nay rather, made after the likeness of Christ's glorious Body.

And then the question of the respective numbers on each side, *i.e.*, of the lost in Adam, and the saved in Christ, though ignored by most commentators, ought to be honestly faced; for to all appearance those who continue in the grace of Baptism are very small compared to those who fall away, and then by far the greater part of the inhabitants of the world are not even nominal Christians, but are Buddhists, or Mahometans, or Idolaters: and as to those who are esteemed believers by the Evangelical commentators on this Epistle, we may safely say that they are not one in ten of those who heartily believe the creed, and strive in God's strength to keep the commandments.

We will, first of all then, endeavour to see how the abounding grace of God in Christ in those who receive it exceeds the evil transmitted by Adam to his descendants. First, they have an union with God in Christ, and a security of soul against temptation infinitely exceeding that of Adam, if these things could at all be predicated of him. Adam seems to have yielded at once —indeed, if we take the short account in Gen. iii., there was little or no moral or spiritual struggle. Adam, perhaps perceiving that his wife did not die as soon as she sinned, seems to have taken and eaten without the smallest misgiving. Then, after the sin, there was no repentance, only the fear generated by alienation, and such was their view of God's Omniscience that they thought a few thick bushes would effectually conceal them from Him. Then there was no trace of repentance, Adam at once laying all the blame upon his helpmeet—or rather upon God for having given to him such an one ("the woman whom thou gavest to be with me") —Eve also taking not the smallest blame to herself, but laying all on the serpent. Now contrast this with the conduct of any sincere Christian under temptation. First see his watchfulness and prayer—then his pleading the Name and Merits of Christ, and if, through the weakness of his nature, he has fallen—see

CHAP. V.] BY ONE MAN, JESUS CHRIST. 107

Jesus Christ, hath abounded ᶻ unto many. ᶻ Is. liii. 11.
Matt. xx. 28.
& xxvi. 28.

15. " Unto many ; " rather, " unto the many."

his shame, his unbaring his breast to the scrutiny of the Searcher of hearts, to cleanse the thoughts of his heart—then his casting aside any and every excuse, and taking to himself alone all the blame. Now this insight into ourselves, this fear of ourselves, this running to meet God with confession and tears, is, under the circumstances, the greatest blessing in which " the grace of God and the gift by grace by Jesus Christ " can abound to a man. It is one who has the knowledge of good and evil, holding fast to God and abhorring the smallest trace of evil.

It is impossible to go further with this comparison, because nothing is told us respecting the spiritual state of Adam, except his conduct under the one temptation; but we know the further life of the Christian, how if he is sincere, it is a daily adding to his faith, virtue, and to virtue knowledge, and to knowledge, temperance, &c.

And then with respect to the body. Christ brings to it an immortality not in a gross and earthly, but in an ethereal body, "sown in corruption and raised in incorruption; sown in weakness and raised in power; sown in dishonour, raised in glory; sown a natural, and raised a spiritual body," equal to the frames of the angels—nay, changed by the power of Christ, that it may be like unto His glorious Body; the Lord Himself predicting of it that the righteous shall shine forth as the sun, in the kingdom of their Father. (Matth. xiii. 43.)

Such is " the grace of God, and the gift by grace, which is by one man, Jesus Christ, abounding" in soul and body unto the many—taking the many to be the righteous, *i.e.*, true Christians and sincere believers.

But about the numbers in Adam and in Christ respectively, and by " in Christ," I mean, of course, those who are new creatures in Him—at first sight the number of those who are in Adam only seems enormously greater than those who are beneficially and spiritually in Christ; but we must remember that this is a matter, not of 1,800 years, but of untold ages, even the ages of eternity. We must remember that evil, if not annihilated, will be cast out, confined—in fact, as the Vision in the Revelation tells us, chained, whereas good, and this good the goodness of Christ in His own, will be ever growing and increasing, doubtless in other worlds besides this.

With respect to the numbers partaking of the grace of God by Christ, one who is undoubtedly of all English commentators " of the straitest sect of our religion," Thomas Scott, has some words, which though of no particular weight in themselves, are valuable as coming from one whose prejudices lead him to make the number of the saved as few as possible. He writes: " If we omit the consideration of the *number* who perish in 'the first Adam,' or are saved in the 'second Adam,' if we wholly leave this to the wise, righteous, and merciful Creator, and Judge of all men, as one of those secret things which belong to Him, and not to us; and if we exclusively consider the benefits which *believers* derive from Christ, as compared with the loss sustained in Adam *by the human race*, we shall then see the passage open most perspicuously and gloriously to our view. For the thought of the *supposed* immense majority of those who shall eventually perish, is apt to encumber the mind in these contemplations. I say *supposed, for possibly we shall find our calculations erroneous,* when the doom of men through all ages and nations shall be finally determined."

These verses, 15-21, look not to individuals merely, but to the future of the race, and certainly the last two chapters of the book of the Revelation open out to us a very different prospect to that which we receive from the popular idea, that the earth is to be annihilated, that the saved—a very small remnant—are draughted away as they die to a far-off heaven, and that the lost, the infinitely greater number, are all alike shut up in a Gehenna of inexpressible torment. The Apostle, in these verses, does not teach universal salvation, for, in another place, he contemplates the case of those who finally "know not God, and obey not the Gospel of our Lord Jesus Christ." The grace of God and the gift by grace in Jesus Christ has, through their own fault, not abounded to them, for they shall be punished with everlasting destruction from the presence of the Lord, and from the glory of his power (2 Thess. i. 7, 8, 9); but he assuredly contemplates a final result of blessing to the whole race, which far exceeds the highest views of those who are most hopeful respecting the future of mankind.

16. "And not as it was by one that sinned . . . many offences unto justification." It was the one sin of Adam which brought

CHAP. V.] NOT AS BY ONE THAT SINNED. 109

16 And not as *it was* by one that sinned, *so is* the gift: for the judgment *was* by one to condemnation, but the free **gift** *is* of many offences unto justification.

17 For if ‖ by one man's offence death reigned by one; much more they which receive abundance of grace and of the gift of righteousness shall reign in life by one, Jesus Christ.)

‖ Or, *by one offence.*

---

condemnation; but the redemption by Christ atones for not only that one sin, but all other sins, which we must account to be absolutely innumerable. It was, in the words of our Consecration prayer, "a full, perfect, and sufficient sacrifice, oblation, and satisfaction for the sins of the whole world."

Adam brought himself under condemnation and death by one sin, whereas the Redemption of Christ has atoned for the evil lives of all Adam's posterity. For before he had said, that if one man's sin slew all, much more will the grace of One have the power to save. After that he shows that it was not that one sin only that was done away by the grace, but all the rest too, and that it was not that the sins were done away only, but that righteousness was given. And Christ did not only do the same amount of good that Adam did of harm, but far more and greater good. (Chrysostom.)

17. "For if by one man's offence death reigned by one . . . life by one, Jesus Christ." Here another idea is brought in—that of reigning in a kingdom. One man's sin brings in the reign of death. Jesus Christ, through the abundance of grace and the gift of righteousness, brings in the reign in life of those who accept His gifts, who, from all that we can learn from this chapter, will ultimately be very many. There is an immense amount of unreality connected with this idea of Christians *reigning* with Christ. The future state is assumed to be one immense assembly congregated in one vast hall. Now if this be all, there can be no reigning, in the proper sense of the word, in such a state—indeed, one good man explains it that we shall rule over ourselves or our passions; but if we take as our guide to the future state of the blessed, the Lord's promises in the parable of the Pounds: "Be thou ruler over ten cities," "Be thou ruler over five cities," or, as in the parable of the Talents, "I will make thee ruler over many things," or the hint given to us in 1 Cor. vi. 3, that we shall judge angels,

18 Therefore as ‖ by the offence of one *judgment came* upon all men to condemnation; even so ‖ by the

| Or, *by one offence.*
| Or, *by one righteousness.*

---

then the case is altered. There is a sphere or spheres in which reigning in the true sense of the word is possible, which cannot be conceived of under the common notions of heaven. Suppose, then, that we take this "reigning" to mean exerting the most widespread and kingly influence for good, then in the ages of eternity the power for good of those who reign through Christ, may far exceed the power for evil of the one man Adam through his sin.

Notice particularly that it is not the grace and the gift of righteousness which reigns, but those persons who receive this grace and gift of righteousness.

18. "Therefore as by the offence of one (judgment came) upon all men to condemnation . . . justification of life." First, with reference to the exact translation of this verse.

Most expositors now render the words, "the offence of one," by the words "one offence," and "by the righteousness of one" by the words, "by one righteousness." But there is a considerable difference about the meaning of "the one righteousness." Some (Vaughan, and Godet, and Alford) explain it as "by one righteous act," *i.e.*, the Death of Christ as the acme of His obedience. Others "one justificatory sentence," as if on the Resurrection of Christ a sentence of justification was passed upon all, which each particular soul receives a part in on its believing. It seems to me rather the former, in which case one transgression issuing in condemnation is counteracted by one righteousness of Christ issuing in justification of life.

Then we have to consider what are the words which have to be supplied to complete the sense of each clause. Our translators render in italics "judgment came" in the first clause, and "the free gift came" in the second. But that which we supply in each clause should be, if possible, the same; and so it is rendered by some "as by one offence the issue came upon all men to condemnation, so by one righteousness the issue came," &c.

"Justification of life," not merely justification which issues in eternal life at last, but a present justification of life as opposed to the "condemnation" of the previous clause. It consequently must include all that we receive by virtue of our union with Christ; and,

CHAP. V.] BY ONE RIGHTEOUSNESS. 111

righteousness of one *the free gift came* ᵃ upon all men unto
justification of life.
ᵃ John xii. 32.
Heb. ii. 9.

---

as I shall show in an excursus at the end of this volume, it must be life from Christ as the Second Adam—that life which is power to fulfil the holy law or will of God (viii. 1-4). This is admirably expressed in the words of an exposition of this Epistle by a priest of a sister Church, " Condemnation—Justification. The words must be taken with all which they imply: the condemnation of Adam conveys to us the idea of his sentence, and also of all its consequences, misery, sorrow, depravity, Physical and Spiritual Death. So the word Justification expresses, first, the act of pardon and forgiveness, and then includes the gift of the New Life, the sanctifying and cleansing of the inner man, as well as the sealing of the mortal frame for a blessed and happy resurrection " (Rev. Morgan Dix).

The numerical comparison in this verse is the strongest of any in this part of the epistle, for " the free gift upon *all* men " is put over against the "judgment upon all men." Now two remarks may be made upon this; 1st, that it is impossible to suppose that the Apostle meant that all men in his day were justified, for he constantly assumes that even his converts may be falling into deadly sin, as, for instance, the Corinthians, where he says to them, " Know ye not that the unrighteous shall not inherit the kingdom of God," and this with express reference to the unrighteousness amongst themselves, from which they had been cleansed, and yet into which they were continually relapsing.

2ndly. It is impossible to imagine that he should have made this comparison at all between all men [εἰς πάντας ἀνθρώπους] on the one side, and all men [εἰς πάντας ἀνθρώπους] on the other, if he considered that those in Christ the Second Adam were only that exceedingly small number whom Evangelical commentators, such as Godet and Philippi, and, amongst ourselves, T. Scott, Bishop Ryle, and others designate as " believers; " or such as Romanists would consider to be saved by reason of their accepting the Roman obedience in addition to the Catholic faith. The Holy Spirit, Who, if He inspired any part of Scripture, inspired these words, seems to have regard to some hidden mystery respecting the diffusion of the grace of Christ which God has withheld from us.

19 For as by one man's disobedience many were made sinners, so by the obedience of one shall many be made righteous.

^b John xv. 22.
ch. iii. 20. &
iv. 15. & vii. 8.
Gal. iii. 19, 23.

20 Moreover ^b the law entered, that the offence

20. "The law entered;" rather, "the law came in beside." See notes below.

19. "For as by one man's disobedience many were made sinners, so by," &c. This verse contains the last of these astonishing parallels, and it fixes the meaning of them, especially the last, and in this respect: By Adam the many were made sinners, not by imputation, but actually through the transfusion of his sinful nature into all who were his descendants; they were made sinners because, through their connection with him, the evil nature which they received at their conception developed into some sin or other, even in the most righteous. Now Christ is said to be through His righteousness the remedy of this state of things, and so, it is said, through the obedience of One shall many—the many—be made righteous—"made righteous," of course, in the sense that the many were made sinners—that is, by having righteousness transfused into them, by their being grafted into Christ, and so made partakers of His righteousness, so that they might bring forth fruit, the fruit of holy lives and good works.

This fixes the meaning of the Justification of the previous verses. It cannot be merely, or even chiefly, the imputation of another righteousness; it must be the transfusion into them of that righteousness which they need. It must, as I have shown, be life, the life of the New Man, to the end that the righteousness of the law may be fulfilled in those who walk not after the flesh, but after the Spirit.

20. "Moreover the law entered that the offence might abound . . . grace did much more abound." Here the Apostle returns to the subject of verse 13. Sin which was in the world *before* the law, *by* the law was not only shown to be sinful, but was actually increased in intensity, because men's natural corruption chafed against the good and holy commandment of God, and so their guilt was increased. It was, at first—that is, before the law was given—simply transgression against a feeling of right within them, which was at the best feeble, of which feeling of right they did not know the author, and so did not recognize the sanction.

might abound. But where sin abounded, grace did much
^c more abound: ^c Luke vii. 47.
1 Tim. i. 14.

When the law was given, it was seen clearly to come from God, and was promulgated under the most tremendous of sanctions—the anger of God if they disobeyed—the favour of God if they were obedient. Now God knew that the children of Israel would not obey; why, then, did He give the law, seeing that He clearly foresaw that it would increase transgressions, and make sin more sinful? He did it to prepare men for—and, as St. Paul expresses it (Gal. iii. 23), shut them up to—the faith which should afterwards be revealed. He acted as good physicians do who know that their patients cannot be healed unless the disease comes to a crisis, and He gave that which would hasten the crisis, and so the sooner bring in health.

Still it may be objected, Did God mean when He said " Thou shalt not commit idolatry or adultery" to restrain men from worshipping idols or defiling their bodies? Yes, undoubtedly He did; but His commands against these sins were only received and acted upon by a remnant, and the great mass of His people disregarded them. God foresaw this, and yet He gave the commandment. Why? Evidently that by the action of the commandment a state of things might eventually be brought in which established, as nothing else could do, purity of worship and purity of life. "The law came that the offence might abound, or as we might express it, that men might awaken to their real state " (Jowett).

Here we have to notice the expression "entered;" it really means "entered beside," *i.e.*, by the way, parenthetically. It was not the original state of things, nor was it the final. It came in as if by the way, and for a particular purpose (Vaughan); which purpose, however, was necessary in order that men might see the absolute necessity of something which could give life and power. It was an experiment, as it were, God showing in the case of a particular people whom He had placed under the most favourable circumstances for obeying Him, that without the gift of a new nature in a Second Adam, they could not. And so the way was prepared for the reign of grace, that where sin abounded, as in the case of those under the law, grace might much more abound, as it did even in the lifetime of the Apostle in those who accepted the Gospel.

21 That as sin hath reigned unto death, even so might grace reign through righteousness unto eternal life by Jesus Christ our Lord.

---

21. "Unto death;" rather, "in death."

21. "That as sin hath reigned unto death, even so might grace reign through righteousness unto eternal life by Jesus Christ our Lord." This is the last parallel, and sums up all.

Sin and grace here are directly opposed; sin reigning in, or by, death, grace reigning through life. Theodoret takes this as meaning that sin reigned in mortal bodies, bodies made mortal through it, and so showed its destructive power for a time, but that grace in its reign far exceeds this. Grace reigns through righteousness, righteousness being, as it were, the instrument by which grace reigns, and reigns not for a short time, some three score years and ten, but unto eternal life, through countless ages.

Notice how grace reigns, not instead of, but through righteousness: the reign of grace was, or rather, is, to produce righteousness in each soul, without which there can be no real reconciliation of each soul to God, and consequently no eternal life; and this "through Jesus Christ our Lord," not merely through His merits but through His Person, Himself Incarnate, Crucified, Risen, Ascended, and so transmitting His good and holy Nature into His brethren.

CHAP. VI.

^a ch. iii. 8. ver. 15.

WHAT shall we say then? ^a Shall we continue in sin, that grace may abound?

---

1. "What shall we say then? Shall we continue in sin, that grace may abound?" The Apostle here meets, and shows the wickedness of, that perversion of the doctrine of free grace which through the corruption and love of sin of the human heart naturally accompanies the Gospel. This perversion we call Antino-

WE WHO DIED TO SIN.

2 God forbid. How shall we, that are ᵇdead to sin, live any longer therein?

ᵇ ver. 11. ch. vii. 4. Gal. ii. 19. & vi. 14. Col. iii. 3. 1 Pet. ii. 24.

2. "Are dead." Rather, "died;" *i.e.* they may not be dead now, but they died once.

mianism, and it is now as rife in Christian England as it could have been in Rome or Corinth in Apostolic days.

There are people in this very town in which I am writing who say, and who are encouraged by their teachers to say, "If I believe I can no longer sin—sin is not sin in me, since Christ died for me and I believe in Him." There are persons who even go so far as to say that fornication is not sin in the believer, and they certainly show no shame for having committed it. The Apostle in asking this question very probably has in his mind what he had said in ch. v. 20, "The law entered that the offence might abound. But where sin abounded grace did much more abound." If this took place before the gift of Christ, why not after?

2. "God forbid. How shall we, that are dead [died] to sin, live any longer therein?" To this the Apostle answers that the grace of God through Christ is, in its whole nature and power and manifestation, against sin and for righteousness. It is not mere favour or kindness, as men may be favourable or kind to one another, quite apart from their moral character. So far from being indifferent to sin, it is death to it; so far from being indifferent to righteousness, its end is righteousness.

"We, that are dead to sin." The right translation is, "how shall we who died to sin?" not "are dead" to it. If all who are baptised into the Name of Christ are dead now to sin, then there need be no protest against any sort of Antinomianism; for there could be none, if all Christians were as indifferent to sin as a dead body is to the lusts and appetites which ruled it when it was yet alive.

The words "died to sin" must refer to some period in the past when this took place. Now in an important sense all died to sin when Christ died. He died because of sin, for He died to put it away, and to destroy it, and He was the representative Man, the Head of the race, so that His Death to sin has opened the way to the salvation of all mankind from sin; so that each one to whom His Death is proclaimed should actually and morally die to sin by believing in Him and being united to Him.

116   BAPTIZED INTO HIS DEATH.   [ROMANS.

3 Know ye not, that ^c so many of us as ‖ were baptized into Jesus Christ ^d were baptized into his death?

c Gal. iii. 27.
‖ Or, *are*.
d 1 Cor. xv. 29.

3. "Know ye not, that so many of us as were baptized." Rather, as Revisers, "Or are ye ignorant that all we who were baptized." All have been baptized, and all baptized into His death ; none are excluded.

It is, however, as clear as possible that whatever secret effects known only to God, the Death of Christ may have on the whole race, yet wilful sinners, slaves of sin, not only have no present benefit from that Death, but crucify afresh Him Who died for them. Can there then be another and a further meaning of this term "died to sin"? Yes, the Apostle proceeds to show that there can.

3, 4. " Know ye not, that so many of us as were baptized unto Jesus Christ . . . . newness of life."

To be baptized into Christ, is to be baptized so as as to become a member of Christ, so that a part in the past death of Christ to sin and the present life of Christ to God becomes ours. This is well expressed by Philippi, a German Evangelical : "He refers to the Baptismal act, because by it the Christian has been taken into union with Christ. From its import, therefore, the nature of the Christian position must needs be clearly apparent. If, according to St. Paul's mode of view, Baptism was merely a symbolical attestation to the fact of regeneration which has previously taken place, and not rather, as is expressly stated (Titus iii. 5 ; Ephes. v. 26), the effectual medium by which the new birth is accomplished, the Apostle would more aptly have reminded the Church of the moment of their believing, than of the moment of their Baptism. . . . Elsewhere also Paul reminds the churches of Baptism as the Sacrament of their initiation into communion with Christ (Gal. iii. 27, Ephes. iv. 5), and the passage analogous to the present one is Col. ii. 11, 12."

" While then in the preceding verse he only said in general terms that they actually died to sin, in this verse he intimates that this took place in Baptism, because what took place in them as Christians must certainly make itself known as having taken place in Baptism, the sacrament of their incorporation into Christ. This holds true especially of Infant Baptism preceding the ministry of the word. But even the word which precedes the Baptism of

CHAP. VI.] BURIED WITH HIM BY BAPTISM. 117

4 Therefore we are ^e buried with him by baptism into death: that ^f like as Christ was raised up from

^e Col. ii. 12.
^f ch. viii. 11.
1 Cor. vi. 14.
2 Cor. xiii. 4.

4. "Are buried;" properly, "were buried." The Authorized rather implies that we continue buried, whereas in the same baptism we have emerged from the tomb.

adults is merely preparatory to Baptism as the real crowning act, just as the word following Baptism simply points back to Baptism, by way of continuous exposition and application. The word that goes before offers to all collectively the gracious gift which Baptism conveys to the particular definite individual. Faith *before* Baptism accepts for itself also the gift promised in the word to all: faith in and after Baptism accepts the blessing given by God Himself to it specially. In the former case takes place a subjective and human (though one willed and brought about by God) in the latter an objective and divine individual application of the blessing of salvation."

4. "Therefore we are buried with him by baptism into death: that like as Christ was raised up," &c. The former verse says, "we were baptized into his Death," *i.e.*, His Death to sin—His atoning Death, the Death which reconciled us to God.

Now Christ's Death culminated in His Burial in the sealed and guarded tomb in which His Body slept for a short space till, on the third day, He broke the bands of death on His Resurrection, and came forth endowed again with life.

Now we were buried with Him in Baptism not that we should continue dead merely, but that we should rise again with Him. Christ descended into the grave in order that He might emerge from it endowed with a new and almighty power of Life, and we share the one with Him, the Death and Burial, in order that we may share the other—the newness of Life.

This verse must be compared with Col. ii. 12, where the rising from the dead with Christ in the sacrament of Baptism is expressly declared: "Buried with him in baptism, wherein also ye are risen with him through the faith of the operation of God Who hath raised him from the dead." So putting the two statements (Rom. vi. 4 and Coloss. ii. 12) together, the verse before us comprehends both Death and Resurrection with Christ—a share in His Death and a share in His Resurrection. Whatever difficulty there is about the meaning of this verse arises not from want of intelligibleness in the passage, but from our want of faith—the plain mean-the dead by ᵍthe glory of the Father, ʰeven so we also should walk in newness of life.

<small>ᵍ John ii. 11. & xi. 40.
ʰ Gal. vi. 15. Eph. iv. 22, 23, 24. Cor. iii. 10.</small>

---

ing of the verse being that in Baptism there is a mystical Burial and Resurrection with Christ, that we may be dead to sin through His Death and alive unto God through Christ's new Life imparted to us. Now it is clear from this that the Baptismal Death and Burial with Christ are not figurative but real. A spiritual reality takes place in every Christian's Baptism, by which the benefits of the Death and Resurrection of Christ are made his; so that for the future he should not only no longer live to sin, but live a new and holy life to God.

Now all this, of course, is a matter of faith. It pertains to our Justification by faith—to our Salvation by grace through faith. In order to see this we have only to ask such questions as, Who was He Who ordained Baptism? For what purpose did He ordain it? Is He or His Spirit everywhere present to see to it that a rite ministered by weak human beings should be accompanied by an act of His power in which He grafts us into Himself, the true Vine, and makes us members of His Body?

But can we believe in such exuberance of grace? We can, if we believe what St. Paul has just written: " Where sin abounded grace did much more abound." Who ordained the Sacraments? If it was the Eternal Son of God, is it safe to take as low a view of their operation as we can? Is not the highest view, if consistent with faith and holiness, the one most in accord with the mystery of the United Godhead and Manhood—the Holy Incarnation of Him Who ordained them?

To believe respecting Baptism, that it is a mystical Death and Burial and Resurrection with the Lord, requires, of course, a special act of faith—a faith in Christ, God and Man, as everywhere present, and everywhere operative. This special faith is clearly recognized in the Catechism of the Church of England: " What is required of persons to be baptized? Repentance whereby they forsake sin, and faith whereby they steadfastly believe the promises of God made to them in that Sacrament."

But I shall dwell upon this, and also upon the application of it to that form of Baptism which is almost universal amongst us—the Baptism of Infants—at some length, further on.

OUR OLD MAN CRUCIFIED.

5 ¹ For if we have been planted together in the likeness of his death, we shall be also *in the likeness* of *his* resurrection.

6 Knowing this, that ᵏ our old man is crucified

¹ Phil. iii. 10, 11.

ᵏ Gal. ii. 20. & v. 24. & vi. 14. Eph. iv. 22. Col. iii. 5, 9.

5. "Planted together." Rather, "united" or "grafted." See below.
6. "Is crucified." Rather, "was crucified."

"By the glory of the Father." This, probably, means by the power of the Father, or by the Spirit of the Father. Chrysostom explains " Them he also glorified " in chap. viii. 30, by "to whom He gave His Spirit."

"Newness of life." This does not mean the outward life ($\beta i o \varsigma$) considered as so much time lived, but the principle of life, $\zeta \omega \dot{\eta}$, as when we say that such a thing begins to show signs of life. Our new life is the infusion into us of the Resurrection Life of the Lord.

"For if we have been planted together in the likeness of his death." Planted together does not mean planted side by side with Him as trees are planted side by side in a wood, but it means nearly the same as being grafted, for it signifies being united to Him so as to grow in Him, and together with Him. If we have been united to Him in, or by, the likeness of His Death, we shall be also in that of His Resurrection. Others translate it, " If we have been," or, " as surely as we have been " (for no doubt is insinuated), —as surely as we have been united in the likeness of His death we shall be also in His Resurrection. There is a difference between the likeness of His Death and that of His Resurrection : His actual Death is past and gone, so we can only be united to Him in its *likeness;* but His Resurrection is present. He lives now in the power and vitality of it, and so we are united to it not figuratively but actually. "If thou hast shared in Death, much more wilt thou in Resurrection and Life. For now that the greater is done away with, the sin I mean, it is not right to doubt any longer about the lesser, the doing away of death " (Chrysostom).

6. "Knowing this, that our old man is [was] crucified with him." We who are united to Christ, or grafted into the likeness of His Death, have two natures, the old and the new. It was the old nature—the body of sin and death—which was crucified with Christ, that is, which partook of His Crucifixion, and to this end,

with *him*, that ¹the body of sin might be destroyed, that henceforth we should not serve sin.

7 For ᵐ he that is dead is † freed from sin.

¹ Col. ii. 11.
ᵐ 1 Pet. iv. 1.
† Gr. *justified*.

---

6. " Might be destroyed." " Might be done away," Revisers.

that the body of sin might be destroyed. It might be wickedly said that, since Christ was crucified for us, we need have no care about mortifying our evil propensities. "No," says the Apostle, "our old man was crucified in His Crucifixion, that the body of sin might be destroyed." St. Paul here uses a figure which is reproduced in Coloss. iii. 5, where the totality of sin is supposed to be a body, and the different particular sins the various members of that body: well, our old man is crucified with Christ, that all these members of the body of sin should be destroyed, that "henceforth we should not serve sin." When the body of sin within us uses any of these its members (and the Apostle particularizes them in Col. iii. 5)—fornication, uncleanness, inordinate affection, concupiscence and covetousness—then it serves sin, and it has been crucified in Christ's Crucifixion for this one purpose, that it should not serve sin. If we had continued innocent, we should have had no old man, and Christ need not have died, and we need not have been baptized into His Death; but since the human race fell in Adam it was needful that a Second Adam should be given, in Whom the sin of the race should receive its penalty, and so each one of us received that penalty in our Head for this purpose, that we should contract no further guilt by yielding to sin.

"That henceforth we should not serve sin." I take this to mean that Christ must suffer for sin, and we, *i.e.*, our old man of sin, must suffer in Him before He could be raised from the dead, and we partake of His Resurrection Life. This verse seems to re-embody the idea of v. 10, "If when we were enemies, we were reconciled to God by the death of his Son, much more being reconciled we shall be saved by his life." The Death of Christ does not impart to us of His Life, but the Death is the necessary prelude to that Resurrection by the power of which we are enabled to live by His Life, and so to serve sin no longer.

7. "For he that is dead is freed from sin," that is, is justified from sin.

CHAP. VI.] CHRIST DIETH NO MORE. 121

8 Now ⁿ if we be dead with Christ, we believe that we shall also live with him: n 2 Tim. ii. 11.
9 Knowing that º Christ being raised from the o Rev. i. 18. dead dieth no more; death hath no more dominion over him.

8. "Now if we be dead." Rather, "if we died."

St. Paul here seems to mean that as long as men have unrepented and unforsaken sin upon them, they are under the dominion and penalty of sin. This penalty is removed on their repentance, whereby they forsake sin, and on their faith, *i.e.*, their accepting the promises of deliverance from the guilt and power of sin, which are embodied in Baptism. Christ is assumed to have died with the weight of our sins upon Him. He discharged this debt by His Death, and emerged from the tomb free from the burden of our sins. And as He was then by death freed or justified from sin [our sins], so we who are in Him are freed from, or justified from, our sins in and by His Death, for we were baptized and so made one with Him in His Death.

8. "Now if we be dead [died] with Christ, we believe that we shall also live with him." Christ ordained the Sacrament of Baptism as the means whereby we should be united to Him in His Death to sin, and so be partakers of the atonement wrought by that Death; but the Baptism which Christ ordained is into a Death followed by a Resurrection. We continue under the water, or have the water poured over us, only for a moment—we emerge from it, and that emerging is also with Christ, that we may partake of the Life which He assumed on the third day.

9, 10. "Knowing that Christ being raised from the dead . . . . he liveth unto God." Why does Christ, once raised, die no more? Because His Death has been an all-sufficient atonement. Christ was such a representative Man—a Second Adam—that, if it be lawful to utter such a thing, if any sin had remained He would have yet been subject to death; but His Resurrection, after He had taken upon Him and borne our sins, was the outward visible sign that sin was put away, and God reconciled.

"Death hath no more dominion over him." Death had dominion over Him for a very short time, but such was the Godhead, such the holiness, such the merit, of Him over Whom it had this three days' dominion, that its very conquest destroyed itself.

10 For in that he died, ᵖ he died unto sin once: but in that he liveth, ᑫ he liveth unto God.

11 Likewise reckon ye also yourselves to be

ᵖ Heb. ix. 27, 28.
ᑫ Luke xx. 38.

---

10. "For in that," &c. Revisers translate, "The death which he died, he died unto sin once, but the life which he liveth, he liveth unto God."

10. "For in that he died, he died unto sin once," &c. Most commentators are agreed that this should be rendered by "The death which he died he died unto sin once," and "in that he liveth" by "the life which he liveth," &c.

"He died unto sin once," once for all, that is, as we commonly say, "it is done with." He suffered and died, and all that is done with, so far as regards its pain and shame. It is impossible to imagine that it can occur again. His Death was momentary and all-sufficient, but not so His Life. It is eternal. "He liveth." He ever liveth to God. "I am he that liveth, and was dead, and behold I am alive for evermore." He liveth an endless life, in which He carries out the purposes of God towards the Church and the Universe. And the Apostle tells us that it is by the power of this endless life that we live. God, when we were dead in sin, hath quickened us—hath, that is, made us alive with or in Christ (Ephes. ii. 5-7). So in Coloss. iii. 1-3, "Christ who is our life," "Christ liveth in me," and our Lord tells us the same, "Because I live ye shall also live."

11. "Likewise reckon ye also yourselves to be dead indeed unto sin," &c. This is the practical conclusion of this whole matter respecting Christ's Death and Resurrection and our Baptism. We are to reckon, to think, to assume, ourselves dead indeed unto sin, but alive unto God. Now we cannot get a true and firm grasp of the whole matter unless we realize what this death to sin means.

There are three ways in which a man may be "dead to sin."

1. He may be dead to sin by being actually and physically dead, i.e., his body may be, for if he has died in sin, sin in terrible ways may have dominion over him in the world of spirits. However, his body, if he be dead, is actually dead to sin, as to everything else. If the temptation to his most darling sin is brought close to his body, he has no consciousness of it, and is unmoved by it.

2. A Christian may be dead to sin, because he has so subdued it, so crucified it, that he no longer feels its suggestions. Such Chris

DEAD TO SIN.

^r^ dead indeed unto sin, but ^s^alive unto God through

^r^ ver. 2.
^s^ Gal. ii. 19.

tians are perfect Christians, and they are very few indeed. But it is very frequently the case that a man through Divine Grace, or through self-discipline, or through age, may be quite dead to the power of some particular temptation; but even in such cases it may revive, which shows that there is not an absolute and complete death.

Now this death, or any form of it, cannot be what the Apostle means, for he alludes to something which is now making itself felt, and must be fought and prayed against, or it may reassert its dominion. We have been baptized in order that the body of sin may be destroyed, and yet notwithstanding our Baptism, and its grace of co-burial and co-resurrection in Christ, we may forget it, and fall from it, and again serve sin. It is the height of inconsistency in a human being which has been united to Christ, even in figure, so to do; but at every point we have to assume the existence of, and to meet, human inconsistency. The old man exists yet, not only in the baptized, but in the converted, in those who give every sign of having had some conscious change in them. There is apparently no Christian who has not some need of the exhortations, "Put off the old man," "Be renewed in the spirit of your mind," "Put on the new man."

3. What then is this death to sin? It is a Sacramental Death, an union with Christ in His atoning Death, so that we die in Him, and in the same short moment of Baptism are raised again with Him, and so partake of His Resurrection Life. When then does a man reckon himself dead to sin, and alive unto God? When he remembers that at a certain time of his past life, when he was brought under the Christian covenant and made a member of Christ, he was endowed with a power against sin which he has to fall back upon, as it were, and to plead with God, and to stir up by prayer and faith (2 Tim. i. 6).[1] We have need constantly to make an act of faith in God's work in us in our Baptism, that God did actually then make us members of a Christ once dead, but now alive with a Life in which we have received a part.

---

[1] This passage, 2 Tim. i. 6, refers to the grace received in ordination; but it must be applicable to every other rite or Sacrament, such as Baptism and Confirmation, which is only administered once in a life-time.

Jesus Christ our Lord.

11. " Through Jesus Christ ; " or, " in Jesus Christ."

This seems to me to be what the Apostle alludes to when he says in the sister passage in the Epistle to the Colossians, " Buried with him in baptism, wherein also ye are risen with him through the faith of the operation of God, who hath raised him from the dead" (ii. 12). Baptism meets our faith in the Resurrection of Christ as being for us. The heathen, or unbaptized convert, saw in the Baptism which he sought, the likeness of the Death and Resurrection; but not a mere outward typical likeness, but an efficacious one, efficacious to infuse into him a new power of life, through the same power and will of God by which Christ Himself was raised ; but inasmuch as Baptism was only administered once in a man's life, in order that it might be efficacious through the remainder of his life, he must renew its power by faith—by conscious acts of faith in that Resurrection of Christ into the power of which he was baptized.

And now an objection occurs, which must be fully met and answered. Those who came to receive Holy Baptism in St. Paul's time were (it is supposed) mostly adults, exercising conscious faith, and those who come now, come through the faith of others. It has been asserted, then, by writers on this very passage, that the benefits ascribed to Baptism belong only to that of penitent and believing adults, and that the same cannot be said of the Baptism of Infants—so that though a man baptized in riper years, can and ought to reckon himself to have died to sin and risen again with Christ, a person baptized in infancy cannot, and has no warrant for exercising any such faith, or at least that there is such doubt about it that any reference to his Baptism is practically useless.

Let the reader give due attention to the following questions :—

Did Christ intend His Baptism to be a permanent institution? Did He intend that it should be this in its fulness, so that throughout all time till His second coming, successive generations of baptized men should become members of His Body, and reckon themselves for moral and spiritual purposes to be such? He must have foreseen that in a few generations His Church would not consist (except in a few instances) of those who received Christianity in riper years, but of those who, being born of Christian parents, were

LET NOT SIN REIGN.

12 ᵗ Let not sin therefore reign in your mortal body, that ye should obey it in the lusts thereof.   ᵗ Ps. xix. 13. & cxix. 133

12. "Obey it in the lusts thereof." So K., L., P., and most Cursives; but ℵ, A., B., C., a few Cursives, 4, 39, 47, 67, 80, 137, 179, Vulg., Sah., Copt., Syriac, &c. read, "obey the lusts thereof."

brought up in it. He must have also foreseen that from the Apostles' times successive generations of Christians, professing to receive it from them, would practise Infant Baptism.

If then, Infant Baptism be either a mutilated rite, deprived of the grace accompanying Baptism in the Apostolic times, or if the grace associated with it by St. Paul and his brother Apostles be a matter of uncertainty, then we should have expected some caution against the practice, but we have none.

On the contrary, the conduct of our Lord to infants in blessing them before they could understand the blessing they received, the notices of the Baptism of households in the Book of the Acts, the analogy of circumcision, and, above all, the doctrine of the Lord being the Second Adam, so that as the first Adam communicates his sinful nature to all in a state of infancy, so the Second Adam would find means to communicate His Nature also to those in the same state, in order that they might grow up in Him—all this seems to necessitate that the doctrine contained in this chapter should be as applicable to those baptized in a state of infancy as to those baptized in riper years.[1]

The extreme importance of this verse 11 must be my excuse for having considered it at such length. It is the practical application of all that has gone before.

12. "Let not sin therefore reign in your mortal body, that ye should obey it," &c. This is a continuation of the same argument. If you had no power from Christ your Head against sin, then it might reign; but you have this power, and you must as you value the continuance of your union with your Head, both here and hereafter, see that sin does not reign within you.

"That ye should obey it in the lusts thereof." There is a remainder of sin which, at times, will make itself felt through its

---

[1] For the full explication of this I would direct the reader to two works published by myself many years ago, "The Sacrament of Responsibility" and "The Second Adam and the New Birth;" also to a chapter on the Scripturalness of the Baptismal Services of the Church in "Church Doctrine Bible Truth."

13 Neither yield ye your ᵘmembers *as* †instruments of unrighteousness unto sin: but ˣyield yourselves unto God, as those that are alive from the dead, and your members *as* instruments of righteousness unto God.

ᵘ ch. vii. 5.
Col. iii. 5.
Jam. iv. 1.
† Gr. *arms,* or, *weapons.*
ˣ ch. xii. 1.
1 Pet. ii. 24.
& iv. 2.

---

13. "Instruments." Properly, "arms." "Neither yield ye your members unto sin as instruments of unrighteousness." Personifying the arms.

"As those that are alive from the dead." So D., E., F., G., K., L., P., and most Cursives; but ℵ, A., B., C., and four Cursives, 16, 47, 73, 93 read, "as if alive from the dead."

suggestions to indulgence. If through faith in the power of Christ within you, you deny and so mortify these desires, then you will not obey it; on the contrary, you will conquer it, and through Christ's aid cast it out. "The law of sin lives in the greatest saints during this life: Who has not reason to tremble? Who will dare exalt himself? but it reigns only in him who yields thereto, and who by sinning becomes its slave."

13. "Neither yield ye your members as instruments of unrighteousness unto sin: but yield yourselves unto God," &c. This implies that there are the two men—the old and the new—within us, each issuing his commands; we yield to the one, or to the other, by yielding our members to fulfil the behests of the one or the other.

The word "instruments" signifies "arms." If we [*i.e.*, our wills, the ego within us] yield our members so that they commit sin, then we fight against God and Christ; but if we yield ourselves to God as those that are living with the life of Christ, then we yield our members also as arms of righteousness to fight on the side of God and Christ.

But notice, we yield our members as arms in the service of unrighteousness, but in the other case we yield ourselves first to God as those alive from the dead. Let us ever remember the words, "I beseech you . . . that ye present your bodies a living sacrifice, holy, acceptable unto God." When we do this we yield our members as instruments of righteousness to fight God's battles. By yielding ourselves to God, if we do it sincerely, we engage His help, and shall be victorious. Chrysostom has a noble passage bringing out this: "See how by his bare words he exhorts them—on that side naming sin, and on this God. For by showing what a difference there is

CHAP. VI.] UNDER GRACE. 127

14 For ^y sin shall not have dominion over you: for ye are not under the law, but under grace.

15 What then? shall we sin, ^z because we are not under the law, but under grace? God forbid.

16 Know ye not, that ^a to whom ye yield yourselves servants to obey, his servants ye are to

y ch. vii. 4, 6. & viii. 2. Gal. v. 18.
z 1 Cor. ix. 21.
a Matt. vi. 24. John viii. 34.
2 Pet. ii. 19.

---

between the rulers, he casts out of all excuse the soldier that leaveth God, and desireth to serve under the dominion of sin ... For consider, says he, what you were and what you have been made. What then were ye? Dead and ruined by a destruction which could not from any quarter be repaired. For neither was there any one who had the power to assist you. And what have ye been made out of these dead ones? Alive with immortal life. And by whom? By the all-powerful God. Ye ought therefore to marshal yourselves under Him with as much cheerful readiness as men would who had been made alive from being dead.... For this reason we need strong armour, and also a noble spirit, and one acquainted too with the ways of this warfare, and above all we need a commander. The Commander, however, is standing by, ever ready to help us, and abiding unconquerable, and has furnished us with strong arms likewise. Further, we have need of a purpose of mind to handle them as should be, so that we may both obey our Commander, and take the field for our country."

14. "For sin shall not have dominion over you: for ye are not under the law, but under grace." This is one of the most absolute promises of the Word of God, and most precious to the struggling Christian. Every Christian should have it constantly in mind—to plead it with God, and to encourage himself by it. Observe the reason why sin is not to have dominion. We are not under the law, but under grace. The law can only threaten and terrify, and judge, and condemn. It is uttered, but there is no grace, no power to fulfil it, accompanying the utterance; whereas the moment the Christian is brought under the New Covenant, grace to do the will of God is assigned to him.

15, 16. "What then? shall we sin, because we are not under the law .... obedience unto righteousness." To understand the force of this appeal we must remember what St. Paul considered to be liberty, and what he considered to be slavery. What the

whom ye obey; whether of sin unto death, or of obedience unto righteousness?

17 But God be thanked, that ye were the servants of sin, but ye have obeyed from the heart [b] that form of doctrine † which was delivered you.

[b] 2 Tim. i. 13.
† Gr. *whereto ye were delivered.*

---

17. "That ye were." Properly, "that whereas ye were the servants of sin, ye have obeyed," &c.

world calls liberty he would call slavery. The world would call the power to follow, if we chose to do so, the lusts of our unregenerate nature, liberty; and so the man who does so to the full is called a libertine; but St. Paul would call this slavery, because if we yielded our members servants to sin to do the will of the flesh, we, *ipso facto,* become the servants of sin. But the carnal mind may urge, May I not commit sin when I please, and do good when I please, and is not this liberty? No, because, as the Lord has said, Ye cannot serve two masters, and He for His part will accept no such divided service. On the contrary, those who attempt thus to serve God and sin, He will at once deliver up to the power of sin, so that they shall be its slaves. There is no middle position— no neutrality—in this war. If ye yield yourselves unto sin in any the least degree (consciously, that is) then ye yield yourselves unto death, ye forfeit your part in the Life of Christ both here and hereafter. But if, on the contrary, ye yield yourselves unto obedience, then it will be to righteousness, to conformity with the will, and consequently to enjoy the everlasting favour, of God.

17. "But God be thanked, that ye were the servants of sin, but," &c. Ye were the servants of sin, *i.e.*, in your heathen state, just as the Colossians were to whom the Apostles wrote as walking and living once in fornication, uncleanness, and other vices (Coloss. iii. 5, 8).

" But ye have obeyed from the heart that form of doctrine," &c. The form of doctrine was the Gospel of Christ Incarnate, Crucified, Risen, Ascended, and coming again to judge. In all probability it was put into a few simple words or propositions that a Christian could easily remember, and repeat to himself. This form of doctrine must have been respecting God's Son, Jesus Christ, as St. Paul says in i. 3 that his Gospel was. It was given not only to be

CHAP. VI.] YIELD YOUR MEMBERS. 129

18 Being then ^c made free from sin, ye became the servants of righteousness.

19 I speak after the manner of men because of the infirmity of your flesh: for as ye have yielded your members servants to uncleanness and to iniquity unto iniquity; even so now yield your members servants to righteousness unto holiness.

_{c John viii.
32. 1 Cor. vii.
22. Gal. v. 1.
1 Pet. ii. 16.}

---

believed in, but to be obeyed, and the obedience to it was the renunciation of sin and the cultivation of holiness.

The best translation of the latter part of this verse is, "Ye have obeyed from the heart that form of teaching to which ye were delivered." The idea is supposed to be suggested by the founding of brass statues in Corinth, from which city the Apostle wrote this Epistle. "You readily obeyed the mould of Christian faith and practice, into which, at your Baptism, you were poured, as it were, like soft, ductile, and fluent metal, in order to be cast, and take its form. You obeyed this mould, you were not rigid and obstinate, but were plastic and pliant, and assumed it readily" (Wordsworth).

18. "Being then made free from sin, ye became the servants of righteousness." "Free from sin," by having the sins of your past life forgiven, and by being yourselves endowed with grace sufficient to free you from the love of sin, and enable you to please God with a willing service.

Notice how the service of righteousness and the service of God are the same. We can only serve God by doing His will, which is some form of righteousness.

19. "I speak after the manner of men because of the infirmity of your flesh: for as ye have," &c. This expression, "I speak after the manner of men," is very difficult. It may mean, you are not yet perfectly spiritual—the infirmity of your flesh, its weakness, owing to sin remaining in it, makes you unable to take in spiritual truths as they are, and so they must be presented to you under such figures as I am now using, particularly this contrast between liberty and slavery — slavery to sin, and liberty to righteousness. Perhaps he means to hint that there can be properly no slavery to righteousness, because in his view righteousness is

K

20 For when ye were ᵈ the servants of sin, ye were free †from righteousness.

21 ᵉ What fruit had ye then in those things whereof ye are now ashamed? for ᶠ the end of those things *is* death.

ᵈ John viii. 34.
∗ Gr. *to righteousness.*
ᵉ ch. vii. 5.
ᶠ ch. i. 32.

---

21. "What fruit had ye then in those things." "What fruit then had ye at that time in the things," &c.

freedom (as we have in our Collect, "Whose service is perfect freedom").

Or it may mean, on account of the weakness of your flesh through original sin yet being within you, I lay upon you no heavier burden than what, with God's help, ye are well able to bear, and that is, that your service of righteousness should correspond to your former service of iniquity (or lawlessness, ἀνομία). As ye yielded your members servants to uncleanness, so now yield the same members servants to righteousness. In Cornelius à Lapide we find a good exposition from Anselm, following Augustine: "No fear in your former days drove you to sin, but the lust of it, and the delight of committing it. So let not the fear of punishment urge you to live righteously, but let the delight in righteousness and the love of it lead you so to do. For as he is most wicked whom not even temporal punishments deter from the filthy works of degraded pleasures, so he is most righteous whom not even the fear of temporal punishments recals from the holy works of the brightest charity."

20. "For when ye were the servants of sin, ye were free from (or to) righteousness." The serving of sin of course implies the serving it as its slave. And as no one can have two masters, when they served sin they did not serve righteousness, that is, they were free as respects the service of righteousness. If rendered "ye were free with respect to righteousness," it must not be taken to mean "ye were free to do righteousness when ye pleased," for that is just what they were not, but they obeyed sin as their master, and did not obey the commands of righteousness.

21. "What fruit had ye then in those things whereof ye are now ashamed?" What fruit or advantage had ye in the gratification of sinful appetites? No fruit except your own degradation. Now that ye have come to a better mind, ye are ashamed of them, and

CHAP. VI.] FRUIT UNTO HOLINESS. 131

22 But now ^g being made free from sin, and become servants to God, ye have your fruit unto holiness, and the end everlasting life.

23 For ^h the wages of sin *is* death; but ⁱ the gift of God *is* eternal life through Jesus Christ our Lord.

g John viii. 32.
h Gen. ii. 17. ch. v. 12. Jam. i. 15.
i ch. ii. 7. & v. 17, 21. 1 Pet. i. 4.

---

earnestly wish that the time spent in this indulgence might be restored, so that ye might live it over again profitably.

"The end of those things is death." And punishment afterwards. So that all that you got was shame when you looked back at your past sinful enjoyments, and unless the grace of God had separated you from this shameful past, the fruit would have been eternal ruin.

22. " But now being made free from sin, and become servants to God, ye have your fruit unto holiness." Every service which in our justified or Christian state we render to God, is fruitful. It is fruitful in our own progress in holiness, and our progress in holiness is our progress in the love of God, and the capacity for sharing His happiness. The works of the servants of God follow them into the eternal world. They are all in the mind and memory of God, and the least of them shall be sensibly felt in the sum of the eternal recompense.

"And the end everlasting life." Here the Apostle repeats what he had written before. " To them who by patient continuance in well doing seek for glory, honour, and immortality, God will render eternal life": but not in the way of wages which a man has earned, but as a gift to one who by God's grace has fitted himself to receive it and enjoy it, for the Apostle concludes :—

23. " For the wages of sin is death; but the gift of God is eternal life," &c. Notice how wages and gift are contrasted. Wages are earned and are due, and by serving sin men earn death. They will not be able to refuse it when the time of payment comes, they must receive it.

Whereas eternal life is not wages, but a gift. How is this ? Is it not said in the place I have just quoted that God will " render to every man according to his deeds"? Yes, but the shape and aspect which eternal life assumes is infinitely beyond the reach of any service which a creature can render. For it is not a dreamy life—the existence of a shadow in a heathen Elysium—or even of a blessed soul in a Jewish paradise; but it is a share in the Life of the Only Begotten Son. It is being made a veritable member of His Body. It is actually eating His Flesh and drinking His Blood to eternal life. It is being raised up in the likeness of His Resurrection. It is our vile body being raised up in the likeness of His glorious Body. No service can win this as its wages. It must in the nature of things be a gift—the gift of God—the highest gift which God can give.

As we have now finished the examination of the chapter in which is set forth the fact of sacramental union with Christ and its practical bearing, it will be necessary to draw attention to two or three matters involved in the Apostle's reasoning.

1. It is clear that the Apostolic doctrine of our union with Christ in Baptism is a part of the Gospel, if this Epistle is occupied with the Gospel, and consequently that no one who does not preach or teach it, preaches or teaches St. Paul's Gospel. We ought to esteem it "good news" that at the very outset of our Christian career, whether it is to be dated from the time of our Baptism as infants, born in a Christian land or community, or from the time of our Baptism as heathens, first having the Gospel presented to us in our riper years—from the very first we were made members of Christ, so that we should be brought up and educated as members of Christ. So that not only should parents rejoice in the fact that in the Baptism of their children Christ took them up in the arms of His mercy, whereby they were sure of being saved, if they were prematurely cut off, but the same parents should see to it that they guard their children from every evil influence—that they should pray for their children, not as they would pray for heathens who had to be converted, but they should pray that they might continue in the grace into which Christ has brought them; and that they should instruct their children in the knowledge of such truths as that they have already been brought into the Church or Body of the Redeemer, and try to convince them in a simple way of the holiness of the Christian's body, because in a measure a part of Christ's Body.

And now with respect to Baptism and conversion. Their relations to one another may be illustrated by the following anecdote. A celebrated revivalist asked a brother clergyman whether he had

CHAP. VI.] BAPTISM AND CONVERSION. 133

been converted? "Yes," he said, "I am ashamed to say that I was converted when I was twenty years old." "Ashamed!" the revivalist exclaimed with a start. "Yes, ashamed, for what was I doing between the time of my Baptism, and the time of my conversion? I will tell you what I was doing. I was contracting habits, the evil savour of which at times makes itself felt even now, when I am free and am the servant of God." "But were you never reminded of your Baptismal obligations?" "Never," was the reply. "To my certain knowledge I never heard Baptism alluded to except in the way of warning us lest we should connect any grace of God with it."

It may be said against this, was there not all this time instruction in the Catechism?[1] There might be, but it was understood that the Church formularies respecting this Sacrament contained many remnants of Popish error, and to say the least, that many of these statements must be received with extreme distrust.

2. Then, in the next place, it is clear from the whole reasoning throughout this chapter that the Apostle assumes that in all cases God accompanied Baptism with grace, whatever that grace might be. Whatever individual Christians might be deficient in, they all had Baptism, and they all had that particular grace of Baptism, which the Apostle expresses in such unique and extraordinary terms as being co-buried and co-raised again in Christ. We were all buried with Him, and all raised again with Him, that we might all walk in newness of life. Now unless this connection (as a rule) of the outward sign with the inward grace is recognized, we are unable to make the smallest use of the doctrine of Baptism, as a doctrine binding all Christians to be holy in body and soul. Some years ago, at the time of what is called the Gorham controversy, a very large party in the Church of England, headed by some of the best men of the day, contended that the outward visible sign and the inward spiritual grace need not be, and (I think I am not doing these good men wrong in saying this) as a rule were not, united; that they were only united when a decree (secret to us) had been pronounced by God in favour of the union, so that it never could be known in

---

[1] An evangelical clergyman of the deepest piety and highest position, in fact one of the leading men of his county, told me that he once thought it necessary to say some words respecting the doctrine of Baptism in a sermon; and that from that day he lost one of his leading parishioners, who informed him that he could not stay in a Church where he might be subjected to hearing such superstition.

the case of any child, whether the administration of Baptism had been a Christian sacrament or an empty ceremony, and so the doctrine of Baptism in this Epistle of St. Paul never could be brought to bear upon any professing Christian, and as far as my experience went, it never was.

Now the mischief of this is known only to God, for in His word, baptismal obligations depend upon baptismal grace, and cannot be enforced without the assumption that it has been received. "Know ye not that so many of us," *i.e.*, all the baptized, "were baptized into His death that we might walk in newness of life?" The obligation contracted in Baptism to live holily does not depend upon any vows taken in it, but upon grace bestowed in it, so that if the bestowal of grace is uncertain so is the obligation.

3. Then, in the last place, what is the relation between faith and Baptism? To which we reply, the most direct and intimate possible. Baptism, of course, may be received without a particle of faith by parents who solicit it for their children, and by persons of riper years, who think that in their case something has been omitted which ought to be supplied; but for any one in his own case to realize the grace of Baptism in the shape in which the Apostle presents it in this chapter, that he is to reckon himself dead to sin and alive unto God, requires in these days, when the doctrine of Baptismal grace is so extensively denied in the religious world, a high degree of faith.

But this faith will not be difficult, if a man begins at the beginning, and ascends step by step as God in the Scriptures leads him up. Does a man believe that God's own and very Son came into the world in the way of the Incarnation; that He took our flesh and blood; that He died for us all; that He rose again for us all; that He ascended for us all; that He sits at the right hand of God; that before He left the world He ordained a Church or Society which was to have a certain mysterious relation to Himself, just as the branch of a vine has to its stem, and the body to its head; that He ordained Baptism to be the outward and visible entrance into this Vine, this Body; that being God and Man He is always present in the plenitude of power to make every Baptism a reality—so that the Baptism of the nineteenth century should be the same in grace as that of the first, so that the Baptism of the deacon, or indeed layman, should be the same as that of an Apostle, so far as this, that the person baptized should be received into an Evangelical state or condition in which he is by an act of faith to reckon himself dead to sin and alive to God?

There is no difficulty in all this if we take the first step, if we believe in the mystery of our Lord's Holy Incarnation, for if the Eternal Son came amongst us, then everything must be in consonance with such a mystery of grace. His Life must be the Life of God amongst us, His Death must be all-atoning, His Resurrection must be life-imparting; and if He ordained any kingdom or church, then it is only likely that this kingdom or church, though existing in this fallen world, and administered by feeble, fallible men, should be alive with His Life, and permeated with His power. If it is a part of faith to believe that He is the Son of God, and Saviour of the world, it is equally a part of faith to believe in the permanency of His presence to make His Sacraments good to the end.

Does, then, the grace of the sacraments depend upon the faith of the receiver? Certainly not; because, if so, the sacraments would be no sacraments. We could exercise no faith in the promises of God made to us in them. But though the grace of sacraments depends not on our faith, the beneficial consideration of them does, The grace which God gives them has to be stirred up by acts of faith and prayer. And this seems very easy, for when a man is tempted to commit sin, or to be slothful, or to neglect any Christian obligations, he has to say to himself, as in the sight of God, "I reckon myself dead unto sin, but alive unto God through Jesus Christ my Lord. I desire that God would renew in me whatsoever has been decayed by the fraud and malice of the devil, or by my own carnal will and frailty."

This is unquestionably the Evangelical use of Baptism in after life, and we must take care that no other consideration respecting Baptism supersedes it. For instance, there is a great temptation amongst a certain class of Church people to base the obligations of Baptism on the vows undertaken in the name of the child, and afterwards ratified in Confirmation. This is a fatal mistake. It goes far to make Baptism a legal rite, in fact mere circumcision under another form. It transfers Holy Baptism out of the province of the Gospel into that of the law. The great consideration respecting Baptism is not that we vow either by ourselves or by proxy, but that we are grafted into the second Adam, that we may partake of His Life.

One more objection must be met.

If such grace is bestowed on all the baptized, how is it that so many fall away? We answer unhesitatingly: in no one case because God has withheld His grace. In every case the lapse took place through the fault of man, or indifferent teaching, in many cases unbelieving, in many anti-sacramental; or through evil example, or through the fault of the Church itself, its laxity, its worldliness, its want of discipline; in every case must we ascribe a lapse to the fault or sin on the part of man, in no case to the withdrawal of grace on the part of God.

CHAP. VII.

KNOW ye not, brethren, (for I speak to them that know the law,) how that the law hath dominion over a man as long as he liveth?

---

1. "Know ye not, brethren, (for I speak to them that know the law)." The Apostle uses this interrogative form as implying that those who were ignorant of what he asserts must be in a state of extreme ignorance indeed; so vi. 3 and 16.

"I speak to them that know the law." This need not imply that all the Roman Christians were of Hebrew origin, and so educated in Judaism. We must remember that the Jewish Scriptures, interpreted according to the light of the Gospel, were the principal spiritual nourishment of the Gentile Churches for many years before the books of the New Testament were collected and distributed amongst the Churches.

The first seven verses of this chapter belong, so far as the argument is concerned, to the former chapter. Both are concerned with bearing fruit to God. In the preceding chapter the idea is the graft growing up with Christ in the likeness of His Death and His Resurrection—in this it is our being delivered from our marriage union with the law, that we should be married to another, even to Christ, and so bring forth worthier fruit to God.

"How that the law hath dominion over a man as long as he liveth?"

CHAP. VII.] DEAD TO THE LAW. 137

2 For ^a the woman which hath an husband is bound by the law to *her* husband so long as he liveth; but if the husband be dead, she is loosed from the law of *her* husband. a 1 Cor. vii. 39.

3 So then ^b if, while *her* husband liveth, she be married to another man, she shall be called an adulteress: but if her husband be dead, she is free from that law; so that she is no adulteress, though she be married to another man. b Matt. v. 32.

4 Wherefore, my brethren, ye also are become ^c dead to the law by the body of Christ; that ye should c ch. viii. 2. Gal. ii. 19. & v. 18. Eph. ii. 15. Col. ii. 14.

---

2. "For the woman which hath an husband . . . . law of her husband." There may be some confusion in the understanding of this verse, owing to the translation "man" in the first verse. The word (τοῦ ἀνθρώπου) thus translated means "man" as representing any human being; and to avoid any possible misunderstanding should perhaps be rendered "person." "Know ye not that the law hath dominion over the person who is born in it, and is initiated into its covenant, so long as he (or she) liveth?" and he illustrates it by the covenant of marriage. The married woman is bound to one husband so long as that husband liveth, but, if the husband be dead, her former marriage contract no longer exists.

"She is loosed from the law of her husband." That is, she is loosed from the contract which obliges her to have one husband only, and that the man she was married to, and then the Apostle proceeds:—

3. "So then if, while her husband liveth, she be married to another man, she shall be called an adulteress," &c. The marriage contract does not reach into the future state. Death at once, and for ever, does away with it, because, in the Resurrection state, they neither marry, nor are given in marriage, *i.e.*, carnally, but are as the angels of God.

4. "Wherefore, my brethren, ye also are become dead to the law by the Body of Christ; that ye should be married to another . . . . bring forth fruit unto God." From what has gone before we should

be married to another, *even* to him who is raised from the dead, that we should ^d bring forth fruit unto God. 5 For when we were in the flesh, the † motions of sins, which were by the law, ^e did work in our members ^f to bring forth fruit unto death.

^d Gal. v. 22.
† Gr. *passions*.
^e ch. vi. 13.
^f ch. vi. 21.
Gal. v. 19.
Jam. i. 15.

---

have expected that the Apostle would have proceeded to speak of the law having died ; but, instead of this, he speaks of the Church having itself in Christ died to the law. The severance from the dominion of the law is not effected by the cessation of the obligation of the law, because the obligation of the moral law never ceases. It ceases as the means of justification, but not as the rule of sanctification ; on the contrary, it is never truly fulfilled except by those in Christ—then, when we are truly abiding in Him, the righteousness of the law is fulfilled in us. But the severance is made by Christ having borne the penalty of the law by His Death ; and we are in the same position as regards the law, by our union with Him in our Baptism into His Death, as He is.

We have become dead to the law by the death of the Body of Christ, Who died to the law (Christ hath redeemed us from the curse of the law, being made a curse for us), that, passing through Death, He might rise from the dead into a sphere for serving God, and with powers for serving God, to which His sphere and His powers when living upon earth under the law were as nothing ; as He Himself intimates when He says : " I have a baptism to be baptized with, and how am I straitened till it be accomplished " (Luke xii. 50).

And now we, in and through His Death, are dead to the law and to every other system which is apart from Him, that we should be united to another, even to Him that is raised from the dead. As the Apostle had said : " If we are planted together in the likeness of his Death, we shall be also in the likeness of His Resurrection," so now he says, If we, once married to the law, have died with Christ to the law, it is not that we should be barren, but that we should be the wife of Him Who was raised from the dead, that we should bring forth fruit unto God.

5. " For when we were in the flesh, the motions of sins, which were by the law," &c. " When we were in the flesh." That is, in our unrenewed or unregenerate state. St. Paul describes this as

CHAP. VII.]   IN NEWNESS OF SPIRIT.   139

6 But now we are delivered from the law, ‖ that being dead wherein we were held; that we should serve ᶠ in newness of spirit, and not *in* the oldness of the letter.

‖ Or, *being dead to that.*
ᶠ ch. ii. 29.
2 Cor. iii. 6.

6. א, A., B., C., K., L., P., seventy Cursives, Vulg., Syriac, Copt., Arm. read as in margin, "being dead to that in which we were held."

belonging to Jews and Gentiles alike in Ephes. ii. 3: "Among whom also we all had our conversation in times past in the lusts of our flesh, fulfilling the desires of the flesh and of the mind." When we were in this state, the motions or passions of sin, which were by the law (that is, were shown to be sin, and so made sin, and were also, owing to the rebelliousness of our nature, aggravated and incited to sin by the law) these motions or passions worked in our members, so as to produce actions worthy of death —they deadened our souls to God and righteousness, and they earned for us the wages of sin, which is death.

6. "But now we are delivered from the law, that being dead" [or rather, "being dead to that in which we were held"], &c. We should rather have expected that the Apostle would have written being delivered from sin, rather than from the law; but the reason why he specifically mentions the law is, that he looked to the service with which, when we were in union with Christ, we should serve God—that it should be in a far more exalted spirit, and have a far wider range of action. This he describes as newness of the Spirit as distinguished from oldness of the letter. The Jew, *i.e.* the typical Jew, thought he served God well if he kept to the letter; the Christian is altogether unsatisfied with mere literal obedience, but desires to go far beyond the letter, and reach to the spirit of each command.

7. "What shall we say, then? Is the law sin? God forbid. Nay I had," &c. The remainder of this chapter seems to have been written for two purposes.

(1.) To rectify any wrong conclusions which the readers of his Epistle might have drawn from St. Paul's words respecting the law, as if it were sinful in itself. He had said that "by the deeds of the law should no flesh be justified;" he had also said that "the law entered that the offence might abound;" he had also said that sin should not have dominion over Christians, "for they were not under the law but under grace." It might then be asked, Was the law something evil in itself? and, in order to answer this, he shows, v. 7—14 or 16, that it was not. But then he feels himself obliged to go further. (2.) The Gospel had not done in man, *i.e.*, in all men, all that might have been expected. St. Paul had said, " Much more having been reconciled, we shall be saved through His life." He had said respecting all Christians, " We have been buried with Him by Baptism into death, that like as Christ was raised up from the dead by the glory of the Father, even so we also should walk in newness of life." He had said universally to all the Roman Christians, " Reckon ye also yourselves to be dead indeed unto sin, but alive unto God ; " and " Sin shall not have dominion over you, for ye are not under the law, but under grace." Now that the Gospel had not produced its full and perfect effect is clear from this, that the Apostle had occasion to say to these very Roman Christians, " Let not sin reign in your mortal bodies, that ye should obey it in the lusts thereof. Neither yield ye your members as instruments of unrighteousness unto sin, but yield yourselves unto God." If St. Paul saw it needful to speak such words to these Roman Christians, there must have been a need, and what was that need? We have it in the last words of this chapter. After he had given thanks for the victory, or rather for the deliverance, he yet concludes with, " So then with the mind I myself serve the law of God, but with the flesh the law of sin." And this is said, not merely with reference to the legal, but to the evangelical state ; for he says to them in viii. 13, " If ye live after the flesh ye shall die; but if ye through the Spirit do mortify the deeds of the body, ye shall live."

One more question must be answered, or an attempt must be made to answer it. Of whom does the Apostle speak when all through he uses the first person singular, and in the latter part the present tense ? Does he speak of himself, or of some other man? To which we answer, he speaks of himself, or in his own person, but in this way : he throws himself, with a power and sincerity which no other human being, except the Lord, ever possessed, into the position of all his brethren—all the children of Adam—whom God has enlightened as to such things as sin, God, salvation, redemption. In all men—heathen, Jew, or Christian—thus enlightened by God with any portion of that " life which is the light of men," there must be a seeming duality, the higher nature, the

7 What shall we say then? *Is* the law sin? God forbid. Nay, [h] I had not known sin, but by the law: for I had not known ‖ lust, except the law had said, [i] Thou shalt not covet.

[h] ch. iii. 20.
‖ Or, *concupiscence.*
[i] Exod. xx. 17. Deut. v. 21. Acts xx. 33. ch. xiii. 9.

---

spirit which has received the light, asserting its rightful dominion, and demanding obedience; and the lower, called the flesh, including, of course, the fleshly or animal soul, as well as the body, rebelling or refusing obedience, or yielding it reluctantly, or so mortified and subdued as to be well nigh crushed, but never apparently absolutely dead, so as to be incapable of revival, till the day of the resurrection of the body.

We shall now proceed to the examination.

"What shall we say then? Is the law sin? God forbid. Nay, I had not known sin," &c. Sin can only be revealed by contrast with righteousness, which is the opposite to sin. If the law were sin it would share in the inherent deceit of sin, and so sin and the law would, joined together, add to the deceit practised on the victim; but the first thing which the law does is to undeceive. It strips off the disguise of sin, and shows it to the human spirit in its true light, as contrary to God and to man's highest nature and best interests.

"I had not known sin, but by the law." Sin is in mankind, but they only know it to be sin because the law of God, either written in their hearts, or given by revelation, shows it to be contrary to the rule of right. The inferior creatures with which we are surrounded cannot be said to sin in the true sense of the word, because God has not revealed to them either Himself or His will. Sin is the transgression of God's law. It is opposition to His will, as the will of the Supreme. What appears to be sinful in animals, as the ravening in wild beasts, is so far from being sin, that it is an instinct implanted in them by God to enable them to keep down the number of other creatures, who would otherwise increase and multiply beyond their means of subsistence.

"For I had not known lust, except the law had said, Thou shalt not covet." This would with more clearness be rendered, "I had not known lust, except the law had said, Thou shalt not lust." The law against evil lust or inordinate desire is in the tenth commandment. It is the natural guard and enforcement of the sixth,

8 But ᵏ sin, taking occasion by the commandment, wrought in me all manner of concupiscence. For ˡ without the law sin *was* dead.

9 For I was alive without the law once:

ᵏ ch. iv. 15. & v. 20.
ˡ 1 Cor. xv. 56.

---

8. "By the commandment," &c. The Revisers point this, "But sin, finding occasion, wrought in me through the commandment all manner," &c.

9. "Without the law;" *i.e.* apart from the law, before it came to me in moral power.

seventh, and eighth commandments, *i.e.*, the commandments upon which human society, with all its advantages, depends. God, for the infinite good of mankind, endowed man with certain rights—the right of life, the right of the family, the right of property; and the tenth commandment shows that the evil desire to transgress these commandments is contrary to the will of God, because it tends to destroy His own ordinance of human society, and so is sin.

8. "But sin, taking occasion by the commandment, wrought in me," &c. Sin is here represented as an evil living thing which before the coming of the law was in a dormant state, but when the commandment came it roused itself into activity: it took occasion, it seized the opportunity afforded it by that secret wrong desire of the soul to do what is forbidden simply because it is forbidden, to work all manner of concupiscence.

"For without the law sin was dead." Dormant, motionless,—waiting for the coming of law to the conscience to be raised into activity. Could not then a man, before the coming of law to his conscience, commit sin? If we remember that law here includes the law written in the heart, as well as the law properly so called, he could not. He would be like an animal, and God would hold him to be such, and not judge and condemn him according to a law of which he was not conscious. There never was a time in the history of the race when this was so. But it was quite possible that there could be this state in each particular man sufficient for St. Paul's argument, and so he says:—

9. "For I was alive without the law once." I cannot but think that this was the state of childish innocence. In childhood a man speaks as a child, thinks as a child, understands as a child. Theologically speaking, of course there is no such thing as a state of innocence, because all are conceived and born in sin—the sin of

CHAP. VII.]   SIN REVIVED AND I DIED.   143

but when the commandment came, sin revived, and I died.

10 And the commandment, ^m which *was ordained* to life, I found *to be* unto death.

^m Lev. xviii. 5. Ezek. xx. 11, 13, 21. 2 Cor. iii. 7.

Adam. But neither did our Blessed Lord, nor do we, treat children otherwise than as in a state of comparative innocence. Things which we should punish very severely in men and women, we never think of visiting upon children. Some, however, explain this differently. "I was alive," that is, "in mine own eyes." I thought it was well with me—I seemed to myself to live and to be safe, because I had not yet realized God, and His will, and His judgments.

"But when the commandment came, sin revived, and I died." When the commandment, in which I had probably been instructed, came home to me, when I perceived that the keeping of it was a matter between me and God; "sin revived"—was seen to be sin —the transgression of God's law. "Revived" means, came to life again. "It was not the birth of sin, but only its revival, the beginning of its action in the form of positive transgression." (Vaughan.)

"And I died." In the sense that Adam did when he had eaten of the forbidden fruit. He died in spirit to God, being alienated from Him, and the sign of this was that he hid himself from the presence of the Lord God. Does this "coming home" of the commandment mean conviction of sin? No. Conviction of sin, as we always understand the term, is the first step in repentance unto life; and St. Paul does not mean that he began to repent, but that he began to live consciously apart from God.

10. "And the commandment, which was ordained to life, I found to be," &c. God expressly tells us this in several places in the Old Testament. Thus Levit. xviii. 5, "Ye shall therefore keep my statutes and my judgments, which, if a man do, he shall live in them;" and Ezek. xx. 11, "I gave them my statutes, and shewed them my judgments, which, if a man do, he shall even live in them." And our Lord Himself says: "If thou wilt enter into life, keep the comandments" (Matth. xix. 17). This place is of very great importance, as showing indisputably that notwithstanding any perverse interpretation which Antinomians put on such expres-

11 For sin, taking occasion by the commandment, deceived me, and by it slew *me*.

a Ps. xix 8.
& cxix. 38, 137.
1 Tim. i. 8.

12 Wherefore ⁿthe law *is* holy, and the commandment holy, and just, and good.

---

sions as "The law entered that the offence might abound," yet St. Paul most thoroughly believed and realized that God gave men the law for one purpose, that they should obey it. It has another purpose—to convince men of their sin and weakness, and to lead them to Christ, but this is only fulfilled in those who attempt to obey the law sincerely.

"I found to be unto death." I found that, owing to my transgression of it, so far from having obtained eternal life through it, I was brought by it under the sentence of death.

11. "For sin taking occasion by the commandment, deceived me, and by it slew me." Sin is so personified here as deceiving before it slew, that we cannot help remembering how the author of sin deceived our first parents before he was able to slay them. He deceived them with respect to the commandment, *i.e.*, he used it as his means of attack in two ways. He represented it to be a commandment which was contrary to their happiness, "Yea, hath God,"—your good God—"said, ye shall not eat of every tree?" and he also told them that if they transgressed it, God would not hold to His threat that they should die. And the same deceit is re-enacted whenever men begin a course of sin. Satan represents the prohibitions of God's law as hard and unjust in depriving men of pleasure in the fruition of their desires, and he also tells them that God will not be so severe as to visit their trifling indulgence in the desires which they inherit by their very nature, with so terrible a penalty as death.

12. "Wherefore the law is holy," &c. The law seems to mean the whole law, which contained various commandments, and sanctions, and examples.

"And the commandment holy, and just, and good." The commandment is holy, as proceeding from a holy God, and designed to make men partakers of His holiness.

"And just." As defining, on righteous or just principles, men's duties to God, to one another, and to themselves.

"And good." Good, as looking to the best interests of God's

SIN WORKING DEATH IN ME.

13 Was then that which is good made death unto me? God forbid. But sin, that it might appear sin, **working death in me by that which is good; that sin by the commandment might become exceeding sinful.**

14 For we know that the law is spiritual: but I am carnal, ° sold under sin.

° 1 Kings xxi. 20, 25. 2 Kings xvii. 17.

---

reasonable creatures, as restraining them from what will ultimately destroy their happiness, as leading them on to attain to the character and enjoy the favour of God.

13. "Was then that which is good made death unto me? God forbid. But sin," &c. This verse may be explained thus. The holiness and goodness of the law had been laid down in the last verse. Could then, this good holy thing become the cause of death? No, on no account. It was sin which became the cause of death, and God allowed sin to be the cause of death, that it might be set forth in its true light, as a thing so evil that it worked death in me not by what is evil, but by what is actually holy and good, so that sin, by means of the holy commandment which it tempted me to transgress, is shown to be very deadly indeed, for it can make that which God ordained for life its instrument, or occasion, to inflict upon me death.

14. "For we know that the law is spiritual: but I am carnal, sold under sin." We now come to by far the most difficult part of this extraordinary argument, and its difficulty, compared to the difficulty of that which has gone before, seems mainly this—that the tense is changed. The Apostle to this time has been describing a past experience—" Sin wrought in me all manner of concupiscence;" " I was alive ; " " Sin revived, and I died ; " " Sin taking occasion by the commandment deceived me ; " " Slew me." But now he begins to speak of what is apparently his present experience—" I am carnal, sold under sin ; " " That which I do, I allow not ; " " The good that I would, I do not ; " " I delight in the law of God, after the inward man ; " " I see another law . . . . bringing me into captivity to the law of sin." Could this have been the experience of the Apostle at the time when he wrote the Epistle ?

Now, in order to arrive at the only possible solution of this—and a solution which will be found, on examination, to be eminently practical—I will examine the meaning of the concluding words of

L

these ten verses—" So then with the mind I myself serve the law of God, but with the flesh the law of sin " (verse 25). Can we put into other words the meaning of this? Certainly we can; he means to say, "My spirit is renewed, but my flesh is not. My spirit is renewed by the action, or, rather, the indwelling, of the Holy Spirit, but my body is yet under the bondage of corruption."

Now we will suppose one coming to the Apostle, and saying to him after he had written this, or something in all respects answering to it, " O holy Apostle, I have read your letter. Do you mean that in mind and thought you serve the law of God, you delight in its excellence, you acknowledge its purity, you contemplate it inwardly as the transcript of the Holy Character of God, and yet in your flesh you wilfully sin, you indulge the desires of the flesh, you gratify your carnal lusts, and you absolve yourself with the words, 'It is no more I that do it, but sin that dwelleth in me.'" The Apostle hears this, and rejoins, " I have heard you patiently, notwithstanding the exceeding foolishness of your way of misrepresenting my teaching. I can only say that, in all godly sincerity, I desire to practise what a little further, if you will read all my letter, you will see that I say to you: 'If ye live after the flesh ye shall die, but if ye through the Spirit do mortify the deeds of the body, ye shall live.' I, through the Spirit, not in my own strength, but in the power of God's Spirit, mortify the deeds of the body, and (I say it in no boasting spirit) I live." " Well, but," the man rejoins, " If you thus live in the Spirit, how can you say such things of yourself, as that you are carnal, sold under sin, that what you hate, that you do, that in you there dwelleth no good thing?" "Stay," says the Apostle, interrupting the questioner, "you do not reproduce what I said. I did not say absolutely 'in me dwelleth no good thing,' but I was careful to say in me, that is, *in my flesh*. I should deny the gift of God if I were to say that there was nothing good in my spirit, for God has filled my spirit with the knowledge of His Son my Lord, but this knowledge is not in my flesh. When I am raised up in the likeness of my Lord's Body, there will be what is good in my flesh, but at present it is not so. My flesh is not yet renewed. I know that it will be, but at present it is not. So that I say 'in me, that is, in my flesh' (and the 'I' within me, my person, is not spirit only but flesh), there dwelleth no good thing."

" But, O holy Apostle," the questioner rejoins, "you have seen the Lord with your bodily eyes. The Lord has constantly appeared to you and conversed with you. You have been caught up into Paradise—you have heard the unspeakable words—is your flesh the same as ours who are far behind you in nearness to God?"

"Yes, yes," rejoins the Apostle, "that is precisely what I am saying in these words respecting which you are questioning me. You may have but lately presented your body a living sacrifice to God, and I may have presented mine years ago. You may be but a private, obscure member of the Church, and I may be in some respects its foremost minister, an Apostle of the world, having the care of all the Churches, but I have written what you have read to assure you that there is no difference at present in our flesh—mine, so far as sin and death are concerned, is the same as yours, and yours as mine. Does your flesh require subduing, so does mine; does my flesh require discipline, self-denial, watchfulness, so does yours. Though not experiencing at every moment, or now at any moment, the full bitterness of what I have written, I might at any time experience it partially or wholly, if God were for one day to withdraw His grace. I know He will not take His Holy Spirit from me. I know that He will assuredly keep that which I have committed to Him till the day of the Lord; but if He did see fit, even for a short time, to withdraw His Spirit, then my flesh, that flesh which is still unrenewed, whose Redemption I wait for—that flesh at once resumes its supremacy. It becomes the sole 'I myself' within me, and if I am to be saved I have to begin all over again."

"But, O holy Apostle, do you not exclaim, O wretched man that I am, who shall deliver me from the body of this death? And do you not praise God for deliverance, when you say, I thank God through Jesus Christ our Lord?" "Unquestionably I do, for He has delivered me; but what is the deliverance? He has not slain the flesh, He has not wholly expelled sin from the flesh, He has not renewed the flesh, but He has renewed my spirit, and given that spirit the command over the flesh, and all my allegiance to Christ is in maintaining that command."

"But, O Father in Christ, is sin still so near to you, Apostle as you are, that it is in your flesh? Cannot you drive it far away and put frontiers, and armies, and walls between it and you?"

"No," rejoins the Apostle, "I have written these verses to show you that the warfare with sin and the subjugation of sin is not to be looked upon in this light. It is not a battle with an external foe, but a struggle with an internal one. The enemy is part of yourself, for it is in you, in your flesh. It is your old self, your old man, your lower animal nature, your flesh not yet incorruptible. It reigns in your natural body because that body has not yet become a spiritual body."

"But, O holy spiritual father, is it ever to be so? is our fight with sin within only to cease with our lives?" To which the Apostle may reply, "My son, I cannot say; God has not shown to me His dealings with each and every particular soul. Only this I say, that if I could decline my warfare, my future reward as a good soldier would be proportionably diminished. It must be so if it was the Holy Ghost Who inspired me when I wrote 'Every man shall receive his own reward according to his own labour.'"

"O holy Apostle," the questioner asks, "I will say but one word more. What instruction in righteousness are we to gather from this your description of our state?" "I marvel," the Apostle would rejoin, "at your want of discernment. I marvel at your forgetfulness of what I so constantly preach. I have written to other Christians, and in some form or other I have taught it daily to you what we are to do in the face of all this. I know that I have to keep under *my* body, and bring it into subjection, lest by any means having preached to others I myself should be ἀδόκιμος, unaccepted at last. This is my work, and however spiritual you think yourself, I would urge you to make it yours."

We can now, I trust, having examined the scope and conclusion of the whole passage, consider each verse separately.

14. "For we know that the law is spiritual, but I am carnal," &c. "The law is spiritual," that is, it is addressed to the spirit—to that part of us which can recognize God, and consciously obey His will.

"But I am carnal, sold under sin." We must necessarily understand here the words of verse 18, "in my flesh." "I am as regards my flesh, in my lower nature, sold under sin." These words were written of Ahab, of whom it was said that "there was none like unto Ahab, who sold himself to do evil." How could they possibly be applied, even remotely, by St. Paul to himself? To which we answer, "What was the difference between St. Paul and Ahab, for the spirit of each was capable of receiving the law of God,

CHAP. VII.] WHAT I WOULD I DO NOT. 149

15 For that which I do I †allow not: for ᵖwhat I would, that do I not; but what I hate, that do I.   † Gr. *know*, Ps. i. 6.
ᵖ Gal. v. 17.

---

and the flesh of each was unredeemed, sold under sin? The difference might all be comprised in this one word—the one lived after the flesh and died, the other, through the Spirit, mortified the deeds of the body, and lived."

15. "For that which I do I allow not: for what I would, that do I not," &c. "I allow not," properly, "I know not."

If it is to be explained "I allow not," then, after Augustine, we take up an old and familiar use of the word "know," which we find in the first Psalm, "The Lord knoweth the way of the righteous."

But Chrysostom and most moderns explain it as if, owing to this conflict within him, the man with whom St. Paul identifies himself knows not what he is doing. "What then is this *I know not?* I get dizzy, he means, I feel carried away, I find a violence done to me, I get tripped up without knowing how. Just as we often say such an one came and carried me away with him without my knowing how; when it is not ignorance we mean to allege as an excuse, but to show a sort of deceit, and circumvention, and plot."

"For what I would that do I not (or practise not), but what I hate," &c. This latter clause may be taken in a higher or a lower sense, according as St. Paul speaks of what he is conscious of in himself, or of what through his power of sympathy he knows to be in his more imperfect brethren. If taken in a higher sense, as if St. Paul spoke from his own experience at that time, then it may be referred to concupiscence or evil desire, or immoderate anger, which may rise almost unobserved in the old nature, and be instantly and energetically expelled, and yet may have been so dwelt upon, though but for a short time, as to cause deep distress and a consciousness of failure, if not sin. If taken in a lower sense, it may be an actual fall, not into deadly sin, but into something on the way to such sin. The thought of this is hateful, the memory of it shameful, the reproof of the conscience deeply felt. It may, perhaps, be illustrated by the fault or sin of the Corinthian Christians in their criminal laxity in dealing with the incestuous person (2 Cor. vii. 8-12). The former clause, "What I would that do I not," is the constant confession even of good Christians, who never

16 If then I do that which I would not, I consent unto the law that *it is* good.

17 Now then it is no more I that do it, but sin that dwelleth in me.

---

seem to themselves to accomplish the full purpose of grace, and if they can accomplish something, it but too often seems to them a very little compared to what might have been expected, and that little not carefully, not humbly, not devoutly brought about.

16. "If then I do that which I would not, I consent unto the law," &c. The first "I" here signifies the lower nature or natural man which for the moment, under some sudden gust of passion, takes the lead; the second is the spiritual man, who is displeased at, and ashamed of, and repents of the evil the moment it is done, because he delights in the law of God. So there is no emphasis to be laid upon the "law" here, as the law of Moses, or the Decalogue. It means simply any precept or indication of the will of God which is contrary to the natural man or old Adam which remains in the unrenewed body.

17. "Now then it is no more I that do it, but sin that dwelleth in me." This is one of the most difficult places in the whole range of Scripture, for where are we to draw the line in its application? We require for its perfect elucidation not a logician, not a grammarian, not even a theologian, but rather some discreet and learned minister to whom men and women have constantly "come and opened their griefs," one ripe in administering "ghostly counsel and advice to the quieting of consciences."[1]

Now in the first place it is quite clear that St. Paul in this verse does not contemplate any deliberate sin, for if any man plans any such sin as an act of malicious injury, or fornication, or fraud, then that sin is his own.

Now this is to be held to, and to be put forth very strongly, and very frequently, and very unhesitatingly by all who claim to be preachers of righteousness. It is astonishing to me how commentators keep themselves ignorant of the under-current of Antinomian

---

[1] Several sermons of exceeding value upon particular verses of this passage are to be found in volumes by Dr. Pusey, particularly one in vol. ii. of "Parochial Sermons," Sermon xviii., on verses 22 and 23, entitled, "Victory amid Strife;" but there is not, what we desiderate, a short treatise on the whole passage.

CHAP. VII.]   SIN THAT DWELLETH IN ME.   151

feeling which pervades the popular and seemingly religious life in all classes. The misunderstanding of this verse is reproduced daily in the words, "Sin is not sin in believers," that is, fornication, and fraud, and lying, and evil speaking, are no longer sins if a man has "accepted Christ." Now those who desire to preach and teach the Christ of the New Testament, must have no hesitation in preaching and teaching, that if there is any the slightest deliberation or planning of any sin, great or small, then instead of "The evil that I would not, that I do," the Apostle's words are changed into, "The evil that I would, that I do."

But we must now turn to the other side—the side of consolation and good hope. What is that which we earnestly desire not to do, and yet it is done within us, and we look upon it as if it was all our own, and are far more grieved and sorry and ashamed than the man who has planned his sin, and determined in his mind to do it and so made it wholly and entirely his own ? There seems to be no room for doubt about the matter—it is that which takes place in the man which (being contrary to the will or self which consents to the law, if it is not he that does it, but sin that dwelleth in him), must be unpremeditated before it takes place, and must be instantly and energetically disallowed the moment it has taken place. If done against another person, or in the sight of another, or so that another is cognizant, instant confession, or reparation, or acknowledgment, must be made. The longer the time that this is deferred the more likely it is that the wrong thing should be laid at the door of the man himself, as if he consented to it, and so the more place is given for scandal. With respect to some secret thought of envy suddenly rising up, or causeless anger, or malicious feeling, or concupiscence, or pleasing memory of past sin, there must be a momentary act of penitent acknowledgment.

I am glad and thankful that I can reproduce words not my own, but those of one to whom men came from far and near to unburthen their souls. No words of man can be more judicious, none more sympathizing. "This infection within us, although of 'the nature of sin,' still unless our will consents to its suggestions is not sin. So long as by God's grace we master it, it is not sin, but the occasion of the victories of His grace. People distress themselves by not owning this ; they deceive themselves if they make it the occasion of carelessness. The one says, "My nature is sinful, and therefore I am the object of God's displeasure, and all is ill with me.' The other says: 'My nature is sinful, and therefore I cannot help it, and am not the object of God's displeasure, although I do what is wrong.' The one mistakes sinfulness of nature for actual sin, and accuses himself of that actual sin, on account of that sinfulness of nature. The other excuses actual sin as though it were unavoidable, because his nature is sinful. Each is untrue. A man is not the object of God's displeasure, on account of the remains of his inborn corruption, if he in earnest strives with it. If he strive not in earnest with it, he is the object of God's displeasure, not on account of the sinfulness of his nature, but on account of his own negligence as to that sinfulness of nature, or as to his sinful concurrence with it. Nothing is sin in us which has not some consent of the will. What is done without or against our will rather takes place *in* us than is done *by* us. Even although it be the result of past actual sin it is not sin to us now unless our will in some way go along with it . . . . It is miserable to have allowed (in time past) sinful tempers which might have been nipped in the bud to grow to be full blown. Thou canst not nip them in that easy way now. Still they are *suffering*, not *sin*. Nay, so long as they are suffering, they are not sin: because what thou willest not, so that thou steadfastly resistest, is not sin.

"Thou hast then these two opposite sides, on which by God's grace to guard thyself. Think not lightly of the power of sin, for it threatens thy life. Despond not on account of this power of sin; for God will keep it chained unless thou thyself free it and invite it unto thee. It does not in itself make thee evil, although it is evil in thee. It is *in* thee, but, if thou wilt, it may be subdued unto thee. It is present to thee. It is not *thine*, unless thou make it thine. It does not separate between thee and thy God. 'The law of sin in the members,' although evil, is not *thy* evil, unless thou will it, and encourage it, and make it the law of thy mind. The law of God, if thou delight in it in the inner man, is God's good in thee, and thine, if thou will it. And mightier will be God's good in thee, His power, His grace, His love, His Holy Spirit which He has placed within thee, than the evil of thy nature within thee. No risings then of any passion, yea, though it should rise again and again against thee, and by rising weary thee and almost wear thee out; no thought by night, when thou hast not power over thy soul, and thy will is not conscious; no thoughts by day which come to thee again and again, and besiege thee and torment thee, and would

CHAP. VII.] HOW TO PERFORM I FIND NOT. 153

18 For I know that ^q in me (that is, in my flesh,) dwelleth no good thing: for to will is present with me; but *how* to perform that which is good I find not.

^q Gen. vi. 5.
& viii. 21.

---

18. "I find not." So D., E., F., G., K., L., P., most Cursives, Vulg., Syriac; but ℵ, A., B., C., 47, 67**, 80, Copt., Arm., omit " I find " ("how to perform that which is good not ").

---

claim thee for their own; no distractions in prayer, even if they carry thee away, and thou lose thyself and awake as it were out of a dream, and thy prayer be gone—none of these things are thine. Nothing without thy will is thine or will be imputed unto thee. It is not the mere presence with thee of what thou hatest: it is not the recurrence again and again of what thou loathest, which will hurt thee; not even if it seem to come from thy inmost self, unless thy will consent to it." (Pusey, "Parochial Sermons," ii. 18.)

The reader will thank me for this extract. I know no words which enter so deeply and so satisfactorily into the meaning and spirit of a passage which deals more closely with the conditions under which sin dwells within us than any other in Scripture.

18. "For I know that in me (that is, in my flesh,) dwelleth no good thing, for to will," &c. Notice how the Apostle considers the flesh, that is, not only the mere visible tangible flesh of bones and muscles, but the fleshly soul or psyche which is its life and activity —a part of himself. We are compound beings of flesh with its carnal soul, and of spirit in which the Spirit of God, or a spirit utterly antagonistic to God, dwells. The Ego—the I, the will, may be in one or the other. If the will, the I is in the spirit, informed and inhabited by the Spirit of God, then the man looks down upon the lower self—the "me, that is, my flesh,"—as depraved and condemned, and not a fit organ for the spirit. In the spirit is the good Spirit of God, but not as yet in the flesh, for "He that raised Christ from the dead hath not yet quickened our mortal bodies by His Spirit which dwelleth in us."

Consequently the will to do all manner of good is present, but how to perform it the man knows not: for the body is the instrument of the spirit, but the body is corrupt and unrenewed, and so weak, and cannot rise to the heights of the spirit, or fly with the swiftness of the spirit, or watch with the wakefulness of the spirit. The illustration of all this is the slumber of the Apostles in Gethsemane: "The spirit truly is willing, but the flesh is weak."

19 For the good that I would I do not: but the evil which I would not, that I do.

20 Now if I do that I would not, it is no more I that do it, but sin that dwelleth in me.

21 I find then a law, that, when I would do good, evil is present with me.

"No good thing." No supernatural strength, no self-denial. If the flesh is subdued, it is by the power of the mind or spirit, not of its own inherent power. The body, by its very nature, is all on the side of appetite.

"But how to perform that which is good I find not," *i.e.*, I find it not in my flesh. I cannot look to my flesh for help or strength, I must look to the Spirit of God.

19, 20. "For the good that I would I do not: but the evil.... sin that dwelleth in me." This 19th verse is not a mere repetition of verse 15, or of the latter part of it: for good and evil are here expressly mentioned; it is not merely "What I would that I do not," but "The good that I would I do not;" and not merely "What I hate," but "The evil which I would not." The latter part of verse 20 is an exact repetition of part of verse 17. Why is this? I can see but one reason. The Apostle desires to emphasize as strongly as possible his participation in that common nature of a fleshly and spiritual self, which is the lot of the weakest brother with whose warfare he identifies himself.

21. "I find then a law, that, when I would do good, evil is present with me." This has, by some, been explained as meaning, "I find then as respects the law—*i.e.*, the Mosaic—that when I would or desire to do good, the law is no assistance, but evil is present with me."

But the rendering of the Authorized, which is usually followed, seems the best, taking law to mean a force, or an observed sequence, which must be under some regulating power, as the law of gravitation. "I find, then, the law, that when I desire to do good, evil is present with me. It is so present with me as to hinder me doing good, or marring the good which I would fain do."

22. "For I delight in the law of God after the inward man." The inner man which delights in the law can only be, one would think, the mind or spirit informed and renewed by the Spirit of

CHAP. VII.] ANOTHER LAW IN MY MEMBERS. 155

22 For I ʳdelight in the law of God after ˢthe inward man:

23 But ᵗI see another law in ᵘmy members, warring against the law of my mind, and bringing me into captivity to the law of sin which is in my members.

ʳ Ps. i. 2.
ˢ 2 Cor. iv. 16. Ephes. iii. 16. Col. iii. 9, 10.
ᵗ Gal. v. 17.
ᵘ ch. vi. 13, 19.

23. "To the law of sin." So A., C., L., most Cursives, Syriac, Arm.; but א, B., D., E., F., G., K., P., fifteen Cursives, d, e, f, g, Vulg., Goth. read, "by the law of sin" [ἐν τῷ νόμῳ].

God. Only such a man within us can *delight* in the law of God. We cannot suppose that by " delight in the law of God " the Apostle means only a recognition of the law as good, ending in mere barren fruitless acknowledgment or admiration. He must mean such a delight as would lead us to obey it, and fulfil it in ourselves.

23. " But I see another law in my members, warring against the law," &c. I see another, *i.e.*, a different law. Here law means the same as in verse 21, and may be translated " principle of action."

" In my members," that is in my unrenewed body. The body is composed of members, each having its separate concupiscence, but all obeying the law or principle of sin.

" Warring against the law of my mind," *i.e.*, the principle of action which governs my mind or inner man, which is, of course, the law of God which the mind has adopted for its own.

" And bringing me into captivity to the law of sin which is in my members." A very important question arises here. Does this law of sin in the members, which wars against the law of the mind, actually bring the I—the Ego—the persons enlightened as to the law of God and delighting in that law, into captivity to the law of sin, or has it a tendency to do so ? St. Paul personally, in his own case, no doubt understands that it has a tendency; but then he thwarts this tendency, and prevents it leading to a victory, and such consequent captivity as that he is again under the dominion of sin. But then the blessed and holy Apostle, all through this wondrous argument, identifies himself with the weakest and most unstable of all his brethren. He constantly speaks, not as the strong, but as the weak : " I am carnal," "That which I do I know not," "What I hate that I do," " Evil is present with me ; " and so here, if he were asked, "Are you brought into captivity yourself?" he would answer, "No, not as you my questioner mean; but if I were to

24 O wretched man that I am! who shall deliver me from
| Or, *this body of death.* ‖ the body of this death?

---

relax my hold on Christ, and my looking to Christ, and my watchfulness and prayer, at any moment I might be led captive. But I desire to identify myself with my brethren who struggle and make little way, and are often overcome, and so, as I have written elsewhere, 'to the weak become I as weak, that I may gain the weak. I am made all things to all men, that I may by all means save some'"[1] (1 Corinth. ix. 22).

24. "O wretched man that I am! who shall deliver me from the body of this death?" The best way of understanding the expression "body of this death," because most accordant with the reasoning of this chapter and the next, is to take the body here as the actual body or flesh, in which resides sin and consequently death. This is one of those "groans" to which the Apostle alludes when he writes: "We which have the first fruits of the Spirit, we ourselves groan within ourselves, waiting for the adoption, to wit the redemption of our body" (viii. 23); and, again, "In this (building) we groan, earnestly desiring to be clothed upon with our house which is from heaven" (2 Corinth. v. 2).

It can hardly allude to any deliverance before the Resurrection, such as a deliverance from sin so perfect that its motions are no longer felt, and are incapable of being revived. There is no word of such a deliverance till the adoption, the renewal, the Redemption of the body (viii. 23).

Does, then, the Apostle long for death? No, he longs for the Second Coming and the Resurrection of the body. "From heaven we look for the Saviour, the Lord Jesus Christ, who shall change our vile body that it may be fashioned like unto his glorious body" (Phil. iii. 20, 21).

25. "I thank God, through Jesus Christ our Lord." Now for what specific blessing does the Apostle here thank God? Evidently for deliverance from "the body of this death." What was the body of this death which made the Apostle cry out for very

---

[1] Some Romanist commentators, as Cornelius à Lapide and Bernardino à Piconio, understand this "other" law as concupiscence, and that St. Paul was only led into captivity in so far as he yet felt in his mortal and unrenewed body the motions of concupiscence; but surely of such motions he would say, "It is no more I that do it, but sin that dwelleth in me."

CHAP. VII.] WITH THE MIND, WITH THE FLESH. 157

25 ˣ I thank God through Jesus Christ our Lord. So then with the mind I myself serve the law of God; but with the flesh the law of sin.

ˣ 1 Cor. xv. 57.

---

25. "I thank God." So ℵ, A., K., L., P., most Cursives, Syr., Goth.; but B. and Sah. read, "thanks to God" [χάρις τῷ Θεῷ], similarly D., E., 38, d, e, Vulg.

wretchedness? It was the long continued violence of the conflict within him between the flesh and the Spirit. What, then, was the deliverance—the victory? It was the subjugation of the flesh to the Spirit, so that the Apostle could say, " I keep under my body, and bring it into subjection." Was this a victory once for all, so that from that time he felt no more consciousness of sin within him? No, it was not; for, after giving thanks for the deliverance, he yet writes—

" So then with the mind I myself serve the law of God; but with the flesh, the law of sin." Looked at in the light of all that goes before, and of all that comes after, in the eighth chapter, this place has a very simple meaning. It means that the mind or spirit is renewed, and that the body, even of the Apostle, continues unrenewed. The mind or spirit of the Apostle is such that it is altogether conformed to the will of God; but the body of the Apostle, as of all other Christians whatsoever, is such that he says with truth of himself a little further on, " Ourselves, which have the first fruits of the Spirit, even we ourselves groan within ourselves, waiting for the adoption, to wit, the redemption of our body."

Again, in another place he says, " We that are in this tabernacle do groan, being burdened: not for that we would be unclothed, but clothed upon, that mortality might be swallowed up of life " (2 Cor. v. 4). Now what was the reason why the Apostle exhibited this desire, amounting to such strength and painful longing that it could with any propriety be called " groaning "? Was it merely his desire to be shining in light proceeding from him as from his Lord on His Transfiguration? Was it merely his desire to be distinguished above his fellows by a brighter crown? No, it was because he desired to be clothed with a spiritual, and, therefore, sinless body; a body respecting which he need no longer say, " I keep under my body." He desired to put off a body which was a clog, a dead weight, an hindrance to, and to put on a body which should be an assistance, an helpmeet for, his renewed and glorified spirit.

CHAP. VIII.

THERE is therefore now no condemnation to them which are in Christ Jesus, who ᵃ walk not after the flesh, but after the Spirit.

2 For ᵇ the law of ᶜ the Spirit of life in Christ

ᵃ ver. 4. Gal. v. 16, 25.
ᵇ John viii. 36. ch. vi. 18, 22. Gal. ii. xix. & v. 1.
ᶜ 1 Cor. xv. 45. 2 Cor. iii. 6.

1. "Who walk not after the flesh, but after the Spirit." Omitted by א, B., C., D., F., G., 47, 67**, 177, d, g, Sah., Cop., Æth.; but E., K., L., P., most Cursives, e, retain the whole; and A., D.**, 137, d**, f, m, Vulg., Goth., Syriac, omit "but after the Spirit."

1. "There is therefore now no condemnation to them which are in Christ Jesus," &c. "No condemnation," *i.e.*, no wrath of God abiding on them here, and no punishment in the future state, though they may be conscious of "another law in their members warring against the law of their minds."

"To them which are in Christ Jesus," *i.e.*, to those who are members of His Body—not only to those once grafted into It, but to those who abide in It, according to the Lord's own words, "Abide in me, and I in you. As the branch cannot bear fruit of itself except it abide in the vine, no more can ye, except ye abide in me" (John xv. 4).

The Apostle dates the engrafting—the commencement of the corporate union—from Baptism; but he makes the continuance to depend upon our putting off the old man, and putting on the new.

"Who walk not after the flesh, but after the Spirit." This sentence has but little manuscript authority; but it must be understood, and it is so important, that it is well to insert it parenthetically here, though it is probably taken or anticipated from verse 4. Chrysostom comments upon it as though it were a part of the text.

2. "For the law of the Spirit of life in Christ Jesus hath made me," &c. We must consider very closely what this "law of the Spirit of life" is, or we may come miserably short of grasping its significance. It is evidently something which is called a law in

CHAP. VIII.] FREE FROM THE LAW OF SIN. 159

Jesus hath made me free from [d] the law of sin and death.

[d] ch. vii. 24, 25.

2. "Hath made me." So A., C., D., E., K., L., P., all Cursives, d, e, Vulg., Goth., Sah., Arm.; but א, B., F., a, f, g, Syriac, read, "thee" ("made thee free").

the sense of an order of things—a sequence, a principle of action, just as the Apostle had been speaking of the "law of the mind," and "the law of sin in the flesh." Is it, then, the same as the "law of the mind" of vii. 23 ? No, certainly not; though it assists it and may be said to comprehend it. Is it the gift of the Spirit? No, clearly not. It is given by the Spirit, applied by the Spirit, enforced by the Spirit; but it is more than the gift of the Spirit as that phrase is commonly understood. What, then, is it? The Apostle proceeds to tell us. It is the gift of a Person, a Second Adam, the very Son of God Incarnate, "God sending his own Son in the likeness of sinful flesh (or of the flesh of sin—the flesh in which dwells the law of sin), and for sin (or as a sin offering), condemned sin in the flesh, that the righteousness of the law might be fulfilled in us," &c.

The law of the Spirit of Life, then, may be understood as the dispensation of the Spirit of Life, in which the Son of God is revealed to the soul as incarnate, as crucified, as risen from the dead, as ascended, as coming again in the Spirit, as uniting men to Himself as His Body, as making them partakers of His Life, so that in and from Him they have a new life, whereby to live to God and to fulfil His holy Will. All this, and much more, is comprehended in the dispensation of the Spirit, and in it the Spirit applies the atoning virtues of the Death of Christ and the Justifying and Sanctifying power of the Risen Life of Christ to the individual Christian, so that if he yields himself to the influence of the Spirit of God he is grafted into Christ, abides in Christ, partakes of His Body and Blood, subdues the flesh to the Spirit, and lives, grows, and walks in Christ.

This "law of the Spirit of Life," the Apostle says, has made him free from the law of sin and death. That is, it has made him free from the power of sin. He is not free from the presence of sin, so that he need have no care to be watchful, for, as we have over and over again said, his body is not yet made a spiritual body. It will be, but it has not yet been so transformed; but he is free from the law—the command—the powerful influence of sin and death.

160 CONDEMNED SIN IN THE FLESH. [ROMANS

^e Acts xiii. 39.
ch. iii. 20.
Heb. vii. 18,
19. & x. 1, 2,
10, 14.
^f Gal. iii. 13.
2 Cor. v. 21.
∥ Or, *by a sacrifice for sin.*

3 For ^e what the law could not do, in that it was weak through the flesh, ^f God sending his own Son in the likeness of sinful flesh, and ∥ for sin, condemned sin in the flesh:

---

3. "For what the law could not do, in that it was weak through the flesh," &c. As the Apostle says in the Epistle to the Galatians, the law could not give life, because it was a mere command, and a command does not carry with it, in the case of such weak, sinful creatures as we are, the will and power to obey the command. This must be by a Person coming amongst us, and then dwelling in us. And so the Apostle proceeds—

"God sending his own Son"—that Son Who partakes of the Life—Moral, Spiritual, Divine, Eternal—of the Godhead.

"In the likeness of sinful flesh." In the likeness of the flesh of sin—not in sinful flesh, but in its likeness. God did not send His own Son in the mere likeness of flesh, but in the reality of our flesh, howbeit sinless.

"And for sin." Probably as a sin offering, the term περὶ ἁμαρτίας being constantly used in the Septuagint to denote the sin offering: so Levit. xvi. 5. "And he shall take of the congregation of the children of Israel two kids of the goats for a sin offering" (δύο χιμάρους ἐξ αἰγῶν περὶ ἁμαρτίας); so also Ps. xl. 6, "burnt offerings and sacrifices for sin," περὶ ἁμαρτίας.

"Condemned sin in the flesh." Just as the animal sacrificed as the sin offering was treated as if the sin of the offerer was punished and slain in its immolation, so Christ, after He had taken upon Him our nature, suffered as if He was the sin offering of humanity, and bare our sins in His own body on the tree.

"Condemned sin in the flesh." No condemnation of sin can be greater than this, that it required the Death of the Holy One of God to expiate it. But by His expiating it by the suffering of death, it is not only condemned in Him, but in us, who partake of His Death and Resurrection—who died and rose again in and with Him, so that we should no longer serve this condemed thing, but be emancipated from its dominion. Sin is personified, and is supposed to have a sort of right over us—an usurped right, but an acknowledged one. But our Lord, in offering Himself a sin-

CHAP. VIII.] WHO WALK AFTER THE SPIRIT. 161

4 That the righteousness of the law might be fulfilled in us, ^g who walk not after the flesh, but after the   ^{g ver. 1.}
Spirit.

5 For ^h they that are after the flesh do mind   ^{h John iii. 6.
1 Cor. ii. 14.}

---

4. "The righteousness." Perhaps, rather, the requirement, δικαίωμα being not the usual word for righteousness. The rendering of the Revisers, "ordinance," is misleading, as ordinance is now always used in the sense of outward ordinance.

offering condemned it, and delivered us. This is one of the many ways in which the Apostle sets before us Atonement, and our reception of that Atonement. The place exactly parallel to, and illustrative of this is 2 Cor. v. 21: " God hath made him, who knew no sin, to be sin for us; that we might be made the righteousness of God in him."

4. "That the righteousness of the law might be fulfilled in us, who walk," &c. These words, be it remembered, are the words of one who has hitherto been contending for the inability of the law to justify—that Christians, if they are to be justified, are not to be "under the law, but under grace,"—and yet here he tells us that the very end of the Redemption (that Redemption which involves the Incarnation, Death, and Resurrection of the Eternal Son) is that we might fulfil the requirement of that law which he had seemingly so disparaged; so that, paradoxical though it may sound, it is true that we are delivered from the law in order that we may fulfil it. We are delivered from the law as the means of justification, in order that by God's grace we may attain to the heights of holiness to which its spirituality would raise us.

5. "For they that are after the flesh do mind the things of the flesh," &c. This follows and depends upon the last words, that "the righteousness of the law may be fulfilled in us, who walk not after the flesh, but after the Spirit." It was the intention of God in redeeming us by sending His own Son, that we should have His holy will, *i.e.*, the just requirement of the law, fulfilled in us; but the Apostle faces the fact that it is not so with all who are baptized into Christ. Amongst these there are two classes, those who are after the flesh, and those who are after the Spirit.

The flesh is that part of our nature which is yet unrenewed. By its very nature, as flesh, it is led by its appetites, and being yet under the law of sin, and not being itself as yet emancipated from

M

the things of the flesh; but they that are after the Spirit ¹ the things of the Spirit.

¹ Gal. v. 22, 25.

the evil effects of the fall, it is continually rising up against the rightful dominion of the human spirit renewed by the Spirit of God. Those who allow themselves, notwithstanding their baptism and the pledges of deliverance and help then received, to be led by it, are "after the flesh," and "mind the things of the flesh." They are either engrossed with the gratification of worldly lusts, as gluttony and good living, and the decking out of their persons, or if they do not live to gratify these low, sensual appetites, their one object in living is to hoard up money, or to squander it in worldly amusements. They are lovers of pleasure more than lovers of God; or their one thought is how they are to get on in society, or to distinguish themselves. They seek to be popular, to please men, or to take the lead. They have men's persons in admiration, because of advantage to themselves. We have the lusts of the flesh enumerated by this Apostle in another place in an epistle not written to heathen but to Christians, and it runs thus: "Adultery, fornication, uncleanness, lasciviousness, idolatry, witchcraft, hatred, variance, emulations, wrath, strife, seditions, heresies, envyings, murders, drunkenness, revellings, and such like" (Gal. v. 19). By these last words, "and such like," the Apostle affirms that this list is not complete. There are many *similar* evil dispositions, vices, forms of worldliness and vanity, which destroy all spiritual life. They that are after the flesh mind these; they are not suddenly overtaken, and think of their fall, or compliance, with shame and sorrow; but they deliberately *mind* one or other of these evil things. They allow their minds to run unchecked upon them; they look forward and plan the means of gratification.

"But they that are after the Spirit, the things of the Spirit." They constantly turn their minds to, and dwell upon the Coming of the Son of God amongst us, and its attendant circumstances, such as His rejection by the world, His Crucifixion, His Resurrection, His sending the Spirit, His headship of His Church. They delight to meditate in secret upon the mysteries of the faith. They have constantly in mind the increase of the Spirit's influence. They make a serious business of prayer, thanksgiving, and the reading of God's Word. They make time for such things, no matter how

CHAP. VIII.] NOT SUBJECT TO THE LAW OF GOD. 163

6 For ᵏ † to be carnally minded *is* death; but †to
be spiritually minded *is* life and peace.

7 Because † ¹ the carnal mind *is* enmity against
God: for it is not subject to the law of God,
ᵐ neither indeed can be.

ᵏ ch. vi. 21.
ver. 13. Gal.
vi. 8.
† Gr. *the
minding of the
flesh.* So
ver. 7.
† Gr. *the
minding of the
Spirit.*
† Gr. *the
minding of the
flesh.*
¹ Jam. iv. 4.
ᵐ 1 Cor. ii.
14.

6. "To be carnally minded," *prudentia carnis;* "to be spiritually minded," *prudentia spiritus,* Vulg. Nothing can be proposed better than the Authorized or the marginal translation.

---

full of business is their secular life, and into that secular life they desire to bring their religion, so that religion may influence every part of it. Such are some, and only some, of the "mindings" of the Spirit, which occupy the thoughts and govern the outward lives of those who are "after the Spirit."

6. "For to be carnally minded is death; but to be spiritually minded is life," &c. Death here can only mean the separation of the soul or spirit from God, its true Life. The effect of this separation from God is temporal death, and if continued is eternal death, but the first death is that of the soul, by separation from its true Life.

And the converse of this is, that the minding of the things of the Spirit is, by its very nature, life and peace—life, because union with the only source of all life, and peace, because being united or reunited to Him, there is nothing between us and God. There is nothing to hinder His love to us and our reciprocating His love; and in this peace is included peace with one another, because, through the Spirit working in us, we desire the good of all, even of our enemies.

7. "Because the carnal mind is enmity against God." Thus the Apostle in another place, "You, that were sometime alienated and enemies in your mind by wicked works" (Coloss. i. 21). We have a secret dislike to those whom we knowingly and wilfully wrong, and by the commission of sin we wrong God, and turn away from Him, and hide ourselves from Him.

"For it is not subject to the law of God." It is the "other" law in our members warring against the law of our mind.

"Neither indeed can be," *i.e.,* as long as the body is unrenewed. In the body, or animal soul (psyche) of the body, the fall yet

8 So then they that are in the flesh cannot please God.

9 But ye are not in the flesh, but in the Spirit, if so be that ⁿ the Spirit of God dwell in you. Now if any man have not ᵒ the Spirit of Christ, he is none of his.

ⁿ 1 Cor. iii. 16. & vi. 10.
ᵒ John iii. 34. Gal. iv. 6. Phil. i. 19. 1 Pet. i. 11.

---

remains in its evil force, and it will not be otherwise till the vile body is changed into the likeness of Christ's Glorious Body.

8. "So then they that are in the flesh cannot please God." They that are in the flesh, *i.e.*, of course, those who mind supremely the things of the flesh, who live after the flesh, and walk after it. These, in their present state, cannot please God. They may make some show of religion—they may, as Herod, hear the preachers of righteousness, and "observe" them, and "do many things," but if they willingly, and of set purpose serve sin—any sort of sin, whatever it be—they cannot please God—all their service is unacceptable to God.

9. "But ye are not in the flesh, but in the Spirit, if so be that the Spirit," &c. "Ye are not in the flesh," your true self, your Ego is not in the flesh, but in the Spirit, if so be that the Spirit of God "dwell in you." If so Almighty a Person as the Holy Ghost dwells in you, you yield yourselves to Him to be inspired and led by Him, or through your grieving Him, and not obeying His leading, you provoke Him to depart.

"Now if any man have not the Spirit of Christ, he is none of his." Notice how the Spirit of God in the first clause of the verse becomes the Spirit of Christ in the latter. Christ having sojourned upon earth, His character is well known. And the Spirit of Christ, Who proceeds from Him, must be like Christ. He must be not only a pure and holy, but a loving, gentle, forgiving Spirit, and must make, or tend to make, those whom He inhabits not only pure and holy, but loving, gentle, forgiving. Thus among the fruits of the Spirit in Gal. v., we have "peace, long-suffering, gentleness, and goodness."

The dogmatic, or theological teaching of this verse is to be noticed. The Spirit of God is the Spirit of Christ, and this can only be because the Spirit proceeds from the Father and from the Son; the Son undoubtedly acted as if the Spirit proceeded from Himself when He breathed on the Apostles, and here He is said to be the Spirit of both God and Christ.

CHAP. VIII.   IF CHRIST BE IN YOU.   **165**

10 And if Christ *be* in you, the body *is* dead because of sin; but the Spirit *is* life because of righteousness.

11 But if the Spirit of ᵖ him that raised up Jesus from the dead dwell in you, ᑫ he that raised up Christ from the dead shall also quicken your mortal bodies ‖ by his Spirit that dwelleth in you.

p Acts ii. 24.
q ch. vi. 4, 5.
1 Cor. vi. 14.
2 Cor. iv. 14.
Ephes. ii. 5.
‖ Or, *because of his Spirit.*

---

11. "He that raised up Christ" (or, the Christ). So אᶜ, B., Dᶜ, E., F., G., K., L., P., most Cursives; but א*, A., D*, F. marg., 31, 47, 73, d, e, Vulg., read, "Christ Jesus."

11. "By his Spirit." So א, A., C., fifteen or sixteen Cursives, Cop., Arm., Æth.; but B., D., E., F., G., K., L., P., seventy Cursives, d, e, f, g, Vulg., Syr., Sah., read, "because of his Spirit."

---

10. "And if Christ be in you, the body is dead because of sin; but the Spirit," &c. "If Christ be in you." Christ is in the Christian by His Spirit.

"The body is dead." Not physically, but as condemned to death, and perhaps as being reckoned dead, for the Christian continually asks with the Apostle, "How shall we who are dead to sin, live any longer therein?"

"Because of sin," *i.e.*, it is not yet renewed, but serves the law of sin (vii. 25).

"But the Spirit is life, because of righteousness." That is, the human spirit being rendered righteous by the indwelling of God's Spirit, is alive before God.

11. "But if the Spirit of him that raised up Jesus from the dead dwell in you," &c. The connection of thought between this and the last verse is this—Your body is dead, because of sin; it is sinful, weak, inglorious, condemned to death, but it shall not always be so. He that raised Christ from the dead raised Him in a spiritual and glorified Body, and this by the action of that Spirit by Which He had anointed Him, and Which dwelt in Him without measure. This Spirit He has already given to you, to regenerate and sanctify your spirits, and by this Spirit He shall raise you up to an incorruptible and glorious immortality of body. There is a difference of reading in the last clause of the verse, which somewhat affects the sense. If we read with א, A., C., "through his Spirit," then the Spirit is the Agent by which the Resurrection is brought about. Just as the Spirit is the Agent bringing about our Regeneration and the Resurrection of our souls or spirits from the death of sin

12 ʳTherefore, brethren, we are debtors, not to the flesh, to live after the flesh.

13 For ˢif ye live after the flesh, ye shall die:

ʳ ch. vi. 7, 14.
ˢ ver. 6. Gal. vi. 8.

---

to the life of righteousness, so the Resurrection of our bodies will take place by His special working. If, on the contrary, we read with B., D., and later uncials, "because of his Spirit," then the fact of our having received and retained the Spirit, will be the reason for our rising again. The former is theologically far preferable, and the latter does not by any means exclude it, for the Spirit dwelling in us to the end not only entitles us to a Blessed Resurrection of our bodies, but will be the means by which it will be brought about.

A reason given by Chrysostom for the Apostle using the word "quicken" instead of raising again is worth observing. "What, then, is it which is said? All shall rise again, yet not all to life, but some to punishment and some to life [John v. 29, Danl. xii. 2]. This is why he did not say 'shall raise up,' but shall quicken. And this is a greater thing than Resurrection, and is given to the just only. And the cause of this honour he adds in the words, 'By his Spirit that dwelleth in you.' And so if while here thou drive away the grace of the Spirit, and do not depart with it still safe, thou wilt assuredly perish, though thou dost rise again. For as He will not endure then, if He see His Spirit shining in thee, to give thee up to punishment, so neither will He allow them if He see it quenched to bring thee into the Bridechamber."

12. "Therefore, brethren, we are debtors, not to the flesh, to live after the flesh." We are debtors, we are under obligations, but to whom? To God and to Christ, and to the Spirit, and to ourselves. To God, Who has given His Son to redeem us from all iniquity, and from eternal ruin. To Christ, Who has assumed our nature, borne our sins, and made us members of His Body. To the Holy Spirit, Who if not driven out by our sins, yet dwells in us. To ourselves, that we should not throw away our hopes of a blessed Eternity. To these we owe it, that we should not live after the flesh, and so undo the work of God, and the suffering of Christ on our behalf.

13. "For if ye live after the flesh, ye shall die," &c. "The life of the flesh does not consist only in intemperance, fornication, and

but if ye through the Spirit do ᵗmortify the deeds of the body, ye shall live. ᵗ Ephes. iv. 22. Col. iii. 5.

---

the other vices of the body, but likewise in a fond adhesion to corrupt reason, and to our own will, in pride, ambition, and envy." (Quesnel.) The cultivation of the most refined tastes, if not subordinated to the will of God, and the good of Christ's Church, but pursued solely with a view to our own selfish gratification, may be, and often is, a living after the flesh. "Ye shall die." This cannot mean less than "ye shall have no part in the kingdom of Christ and God." How far it involves actual positive punishment for ever and ever, must be left to God—to His justice, His mercy, His wisdom, and the necessities of the moral government of the universe.

"But if ye through the Spirit do mortify the deeds of the body," &c. This means that *we* are, in dependence upon the power and help of the Spirit, "to mortify the deeds of the body." We are not to leave all to the Spirit, and take no trouble ourselves; but we are to use all means set forth in Scripture, such as self-denial, self-discipline, fasting, watchfulness, prayer, confession, devotional reading of Scripture, so that the Word of God may dwell in us richly, avoiding all scenes, and companies, and places which have been in former times occasions of temptations. It is through such things that the Spirit works. The Lord, Who sends the Spirit, says to Apostles—and, if so, much more to us—"Watch and pray, lest ye enter into temptation." He says, too, with fearful emphasis, "If thy right eye offend thee, pluck it out. If thy foot . . . thy hand offend thee, cut them off." And His servant says, "Mortify your members which are upon the earth:" "they that are Christ's have crucified the flesh, with its affections and lusts." These endeavours are to be done relying on the Spirit—praying for the Spirit—laying ourselves open for the reception of all His Holy influences. This doing, we shall mortify the deeds of the body, and we shall live.

If it be rejoined that all this is "work," and that we are saved by simple faith in Christ—simple reliance upon Him, and so on— we rejoin, what means the Apostle when he says, "Work out your own salvation with fear and trembling, for it is God that worketh in you both to will and to do of his good pleasure"? What God works in us by His Spirit is not a reason for mere idle reliance, but for hard and careful work, even with "fear and trembling."

14 For ªas many as are led by the Spirit of God, they are the sons of God.

ª Gal. v. 18.

---

14. "For as many as are led by the Spirit of God, they are the sons of God." This is an inference from the preceding verse, for the Apostle begins it with "for," "for as many as are led," &c. The connection seems to be, "The son of God must live in God's sight, and consequently they who through the Spirit mortify the deeds of the body are led by the Spirit, and live in Him, and are the true sons of God. The Spirit, whatever else He works within them, will certainly lead them to mortify the deeds of the body."

This is a place of the utmost practical importance. The Apostle and the Church after him has ever taught that all the baptized are, in a sense, children of God. "Ye are all the children of God by faith in Christ Jesus, for as many of you as have been baptized into Christ have put on Christ" (Gal. iii. 26, 27). But we have to continue in Him into Whom we have once been engrafted, and this continuance is the condition of our present sonship.

There are, as I have elsewhere taught, four senses in which the children of men are made children of God; each one leading up to that which follows it.

1. We are all children of God, because He made us reasonable beings, capable of knowing and loving Him. Thus Deut. xxxii. 6, Malachi ii. 10.

2. We are all children of God by adoption, sealed to us in Holy Baptism (Gal. iii. 26, 27).

3. But we remain children or sons of God only if we put ourselves consciously under the guidance of His Spirit, and follow His leading. We may take two remarkable illustrations from the Sermon on the Mount. The Spirit of God is emphatically a Spirit of peace and love, and the Lord says, respecting the peace-makers, that they shall be called the children of God, and He also says that we are to love our enemies, that we may be the children of God (Matth. v. 44, 45); and the Apostle writes in the same spirit to the Philippians, "Do all things without murmurings and disputings, that ye may be blameless and harmless, the sons of God," &c. (Phil. ii. 14, 15).

4. And, lastly, those who have made their calling and election sure, are established as the sons of God for ever. Thus our Lord

CHAP. VIII.] THE SPIRIT OF ADOPTION. 169

15 For ˣ ye have not received the spirit of bondage again ʸ to fear; but ye have received the ᶻ Spirit of adoption, whereby we cry, ᵃ Abba, Father.

ˣ 1 Cor. ii. 12.
Hebr. ii. 15.
ʸ 2 Tim. i. 7.
1 John iv. 18.
ᶻ Isai. lvi. 5.
Gal. iv. 5, 6.
ᵃ Mark xiv. 36.

15. "Whereby we cry;" or, perhaps, "wherein we cry."

says they which shall be accounted worthy to obtain that world and the Resurrection from the dead . . . . are equal to the angels, and are the children of God, being the children of the Resurrection (Luke xx. 36, Rev. xxi. 7).

15. "For ye have not received the spirit of bondage again to fear." This seems to mean "Ye, by receiving Christ, have not received a second mere law to which ye will be in bondage as slaves are, and so be again led by a spirit of bondage to the letter, as the Jews were: but, by being brought into Christ, the beloved Son, ye have received the adoption of sons, and so God has given to you a spirit answering to your new privileges. Along with adoption in Christ ye have received the spirit of adoption—the filial spirit—which makes you regard God as a Father, and address Him as a Father." The Apostle, no doubt, had in his mind the Lord's Invocation of His Father at Gethsemane, for the words in Syriac and Greek are identical. And no doubt also he remembered the prayer in which the Lord had taught him to invoke God, as no Jewish prayer ever did, for it begins with "Our Father." Nothing can be more remarkable than the paucity of the use of this word "Father" as addressed to God in the Old Testament, particularly when we consider the dear and intimate relations which the Jews had towards Him, and the extreme fervency with which at times they expressed those relations. Take the beginning of the 18th Psalm. "I will love thee, O Lord, my strength; the Lord is my stony rock and my defence: my Saviour, my God, and my might, in whom I will trust, my buckler, the horn also of my salvation, and my refuge." How remarkably the term father—the one most familiar with us—is avoided. It seems to be because He had not been revealed as a real actual begetting Father in the manifestation of the Son. The sonship of Christians wholly depends upon the Sonship of Christ. "To as many as received him, to them gave he power to become the sons of God" (John i.), as if it was a new power [ἐξουσία] given by the Son. And, if so, the privilege of adoption or sonship, or at least

16 [b] The Spirit itself beareth witness with our spirit, that we are the children of God:

[b] 2 Cor. 1, 2. & v. 5. Ephes. i. 13. & iv. 30.

---

the full and clear revelation of it, must be reserved till He was revealed in Whom we are sons.

Still it is to be remembered that many in the old dispensation served God in the spirit of sons, whilst many in the new serve God in the spirit of the most abject bondage. And in households and in families many a servant far surpasses in natural and dutiful affection the proud, self-asserting, self-reliant son or daughter.

16. " The Spirit itself beareth witness with our spirit." " With our spirit," *i.e.*, both the Spirit of God which God has given to us and our own spirit within us bear a joint testimony to this, that we are the children of God.

Two questions must be considered.

What is the witness of God's Spirit—and what is the witness of our own as distinguished from God's Spirit.

By some the witness of the Spirit has been taken to mean the witness of the dispensation which is altogether the work of the Spirit revealing the Son of God, and the means by which we are made partakers of His Nature and Grace, and in a most important sense this is true, and by no means sufficiently realized by Christians— that the Church and its witness to Christ crucified, risen and ascended, and the Scriptures, and the means of grace all testify to the Christian that he is chosen of God, for it is only through the providence of God that he is in the Church, and believes its testimony to the Son of God, and accepts the Scriptures, and receives the Sacraments, and he must rely upon God's providence as having thus revealed to him God's gracious intentions respecting himself. This then is the outward objective testimony of the Spirit: but I do not think that it is here so much in the mind of the Apostle, as the unmistakable evidence of the Spirit in the workings to which he had alluded in the last three verses. He had said that true Christians through the Spirit mortify the deeds of the body, that they are led by the Spirit, and that they have received a Spirit which makes them consider God to be, and to invoke Him as, their Father. All this cannot have come from beneath—from the world, from themselves—and it corresponds to and coincides with the

THE WITNESS OF THE SPIRIT.

testimony of their own spirit which they examine in a humble and honest and devout way, which spirit of theirs clearly testifies to them that notwithstanding shortcomings, and temporary declensions, and infirmities owing to the fact that they dwell in unrenewed bodies, they are yet on the side of God, and of Christ, and against sin and the world. But does not the Holy Spirit speak directly to the soul? Yes; but this speaking is undoubtedly in accordance with His acting and His indwelling. I do not see how He can witness to the sonship of those who do not put themselves under Him to be led by Him, or to the sonship of those who do not sincerely labour to mortify the deeds of the body.

The present personal application of this verse in our times is very difficult. There are a number of seemingly enlightened and religious persons amongst us who claim to have the witness of the Spirit not only to their present sonship, but to their final acceptance, no matter what their conduct between now and judgment be —and there are others, including many deeply-religious Catholic-minded persons, who seeing how dishonestly and dangerously this passage is perverted, all but ignore its teaching altogether.

Now this should not be. Those who realize the Incarnation, the all-atoning Death, the Resurrection, the present Intercession, the Headship of Christ to the Church—the Sacraments, especially the Eucharist, as bringing about the highest Union betwixt Christ and the Christian, those who realize too that the whole Christian work and conflict requires constant watchfulness, self-denial, and self-discipline—have a right to the comfort and consolation and good hope of this passage, whereas those who look upon Christ principally as a substitute, who believe that He has done all for them in the sense of saving them trouble, and conflict, and self-crucifixion— who look upon salvation as the matter of a moment, not of a lifetime—such, it seems to me, have no right to the supposed assurance of this place. Nothing but cherished sin ought to prevent a Christian from having this witness of the Spirit. If we are sincerely putting ourselves under the leading of the Spirit, and striving by the same Spirit to live in the Spirit of adoption, then the Spirit will be ready to witness with our spirit. If, for instance, the Magnificat is true to us, and if we through the grace of the Incarnation can claim it in some degree as the expression of our state, then, indeed, our souls must say, "He that is mighty hath magnified me, and holy is His Name."

17 And if children, then heirs; heirs of God, and joint-heirs with Christ; if so be that we suffer with him, that we may be also glorified together.

^c Acts ii. 18.
Gal. iv. 7.
^d Acts xiv. 22.
Phil. i. 29.
2 Tim. ii. 11, 12.

17. "And if children, then heirs." This is the natural consequence amongst men; the children inherit the property of their fathers on their death, but in spiritual and eternal things, it is far more than this: God is the possessor and owner of all things, and His kingdom and power are boundless, so that He can always give to His children as much as their capacities for enjoyment will allow. "All things," says our Apostle to the Corinthians, "are yours."

"Heirs of God, and joint-heirs with Christ." Because we are through His Incarnation, and the possession of His Spirit, His brethren. Thus He describes Himself as saying at the last day, "Inherit the kingdom prepared for you." Eternal blessedness by being called an inheritance is described as much more than a gift given, as it were, on the spur of the moment. It has long been intended for us, prepared for us, laid up for us. God grant that we may not forfeit it (Hebrews xii. 15, 16, 17).

"If so be that we suffer with him, that we may be also glorified together." If we suffer with Him. This sentiment is repeated by the Apostle in one of his last letters. "If we be dead with him, we shall also live with him: if we suffer we shall also reign with him" (2 Tim. ii. 11, 12). When can we be said to suffer with Christ? When we take what He lays upon us patiently, and as from God (as He said, "The cup which my Father hath given me, shall I not drink it?")—when in all our sufferings we remember His, and how by them He atoned for our sins, and was perfected by suffering to be our sympathizing Mediator and Intercessor; when we esteem it a token for good that we partake of the pain which He did. Quesnel writes, "Let us always remember that we are the heirs of the living God Who dwells in heaven, that so we may despise all earthly things. But let us at the same time remember that we are joint heirs with God Who died on the Cross, that so we may not refuse to die with Him on ours. We can have no part in His inheritance if we have none in His sufferings. This is an indispensable condition of the New Covenant. This inheritance costs dear to flesh and blood, but does not damnation often cost it dearer?"

18 For I reckon that ᵉ the sufferings of this present time *are* not worthy *to be compared* with the glory which shall be revealed in us.   ᵉ 2 Cor. iv. 17. 1 Pet. i. 6, 7. & iv. 13.

19 For ᶠ the earnest expectation of the creature waiteth for the ᵍ manifestation of the sons of God.   ᶠ 2 Pet. iii. 13. ᵍ 1 John iii. 2.

---

18. "For I reckon that the sufferings of this present time are not worthy," &c. "I reckon," that is, "I consider." It has not the smallest tinge of deliberation through uncertainty.

"That the sufferings of this present time." Compare the words "Our light affliction, which is but for a moment, worketh for us a far more exceeding and eternal weight of glory" (2 Cor. iv. 17).

"The glory which shall be revealed in us." Glory both of body and spirit. The body shall be raised up in the likeness of Christ's glorious body, in incorruption, in glory, in power; and the spirit, no longer hampered with an unrenewed frame, shall be clearly seen to reflect the perfect likeness of its Maker. To take the comparison of the present distress with the future joy, what will be even years of disease with an eternity of health and strength? What decrepitude and old age with an eternity of perpetual youth? What the short pains of martyrdom, terrific though they be for the moment, with the being with, and reigning with, Christ a thousand years?

19. "For the earnest expectation of the creature waiteth for the manifestation," &c. The creature, *i.e.*, the whole creation, is personified, and is supposed to be waiting with outstretched neck, for the renewal which is coming, as spectators stretch their necks to see the runners in a race.

"Waiteth for the manifestation of the sons of God." Waiteth, that is, not for destruction or annihilation, but for the manifestation of the highest and best part of the creation.

What is the creature ($\kappa\tau\iota\sigma\iota\varsigma$) of this and the following verse? I think there can be no doubt, if we take into full consideration the significance of the contrast in the beginning of verse 23, "and not only they, but ourselves also, who have the firstfruits of the Spirit," that it is the unrenewed creation. First, then, the creation or creature is man, then the creatures nearest to him, who seem to have souls in sympathy with his, who can in some small degree enter into some of his purposes, and who seem to partake both of

20 For ʰ the creature was made subject to vanity, not willingly, but by reason of him who hath subjected *the same* in hope,

ʰ ver. 22.
Gen. iii. 19.

21 Because the creature itself also shall be delivered from the bondage of corruption into the glorious liberty of the children of God.

---

20. "Who hath subjected the same in hope, because," &c., or, "who hath subjected the same in hope that the creature" (Revisers). The Authorized is far preferable.

21. "Because," διότι. So ℵ, D., F., G.,; but A., B., C., E., K., L., P., and all Cursives, read "in hope that," ὅτι.

his virtues and of his vices; and the rest of the creation cannot be excluded, but is affected according to its nearness to man or its dependence upon him.

20. "The creature was made subject to vanity." This cannot mean vanity in the sense of mere emptiness, nor can it mean corruption, decay and death, though these contribute to the "vanity" of the state; but I think it rather means aimlessness, want of true purpose—the creature is out of gear, so to speak, and awaits the restoration of its true aim and significance at the restoration of its head, even man.

"Not willingly." Here there seems a reference to Adam, who willingly ate of the forbidden fruit, and so willingly subjected himself to evil, whereas the rest of the creation was subjected from without, that is by God, to the effects, or some of them, of Adam's fall.

"But by reason of him who hath subjected the same in hope." The extension of the evil of the fall, and its dislocating effects on other creatures beside man was not ordered by God that it should continue so for ever; as man was subjected to sin in hope that he should be redeemed, so the creation was made subject to vanity in hope that in the fulness of time it might partake of his redemption.

21. "Because the creature itself also shall be delivered from the bondage of corruption," &c. This is a great mystery, but it is in accordance with many very distinct intimations of Scripture, as Isaiah xi., where the principal creatures seem to have their natures changed (also Isaiah lxv. 17, 25 ; Hosea ii. 18).

There is no reason why it should not be so, if we believe in the omnipotence and infinite goodness of God.

"Corruption" must be here decay and death, and from this it is

CHAP. VIII.]   ALL CREATION GROANETH.   175

22 For we know that ‖ the whole creation ¹groaneth and travaileth in pain together until now. ‖ Or, *every creature,*

23 And not only *they*, but ourselves also, which Mark xvi. 15. Col. i. 23.

¹ Jer. xii. 11.

---

delivered, and into nothing less than the glorious liberty of the children of God. So that there is a most glorious future for this "creature," this κτίσις, whatever it be, and it must be beings living upon this earth, whether men or animals, who do not at present partake of regeneration.

"Into the glorious liberty of the children of God." Rather into the liberty of the glory, the bondage of corruption being set against the liberty of glory, glory being here all the moral and physical attributes of the renewed and glorified saint. Of all intelligent beings the children of God (angels or saints) are the freest, because they are under the dominion of nothing which can hurt them, and they are free to do what is in accordance with the most exalted aspirations that created intelligences are capable of.

22. "For we know that the whole creation groaneth and travaileth in pain," &c. Here we have a further illustration of the expectant state of the lower creation. Before (verse 19) it was "earnest expectation;" now it is the groaning and travailing in birth of a woman with child expecting to be delivered. The old creation is supposed to be in the pains of labour, ready to give birth to the new. The sense of want, and imperfection, and distress which permeates a world created by God and pronounced very good by Him cannot remain unsatisfied. The sense of need in the kingdom of so Almighty and good a God points to the satisfaction of that need—the sense of imperfection to the attainment of perfection, of pain to a state of enduring joy.¹

The words "until now" cannot be taken as if there was a cessation or respite at the Lord's first coming. On the contrary, the gift of the Spirit makes the yearning and longing for the final deliverance more urgent.

23. "And not only they, but ourselves also, which have the firstfruits of the Spirit," &c. "Ourselves who have the firstfruits of the Spirit," must be held to include all who through the coming of Christ and the preaching of His Gospel, are partakers of the

---

¹ See a sermon of J. Wesley on "The New Creation," No. lxiv.

have ᵏ the firstfruits of the Spirit, ˡ even we ourselves groan within ourselves, ᵐ waiting for the adoption, *to wit*, the ⁿ redemption of our body.

24 For we are saved by hope: but ᵒ hope that

ᵏ 2 Cor. v. 5. Ephes. i. 14.
ˡ 2 Cor. v. 2, 4.
ᵐ Luke xx. 36.
ⁿ Luke xxi. 28. Ephes. iv. 30.
ᵒ 2 Cor. v. 7. Hebr. xi. 1.

24. "We are saved;" literally, "We were saved."

Spirit. Abundant though the gifts of the Spirit were in the Apostolic age, they were only the *first* fruits, and the full harvest will not be till the resurrection of our bodies at the time of the restitution of all things.

"Even we ourselves groan within ourselves, waiting for the adoption," &c. The expression of these groans in words is to be found in the concluding verses of the last chapter: "I delight in the law of God, after the inward man, but I see another law. O wretched man that I am," &c. And also particularly in 2 Corinth. v. 2, 4: "In this tabernacle we groan, earnestly desiring to be clothed upon with our house which is from heaven. We that are in this tabernacle do groan, being burdened," &c.

It is very necessary for the Christian to see that he has something of this experience. If his spirit is truly and really renewed, or in the process of renewal, it stands to reason that he must, at times at least, have the same inward feelings respecting the unrenewed state of his body and the law of sin in his members, which the Apostle predicates of himself and of those with him who have the firstfruits of the Spirit. If we have no inward conflict, no earnest expectation, nothing that can be called earnestly desiring or "groaning, being burthened," have we not reason to fear that our lot is not with St. Paul and the saints whom he joins with himself in this experience?

"The adoption, to wit, the redemption of our bodies." Notice how the body is to share in the adoption of the Spirit, and also how Redemption is not yet completed. The full price, even the Blood of Christ, is paid, but corruption and the grave have not yet surrendered the bodies which, as well as the souls or spirits inhabiting them, belong to Christ.

24. "For we are saved by hope: but hope that is seen is not hope." This verse and the following seem to depend upon the mention of "waiting" in the previous verse: "We who have the firstfruits of the Spirit, groan, waiting, as they who are in prison

CHAP. VIII.] WE HOPE FOR THAT WE SEE NOT. 177

is seen is not hope: for what a man seeth, why doth he yet hope for?

25 But if we hope for that we see not, *then* do we with patience wait for *it.*

26 Likewise the Spirit also helpeth our infirmities: for

---

26. "Our infirmities." So K., L., P., most Cursives, &c.; but ℵ, A., B., C., D., some Cursives, d, Vulg., Syriac, read, "our weakness" (singular).

groan, waiting to be set free." Now this waiting (ἀπεκδεχόμεθα) is the very substance and essence of hope; our full salvation is not yet, it is in, and by, hope. When we believed in Christ, we believed in One Who will return and receive us to Himself. When we were baptized into Christ we were baptized into One Who died and rose again, in the assured hope that if we have been planted into the likeness of His Death, and been made partakers of it, we shall be also in the likeness of His Resurrection, and be made at last fully partakers of it.

This is in no way contrary to justification by faith, for, as Dean Alford, quoting Tholuck, says, " Hope is, in fact, faith in its prospective attitude. We should not have come to Christ or submitted ourselves to Him unless we hoped to receive salvation from Him. Now this salvation is in part present, inasmuch as we receive justification and renewal now from Him; but, as regards the adoption and redemption of our bodies, it is future, and so is an object of hope, and so faith, so far as regards the renewal and spiritualizing of the body, is the 'substance of things hoped for.'" (Hebrews xi. 1.)

"Hope that is seen is not hope." Hope is here put for the object hoped for, and "seen" means in possession. If we saw and so possessed our spiritual bodies, they would no longer be objects of hope.

25. "But if we hope for that we see not," &c. This is the practical conclusion from what has gone before. If our hope is a firm, strong, good hope, then we wait with patience for its accomplishment. If our hope is weak, then our faith is weak, and we have no firm hold on the glorious future.

26. "Likewise the Spirit also helpeth our infirmities (or infirmity): for we know not," &c. Here is another source of consolation and good hope; for the Christian, owing to the conflict within him, is sometimes distracted with the sense of his utter weakness; he cannot even pray as he ought, so ignorant is he of what is really

p Matt. xx. 22. Jam. iv. 3.
q Zech. xii. 10. Eph. vi. 18.
r 1 Chron. xxviii. 9. Ps. vii. 9. Prov. xvii. 3. Jer. xi. 20. & xvii. 10. & xx. 12. Acts i. 24. 1 Thes. ii. 4. Rev. ii. 23.
| Or, *that*.
s 1 John v. 14.

ᵖ we know not what we should pray for as we ought: but ᑫ the Spirit itself maketh intercession for us with groanings which cannot be uttered.

27 And ʳ he that searcheth the hearts knoweth what *is* the mind of the Spirit, || because he maketh intercession for the saints ˢ according to *the will of God.*

---

necessary for him; and so God, Who has given him an Intercessor in heaven at His right hand, in the Person of His Son, now gives him an Intercessor within him, in the Person of the Holy Spirit. This Spirit helps him in this his utter weakness. The Holy Ghost leads him to desire things, or, rather, to feel desires which he cannot put in words. He can only express them by inarticulate sighs and moans, but, so far from this weakness of expression being displeasing to His heavenly Father, it is acceptable to Him. He discerns in these inarticulate longings the voice of His Spirit Who has inspired the man with these fervent desires, which, to use a common expression, are too big for utterance. The man knows not what he means in these sighings, but God does. He sees in them the work of His own Spirit, Who has so enlarged the man's desires that his tongue cannot find means to utter them intelligibly.

"He that searcheth the hearts knoweth what is the mind of the Spirit." God looking into our hearts distinguishes between what is our own and what is the work of His Spirit. Our fellow-creatures, if they could read our hearts, would ascribe this venting of desires in sighs, this want of ability to express ourselves in words, to our weakness, whereas God discerns in it the presence and working of the Spirit, and answers it because, as the Apostle goes on to say, the intercession is according to the will of God.

This whole passage is very conclusive as regards the doctrine of the true personality of the Holy Spirit. He is distinguished from Him Who knows what His, the Spirit's, Mind is, and He is distinguished from the human spirit which He assists and intercedes in as a greater Spirit dwelling in and instructing the lesser—the Divine in the human.

We have also here the love of the Spirit. He intercedes in us and for us. He is often grieved, and resisted, and some even desire to quench Him; but, notwithstanding these provocations, He continues in us, helping our infirmities, exciting our languid affections, convincing, reproving, comforting, and at the last will be the Divine Agent in accomplishing that for which above all else He makes us long—even the redemption of our bodies.

28. "And we know that all things work together for good to them," &c. This is a third and last reason for consolation and good hope for true Christians. The witness of the Spirit within them, the groans for deliverance in which all creation joins, the ever animating hopes, are all tokens that they are true children of God.

And now there is another and further consideration by which they may take abundant comfort, which is no other than this, that their salvation, in all its various stages, is not a thing of chance, but a matter of God's pre-determination and pre-ordination. This and the following verses are an application to the Roman Christians of the words of St. James: "Known unto God are all his works from the beginning of the world" (Acts xv. 18), and of St. Paul's words to the Philippians, "Being confident of this very thing, that he who hath begun a good work in you will perform it until the day of Jesus Christ" (Phil. i. 6).

These words (verses 28, 29, 30, 31) are no doubt predestinarian words, and if we deprive them of their predestinarian meaning we deprive them of all the comfort which God Who inspired them designed holy souls to receive from them. They have been miserably, indeed, one may say, wickedly perverted, but they are in accordance with Catholic truth, and the greatest doctors of the Church—Augustine, Bernard, Anselm, Thomas Aquinas—have used them as setting forth the security of true Christians, and the comfort and joy which such ought to have from the sense of that security.

I desire, then, that the reader should understand that in what I am writing I desire not for a moment to deny that they must be understood in their natural sense—that God designs salvation for certain persons whose marks are here described, and that, if I show the limitations under which this truth is to be understood, it is to make the truth itself more certain, which is imperilled if it is built on a basis which is partially insecure.

Before examining the verses word by word, two or three observations will be necessary.

First then, the Apostle in what he writes has not the least

intention of dividing the Church of Rome, to which he writes, into two classes—the elect, and the non-elect. On the contrary, he assumes the election of all of them; for his Epistle is written to "all that be in Rome, beloved of God, called to be saints," and he assumes also that they, as a body, are in a fit state to receive his benediction of grace and peace from God the Father, and the Lord Jesus Christ. If it be answered that this might be dangerous to some Christians of Rome who might presume upon this election when they had no grounds for so doing, we answer, that there are two dangers connected with this matter: 1. To consider election certain when it is not, and 2. To doubt about it, or disbelieve it, or ignore it when it is certain.

Then, in the next place, we are to remember that the doctrine of Predestination was in no respect a peculiarity of the teaching of St. Paul. It was held by his brother Apostle, St. Peter, as absolutely as he held it, if we are to judge from the teaching of his first Epistle, where he speaks of Christians as "elect according to the foreknowledge of God the Father, through sanctification of the Spirit, unto obedience and sprinkling of the blood of Jesus Christ" (1 Peter i. 2); and he further carries it out in the inference that such elect ones are "kept by the power of God unto salvation" (verse 5). But in saying that Predestination or Election was in no respect distinctively Pauline, I mean that it was a Jewish doctrine derived from the Old Testament, in which, in one shape or another, it occupies a most prominent position both in the Law, properly so called, and in the prophets. First of all God chose certain persons before they became nations, and in order that they might become nations; then in the elect families He chose certain children, and passed by others—in the case of Ishmael and Isaac, and then of Esau and Jacob, passing by the elder and selecting the younger. Then Election and Predestination is the theme of the whole latter part of the prophecy of Isaiah. According to his prophecy it extends to the heathen as well as to the Election proper. Cyrus is elected as absolutely as Josiah or Jeremiah, though of course not for the same purpose. I do not, of course, mean that the election of the Old Testament is the same as that of the New: the election of the New is spiritual and not national, though the election of Israel after the flesh was for high moral and spiritual purposes; but the essential feature was the same, in that God chose or elected men to fulfil His purpose before they came into existence.

28 And we know that all things work together for good to them that love God, to them ᵗ who are the called according to *his* purpose.

ᵗ ch. ix. 11, 23, 24. 2 Tim. i. 9.

---

28. *"* We know that all things work together for good to them," &c. So ℵ, C., D., F., G., K., L., P., all Cursives, Vulg., Syriac, Copt., Arm.; but A., B., add, "God," "We know that God worketh all things with them for good."

A third point is, why did St. Paul bring in here the doctrines, and use the Predestinarian terms? Evidently to vindicate the right of all those in Rome who loved God and were members of His Church, to the comfort of the doctrine. He must have had in his mind that a large number of his co-religionists would absolutely deny to any Roman Christian, no matter what his love to God, any part in God's Election, just as they would deny that he was justified unless he was circumcised and kept the law: here, then, the Apostle claims for true Christians the true and spiritual Election, just as he claims for the same Christians that they only who are justified by faith are the truly justified.

28. "And we know that all things work together for good," &c. Some of these "all" things are enumerated in verse 35: "Tribulation, distress, persecution, famine, nakedness, peril, the sword."

"Work together for good," *i.e.*, for their ultimate good, their eternal well-being.

"To them that love God, to them who are the called according to his purpose." "To them that love God." Let the reader particularly notice that all things work together for good, not to those who believe, but to those whose belief works by love, *i.e.*, to those whose faith is effectual for the purpose for which God gave it to them.

This is to be particularly borne in mind. There may be a mistake about faith, and too often there is; there may be often a difficulty about distinguishing between a notional, or an historic, and a deep-seated and genuine faith; but there can be no mistake about love—the love of God—if we attend to the marks of it, for it never is used to signify a mere emotion, but always an obediential reality.

"To them who are the called according to his purpose" (or, according to purpose). Those who love God are not merely seekers after God who have not yet found Him, but they are those who, by the preaching of the word, have had the Father presented to them

29 For whom ^u he did foreknow, ^x he also did

<small>u See Exod. xxxiii. 12, 17. Ps. i. 6. Jer. i. 5. Matt. vii. 23. ch. xi. 2. 2 Tim. ii. 19. 1 Pet. i. 2.
x Ephes. i. 5, 11.</small>

as the Father of Jesus Christ, and, because they have seen His love to lost mankind in His Son, have had their hearts attracted to Him, and have begun to love Him.

Now this calling was not, as a rule, at least, a secret calling alone, but it was an outward calling, through the ministers of the word, *i.e.*, through human agents who preached the Gospel, and baptized into the Church, for the calling was not a calling to individual religion only, but into a fellowship, according to the words of the Apostle, "God is faithful, by whom ye were called to the fellowship of his Son Jesus Christ our Lord" (1 Cor. i. 9; Ephes. iv. 1-4).

"According to his purpose." What is this purpose? It seems to mean design or determination. The key to the meaning of it is to be found in Ephes. iii. 11, "According to the eternal purpose which he purposed in Christ Jesus." But what was *this* purpose— I mean the one alluded to in this latter passage? The Apostle tells us in the verse before, "To make all men see what is the fellowship (or dispensation) of the mystery, which from the beginning of the world hath been had in God who created all things ... to the intent that now unto the principalities and powers in heavenly places might be known, by the Church, the manifold wisdom of God."

The idea, then, seems to be this: God had a design in constituting the Church of Christ, and that was, to make known throughout the universe His manifold wisdom; but to this end those gathered into the Church must be calculated to forward this design (which in its integrity is known only to God). The persons in the Roman and other Churches who were brought into the Body of Christ, did not drop in, as it were, haphazard, but all were chosen with a view of their fulfilling their place in the Church. All this is clearly indicated in 1 Cor. xii. 11-31. If, then, the Church of God was to answer God's all-wise purpose, the members of it must be chosen "according to his purpose;" and the Apostle here declares that they were so chosen, and so, in strict logical sequence, he proceeds—

29. "For whom he did foreknow, he also did predestinate to be conformed," &c. Some commentators explain this as meaning

CHAP. VIII.]   THE IMAGE OF HIS SON.   183

predestinate ʸ *to be* conformed to the image of his   ʸ John xvii. 22. 2 Cor. iii. 18. Phil. iii. 21. 1 John iii. 2.

"whom He did foreknow would be conformed to the image of His Son, them He did predestinate to be so conformed;" but this cannot be. It would be a sort of truism, it would be inconsistent with the gravity of the passage. It would make the will of God in predestinating to depend upon something which, though good, was independent of God. It seems rather to mean—those whom God foreknew would answer His high purpose, those He predetermined to advance another stage in the direction of the accomplishment of His purpose ; and this was that He predetermined that they should not serve His purpose in heathenism, or in unbelieving Judaism, but in true spiritual Christianity—in union with His Church under its Head, and under the guidance of His Spirit. For in such an age as the first age, many might ask, "Why cannot I serve God by remaining as I am, by more or less secretly believing and acting on my fellow-men, apart from the Elect Body ?" "No," the Apostle says, "you cannot. Those whom God foreknows as fit to fulfil His designs, He predetermines that they should be conformed to the image of His Son." This does not merely mean that they should be like His Son in character, but it also means that they should be in a measure conformed to His Son's example in openly opposing the world, and enduring its contempt, enmity, and persecutions. And there is a further meaning. The Apostle in writing this cannot have shut out from his mind the sort of conformity to Christ's Death and Resurrection which he had insisted on so strongly such a short time before, that they should die and be buried, and be raised again in the image of His Death, Burial, and Resurrection.

"The image of his Son." There would have been nothing like the deep-rooted dislike which many religious persons have exhibited towards the doctrine of Predestination, however stated, if it had been borne in mind that the image, to which we are predestinated to be conformed, is the image of Christ—of the Son of God— of the meek, lowly, loving, sympathizing, patient Son of God. On the contrary, the characters of those who have at and since the Reformation, most uncompromisingly set forth the doctrine of God's decrees, have been, as a rule, of the most repulsive and uncharitable type that a Christian can possibly have, and yet be

Son, *that he might be the firstborn among many brethren.

[*] Col. i. 15, 18. Hebr. i. 6. Rev. i. 5.

30 Moreover whom he did predestinate, them he also

---

entitled to the name of Christian, and so such men have been morally unable to set forth the character of Christ as portrayed in the Gospels.

"That he might be the firstborn among many brethren." Who are Christ's brethren? Many answers may be given. They who are sanctified: "Both he that sanctifieth, and they who are sanctified are all of one, for which cause he is not ashamed to call them brethren." Then they who do the will of God: "Who is my mother? and who are my brethren? And he stretched forth his hand toward his disciples, and said, Behold my mother, and my brethren. For whosoever shall do the will of my Father which is in heaven, the same is my brother, and sister, and mother" (Matth. xii. 48-50).

But, no doubt, this "many brethren" denotes that they should be all one family, one Church, united in upholding the honour, and following the leadership of the great Elder Brother.

30. "Moreover, whom he did predestinate, them he also called." "Them he also called," that is, as I said, not by a call in their secret chambers, or in the recesses of their hearts only, but by an outward, audible call, in which Christ spoke through ministers, or prophets, or evangelists, and accompanied the words of His minister with a power exercised upon their wills, so that they accepted the Lord as the Son of God, and surrendered themselves to Him, so as to be enrolled in His Church, and be made members of His Body.

If it be objected that I ought not to insist on this latter, as involved in the calling, I answer, it is so insisted on by the Apostle himself when he writes to the Ephesian Christians, "I beseech you, that ye walk worthy of the calling wherewith ye are called, with all lowliness and meekness, with long-suffering . . . endeavouring to keep the unity of the Spirit in the bond of peace. There is one body and one Spirit, even as ye are called in one hope of your calling, one Lord, one faith, one Baptism," &c. (Ephes. iv. 1-5.) The calling was not a calling to a place in some infinitely distant heaven when they died, but to a place in Christ's mystical Body on earth whilst they lived.

Those, then, whom God predestinated He called, that they might

CHAP. VIII.] CALLED, JUSTIFIED, GLORIFIED. 185

[a] called: and whom he called, them he also [b] justified: and whom he justified, them he also [c] glorified.

[a] ch. i. 6. & ix. 24. Ephes. iv. 4. Hebr. ix. 15. 1 Pet. ii. 9.
[b] 1 Cor. vi. 11.
[c] John xvii. 22. Ephes. ii. 6.

hear,[1] might obey the calling, and belong to that mysterious fellowship through, and by means of which, the wisdom of God might be further revealed to the various ranks of angels (Ephes. iii. 10).

"And whom he called, them he also justified." "By granting to them, on their so believing as to obey the call, Justification of Life. The most mysterious of all God's gifts in this world was on their believing bestowed on them, that they should partake of the Resurrection Life of the Lord, so that they might not only be pardoned, but endowed with a new gift of power—even the Lord's Life—to do the will of God. This was bestowed upon them when they were grafted unto Christ—when by Baptism they put on Christ, when as members of the mystical Body they were sanctified and cleansed with the washing of water by the Word, and when they were saved by the bath of Regeneration and Renewing of the Holy Ghost."

"And whom he justified, them he also glorified." There is very considerable doubt respecting the meaning of this "glorified." By some (Chrysostom, Theodoret, &c.), it is held to be a present blessing or glory, and this agrees with the fact that the rest of the stages of salvation are all in past time—He foreknew, He predestinated, He called, He justified. Why then, it is asked, should "He glorified," refer to the future, if an adequate sense of "glorify" can belong to the present state of things? It so happens, though this may be accidental, that the Greek word δοξάζειν is never applied to what takes place in Christians, either at death or at the last day. There can be no doubt that the gift of the Spirit, and the consequent adoption and conformity to the mind of God and the image of Christ, is a glory taking place now, which is con-

---

[1] It is not sufficiently considered that the calling which reached the outward ear depended upon the foreknowledge and predestination of God. Thus, in one chapter of the Acts, we read that God ordained, and, therefore, had predestinated, that two large and important provinces of the Roman world, Asia and Bithynia, should not at that time have the Gospel preached unto them: in other words, that the inhabitants of these provinces should not then be called, justified, and glorified (Acts xvi. 6, 7).

stantly referred to by St. Paul, particularly in 2 Cor. iii., where it is said that the ministration of the Spirit, compared to that of Moses, is so much more glorious, that " the ministration of righteousness exceeds in glory "—that " that which remaineth," *i.e.*, the present dispensation of the Spirit, is " in glory," and finally, " we all," *i.e.*, all who continue partakers of the Spirit, are changed from glory to glory, as by the Spirit of the Lord. Our Lord undoubtedly refers to the sonship which He had conferred upon the Apostles, and not to their final beatification, when He says, " The glory that thou gavest me I have given them " (John xvii. 22).[1]

Again, Ephes. i. 18 and ii. 6, and Coloss. i. 11, " the glory of his power," and again, verse 27, " the riches of the glory of this mystery," all refer to present glory put upon the Church. And again, the reader will remember how Our Lord is said to have been raised from the dead by the glory of the Father, meaning, no doubt, by the Spirit of the Father. These considerations make it exceedingly probable (I think certain) that Chrysostom and Theodoret are right when the first interprets it by " He glorified them by the gift," *i.e.*, by the adoption; and the latter by " those whom He justified He glorified, calling them sons, and giving them the grace of the Holy Spirit."

We will now endeavour to put into other words the Apostle's argument. The tribulations which you endure from without, and the conflict you feel within you between the flesh and the Spirit, at times cast you down, and make you tempted to think that God has no regard for you; but it is not so; for how is it that you love God? It is most assuredly not of yourselves, for first of all you must have been called to the knowledge of Himself and faith in Him. If anything in the world takes place through the providence of God, it is the proclamation of the Gospel to you from without, and the power to accept it working within. And this calling was followed by your regeneration—you were made new creatures in Christ, the old things of your heathen state, your heathen misbeliefs, your dim and uncertain knowledge of the future, passed away, and all things became new; above all, you were gifted with a new power against sin. And you were called to no common fellowship, but to the followship of His own Son. That Son was called to suffering. He endured the cross, despising the

---

[1] This, with Ephes. ii. 6, are the only places referred to in the old marginal references in our Bibles.

31 What shall we then say to these things? ^d If God be for us, who *can be* against us?

32 ^e He that spared not his own Son, but ^f delivered him up for us all, how shall he not with him also freely give us all things?

^d Num. xiv. 9. Ps. cxviii. 6.
^e ch. v. 6, 10.
^f ch. iv. 25.

---

shame, and your partaking of the same sufferings as He did, because of His witness for God, stamps you as one of His many brethren. If God, then, has any plan, any foreseen and fore-ordained plan, in the sending of His Son amongst us, and the foundation and continuance of the Church of that Son which is His Body and His Bride, you are part of that plan. As all things work together for the good of the Church of Christ, as all the providential dispensations of this world are shaped with a view to its final beatification, so all things, no matter how seemingly contrary, work together for your good.

Some further necessary remarks I shall make at the end of the chapter.

31. "What shall we then say to these things? If God be for us, who," &c. "What shall we say?" he asks, and the answer is, "If God be for us, who can be against us?" The reader will notice here, and, indeed to the end of this chapter, that the Apostle never contemplates danger from within, from the remainder of sin, but only from without. He assumes that, no matter how the world rages and persecutes, the spirit cleaveth steadfastly unto God. "The Lord is on my side, I will not fear what man doeth unto me."

32. "He that spared not his own Son, but delivered him up for us all, how," &c. Here the Apostle leaves the particular calling, and election, and predestination, and falls back on that which is at once the root and the crowning mercy of all. "For reflect what goodness it is not to spare even His own Son, but to give Him up, and to give Him up for all, and those worthless and unfeeling, and enemies, and blasphemers. If He gave His own Son, and not merely gave Him, but gave Him to death, why doubt any more about the rest, since thou hast the Master? Why be dubious about the chattels when thou hast the Lord? For He that gave the greater things to His enemies, how shall He do else than give the lesser things to his friends?" (Chrysostom.) "And that person

33 Who shall lay any thing to the charge of God's elect?
g Isai. l. 8, 9.   g *It is* God that justifieth.
Rev. xii. 10, 11.

33. The marginal reading of the Revisers is, "Who shall lay anything to the charge of God's elect? Shall God, that justifieth? Who is he that shall condemn? Shall Christ that died, yea rather, that was raised from the dead," &c.

fears nothing from the world, and hopes for everything from God, who understands, esteems, and cultivates as he ought this unspeakable gift of God." (Quesnel.) Philippi, with very good reason, sees a reference to Abraham not sparing Isaac. God there says to him, οὐκ ἐφείσω τοῦ υἱοῦ σου τοῦ ἀγαπητοῦ, "Thou hast not spared (withheld) thy son, thy beloved son." This correspondence can scarcely be deemed accidental. Rather is it in the highest degree probable that a reference to the passage in Genesis is to be supposed; God Himself has done what, in Abraham's typical act, He declared to be the highest proof of love.

33. "Who shall lay anything to the charge of God's elect? It is God that justifieth." The elect—those, that is, who love God—are here supposed to be brought before the tribunal, and accusations are called for, just as it happened in the case of their Master; but of what worth are such, or any accusations, since God has justified them, that is, has pardoned them, and given them a new life, whereby they live to Him by an holiness surpassing anything that has ever been seen before in this world? Who are supposed to be the accusers? If it is Satan, then God will answer, "I have justified them against you. Their transgressions were against me, not against you, and I have seen fit to pardon them, and to work in them, at their own desire, that holiness which you have lost. A place of repentance and restoration has been found for them, and they have availed themselves of it."

Does the law—do the Jews accuse them? The answer is, they have the true circumcision, the all-availing Blood of Atonement, and the law written in the heart.

Do the heathen accuse them as being atheists, and neglecters of the gods? The answer is, they neglect gods that are no gods, and worship Him Who liveth for ever and ever.

Do their consciences accuse them of past sins? The answer is, they have a Blood which was shed for the remission of sins that are past, and which now purges their consciences from dead works to serve the living God.

CHAP. VIII.] CHRIST THAT DIED. 189

34 ʰ Who *is* he that condemneth? *It is* Christ that died, yea rather, that is risen again, ¹ who is even at the right hand of God, ᵏ who also maketh intercession for us.

35 Who shall separate us from the love of

ʰ Job xxxiv. 29.
ⁱ Mark xvi. 19. Col. iii. 1. Hebr. i. 3. & viii. 1. & xii. 2. 1 Pet. iii. 22.
ᵏ Hebr. vii. 25. & ix. 24. 1 John ii. 1.

---

34. "It is Christ that died." So B., D., E., K., most Cursives, d, e, Syriac; but ℵ, A., C., F., G., L., 5, 17, 31, 33, 67**, 73, 80, f, g, Vulg., Copt., Arm., Æth., read, "Christ Jesus."

34. "Risen again." So B., D., E., F., G., K., L., most Cursives; but ℵ, A., C., 17, 31, 39, 73, 115, Cop., Æth., add, "from the dead."

34. "Even" (καί). Omitted by ℵ, A., C.; retained by B., D., E., F., G., K., L., most Cursives, e, f, g, Vulg. (Cod. Amiat.), &c.

35. "From the love of Christ." So A., C., D., E., F., G., K., L., most Cursives, d, e, f, g, Vulg., Goth., Syriac, Cop., Arm., Æth.; but ℵ, B, 7, 74, 76, 91, 123, 238, &c., read, "of God."

---

34. "Who is he that condemneth?" No human tribunal, no earthly judge can condemn. All judgment is committed to the Son. And He died to save them from being condemned for sins which they repent of. Nay, rather, He is risen again to exhibit to all the efficacy of His Death, and to endow them with a new life, *i.e.*, a new power against sin and for God.

"Who is even at the right hand of God" as Head of that mystical Body of which He has made them members. "Who also maketh intercession." In heaven He appears as the Lamb standing as slain, to plead on our behalf the efficacy of His sacrifice.

An alteration has been suggested in the punctuation, making the second clauses questions. Who shall lay anything to the charge of God's elect? Is it God that justifieth? Can He at once justify and accuse? Who is he that condemneth? Is it Christ that died and rose again? Can He at the same time condemn and intercede? But the sense is, as far as I can see, not altered.

35. "Who shall separate us from the love of Christ? shall tribulation," &c. It is singular that there should have been two opinions respecting the import of this question. It seems to mean, "Can any thing whatsoever which happens to us in this world diminish Christ's love to us, much less destroy it?" It has been urged that such a question is futile. Who would ever imagine that any suffering which we endure should ever prevent Christ's love from reaching us and resting on us? To this we answer that in times of

Christ? *shall* tribulation, or distress, or persecution, or famine, or nakedness, or peril, or sword?

¹ Ps. xliv. 22. 1 Cor. xv. 30, 31. 2 Cor. iv. 11.

36 As it is written, ¹For thy sake we are killed all the day long; we are accounted as sheep for the slaughter.

---

persecution with us, who have within ourselves such a strange mixture of belief and unbelief, nothing is more common than to think, and even to exclaim, that we are deserted, or cast off, by God, which is the same as saying that we are separated from the love of Christ, Who is our Intercessor with God. The other meaning given is, "What shall diminish or destroy our love to Christ?" but the Apostle all through the chapter is dwelling upon God's love to us, God's hold upon us, God's constancy to us, so that the first meaning seems on all accounts preferable.

"Shall tribulation, or distress, or persecution, or famine," &c. All these are tribulations from without, and some of them, as persecution, would come upon Christians, owing to their open profession of the faith of Christ. It is to be remembered that the law of Moses promised freedom from distress and abundant temporal blessings as the reward of serving God faithfully, and the heathen converts had been brought up in the belief that such things as distress, famine, and the sword, were undoubted signs of the anger of the gods against those who had displeased them. In the case of Christians in the Apostolic and following ages, the whole significance of God's dealings was reversed. The key to all is in such passages as, "If we suffer we shall also reign with him," "What son is he whom the father chasteneth not?" (2 Tim. ii. 12; Heb. xii. 7).

36. "As it is written, For thy sake we are killed all the day long." The Apostle quotes this as showing that even in the times of the old dispensation the people of God were hated and persecuted. He quotes it, however, as simply proving the fact, for the tone of the Psalm is one of remonstrance—the people of God had faithfully adhered to Him, and why, then, did He allow them to be trampled on?—showing that in times of persecution we may pray to God for the removal of the present distress and the triumph of His Church.

37. "Nay, in all these things we **are more than conquerors**," &c.

CHAP. VIII.]   MORE THAN CONQUERORS.   191

37 ᵐ Nay, in all these things we are more than conquerors through him that loved us.

38 For I am persuaded, that neither death, nor life, nor angels, nor ⁿ principalities, nor powers, nor things present, nor things to come,

ᵐ 1 Cor. xv. 57. 2 Cor. ii. 14. 1 John iv. 4. & v. 4, 5. Rev. xii. 11.
ⁿ Ephes. i. 21. & vi. 12. Col. i. 16. & ii. 15. 1 Pet. iii. 22.

38. " Nor powers." ℵ, A., B., C., D., E., F., G., 37, 47, 73, 137, 179, d, e, f, g, Vulg. (Amiut.), Copt., place this after " things to come ; " but K., L., and most Cursives retain it in its place in the Authorized after "principalities."

Alford translates this, "we are far the conquerors." " The wrath and persecutions of our adversaries only add to the brightness of our crown. This was a new rule of victory for men to prevail by their adversaries, and in no instance to be overcome, but to go forth in their struggles, as if they themselves had the issue in their own hands."—Chrysostom.

38, 39. " For I am persuaded, that neither death, nor life, nor angels, ... the love of God, which is in Christ Jesus our Lord." It seems absurd, as some do, to take to pieces this sublime passage. It simply means that nothing in God's universe can separate us from the love of Him Who created that universe, if He has seen fit to set His love upon us.

"Death nor life." The mention of death seems to mean that God will see to it that through no pains of death shall we fall from Him. " Though I walk through the valley of the shadow, I will fear no evil, for thou art with me." Life seems to mean the perils, the vicissitudes, the " changes and chances of this mortal life." The interpretation given by Grotius, after Jerome, "neither the fear of death nor the hope of life " is, according to Philippi, a correct paraphrase of the sense ; but I think the former is preferable.

" Nor angels nor principalities." It has been asked whether this means good or evil angels ; good angels would not endeavour to separate us from the love of God, and it is said that evil spirits are never called angels by St. Paul ; but this seems to be said in forgetfulness of 1 Corinth. vi. 3: " Know ye not that we shall judge angels ? " and it cannot be supposed that we shall judge the elect angels. But it is the power, not the character of angelic beings to which St. Paul refers here. If it could be supposed for a moment that they should desire to pluck us out of the hand of God, the

39 Nor height, nor depth, nor any other creature, shall be able to separate us from the love of God, which is in Christ Jesus our Lord.

---

united force of all the armies of heaven or of hell would not be able to do so.

"Nor things present, nor things to come." Nothing in time present or future.

"Nor height, nor depth, nor any other creature (parallel to Phil. ii. 10: "Things in heaven, and things in earth, and things under the earth,") shall be able to separate us from the love of God which is in Christ Jesus." The significance is two-fold. It is the love of God manifested in Christ, more particularly in giving Him through His Incarnation and Death, and it is the love of God to those whom He hath chosen in Christ.

And now let us review the teaching of this passage with respect to that doctrine of election which has been most rife amongst us, viz., Calvinistic Election. I shall here take no notice of dogmatic statements of Divines, and simply confine myself to the bearing of the passage upon what is popularly held with reference to election and predestination by those who hold these doctrines at all.[1] It may be fairly stated to be this, that when once a man has been converted or saved, he is sure to be welcomed into heaven at last, no matter what sins he may commit between the time of his conversion and the moment of his death. If he falls, no matter how grievously, he will certainly be restored before he is called to leave this world. According to this, exactly the same number of those who are foreknown by God are called, all to a man who are called are justified, and all who are justified will be glorified: the past tense of the last being used to denote the absolute certainty—in His eternal purpose He has glorified them as certainly as He has called them and justified them. Now what we have at present to do with is, not whether the passage logically involves all this, according to the fashion with which we apply our logic to the oracles of God—that is another question—but whether it was in the Apostolic mind.

---

[1] The vast mass of those who make a show of using this high and holy doctrine in their daily life, care nothing about the guarded statements and balancings and reservations of the learned; and at once take these passages as they wish to take them, as designed to save them all trouble and anxiety about their final salvation.

It most certainly was not, and for this reason, that in the catalogue of the things which are supposed to be able to separate us from the love of Christ, there is the most significant of all omissions, that is, of the all-important word " sin," or what would be equivalent, of the word "self." Now, it may be asked, is not falling away through sin and self covered by "neither death, nor life," or " by things to come," or by " any other creature "? No, we answer, and for two reasons: first, St. Paul would certainly never call sin a κτίσις, a creature, for by this word he invariably means a creation of God; and, secondly, that at the conclusion of this argument respecting election, in chap. xi. 20-22, the Apostle assumes that sin, or self yielding to sin, may nullify God's election, and separate those who " stand by faith " from the goodness of God : " Thou standest by faith. Be not high-minded, but fear. For if God spared not the natural branches, take heed lest he also spare not thee. Behold, therefore, the goodness and severity of God; on them which fell severity, but toward thee, goodness, if thou continue in his goodness: otherwise thou also shalt be cut off." The reader will see that the Apostle, having up to this point spoken generally, turns to the individual Christian, who stands by faith, and who must therefore be a partaker not merely of outward calling, but of inward grace, and speaks to him as to one having free will, and warns him that God will have respect unto that free will, without which any service of God, Who reads the hearts, must be worthless. Now this part of chap. xi., which I have cited, is part of the same context as the latter part of chap. viii., all having to do with Predestination and Election. It proves this, beyond all doubt, that the omission of the all-important words "sin" and "self" in the two lists, in verses 35, 38, and 39, is not accidental—not an oversight—but intentional on the part of St. Paul, or of the Spirit Who inspired him. But that place (xi. 20, 21, 22) is not alone in the writings of St. Paul in its teaching of humble-mindedness and constant fear of coming short of the Divine goodness; one may say it is but one of fifty, in which the danger of the tendencies of the evil self—of the yet indwelling old man—is recognized. What is to me a far stronger passage than this on the side of Christian security, is followed with the same wise and salutary caution. The Apostle writes to the Philippians: " Being confident of this very thing, that he who hath begun a good work in you, will perform it until the day of Jesus Christ " (i. 6); but in the next chapter the

Apostle sees it necessary to assure them that the working of God within them is a matter on no account to be trifled with: "Work out your own salvation with fear and trembling, for it is God that worketh in you, both to will and to do of his good pleasure" (ii. 12, 13). It is a fearful gift is this free will—this liberty—and the best Christians are often tempted to wish that they had it not, but it is apparently one of the terms of our existence as intelligent creatures fitted to serve God with a willing service. Godet has a very remarkable passage bearing upon the certainty of ultimate salvation, notwithstanding persecution and other incentives to fall away: "It will, perhaps, be asked, if a Christian has never been known to deny his faith in suffering and persecution? Yes, and it is not a mathematical certainty which the Apostle wishes to state here. It is a fact of the moral life which is in question, and in this life liberty has always its part to play, as it had from the first moment of faith. What Paul means is, that nothing will tear us from the arms of Christ against our will, and so long as we shall not refuse to abide in them ourselves." If the Calvinist refuses to accept anything short of final perseverance assigned to him at the first, independent of his own watchfulness and faithfulness, we can only remind him that he cannot in reason expect that Christ will deal with him more favourably than He did with His own Apostles, whose future acceptance He made conditional when He said to them: "If ye continue in my word then are ye my disciples indeed" (John viii. 31); and when He said to them, "As my Father hath loved me, so have I loved you; continue ye in my love. If ye keep my commandments ye shall abide in my love, even as I have kept my Father's commandments, and abide in his love" (John xv. 9, 10).

If any soul says: "I know perfectly that no persecution, or distress, or tribulation shall separate me from the love of Christ. I want something further." "Wait," the Apostle might answer, "in all probability you do not know it, or you would not speak so self-confidently. Your life, compared to that of the Christians for whose consolation I wrote what I have written in this Epistle, has been comparatively easy, painless, untried; human government, human law, human society, which have made your life so serene, put them in danger of death for the sake of Christ every day of their lives. If you had their experience, you might be thankful for their consolations."

CHAPTERS IX.-XI.

Though St. Paul in these chapters may be said to be discussing the doctrines of Predestination and Election, it is upon very different grounds to that on which he rested his arguments in the latter verses of the preceding chapter. There he had before him the consolation and good hope of the Roman Christians in all their trials and persecutions. If they loved God they were the called according to His purpose—foreknown, predestinated, called, justified, adopted to fulfil His gracious purposes in His Church. But now he has to face the fact that God in predestinating and calling a Church from among the Gentiles, was, apparently, changing His purposes; hitherto Israel, after the flesh, had been the election, as Christ Himself had said, "I am not sent but to the lost sheep of the house of Israel." But the exclusive privileges of Israel were to exist no longer. God was now widening the basis, so to speak, of His Election, so that the Gentiles, if they believed in and loved God, were as much the chosen of God and heirs of His promises as the Jews. Now this, in the Apostle's view of matters, required to be proved. But there was another, and a far more fearful fact intimately connected with the election of the Gentiles, and this was the casting away of the Jews. It was not that the Gentiles were elected into the Church along with the Jews, but that, if St. Paul's teaching was true, that the Gentiles were elected in Christ—then the Jews were forfeiting, or had already forfeited, their election as a nation. The mass of them had rejected Christ, so that if, in future, election was to be "in Christ," they were excluded from the ranks of the people of God. The mistake which the Jews made, was the natural but fatal one of supposing that God's election was absolute, and so irreversible, that it had no respect to character or will, or continuance in the favour of God—above all that it was independent of the acceptance or rejection of the Messiah, which Messiah was God's only Son—God manifest in the flesh, God blessed for ever. This was far worse than falling deeper and deeper into sin—for it was rejecting the remedy against sin, it was rejecting the offer of the Life of God to be imparted to them. It was rejecting the highest conceivable manifestation of the love of God.

Again, there was another matter to which St. Paul constantly refers, which is that God's election is not a mere matter of number —nor, in fact, of absolute majorities or minorities. The great majority might fall, but a minority, sometimes a small one, a remnant, might be sufficient for His purposes.

Again, it is very remarkable, and we shall have to revert to this again, that there is throughout the argument of these three chapters the (one might almost say, studious) avoidance of any reference to a future life, to any place in Heaven or Paradise, or in hell or punishment. It is impossible to suppose that if St. Paul's view respecting these high and inscrutable matters was what is commonly called Calvinistic, there should have been such an omission.

The above considerations the reader will find it necessary to carry along with him in the examination of the meaning of these chapters.

CHAP. IX.

a ch. i. 9. 2 Cor. i. 23. & xi. 31. & xii. 19. Gal. i. 20. Phil. i. 8. 1 Tim. ii. 7.

b ch. x. 1.

I ^a SAY the truth in Christ, I lie not, my conscience also bearing me witness in the Holy Ghost.

2 ^b That I have great heaviness and continual sorrow in my heart.

---

1. "I say the truth in Christ, I lie not, my conscience also bearing me witness," &c. Why should the Apostle begin with such strong asseverations respecting his love to his people? Because his adversaries were constantly accusing him of enmity to his c untrymen and disregard of their position among the nations. Thus, when they found him in the temple, they cried: "Men of Israel, help, this is the man that teacheth all men everywhere against the people and the law, and this place" (Acts xxi. 28).

"In Christ." This is more than "as a Christian." It is as if Ch ist—the truth—was the element in which the Apostle lived, and thought, and spoke.

2. "That I have great heaviness, and continual sorrow in my heart." What a world of conflicting emotions must there have been

CHAP. IX.]   ACCURSED FOR MY BRETHREN.   197

3 For ^c I could wish that myself were ‖ accursed from Christ for my brethren, my kinsmen according to the flesh:

4 ^d Who are Israelites; ^e to whom *pertaineth* the

^c Ex. xxxii. 32.
‖ Or, *separated.*
^d Deut. vii. 6.
^e Ex. iv. 22.
Deut. xiv. 1.
Jer. xxxi. 9.

in the breast of the Apostle—perpetually rejoicing in Christ, always being made by God to triumph in Him, thanking God always, and yet continually sorrowing for those out of Christ, particularly his own countrymen, to whom he held that Christ especially belonged.

3. " For I could wish that myself were accursed from Christ," &c. Thus Moses intercedes for Israel in language exactly similar. " Yet now, if thou wilt forgive their sins, and if not, blot me, I pray thee, out of thy book, which thou hast written." The words of St. Paul are by many considered too strong, even approaching to impiety, and so many attempts have been made to deprive them of their obvious meaning, but to no purpose. We are to remember that St. Paul does not say deliberately " I wish," or " I pray," but " I *could* wish—sometimes the thought of their rejection so overwhelms me that I could wish to be separated from Christ instead of them. If it be asked, does St. Paul offer himself to endure eternal condemnation on their account ? we answer, as we said at the commencement of this chapter, that eternal condemnation is not once mentioned throughout this argument, and we have no right to assume nothing short of it here.

" My brethren, my kinsmen according to the flesh." The deepest and most fervent Christianity does not, or is not intended, to destroy the ties of natural affection. They are nothing to the bands which unite us to Christ, but where they can be cherished without disloyalty to Christ they must be.

4. " Who are Israelites ; to whom pertaineth the adoption, and the glory." The word Israelite is compared with Jew—an honourable name. Thus our Lord says of Nathanael, " Behold an Israelite indeed." St. Paul then most appropriately puts it as the first designation of those whose privileges as the people of God he was about to recount. It was also the name of election. " Israel mine elect " (Isaiah xlv. 4).

" To whom pertaineth the adoption." Thus God sent to Pharaoh through Moses, " Israel is my son, my first-born," (Exod. iv. 22 and Jerem. xxxi. 9), " I am a father to Israel," and Isaiah i. 2, " I

adoption, and ᶠthe glory, and ᵍthe ‖ covenants, and ʰthe giving of the law, and ⁱthe service *of God*, and ᵏthe promises;

---

have nourished and brought up children." How is it then that the true sonship seems to be restricted to those who believe in Christ? Perhaps the key may be found in Gal. iii. 23, to iv. 5. "The Old Testament shows us man at the beginning of his sonship, but still under the servile tutorship of the Law—the New Testament on the completeness of his sonship as one of full age."—Philippi.

"And the glory." This may mean the honour which God put upon them by making them His people—His peculiar people—or it may refer to the visible glory which was the symbol of the presence of God Himself in their midst. This glory appeared to Moses, and communicated itself, in a measure, to him, so that when he came down from the mount his face shone. It appeared also to Isaiah (vi.), and Ezekiel (i.), and was seen by the High Priest over the ark when, on the great day of atonement, he went within the veil. It was such a pledge of the peculiar presence of God that He was called the God that dwelleth between the cherubims (Exod. xxv. 20-22). The glory was not the mere shining of a bright light, but the peculiar presence of God, of which it was the pledge.

"And the covenants." Why is it said "the covenants," in the plural? There was a continual renewal of the original covenant with Abraham (Gen. xv. 18) in different forms, as when God gave him circumcision (xvii. 13, 14), and renewed His covenant with the whole house of Israel in blood (Exod. xxiv. 1-8). And may it not be because the New Covenant promised in the times of the Messiah, belonged first to the house of Israel and of Judah also? (Jerem. xxxi. 31-34).

"And the giving of the law." The Apostle here, no doubt, alludes not only to the contents of the law, but to the manner in which God gave it. Never was the Supreme Being manifested with such outward signs of pomp, and terror, and majesty. "Did ever people hear the voice of God speaking out of the midst of the fire, as thou hast heard, and live?" (Deut. iv. 33).

"And the service of God." It was an especial honour that God put upon them that He prescribed their service in the tabernacle

CHAP. IX.] CHRIST, WHO IS OVER ALL. 199

5 ¹Whose *are* the fathers, and ᵐ of whom as concerning the flesh Christ *came*, ⁿ who is over all, God blessed for ever. Amen.

¹ Deut. x. 15.
ch. xi. 28.
ᵐ Luke iii. 23.
ch. i. 3.
ⁿ Jer. xxiii. 6.
John i. 1.
Acts xx. 28.
Heb. i. 8.
1 John v. 20.

5. "Christ came, who is over all, God blessed for ever." The order of words should rather be, "Christ came, who is God over all, blessed for ever." Ὁ ὢν ἐπὶ πάντων Θεὸς being a similar phrase to τὴν τοῦ Θεοῦ δικαιοσύνην, and ἡ ἐκ πίστεως δικαιοσύνη of the next chapter, verses 3 and 6.

The rendering, "God be blessed for ever," severing the connection of the blessing from Christ, is a distinctly Socinian gloss, defensible, as I have shown below, on Socinian grounds only.

---

and temple even to its minutest particulars. He showed Moses the pattern of the tabernacle, and He raised up men specially endowed by His Spirit with wisdom to carry out His directions (Exod. xxxv. 30). He ordained the ministers and the ministry, the sacrifices, the altar, the very vessels of Divine service.

"And the promises." Especially the promises of the Messiah, which almost all belonged to the Jew, as in the 2nd Psalm, "I have set my king upon my holy hill of Sion." The 110th, "The Lord shall send the rod of thy power out of Sion." Isaiah ix., "Unto us a child is born ... of the increase of his government and peace there shall be no end, upon the throne of David," and Jerem. xxiii., "I will raise unto David a righteous branch.... In his days Judah shall be saved and Israel shall dwell safely," &c.

"Whose are the fathers." Abraham, Isaac, Jacob, and the fathers of the twelve tribes, and Joseph and Benjamin. Even the holy men of old whose descent was not reckoned from Abraham, such as Melchizedec and Job, seem to belong to the chosen people rather than to those without the pale.

"And of whom as concerning the flesh, Christ came, who is over all, God blessed for ever." The rendering of our Authorized is in strict accordance with the original, and is required by the sense of the passage. It is the natural translation, and so is rendered by the Fathers, whose vernacular was Greek. Chrysostom, "After taking all these things into consideration, and reflecting how earnest God, along with His Son, had been for their salvation, he lifts up his voice aloud, and says, Who is blessed for ever, Amen. So himself offering thanksgiving for all men unto the only begotten Son of God." Also Athanasius, "This too, in confutation of the Jews hath Paul written in his Epistle to the Romans ('Of whom as concerning the flesh, Christ, Who is over all, God blessed for ever.')"—"Discourses against the Arians" (Disc. i. ch. ii. sec. 2). And Theodoret, "And indeed it was sufficient to declare the Divinity of the Lord Christ, that he had added 'according to the flesh.' But as in the exordium when he had said, 'made of the seed of David according to the flesh,' he subjoined, 'Who was predestinated to be the Son of God with power,' so here when he had said 'according to the flesh,' he added, 'Who is over all God blessed for ever,' both showing the difference of nature, and teaching that he very rightly lamented that whilst He Who was God over all, had, according to the flesh, proceeded from amongst them, they had fallen from such nobility and were estranged from that relationship."

The Vulgate translation also, which was made when Greek was a living language, gives, "Christ, according to the flesh, Who is over all, God blessed for ever (Christus secundum carnem, qui est super omnia Deus benedictus in sæcula. Amen.") And the Syriac, " Christ, according to the flesh, Who is God above all. To Whom are praises and blessings for ever and ever."

The sense of the whole passage also absolutely requires the usually received translation. For St. Paul is recounting the privileges of the Jews, the adoption, the glory, the giving of the law. Amongst these, or, rather, as the last and crowning one, exceeding all, he reckons the Messiah as born of the nation, and he uses the term "according to the flesh." This " according to the flesh " requires, as Theodoret has shown, a something according to the Spirit, or according to the Divine Nature, to correspond to it, for their relationship to the Messiah was no particular honour if He was only " as one of the prophets," and so this " according to the flesh " requires to complete the sense, something like " according to His higher Nature, which Nature is that of ' God over all blessed for ever.'"

The objections to the ancient rendering are dogmatic on the side of Socinianism. It is said, "Had St. Paul ever spoken of Christ as God, he would many times have spoken of Him as such, not once only, and that by accident" (Jowett). Now St. Paul in so many words speaks of Christ as God twice, once here, and once in Titus ii. 13 : " Looking for that blessed hope, and the glorious appearing of the great God and Saviour of us, Jesus Christ," and this is exactly the number of times that He is directly named God in St. John's

NOT ALL ISRAEL.

6 °Not as though the word of God hath taken none effect. For ᵖthey *are* not all Israel, which are of Israel:

° Num. xxiii. 19. ch. iii. 3.
ᵖ John viii. 39. ch. ii. 28, 29. & iv. 12, 16. Gal. vi. 16.

Gospel, John i. 1, xx. 28, and yet St. John's Gospel has in all ages of the Church been considered to have been written for the sake of setting forth the highest conceivable view of the Person of Christ, and of His relations to His Father and to the Universe. St. John's Revelation of the Divine glory of Christ and St. Paul's are identical. Both call Him by the name "God." Both call Him Lord, in the highest Divine sense of the word as the reproduction of the Old Testament word Lord. Both call Him the own Son (ἴδιος) of God, John v. 18, Rom. viii. 3. Both alike ascribe to Christ the three highest works of God—Creation, John i. 3, Coloss. i. 16 ; Salvation, John iv. 42, God our Saviour, Christ our Saviour, Titus i. 3, 4; iii. 4, 6; Universal Judgment, John v. 22, 23; Rom. ii. 3, 16; 2 Cor. v. 10.

Again, what in St. John's Gospel is stronger on the side of the Divinity of Christ than "Who being in the form of God thought it not robbery (or a thing to be tenaciously grasped or held fast), the being equal with God" (Phil. ii. 6), or, "In him dwelleth all the fulness of the Godhead bodily " (Coloss. ii. 9)?

So that what St. Paul has here written, if we understand it as giving Divine glory to Christ, is in perfect accordance with all the rest of his Epistles.[1]

6. "Not as though the word of God hath taken none effect. For they are not," &c. "I have said that I lament with great heaviness and continual sorrow, the defection of a nation on whom God has bestowed such abundant honour. But because I thus lament, and at times would have wished myself accursed if I could not save them, you are not to suppose that I think that the purpose of God has failed. You mistake the purpose of God altogether if you think that it is His unalterable decree that all the fleshly seed of Abraham, no matter what their conduct, should be His instruments for carrying out His purpose."

"For they are not all Israel, which are of Israel." There is a

---

[1] The reader will find at the end of this volume an Excursus respecting the Christology of St. Paul.

7 �q Neither, because they are the seed of Abraham, *are* they all children: but, In ʳ Isaac shall thy seed be called.

q Gal. iv. 23.
r Gen. xxi. 12.
Heb. xi. 18.

8 That is, They which are the children of the flesh, these

---

spiritual Israel, a true Israel of God which alone answers to the high purposes of God, and is the only Israel worthy of the name. And there are intimations of this election within an election all through the history of the Old Testament, and so St. Paul says:—

"Neither, because they are the seed of Abraham, are they all children," &c. When God made promises to Abraham, they were to his seed; but God narrowed this to his seed by Sarah, for when Sarah saw that the Lord had restrained her from bearing, and took her own way of impatience and want of faith, God did not recognize the issue as the true seed to whom He had made the promise, but deferred for some years the fulfilment of His word, which, in some way not revealed to us, depended upon the faith of Sarah as well as on that of Abraham (Hebrews xi. 11). So that at the very outset certain spiritual, or quasi-spiritual, considerations came in, which shut out half of Abraham's seed from the election.

"In Isaac shall thy seed be called." That is, thy true seed shall be accounted to be that of Isaac, not of Ishmael. It may be well to direct attention here to the fact that this election of the seed of Isaac and rejection of that of Ishmael had nothing whatsoever to do with the eternal salvation of their descendants, for if God had intended to shut out Ishmael from His eternal mercies, would He have said, " Behold, I have blessed him, and will make him fruitful," &c. And also " of the son of the bondwoman, will I make a nation, because he is thy seed," Gen. xxi. 13. And a little further, " God hath heard the voice of the lad," and verse 20, " God was with the lad."

To settle it firmly in our minds that non-election on God's part is not for a moment to be held necessarily to imply eternal condemnation, is the first step to enable us to take a calm and dispassionate view of the following verses.

8. "That is, They which are the children of the flesh, these are not the children of God," &c. "That is." It is signified, or typified, or involved, in this rejection of Ishmael and acceptance of

CHAP. IX.] SARAH SHALL HAVE A SON. 203

are not the children of God: but *the children of the promise are counted for the seed. *Gal. iv. 28.

9 For this *is* the word of promise, †At this time will I come, and Sarah shall have a son.   †Gen. xviii. 10, 14.

10 And not only *this;* but when ᵘRebecca also had conceived by one, *even* by our father Isaac;   ᵘGen. xxv. 21.

Isaac, that fleshly descent or natural generation does not make men, whether Jews or Gentiles, children of God, but the children of God are the children of the promise.

9. "For this is the word of promise, At this time will I come, and Sarah," &c. We must very carefully consider the import of this verse. At first sight it seems to undo what the Apostle had just said, that the children of the flesh are not the children of God; for assuredly Isaac as much as Ishmael was begotten by fleshly generation; but the meaning seems to be somewhat of this sort. Abraham, in taking Hagar to have seed by her, had no promise of God for what he did. It was altogether a very fleshly suggestion, and, in its religious aspect, a very doubtful one; whereas, in the case of Isaac, we are expressly told that Sarah's faith came in, as we read, "Through faith also Sarah herself received strength to conceive seed, and was delivered of a child when she was past age, because she judged him faithful who had promised." (Heb. xi. 11.)

"For this is the word of promise." This should rather be translated, "For of promise," as distinguished from mere natural sequence, "is this word."

"At this time will I come [*i.e.*, with miraculous power to annul the barrenness of Sarah], and Sarah shall have a son."

10. "And not only this; but when Rebecca also had conceived by one, even," &c. He now proceeds to take a still more remarkable case, illustrating the perfect freedom of God's election. When Ishmael was rejected, and Isaac elected to be the depositary of the promise, it might be said that this was natural, for Ishmael was, in a sense, illegitimate, being born of a concubine, and Isaac legitimate, being the child of the lawful wife; but, in the case of the twin children of Isaac and Rebecca, such a thing could not be said. When they were in the womb it was pronounced that the elder should serve the younger, and so the election could not have

11 (For *the children* being not yet born, neither having done any good or evil, that the purpose of God according to election might stand, not of works, but of ˣhim that calleth;)

12 It was said unto her, ʸThe ‖ elder shall serve the ‖ younger.

13 As it is written, ᶻJacob have I loved, but Esau have I hated.

ˣ ch. iv. 17. & viii. 28.
ʸ Gen. xxv. 23.
‖ Or, *greater*.
‖ Or, *lesser*.
ᶻ Mal. i. 2, 3. See Deut. xxi. 15. Prov. xiii. 24. Matt. x. 37. Luke xiv. 26. John xii. 25.

---

been because either had fulfilled the demands of the law, or done any works whatsoever. In other words, neither had any claim upon God, and so the case of these two brothers, very early in the sacred history, set aside, and effectually one would think, any such claims as the Jews were continually putting forward, grounded on the supposed fulfilment of the law. It was the strongest precedent conceivable for God to hold Himself unfettered in the matter of the choice of the persons who would serve His purposes.

12. "It was said unto her, The elder shall serve the younger." Here again it is asserted as plainly as possible that what was in the contemplation of the Apostle was not eternal reward or punishment, but fitness to serve the purposes of God.

13. "As it is written, Jacob have I loved, but Esau have I hated." This is taken from the prophet Malachi, and, by turning to the passage, we shall see in what way God's hatred showed itself: "Wherein hast thou loved us? Was not Esau Jacob's brother, saith the Lord: yet I loved Jacob. And I hated Esau and laid his mountains and his heritage waste for the dragons of the wilderness. Whereas Edom saith, We are impoverished, but we will return and build the waste places. Thus saith the Lord of hosts, they shall build, but I will throw down; and they shall call them, The border of wickedness, and, The people against whom the Lord hath indignation for ever." We must assume, then, that the perpetual indignation was because of the great and continued wickedness.

And now let us look more closely into this matter of the election of Jacob and the reprobation of Esau. Why this difference made between two brothers in the womb—the difference affecting the races which sprang from them, until nearly the time of Christ? There must have been a reason, for God cannot act without reason, and this reason must have been one in God's foreknowledge, for He would not act on the mere impulse of the moment, and it must have been one connected with the character of Esau and of his descendants, and Jacob and his descendants, for, assuming the truth of the Revelation of God's character in the Scriptures, no other reason can be imagined. Different reasons have been assigned. Though neither child had done, or could have done, good works, yet Philippi supposes that " the Divine provision, on which election rests, relates not to any work whatever, as being able to establish some merit in favour of the elect, but to his faith, which cannot (?) be a merit, since faith consists precisely in renouncing all merit [In the Scripture it is described as being not the renunciation of merit, but the evidence of things not seen] in the humble acceptance of the free gift. Faith foreseen is therefore a wholly different thing from works foreseen."

Alford pronounces this assigning of foreseen faith to be the Pelagianism of the Romanists, who, by making our faith as foreseen by God the cause of our election, affirm it to be ἐξ ἔργων. But whatever was the secret and mysterious cause in the mind of God, was His choice vindicated by the course of events? Unquestionably it was: for what does the history teach us? In the first place we find in Esau the most utter contempt for the religion of the family, for we read that when he was forty years old he took to wife two Hittites, and it is significantly said that these were a grief of mind to Isaac and Rebecca. Now why this grief? No doubt because all sorts of profanities, of idolatrous rites—very probably of filthy orgies—were going on in the tents of the only family upon earth which belonged to the true God. Then comes the selling of his birthright. He came, faint from hunting, to the tents of his rich and prosperous father. He would not wait two minutes till some slave ran for some refreshment. What good was this ridiculous birthright? He did not believe in it in the least. It was not worth a basin of broth, and so, in boastful and profane contempt, he sold it. Then, so little had Esau impressed any traditions of reverence for Jehovah amongst the people which sprung from him, that Edom refused to allow Israel to pass through his borders on their way to Canaan, or even to drink of the wells on the roadside. The Edomites are always found among the enemies

14 What shall we say then? *Is there* unrighteousness with God? God forbid.

^a Deut. xxxii. 4. 2 Chron. xix. 7. Job viii. 3. & xxxiv. 10. Ps. xcii. 15.

---

of Israel, they seem to have excelled the rest of the heathen in bitter hatred to Jerusalem itself (Psalm lxxxiii. 6 ; cxxxvii. 7; Amos i. 11); and this notwithstanding that in the very law itself there was a command to the Israelites to deal friendly with them (Deut. xxiii. 7), which we have no reason to believe was not acted upon. It is quite clear that if it was the principal design of God in choosing the Israelites, to prepare a place among them for the Messiah, and in a measure to prepare the Gentiles for receiving the knowledge of Him through the dispersion, which kept alive in every city of the heathen a nucleus of true worshippers, some of whom received and acted upon the Apostolic Gospel, such a design could not have been fulfilled by the Edomites; and whereas Israel, notwithstanding all its declensions, gave birth to a long series of illustrious heroes and prophets, the Edomites produced only Doeg and the Herods: so that the wisdom of God, in passing over the eldest brother, is amply vindicated by the course of events.

Their conduct, with reference to the people of God, stands in remarkable contrast with that of the Kenites, and we may say also with that of Tyre and Egypt.

14. "What shall we say then? Is there unrighteousness with God? God forbid." This, following upon what has gone before about Jacob and Esau, means, Was God unrighteous in preferring Jacob to Esau as the depositary of the Messianic promise? And he answers emphatically, "Let not such a thing be imagined," giving as a reason the passage, "For he saith to Moses, I will have mercy upon whom I will have mercy," &c.

This quotation is taken from Exod. xxxiii. 19. The whole verse reads, "I will make all my goodness pass before thee, and I will proclaim the name of the Lord before thee, and will be gracious to whom I will be gracious, and will shew mercy on whom I will shew mercy." It is plain, I think, that St. Paul quotes the passage, not with regard to its context, but as expressing a great general truth, that God will allow nothing to prevent His mercy reaching those whom He, in His wisdom, sees to be in a fit state to receive it. It may be asked why, seeing that God executes judgment as well as mercy, a text is chosen which exhibits only one side of His

CHAP. IX.] I WILL HAVE MERCY. 207

15 For he saith to Moses, ^b I will have mercy on   ^{b Ex. xxxiii.}_{19.}

dealings, and the answer is, that the whole controversy arose out of the exclusiveness of the Jews, who, as far as in them lay, would not allow God to have mercy on the Gentiles. This was, in fact, the crown of their wickedness, as the Apostle writes, " They please not God, and are contrary to all men : Forbidding us to speak to the Gentiles that they might be saved, to fill up their sins alway: for the wrath is come upon them to the uttermost" (1 Thess. ii. 16).

And now with respect to the significance of this verse. A Being Who is infinite in all His attributes, Who has not only absolute power, but absolute wisdom, absolute goodness, absolute foreknowledge, claims to do what He pleases in the matter of showing mercy and if of showing mercy, of course of withholding mercy.

Now on what ground does God claim this, because in vast numbers of cases He tells us the motives which induced Him to adopt such or such a line of conduct, and He has given to us inquiring, intelligent spirits, which compel us, though it may be secretly, to inquire into the reason even for *His* actions ?

Two grounds have been assigned. The one I shall give in the words of Calvin, who states the reason as clearly, as directly, and as dogmatically as it can well be: " It may, indeed, appear a frigid defence that God is not unjust, because He is merciful to whom He pleases ; but as God regards His authority alone as abundantly sufficient, so that He needs the defence of none, Paul thought it enough to appoint Him the vindicator of His own right. Now Paul brings forward here the answer which Moses received from the Lord when he prayed for the salvation of the whole people,[1] ' I will shew mercy,' was God's answer, ' on whom I will shew mercy, and I will have compassion upon whom I will have com-

---

[1] This is a falsehood, and Calvin must have known it to be so when he wrote it. There is no word in Exodus xxxiii. of Moses praying for the salvation of all Israel. God gave the answer to the prayer of Moses, " I beseech thee shew me thy glory ; " and God had (in the four previous verses) as good as declared the acceptance of the whole people as his people. Moses says, verse 15 :—"If thy presence go not with me, carry us not up hence. For wherein shall it be known here that I and thy people have found grace in thy sight? Is it not in that thou goest with us? so shall we be separated, I and thy people, from all the people that are upon the face of the earth. And the Lord said unto Moses, I will do this thing also that thou hast spoken," &c. So that it is absolutely false to assign the meaning which Calvin gives.

whom I will have mercy, and I will have compassion on whom I will have compassion.

---

passion.' By this oracle the Lord declared that He is a debtor to none of mankind, and that whatever He gives is a gratuitous benefit, and then that His kindness is free, so that He can confer it on whom He pleases; and lastly, that no cause higher than His own Will can be thought of why He does good and shows favour to some men, but not to all. The words, indeed, mean as much as though He said: 'From him to whom I have once purposed to show mercy I will never take it away, and with perpetual kindness I will follow him to whom I have determined to be kind.' And thus He assigns the highest reason for imparting grace, even His own voluntary purpose, and also intimates that He has designed His mercy peculiarly for some, for it is a way of speaking which excludes outward causes, as when we claim to ourselves the free power of acting, we say, 'I will do what I mean to do.'"

This passage is remarkable, if for nothing else, for its thoroughness. I will draw attention to one sentence. "No cause higher than His own will can be thought of, why He does good, and shews favour to some men and not to all." But this is directly contrary to the whole of the Scriptures of God—to what Moses, David, Isaiah, Jeremiah, Ezekiel, have written. It is directly contrary to every word of our Lord's teaching. If there be one passage of God's Word to which it is more in opposition than another, it is to the words of the Apostle in this very Epistle, when he writes, "To them who by patient continuance in well-doing seek for glory, honour, and immortality, God will render eternal life." The fallacy in the whole passage is, that Calvin contends not for the Will of God, that is, for a most righteous, most merciful, most wise Will of a most benevolent Creator, but (if the words may be written without sin) for His wilfulness—in fact, that He has a right to deal with spirits into whom He has infused a sense of justice, however that sense of justice may be at times obscured, in a spirit of mere caprice, and that even when it involves their eternal misery through ages of ages.

There must be a way of understanding this declaration of God more in consonance with all His other declarations, and it is not far to seek, for it naturally suggests itself. It is " I am a righteous judge, and My mercy is over all My works; as such I will deal

CHAP. IX.] OF GOD THAT SHEWETH MERCY. 209

16 So then *it is* not of him that willeth, nor of him that runneth, but of God that sheweth mercy.

17 For ^c the Scripture saith unto Pharaoh, ^{c See Gal. iii. 8, 22.}

righteously and mercifully. I will have mercy upon whom I will have mercy, because no one except Myself knows who needs mercy, and the sort of mercy he needs; no one but Myself knows who needs discipline, and the kind of discipline he needs; no one but Myself knows who have so rebelled against My Spirit, that in mercy to themselves I must withdraw Him, lest they add to their condemnation by further resistance. I will have mercy upon whom I will have mercy; that is, I do not at present reveal to you the reasons why I deal in mercy with one and in severity with another; but a time will come when you shall know those reasons, for I have put within you a spirit to which I have given the power of reflecting on My dealings, and even of judging respecting them, whether they are in accordance with what I have told you respecting Myself.

So then it comes to this: when Calvin writes, " No higher cause than His own Will can be thought of," we answer, No. Having regard to the way in which you have put the matter, a much higher cause can be thought of, and that is not the mere will, but the will which is the expression of God's love, justice, mercy, wisdom—in fact, of all the moral attributes of God—which in this passage Calvin, for reasons best known to himself, has kept altogether out of sight.

16. " So then it is not of him that willeth, nor of him that runneth," &c. This place has been taken to refer to the will of Isaac that Esau, the eldest, should receive the blessing, and that Jacob and Esau both hasted to get the savoury meat, but that the issue was that which God had fore-ordained; but it contains an axiom so universal, that it has but one exception. The axiom is that expressed in the terse words of the Book of Proverbs, " There are many devices in a man's heart, but the counsel of the Lord, that shall stand" (xix. 21). There is, however, one exception—an amazing one. It *is* " of him that willeth " if he earnestly wills the salvation of his soul, for then his will meets and coalesces with the Will of Him Who wills all men to be saved. It is of him that runneth if he " so runs that he may obtain."

17. " For the Scripture saith unto Pharaoh, Even for this purpose have I raised," &c. God's dealings with Pharaoh, though they

P

> [d] Even for this same purpose have I raised thee up, that I might shew my power in thee, and that my name might be declared throughout all the earth.

[d] Exod. ix. 16.

17. "Have I raised thee up." This does not mean "brought thee into existence," for then an altogether different phrase would have been used; but "raised thee to thy present high place."

never can be wholly divested of deep mystery, will be rendered much plainer and more entirely consonant with His justice, if we go sufficiently far back in the history. The nation of Egypt had been saved from destruction by an Israelite, Joseph, who, by a course of circumstances in which the finger of God is traceable at every point, was raised to the second place in the kingdom, and had all the affairs of Egypt placed in his hand. Through his counsels the food of the plenteous years was not wasted, as it would have been if he had not been at the head of affairs, but laid up in store for the years of famine. Now the Egyptians repaid this kindness with the blackest ingratitude; they enslaved the nation of their benefactor, murdered their children, and ground them down with oppression and cruelty. But God had foreseen all this, and foretold both the oppression of the Israelites and the manner of their deliverance and the punishment of the Egyptians. "That nation whom they shall serve will I judge, and afterward shall they come out with great substance" (Gen. xv. 14).

The judgment of God on the Egyptians consisted in the plagues, whereby the nation of Egypt, as it deserved, was well-nigh destroyed. And through the fame of these plagues, and the subsequent safe passage of the Israelites through the Red Sea, and the destruction of the Egyptians therein, a warning was given to the guilty races of Canaan, that they should flee from the land which God had given to another people; the memory of which, and its significance, was fresh forty years after, as we learn from the account of Rahab in the Book of Joshua (ii. 10).

Now, in order that the Egyptians might suffer the righteous retribution due to their wicked treatment of Israel, God did not allow His severe judgments to have that effect upon Pharaoh which they were, in the ordinary course of events, calculated to produce. The first two or three plagues would naturally have been sufficient; but God supernaturally upheld him in his resistance to the effect of the signs and wonders which came to pass at the word of

18 Therefore hath he mercy on whom he will *have mercy*, and whom he will he hardeneth.

God's servant, and ceased at his word. This was the *hardening of Pharaoh's heart*. It was more than a natural hardening, more than Pharaoh hardening his own heart. It was an action of God, to uphold him in resistance, so that he was not able to turn back, but must go on in rebellion till the Egyptians had suffered what they deserved, and all the neighbouring kingdoms, Amalekites, Edomites, Moabites, Canaanites, had heard the report of what God was doing on behalf of the seed of Israel, and ought to have set their own houses in order accordingly.

One thing we must be quite sure about, that God would not hold Pharaoh responsible in the spiritual world for that part of his hardening which came through the external action of God, over and above what was due to the action of his own evil spirit on himself. If Pharaoh was reprobate in the matter of future judgment, that reprobation was fully consummated long before his first interview with Moses. Not a word is said throughout the narrative respecting future reward or punishment, or turning to God, or a future Messiah, and such things—the one sole word is, "Let My people go, that they may serve Me," and we have not the smallest right to assume any other.

18. "Therefore hath he mercy on whom he will have mercy, and whom," &c. He had mercy upon Isaac, upon Jacob, upon the twelve sons of Jacob, so that, notwithstanding their provocations —notwithstanding their treatment of their father and Joseph —notwithstanding the profligacy of Judah, and Reuben, and the treachery of Simeon and Levi in the matter of the Shechemites, the promise of the Messiah, and the wondrous future which led to its accomplishment, was theirs.

And He hardened not only Pharaoh, but his servants and his people, for Pharaoh was the representative of his people. They, of course, would not willingly part with several hundred thousand slaves. Their labour was an immense public profit, and in all probability a great private advantage to a great part of the Egyptians. He hardened them so that they were judged for their oppression, and their captives went out with much substance—some very slight repayment for their centuries of bondage.

^a 2 Chron. xx. 6. Job ix. 12. & xxiii. 13. Dan. iv. 35.

19 Thou wilt say then unto me, Why doth he yet find fault? For ^e who hath resisted his will?

19, 20, 21. "Thou wilt say then unto me, Why doth he yet find fault? . . . one vessel unto honour, and another unto dishonour?"

Before entering upon the closer exposition of these verses, it may be well to examine carefully the passages in which this figure of the potter and the clay is used in the sacred writings. At first sight it seems to preclude all action whatsoever, except that of Almighty God. The sinner, or the nation, or the Church, must, we should suppose, be altogether passive, for no will, no action in the way of either obedience or resistance can be supposed to reside in the clay. If it refers to the individual soul, that soul must be moulded totally independently of its own will in the matter of its choice or its after-treatment. There is a basin or vessel of soft clay carefully prepared, so as to be of the same consistence throughout. Into this the potter thrusts his hands, and draws out a portion corresponding to the size of the vessel he intends to make, which vessel, as to its use and size, he must have determined upon beforehand.

So that taking the simple figure by itself, it seems to preclude all power of choice, all power of influencing the Being represented by the potter—above all, all power of remonstrance. For man to remonstrate with God is not so much wickedness as absurdity—as absurd as if the clay under the potter's hands were to remonstrate with him.

Now there are six places in the Scripture—four in the Old Testament, two in the New—in which this figure is used, and in all these places free-will, *i.e.*, the power on the part of the clay to choose for itself whether it will submit to the hand of the potter to be made by him what he is pleased to make it, or resist his action, is very distinctly asserted or implied.

The first of these places is Jeremiah xviii. 1-10. This is by far the most important, as it is the only one in which the potter is supposed to make different vessels of the same lump. I will give it in full. It is certainly the one which the Apostle had principally, if not entirely, in his mind: "The word which came to Jeremiah from the Lord, saying, Arise, and go down to the potter's house, and there I will cause thee to hear my words. Then I went

CHAP. IX.] WHO HATH RESISTED HIS WILL? 213

down to the potter's house, and, behold, he wrought a work on the wheels. And the vessel that he made of clay was marred in the hand of the potter: so he made it again another vessel, as seemed good to the potter to make it. Then the word of the Lord came to me, saying, O house of Israel, cannot I do with you as this potter? saith the Lord. Behold, as the clay is in the potter's hand, so are ye in mine hand, O house of Israel. At what instant I shall speak concerning a nation, and concerning a kingdom, to pluck up, and to pull down, and to destroy it; if that nation, against whom I have pronounced, turn from their evil, I will repent of the evil that I thought to do unto them. And at what instant I shall speak concerning a nation, and concerning a kingdom, to build, and to plant it; if it do evil in my sight, that it obey not my voice, then I will repent of the good, wherewith I said I would benefit them."

So that in the prophecy from which St. Paul takes this figure of the potter dealing with the clay, not only is free-will recognized, but the whole action of the potter, so far as it is appealed to to teach human beings, is made to depend upon the will of the clay. "If that nation, against whom I have pronounced, turn from their evil, I will repent of the evil ... At what instant I shall speak concerning a nation ... to build and to plant. If it do evil ... I will repent of the good," &c. The place, then, in Jeremiah from which the Apostle takes his illustration, bears the strongest testimony imaginable to the fact that, in all His dealings, God has respect to the exercise of free-will on the part of His creatures.

The second place in which the potter and the clay are referred to is very obscure, and the translation difficult. It is in Isaiah xxix. 15, 16: "Woe unto them that seek deep to hide their counsel from the Lord, and their works are in the dark, and they say, Who seeth us? and who knoweth us? Surely your turning of things upside down shall be esteemed as the potter's clay: for shall the work say of him that made it, He made me not? or shall the thing framed say of him that framed it, He had no understanding?" Whatever be the meaning of this verse, it presupposes the energetic free-will of the clay. Matthew Pool, a Calvinist commentator, paraphrases it thus: "Your turning of things upside down; all your subtle devices, by which you turn yourselves into all shapes and turn your thoughts hither and thither, and pervert the order which God has appointed, is no more to me than the clay is to the potter, who can not only discern it thoroughly, but alter and dispose it as he seeth fit; and no less absurd and ridiculous is your conceit, that I your Maker and supreme Governor cannot discover and control all your artifices at my pleasure."

The third place, Isaiah xlv. 9, equally demands the free-will of the clay: "Woe unto him that striveth with his Maker! Let the potsherd strive with the potsherds of the earth. Shall the clay say to him that fashioneth it, What makest thou? or thy work, He hath no hands." Calvin certainly interprets it on the principles of free-will. His words are: "A more simple view appears to me to be to understand that the prophet restrains the complaints of men who in adversity murmur and strive with God. This was a seasonable warning that the Jews, by patiently and calmly bearing the cross, might receive the consolation which was offered to them, for whenever God holds us in suspense the flesh prompts us to grumble, 'Why does he not do more quickly what He intends to do? of what benefit is it to Him to torture us by His delay?' The prophet, therefore, in order to chastize this insolence, says, 'Does the potsherd dispute with the potter? Do sons debate with their fathers? Has not God a right to treat us as He thinks fit? What remains but that we should bear patiently the punishments which He inflicts on us.'"[1]

The fourth place is yet more remarkable, for in it the clay, so far from being impassive, is supposed to pray—to confess God and to earnestly deprecate His wrath (Isaiah lxiv. 8.) "But now, O Lord, thou art our father; we are the clay, and thou our potter; and we all are the work of thy hand. Be not wroth very sore, O Lord, neither remember iniquity for ever: behold, see, we beseech thee, we are all thy people."

The fifth place is still more expressive of the free-will of the clay. It is in St. Paul's own writings—in his second Epistle to Timothy (ii. 20, 21). "In a great house there are not only vessels of gold and of silver, but also of wood and of earth; and some to honour and some to dishonour. If a man therefore purge himself from these, he shall be a vessel unto honour, sanctified, and meet for the master's use, and prepared unto every good work." This is the most re-

---

[1] Thomas Erskine, of Linlathen, explains the place with its context differently. He supposes that it alludes to the rebellious thoughts of the Jews in that their deliverance came through the heathen Cyrus, and not through some divinely-commissioned leader of their own nation.

CHAP. IX.] WHY HAST THOU MADE ME THUS? 215

20 Nay but, O man, who art thou that ‖ repliest against God? ᶠ Shall the thing formed say to him that formed *it*, Why hast thou made me thus?

‖ Or, *answerest again*, or, *disputest with God?* Job xxxiii. 13.
f Is. xxix. 16. & xlv. 9, & lxiv. 8.

markable of all the places we have examined, for instead of regarding the nature and use and destiny of the potter's vessels as fixed from the first, he actually lays it down that a vessel may change itself. By purging himself from false doctrine (that of Hymenæus and Philetus) and *a fortiori* from bad practices, a man from being a vessel of dishonour may become a vessel of honour. The assertion of free-will can scarcely go further.

The sixth and last place is the one in this chapter where, after speaking of the potter having power over the clay to make one vessel to honour and another to dishonour, he speaks of God "enduring with much long-suffering the vessels of wrath fitted to destruction." Now supposing that these vessels were souls whom God had predestinated to destruction in hell, and that for His glory, and had, as certainly as the potter moulds his clay, fitted them for such destruction, could it possibly be said that "He endured them with much long suffering," seeing that by continuing as they were they fulfilled His purpose in making them to dishonour by infusing sin into them? If He endured them with much long-suffering, it must have been because it was in their power to repent and turn, and they would not, according to the Lord's remonstrance: "Ye will not come unto me that ye might have life."

From this examination of the use of this figure in every place in which it occurs, a very remarkable lesson is taught us, viz., that when free-will is not only not asserted, but seems not so much as implied—nay, when it appears contrary to the analogy of the figure employed (for the action of the potter on the clay seems to exclude free-will, or, indeed, anything except the mere power of the potter) —yet, notwithstanding this, free-will may be implied, and not only implied but may regulate the whole action of the Divine Being, Whose absolute Omnipotence in dealing with us is typified by the action of the potter.

We now proceed to the examination of the passage clause by clause.

19. "Thou wilt say then unto me, Why doth he yet find fault, for who," &c. Who is the objector here? It is assuredly not an

21 Hath not the ^g potter power over the clay, of the same lump to make ^h one vessel unto honour, and another unto dishonour?

<small>g Pro. xvi. 4. Jer. xviii. 6.
h 2 Tim. ii. 20.</small>

objector who takes similar ground to a modern anti-predestinarian, or anti-Calvinist, who has been shocked beyond measure at some enunciation of the "horribile decretum," and asks how can such a representation of God's dealings with souls be consistent with the whole teaching of Scripture. Neither can it be an Antinomian who says, " Seeing that God has made me a vessel of wrath, what have I to do but conduct myself as such, and indulge my inclinations to the full? " Such suppositions are simple anachronisms—the crediting of the first century with the perverse interpretations of the sixteenth and seventeenth.

There cannot be the smallest doubt but that the objector is a Jew, who very naturally, but very wrongly, opposed the inference which he would foresee St. Paul was about to draw from God's dealings with the reprobate, *i.e.*, the non-elect, persons he had just alluded to, Ishmael and Esau, and above all with Pharaoh, who so far from resisting God's will, had actually, though unwillingly, carried it out. The Jew could see in a moment what the Apostle was coming to. It was, that, if Pharaoh was hardened, so that he became a vessel of wrath, and yet was the instrument through whom God showed His power, and made His Name declared throughout all the earth, might not the very same action of God be taking place then, even before their eyes, and they themselves be the instruments for bringing God's purposes about? The salvation of the Israelites in the time of Pharaoh was not to be named by the side of what had taken place in their own days. In the matter of the Sacrifice of His Son, and the salvation which sprang directly from it, and the dispersion of the Christians, so that the Word of God was preached everywhere, God made the greatest use, not only of good, but rather of wicked men—of very wicked men. Well, then, the Jew might say, " If we, our chief priests, our elders, the whole populace of Jerusalem, the rulers of our synagogues, everywhere supported by the frequenters of the synagogues, are unconsciously carrying out God's purposes, first in the Sacrifice of Christ, then in the universal diffusion of the knowledge of that Sacrifice, why does God cast us off—treat us as reprobate—as vessels of wrath fitted for destruction?" To which the Apostle

WILLING TO SHEW HIS WRATH.

22 *What* if God, willing to shew *his* wrath, and to

answers, " You do not realize the lesson which your whole history should have taught you, that God makes all things serve His purposes. He desires that men should serve Him willingly, and consciously submit to His will. They are the clay in His hands, but not mere earthy inanimate clay, but clay to which He has given the power of confessing Him, and acknowledging His Fatherhood—clay that can say to Him, 'Now, O Lord, thou art our Father. We are the clay, and Thou our potter, and we are all the work of thine hand.'" Nay, even more than this, if they are already made into vessels of dishonour, by self-purification they can change their spiritual condition, and become vessels unto honour, sanctified and meet for the master's use (2 Tim. ii. 21).

Still, was God just in punishing those who thus carried out His purposes? Certainly, because in the exercise of their free-will they were only intent on carrying out their own wicked purposes—their purposes of covetousness, as Judas—of malice and envy, as the chief priests—of dislike of spiritual truths, as the Scribes—of bloodthirstiness, as the populace. God's intention in making use of them to bring good out of evil did not, in the least degree, diminish their wickedness, and ought not, on principles of pure justice, to diminish their punishment.

22. "What if God, willing to shew his wrath, and to make his power known," &c. To what particular action of God does the Apostle here allude? A moment's consideration will convince us that it must be to something occurring in the present state of things, as God's action in the matter of Pharaoh did. In the case of Pharaoh, God did not show His wrath by exhibiting Pharaoh as enduring the punishment due to him in a future world; and so with the Jews. If God willed to show His wrath and make His power known in them, it must be by some endurance with them here in this present state of things, some respite to them as the ancient people of God; for God keeps the final doom of sinners in Hades known only to Himself, and He could not show His wrath and make His power, in this respect, known, till the consummation of all things. I think, then, there can be but one opinion as to what must be meant by this endurance, with much long-suffering, of the vessels of wrath. What can it be but the forty years' respite between the descent of the Holy Spirit and that final withdrawal of

make his power known, endured with much longsuffering

God's presence, when in the destruction of their place and nation the wrath came upon them to the uttermost?

Our Lord, on two occasions, treats the Jews of His time, *i.e.*, the mass of them—the nation—as reprobate; once in Matth. xiii. 15: "This people's heart is waxed gross ... lest at any time they should see with their eyes, and should be converted," &c. This place is also cited by St. Paul himself in Acts xxviii. 27, and with exactly the same significance. Again, the Apostle St. John cites it in xii. 39, 40, for the same purpose. The reader will find a very full examination of the bearing of this hardening in my notes on these places. Again, the Jews and their rulers are held to be vessels of wrath, who yet carried out the determinate counsel and fore-knowledge of God in St. Peter's address on the day of Pentecost [Acts ii. 23, and in the Apostolic Hymn in Acts iv. 27]: "Against thy holy child Jesus, whom thou hast anointed, both Herod, and Pontius Pilate, with the Gentiles, and the people of Israel, were gathered together, for to do whatsoever thy hand and thy counsel determined before to be done." And yet, to this reprobate nation, to these very vessels of wrath, God was long-suffering, not willing that any should perish, but that all should come to repentance. His Son beheld the city, and wept over it. "If thou hadst known, even thou, at least in this thy day, the things which belong unto thy peace" (Luke xix. 41). The Lord also said, "Ye will not come unto me, that ye might have life" (John v. 40). Again, St. Paul and the other Apostles were sent to the Jews first. Again, the deep and bitter grief, so that Paul almost, at times, desired to be accursed from Christ for his brethren, and his heart's desire for their salvation, were exhibitions of the same long-suffering of God on behalf of reprobate Israel.

There is no use, of course, in our attempting either to solve or to ignore the mystery of God thus dealing in long-suffering with souls that were, to all appearance, doomed. It seems as if God, or Christ, knowing their future, dealt with them exactly as if He did not know it. The case of Judas is, perhaps, the strongest in point, and the clearest. God gave him to His Son to be His Apostle, and so a vessel of the highest conceivable honour, and yet he became the traitor. He became the traitor because he would not, being a vessel of election, purge himself from his love of money. And

CHAP. IX.]   THE VESSELS OF WRATH.   219

¹ the vessels of wrath ‖ ᵏ fitted to destruction: ⁱ 1 Thess. v. 9.
                                                      ⁀ Or, *made up*.
                                                      ᵏ 1 Pet. ii. 8.
                                                      Jude 4.

Christ gave more warnings against covetousness than He did against any other sin. Christ, as God, knowing the end of this man, did not expel him from the elect company, but allowed him to continue in it, though constantly the Lord said to him what, if he had had any feeling, would have made him withdraw himself. Up to the last, *i.e.*, to the moment when he made the bargain, he might have withdrawn. His wickedness was his own—if we are sure of anything we are sure of that—and yet, in God's all-wise and all-merciful purposes, it brought about the Redemption of the world. And if his fall was his own, so were Christ's warnings His own also—all from His heart—all given in all sincerity, all intended by Him to save the man, that, if possible, he should not go to his own place.

Here, then, we have the actual case of a vessel of wrath fitted to destruction, and yet endured with all long-suffering. Now this man was not an inferior, but one of the chiefest instruments in carrying out the determinate counsel of God. He was side by side with Annas, Caiaphas, the other chief priests, and Pontius Pilate. If we had revealed to us, as we may have in the future world, the interior history of this man from moment to moment, from his birth, his first struggles with, or yieldings to, evil, his first hearing of Christ, his first contact with Him—all his thoughts afterwards, as they are known to God—all the thoughts due to his own will— all the thoughts suggested by Satan—all the thoughts infused by the Holy Spirit—every piercing word of Christ, and the process of the quenching of its power within; and if God gave us faculties for comprehending all this, then we should see how perfectly just, and righteous, and kind, and long-suffering God was in dealing with him. So that his fulfilment of God's counsel in the matter of the betrayal was, so far as its wickedness was concerned, in no way due to God. The man brought the wickedness—all the wickedness; God brought, through His providence, the circumstances under which it conduced to Redemption. And as it was with Judas, so it was with Annas, with Caiaphas, with every chief priest, with every malignant scribe, with every Jew who had the power and the will to persecute and so disperse the first preachers of the Gospel, that the Name of Christ might be known everywhere.

23 And that he might make known ¹the riches of his glory on the vessels of mercy, which he had ᵐ afore prepared unto glory,

ˡ ch. ii. 4.
Eph. i. 7.
Col. i. 27.
ᵐ ch. viii. 28, 29, 30.

23. "And that he might make known the riches of his glory on the vessels," &c. This also has a present significance. It means a glory conferred in this life, which might be seen and known of all men. For the work of the Holy Ghost in creating and establishing the Church of Christ was indeed a glorifying work. We again refer to the teaching of 2 Corinth. iii. 9 : "If the ministration of condemnation be glory, much more doth the ministration of righteousness exceed in glory. For even that which was made glorious had no glory in this respect, by reason of the glory that excelleth. For if that which is done away was glorious, much more that which remaineth is glorious." "We all . . . . are changed [of course, now, in this present time], from glory to glory, even as by the Spirit of the Lord." It was, indeed, when we come to think of it, an amazing glory put upon the spirit of man, that one belonging to the narrowest and blindest sect of a narrow and blind nation, should be able to treat upon the ideas which form the substance of this Epistle ; and that Gentiles brought up in ignorance and filthiness, should be so purified as to be able to entertain these ideas. When we consider this astonishing miracle in the matter of knowledge— of knowledge so new, so far extended, so various, so soul-transforming—and when we consider the mythologies, the superstitions, the impurities, the scepticism, and agnosticism in which these converts had been brought up, we cannot but acknowledge what a glory that is with which God has invested man. And when we add to this the miraculous works of the Spirit, and, notwithstanding all opposition, the Gospel spreading everywhere, and godless men having such a knowledge and love of God, and hopeless men having such bright, such transcendent hopes, and a new power in the world against sin and on the side of righteousness, we may well say that the human instruments of all this—the vessels of mercy—made known the riches of God's glory.

"Which he had afore prepared unto glory." That men should carry out such purposes must not be left to chance, to hap-hazard, to blind fate, or there might have been no instruments at all for carrying out the will of the All-merciful God, and so, according as

24 Even us, whom he hath called, ⁿ not of the Jews only, but also of the Gentiles?   ⁿ ch. iii. 29.

25 As he saith also in Osee, ᵒ I will call them   ᵒ Hos. ii. 23.
my people, which were not my people; and her   1 Pet. ii. 10.
beloved, which was not beloved.

---

was before said, they were foreknown, predestinated, called, justified, and glorified.

24. "Even us, whom he hath called," &c. This verse could not well have been written, except St. Paul had chiefly in his mind not abstract principles, but a course of events which was then taking place, which was most distasteful to the Jewish mind, and to justify which he proceeds to appeal to some plain passages in the prophets—first in Hosea.

25. "As he saith also in Osee, I will call them my people, which," &c. Here is a difficulty, because if we turn to Hosea, we shall see that the prophet was not speaking of Gentiles, but of the house of Israel, and not that part of it which had adhered to the covenant of Moses and the house of David, but that which had revolted from God; but the truth, on account of which the Apostle cites the passage, is that which it bears on its surface—that God might so far change His plans, as to make those who were utterly alienated from His people, to be a part of His people. The case of the ten tribes, which is in the mind of the prophet, or rather of God speaking by him, seems much more hopeless than that of the Gentiles. They apostatized from the moment that they became a separate nation. They cut themselves off from their glorious past. They repudiated Moses, Joshua, Samuel, David. They were, by far the greatest part of them, apparently amalgamated with the heathen, and those who adhered to God retained nothing of their former separate nationality, and became Jews. So that the words of the prophet cited by the Apostle, were as applicable to the Gentiles as to such purely heathen Israelites.[1]

---

[1] Whether the descendants of the ten tribes who were dispersed at the Nineveh invasion, yet exist either in separate localities or amalgamated with the tribes of Judah and Benjamin, is known only to God. Dr. Wolff, the Jewish missionary, told me that the Jews of Bokhara were descendants of the ten tribes, but in no way distinguishable from other Jews in ritual or traditions. Of course only those who are totally ignorant of history and of every science connected with it, such as ethnology, can be the dupes of the Anglo-Israelite craze.

A REMNANT SHALL BE SAVED. [ROMANS.

26 ᵖ And it shall come to pass, *that* in the place where it was said unto them, Ye *are* not my people; there shall they be called the children of the living God.

27 Esaias also crieth concerning Israel, ᑫThough the number of the children of Israel be as the sand of the sea, ʳ a remnant shall be saved:

28 For he will finish ‖ the work, and cut *it* short in righteousness: ˢbecause a short work will the Lord make upon the earth.

ᵖ Hos. i. 10.
ᑫ Is. x. 22, 23.
ʳ ch. xi. 5.
‖ Or, *the account*.
ˢ Is. xxviii. 22.

---

28. "For he will finish the work, and cut it short in righteousness: because a short work will the Lord," &c. So D., E., F., G., K., L., P., most Cursives, d, e, f, g, Vulg., Goth., Arm.; but ℵ, A., B., 23, 47, 67, Syr., Copt., Æth., omit "in righteousness: because a short work," so that the verse reads, "For the Lord will execute his work upon the earth, finishing it and cutting it short."

26. "And it shall come to pass . . . children of the living God." Chrysostom's remarks here are much to the point: "But if they should assert that this was said of those of the Jews who believed, even then the argument stands. For if with those who after so many benefits were hard-hearted and estranged, and had lost their being as a people, so great a change was wrought, what is there to prevent even those who were not estranged, after being taken to Him, but were originally aliens, from being called, and, provided they obey, from being counted worthy of the same blessings?"

27. "Esaias also crieth concerning Israel, Though the number of the children," &c. The Apostle now proceeds to cite some prophetic declarations of Isaiah having quite a different significance. In the last two verses he had quoted the prophet as declaring that if the ancient people apostatized from God, He would have a new people, who should be His true children, and fulfil His purpose. Now He declares that the promises to Abraham, Isaac, and Jacob would be continued to the nation, but only through a remnant. No matter how populous the land should be, the mass of the nation will fall away, and the real inheritors of the promises who should transmit them to their descendants would be a small remnant.

28. "For he will finish the work, and cut it short in righteousness," &c. St. Paul here quotes from the Septuagint, but the

CHAP. IX.] WE HAD BEEN AS SODOMA. 223

29 And as Esaias said before, ^t Except the Lord of Sabaoth had left us a seed, ^u we had been as Sodoma, and been made like unto Gomorrha.

^t Is. i. 9.
Lam. iii. 22.
^u Is. xiii. 19.
Jer. l. 40.

30 What shall we say then? ^x That the Gentiles, which followed not after righteousness, have attained to righteousness, ^y even the righteousness which is of faith.

^x ch. iv. 11.
& x. 20.

^y ch. i. 17.

31 But Israel, ^z which followed after the law of righteousness, ^a hath not attained to the law of righteousness.

^z ch. x. 2. &
xi. 7.
^a Gal. v. 4.

---

31. "Not attained to the law of righteousness." "Righteousness" omitted by ℵ, A., B., D., E., G., some Cursives, d*, e, g, Copt.; but retained by F., K., L., P., most Cursives, Vulg., Syriac, Goth.

"work" should rather be translated "word," and the Septuagint may be rendered literally "accomplishing, and cutting short (the) decree in righteousness, because the Lord will make a rapidly accomplished decree in all the world" (or inhabited land, οἰκουμένῃ).

The decree in both clauses signifies the execution of the decree, which on the part of God will be rapid and decisive. It means what the Septuagint expresses quaintly and literally, "a short work will the Lord make upon the earth." Alford interprets it thus:—
"This verse is adduced by the Apostle as confirming the certainty of the salvation of the remnant of Israel, seeing that now as then, He with Whom a thousand years are as a day, will swiftly accomplish His prophetic Word in righteousness."

29. "And as Esaias said before, Except the Lord of Sabaoth had left," &c. This is a verse much to be noted, for it seems to assert that naturally, *i.e.*, in the ordinary course of God's dealings with wicked nations, Israel would have been like Sodom—that is, annihilated, but in order to preserve them as the depositary of His promises, He had decreed in His foreknowledge and brought about by His calling, that there should be a remnant which should, notwithstanding the falling away of the nation, be accounted the true Israel—so that the election is all on the side of mercy.

30, 31. "What shall we say then? That the Gentiles, which followed not," &c. What shall we say then to the fact that the Gentiles are now being accepted by God, and the Jews rejected?

32 Wherefore? Because *they sought it* not by faith, but as it were by the works of the law. ^bFor they stumbled at that stumbling-stone;

33 As it is written, ^cBehold, I lay in Sion a stumblingstone and rock of offence: and ^dwhosoever believeth on him shall not be ‖ ashamed.

^b Luke ii. 34.
1 Cor. i. 23.
^c Ps. cxviii. 22.
Is. viii. 14. &
xxviii. 16.
Matt. xxi. 42.
1 Pet. ii. 6,
7, 8.
^d ch. x. 11.
‖ Or, *confounded*.

32. "By the works of the law." "Of the law" omitted by א, A., B., F., G., f, g, Vulg., Copt.; retained by D., E., K., L., P., most Cursives, Syriac, Arm.

This seems unfair, for the Gentiles have attained that which they did not seek, even righteousness; and Israel, which followed apparently after righteousness, and by the way which God had apparently given them, that is, the law, have not attained to the law, that is, to the true practice of it. This seems unjust. "No," the Apostle goes on to say, "it was perfectly right on God's part thus to deal with them, because they did not seek the true righteousness in the right way. God sent His Son amongst them with every credential as the Messiah which they could possibly expect. They would not come unto Him that they might have life, and so they rejected the counsel of God against themselves."

32, 33. "Wherefore? Because they sought it not by faith ... not be ashamed." The Apostle here amalgamates, as it were, two passages. The first (Isaiah viii. 13-14), in which the Lord of Hosts is said to be given for two purposes. First, for a sanctuary; but then inasmuch as all did not take refuge in Him as their sanctuary, for those who did not so take refuge, for a stone of stumbling and for a rock of offence to both the houses of Israel, &c. In the second passage God says:—"Behold I lay in Zion for a foundation a stone, a tried stone, a precious corner stone, a sure foundation;" and in the Septuagint this verse concludes with:—"And he that believes on him shall by no means be ashamed." So that taking some of the teaching of each passage, the great twofold truth is set before the Jews, that they cannot reject the counsel of God in the giving of His Son with impunity. He is either their sanctuary, into the protection of which they run by faith and are never ashamed; or He is their stone of stumbling and rock of offence, against which they stumble and fall, and lose their calling and election, as the people of God.

CHAP. X.

BRETHREN, my heart's desire and prayer to God for Israel is, that they might be saved.

2 For I bear them record ^a that they have a zeal of God, but not according to knowledge.

3 For they being ignorant of ^b God's righteousness, and going about to establish their own

^a Acts xxi. 20, & xxii. 3. Gal. i. 14, & iv. 17. See ch. ix. 31.
^b ch. i. 17, & ix. 30.

---

1. "For Israel." So K., L., most Cursives; but ℵ, A., B., D., E., F., G., P., a few Cursives (6, 10, 17, 47, 71, 93, 137), d, e, f, g, Vulg., Goth., Syriac, Copt., Arm., read, "for them."

1. "Brethren, my heart's desire and prayer to God for Israel is, that," &c. Why does the Apostle here interject, as it were, this expression of strong desire? It is in the same spirit as the sorrowful longing for the salvation of Israel expressed at the commencement of the last chapter. No doubt because he had just been forced to write severe things respecting Israel after the flesh; and so he strongly reasserts that, though his duty required him to assert bitter and unwelcome truth, his affection for his countrymen was as strong as ever.

"Desire" (εὐδοκία). No better translation can be suggested than that of the Authorized.

"That they might be saved"—literally, "for salvation." The latter rendering is greatly to be preferred, as St. Paul had hitherto, as much as possible, avoided reference to the particular salvation of individual Israelites, and dwelt on the casting away or acceptance of bodies or peoples; and certainly the translation, "for salvation," is more in accord with this than "that they may be saved."

2. "For I bear them record that they have a zeal of God, but not according," &c. A zeal of God, *i.e.*, for His Unity—the purity of His worship, as free from idolatry—the keeping of the Sabbath.

"Not according to knowledge." Knowledge here signifies better, more perfect knowledge. The word is "epignosis," whereas the common word, implying the less perfect knowledge, is "gnosis."

3, 4. "For they being ignorant of God's righteousness, and going

Q

ᵃ righteousness, have not submitted themselves unto the righ-
ᶜ Phil. iii. 9. teousness of God.

---

about to establish. . . . For Christ is the end of the law for righteousness to every one that believeth." God's righteousness here is, of course, "the righteousness of God which is by faith of Jesus Christ unto all and upon all them that believe" (iii. 22). As it is only attained to by believing in Jesus Christ, the Jews had it not, because they rejected Christ.

The Apostle here seems to lay the blame on their ignorance; but it was not likely that God would cast away His ancient people for mere ignorance. There must have been something wilful, something immoral, something even wicked in their ignorance; and in the words of Isaiah, cited by the Lord and by St. Paul, it is said: "They have closed their eyes lest they should see with their eyes," &c.—which implies that it was very wilful, and very determined indeed.

The key to solving the question seems to me in the words, "have not *submitted themselves* to the righteousness of God." The righteousness which the Jew desired for himself was one which, being mainly, if not altogether, external and negative, was one which required no effort, no self-denial, no change of will. It was a righteousness which, above all, fell in with their exclusiveness and pride of privilege on which they could boast themselves, and make a fair show, as they thought, before the sinners of the Gentiles. It consisted in observing the letter of the ten commandments, and, if this was inconvenient, there were means of absolving themselves from obedience even to the mere letter, as our Lord denounces in the matter of the fifth commandment (Matthew xv. 3-8). Whereas the righteousness of God revealed in Jesus Christ, and given in Him, was a very different thing indeed. It was the righteousness, not of mere external or negative commands, but of the Beatitudes. It consequently required a new life, and that the life of a risen Christ *in* the man, and not merely enveloping him. It required regeneration—a grafting into Christ, an union with Him, internal and external.

Now this righteousness was, of course, by its very nature, inseparable from Christ; and the Jewish heads of Church and State, the traditional leaders, as the high priests, and the self-appointed leaders, as the Rabbis, Scribes, and Pharisees, had rejected Christ,

4 For ^d Christ *is* the end of the law for righteousness to every one that believeth.   ^d Matt. v. 17. Gal. iii. 24.

---

crucified Him, and denounced all that believed in Him as apostate and excommunicated.

The Jew, then, if he would be saved, must submit to this righteousness which God offered him through Christ—this humbling, purifying, self-crucifying righteousness, and yet this exalting, ennobling, glorifying righteousness, for it raised him up far above the world, subdued the sinfulness and consequent degradation of his flesh, and made him a member of One at the right hand of God. The acceptance of this, involving the submission of his whole soul and spirit, the idea of which he detested, made him more and more unwilling to accept Jesus as the Christ. He would not give up his little righteousness, which was, indeed, a "dangerous thing" to him, to receive the highest righteousness—the righteousness of God; and so the rejection of righteousness in the rejection of Christ, whilst it seemed to assert morality, was a sign of the deepest immorality, because the most deep-seated alienation from God.

4. "For Christ is the end of the law for righteousness to every one that believeth." The end of the law is, I think, the final purpose of the law—the end for bringing about which the law was given.

Now the Apostle in the last chapter had said, respecting God's ordaining the law, that it was ordained unto life; and though St. Paul found it to be "unto death," that was not because of any fault in the law, for he said that the law was holy, and the commandment holy, and just, and good; but because of his own internal sinfulness, which made the law weak (viii. 3). For what purpose, then, did God give the law? Evidently to prepare men for Christ. God, above all things, desired righteousness—the highest righteousness, even His own righteousness, if it could be communicated to His intelligent creatures. To this end He gave the law which in many ways prepared for Christ. Its types pointed to Him, its sacrifices foreshadowed His; but above all its moral precepts, if men attempted to sincerely obey them, were as the schoolmaster (pædagogus, Gal. iii. 24), to lead men to Christ.

So that Christ was the end of the law, in that if He was received

5 For Moses describeth the righteousness which is of the law, *That the man which doeth those things shall live by them.

* Lev. xviii. 5. Neh. ix. 29. Ezek. xx. 11, 13, 21. Gal. iii. 12.

5. Revised version, "For Moses writeth that the man that doeth the righteousness of the law shall live thereby."

by men, and dwelt in them, then the righteousness of the law would be fulfilled in them—they, of course, walking not after the flesh, but after the Spirit. Christ, then, was the "end of the law" to those who by faith received Him. Because they truly believed in Him, they were grafted into Him, and they abode in Him, and that which He Himself had promised was fulfilled in them: "He that abideth in me, and I in him, the same bringeth forth much fruit, for without me ye can do nothing" (John xv. 5).

5-8. "For Moses describeth the righteousness which is of the law . . . the word of faith which we preach." The Apostle in these verses describes the easy attainment of the knowledge of the Gospel in the same terms in which Moses had described the easy attainment of the knowledge of the law. Both were nigh, both were within reach of the comprehension of the most ignorant. Both consisted—so far, that is, as these first principles were concerned—in household words easily learnt and easily remembered. "Moses describeth the righteousness of the law;" or, according to another reading, "Moses writeth that the man that doeth the righteousness of the law shall live thereby." There were a few plain precepts which no one could fail to understand: "Thou shalt have no other gods but me;" "Thou shalt not make any graven image;" "Thou shalt not kill—commit adultery—steal." And the righteousness of the law consisted in the simple doing of these precepts (Levit. xviii. 5), "Ye shall therefore keep my statutes and my judgments, which, if a man do, he shall even live in them." But the law-giver, in another place (Deut. xxx. 11), describes the nearness of the commandments, in that every Israelite, unless he kept his ears from his very childhood wilfully shut, must know these commandments. "For this commandment which I command thee this day, it is not hidden from thee, neither is it far off. It is not in heaven that thou shouldest say, Who shall go up for us to heaven, and bring it unto us, that we may hear it, and do it? Neither is it beyond the sea that thou shouldest say, Who shall go

CHAP. X.] THE WORD IS NIGH THEE. 229

6 But the righteousness which is of faith speaketh on this wise, ᶠ Say not in thine heart, Who shall ascend into heaven? (that is, to bring Christ down *from above:*) ᶠ Deut. xxx. 12, 13.

7 Or, Who shall descend into the deep? (that is, to bring up Christ again from the dead.)

8 But what saith it? ᵍ The word is nigh thee, *even* in thy mouth, and in thy heart: that is, the word of faith, which we preach; ᵍ Deut. xxx. 14.

---

over the sea for us, and bring it unto us, that we may hear it, and do it? But the word is very nigh unto thee, in thy mouth, and in thy heart, that thou mayest do it." The Apostle applies this with some alterations, and some words thrown in parenthetically, to the Gospel: "The righteousness which is of faith speaketh on this wise." Here "the righteousness of faith—meaning, I think, the dispensation of faith which he personifies—speaketh on this wise: Say not in thine heart, Who shall ascend into heaven? (that is, to bring Christ down from above)." This means Christ is the righteousness of God, because He is the Son of God; and God *has* sent Him down from heaven, and given Him to us to be our righteousness. We have not to ascend into heaven to bring Him down. We have not even to beseech God with earnest prayers to send Him. He is sent, He has come down, He has taken our nature, He is ours.

7. "Or, Who shall descend into the deep? (that is, to bring up Christ again)," &c. The words in Deuteronomy corresponding to this are (Sept.): "Neither is it beyond the sea, saying, Who will go over for us to the other side of the sea, and take it for us, and make it audible to us?" But the Apostle having in mind that Christ went not over the sea, but descended into the abyss, turns it, "Who shall descend into the deep," *i.e.*, to bring up Christ from the dead. The Resurrection of Christ has not to be brought about, but is accomplished, and is ours. We have been even made partakers of it by faith and Baptism.

8. "But what saith it? The word is nigh thee, even in thy mouth," &c. The Apostle here appropriates the word of Moses respecting the nearness of the law, to the nearness of the Gospel. Only in the latter case it is not the word of mere precept—of mere

IF THOU SHALT CONFESS. [ROMANS.

h Matt. x. 32.
Luke xii. 8.
Acts viii. 37.

9 That ^h if thou shalt confess with thy mouth the Lord Jesus, and shalt believe in thine heart

---

hard, powerless precept, but the word of faith—of the Gospel. Believe God's goodness in the gift of His Son, believe that the Son of God has come, has been crucified, has risen. If thou knowest anything, thou knowest this.

9. "That if thou shalt confess with thy mouth the Lord Jesus, and shalt believe in thine heart," &c. The belief must come before the profession, but the confession is here mentioned first, because in the place of Deuteronomy quoted in verse 8, "In thy mouth," comes before "in thine heart." And so the word or profession of the Gospel must be in the mouth as well as in the heart.

9. "That if thou shalt confess with thy mouth," &c. What is this confession? There can be little doubt that the common symbol, or united confession of Christians, was something closely answering to our Apostles' Creed. It certainly was conterminous with the Gospel, and was consequently the Coming of the Son of God in the flesh of the seed of David (Rom. i. 3); the death for our sins, the burial, the Resurrection (1 Cor. xv.), and the Judgment (Rom. ii. 16). But chiefly was it the Resurrection of the Lord. That was the article on which, by St. Paul at least, by far the most stress was laid, for it involved the truth of, or rather what was supernatural in, all the rest. The death of a man by crucifixion might be, and, indeed was, quite natural, but the Resurrection raised the Death of Christ into the highest sphere of the Divine and supernatural, for it transformed a death which the Lord shared with innumerable malefactors, into a Death which was all-propitiatory and all-reconciling.

Now to confess this required at times the greatest possible moral courage; but it must be done, for Christ had said, "Whosoever shall confess me before men, him will I confess also before my Father which is in heaven; but whosoever shall deny me before men, him will I also deny before my Father which is in heaven" (Matth. x. 32). But there must have been some form of words embodying it, which would distinguish Christ from all other men. Caiaphas and Pilate would readily have confessed that they believed that there was a man called Jesus, Who professed to be the Christ. So in fact could every Jew, but what was this worth? The truth which the Christian confessed was, that this crucified Jesus was the Christ of God,

THOU SHALT BE SAVED. 231

that God hath raised him from the dead, thou shalt be saved.

---

and that this was proved by His Resurrection, which showed also that He was the very Son of God, and that He would judge all men at the last day.

For the whole body of Scripture truth respecting the person and work of Christ is involved in the one fact of His Resurrection. By it He was declared to be the Son of God with power, *i.e.*, God's own very Son, sharing, as every real proper son does, His Father's Nature, and so a partaker of all His attributes. By it His Life on earth was shown to be righteous, and His Death the ransom of a world of sinners. By it, united with His Ascension, we are assured that we have part in His Risen Life, and in His Mediation and Intercession, and that we shall be judged by Him at the last. A true belief in the Resurrection involves all this. The belief in the Resurrection of Christ with the heart, accepts all which it involves respecting the glory and power of Jesus.

But it cannot be with the heart only. It must be also with the lips. It must be public and unreserved. Christ Himself requires this when He says, "Whosoever shall confess me before men, him will I confess also before my Father which is in heaven." It was not by a secret doctrine whispered from one man to another, that the Gospel was to be propagated, and men saved. It must be proclaimed upon the house-tops. If God had thus interfered, and Christ had thus humbled Himself, the least that men could do was to confess this, and not be ashamed of it, but glory in it. Now this at times demanded the utmost moral courage. To confess that they received salvation and righteousness through a Jew, a member of the most despised of nations, and through a Jew also put to the vilest of deaths, was at times a work indeed—a work demanding the most determined courage, and the most unreserved self-surrender, even of life; but the Lord Himself demanded it. "He that findeth his life shall lose it, and he that loseth his life for my sake, shall find it" (Matth. x. 39).

But why is "confessing" put before "believing"? Evidently because in the words which St. Paul had just quoted, "in thy mouth," is put before "in thine heart." In the next verse the Apostle observes the more logical order, putting "with the heart man believeth," before "with the mouth confession is made."

10 For with the heart man believeth unto righteousness; and with the mouth confession is made unto salvation.

Let the reader notice what the believer has to believe. Many have said in these latter days that he is now required to believe that Christ died for him in particular, and that his particular sins, as distinguished from those of others, are blotted out; but this is what the Apostles neither say nor mean. They delight rather to believe, and to express the belief, that Christ died for all. "He died for all." "He is the propitiation for our sins." "He himself bare our sins." He died for me is an isolating, a separating formula. He died for all, for the world, for the Church, for the many, is an unifying one. But the Apostle passes on to the Resurrection, and the significance of this is given in this very Epistle, "To this end Christ died, and rose again, and revived, that he might be Lord both of the dead and living" (xiv. 9).

10. "For with the heart man believeth unto righteousness; and," &c. This verse, literally translated, is, "With the heart it is believed unto righteousness, and with the mouth it is confessed unto salvation." All belief, such as God acknowledges, must of necessity be "of the heart." This seems to exclude not an hypocritical or feigned belief only, but an otiose belief—a mere historical assent; and yet this historical assent must be held to, for where it exists there is a foundation upon which, by God's grace, something may be built. We naturally and rightly look upon the so-called nominal believer as in a far different position to the man who rejects altogether the Divine Origin and Mission of Jesus of Nazareth. The latter is an infidel. He rejects of set purpose the Revelation of the love of God in the gift of His Son. He rejects the only remedy worth speaking of for moral evil which has appeared in the world. He deliberately puts from him the honour which God has put upon our race, by causing His Son to take the nature of man upon Him.

"With the mouth confession is made unto salvation." Is this confession, then, to be confined to the repetition of creeds in public worship, or even the reception of the Eucharist? No, by no means. Wherever the name of Christ, or His Salvation, or His Godhead, or Miracles, or Resurrection are called in question, there must be, if we are to be faithful, a distinct counter assertion that what is

CHAP. X.]   THE SCRIPTURE SAITH.   233

11 For the scripture saith, ¹ Whosoever believeth on him shall not be ashamed.

12 For ᵏ there is no difference between the Jew and the Greek: for ˡ the same Lord over all ᵐ is rich unto all that call upon him.

¹ Is. xxviii. 16, & xlix. 23. Jer. xvii. 7. Ch. ix. 33.
ᵏ Acts xv. 9, ch. iii. 22. Gal. iii. 28.
ˡ Acts x. 36, ch. iii. 29. 1 Tim. ii. 5.
ᵐ Eph. i. 7, & ii. 4, 7.

said of Him in Scripture, or accepted by the Church, is true, and for our life, and that it is due to His Father Who gave Him, and to Him Who was given, to believe this, and confess the goodness of God in the whole matter. Must, then, Christians constantly obtrude sacred truth before all societies? No, they must remember the words of the Lord, not to cast pearls before swine; but all Christians, even imperfect ones, cannot be classed as swine, and we must be on the watch for opportunities of asserting the providence of God, and the truth of the Catholic faith, and, if need be, the anger of God against the impenitent and unbelieving.¹

11. "For the Scripture saith, Whosoever believeth on him shall not be ashamed." The stress is to be laid on *whosoever*, i.e., no matter of what nation or people he is: (the word, however, is not in the original Hebrew or Septuagint).

"Shall not be ashamed," *i.e.*, he shall not be ashamed in the sense that those are who have relied on some promise, and are disappointed. The Hebrew reads, "shall not make haste" (יחיש); the Septuagint translators, by the alteration of a letter, changing this into יבֿיש.

12, 13. "For there is no difference between the Jew and the Greek: for the same Lord over all is rich unto all that call upon

---

¹ May I be permitted here to reproduce what I have written on Luke xii. 9, page 319. "In Christian England the confession of Christ has assumed a different form, but it equally requires sincerity and courage to make it: a Christian has now to profess the creating power of God amongst Evolutionists, and the all-ruling providence of God in the company of unbelieving Scientists. In some companies he has to brave the ridicule attached to the belief in miracles. In the society of filthy-minded men he has to uphold the purity of Christ, and in the society of worldlings he may be called upon to uphold the rooted antagonism between the world and Christ. These may seem very poor and mild ways of confessing Christ compared to what our forefathers in the faith had to endure, but they all try the mettle of the Christian. If he is faithful in confessing Christ in these comparatively little matters, he may have a good hope that God would, if called upon, give him grace to make a bolder and more public dangerous confession, if it was laid upon him so to do."

13 ⁿ For whosoever shall call ᵒ upon the name of the Lord shall be saved.

14 How then shall they call on him in whom they have not believed? and how shall they believe in him of whom they have not heard? and how shall they hear ᵖ without a preacher?

ⁿ Joel ii. 32.
Acts ii. 21.
ᵒ Acts ix. 14.
ᵖ Tit. i. 3.

---

him . . . shall be saved." "There is no difference," *i.e.*, notwithstanding the difference in their privileges in the matter of revelation, and of purer worship, they are all personally alike in the sight of God, so that if they come to Him, forsaking their sins, they will be alike accepted by Him.

13. "For whosoever shall call upon the name of the Lord shall be saved." "Call upon the name of the Lord," *i.e.*, invoke His help for deliverance from sin. Calling upon the Name of God is the first and surest sign of belief in Him. The promise is taken from Joel ii. 32, and forms part of a prophecy of the signs and wonders which were to take place on the day of Pentecost.

To call upon the name of the Lord is the first thing we have to do in the matter of our salvation. It is the first act of true belief, and yet, rightly understood, it involves all religion. For to "call upon the name of the Lord," if we continue in this habit of calling, "implies right faith, to call upon Him as He is; right trust in Him, leaning upon Him; right devotion, calling upon Him as He has appointed; right life, ourselves who call upon Him being, or becoming by His grace, what He wills" (Pusey's "Minor Prophets," *in loco*). So that to call upon the name of the Lord includes the first earnest call of the newly-awakened sinner, and the last commendation of his spirit to his Father of the saint ripe for glory and immortality.

14, 15. "How then shall they call on him in whom they have not believed? . . . glad tidings of good things." These two verses entirely depend on the last verse, "whosoever shall call," &c., which sets forth a benefit unspeakably great, and of the first importance to every responsible being who has sinned, and who will have to be judged. If the promise that all who call upon God, and are heard by Him, is for all, it ought to be proclaimed, *i.e.*, preached, to all, because the calling upon God on the part of men depends upon their believing in Him, and their believing in Him depends upon

HOW SHALL THEY PREACH?

15 And how shall they preach, except they be sent? as it is written, ^q How beautiful are the feet of them that preach the gospel of peace, and bring glad tidings of good things!

q Isa. lii. 7.
Nah. i. 15.

---

15. "That preach the gospel of peace." Omitted by ℵ, A., B., C., Sah., Copt., Æth.; but retained by D., E., F., G., K., L., P., and most all Cursives, d, e, f, g, Vulg., Syriac, Arm., Goth.

their hearing about Him and His Salvation. But if they are to hear about God and His Salvation, someone must preach it to them—and the word "preach" signifies to "herald it to them," to act like a herald in proclaiming the message of a sovereign; and if they are thus to be heralded, *i.e.*, to receive the message of the Sovereign's grace, the herald must be sent. Without laying undue stress upon this mission of the herald, or the one sent, it is clear that the Apostle himself considered it of primary importance that he did not go to the Gentiles on the prompting of his own will. He quotes before the Jews the words of Christ, "Depart, for I will send thee far hence unto the Gentiles " (Acts xxii. 21). He is the Apostle, or one sent of Jesus Christ. He is sent "not of men, neither by man, but by Jesus Christ and God the Father, Who hath raised Him from the dead " (Gal. i. 1). We would not forbid anyone going amongst the heathen to proclaim to them Christ; but we would bid such persons remember that they seriously hinder the cause of Christ if they multiply among the heathen the same divisions as we have at home. St. Paul not only proclaimed to all who heard him the same Gospel as did Peter and John, but he united men in the same Church, for he was emphatically the Apostle of the Church's Unity (1 Cor. i. 10-17 ; xii. 12, 25 ; Ephes. iv. 3-6).

"How beautiful are the feet of them that preach the gospel of peace," &c. This passage is quoted, not as bearing upon the mission of heralds or preachers, but on their function of preaching; for it is to be remembered that, as far as we can gather, preaching or heralding was a new thing—certainly the preaching of the Gospel to all was absolutely new. Even in Isaiah, the evangelical prophet, there are comparatively few places which prophecy of an universal proclamation of the Salvation of God.

Here, then, we have not only a prophecy of the fact that a day

236 FAITH COMETH BY HEARING. [ROMANS.

r ch. iii. 3.
Heb. iv. 2.
s Is. liii. 1.
John xii. 38.
† Gr. *the hearing of us?*
‖ Or, *preaching?*
t Ps. xix. 4.
Matt. xxiv. 14,
& xxviii. 19.
Mark xvi. 15.
Col. i. 6, 23.
u See 1 Kin.
xviii. 10.
Matt. iv. 8.

16 But ʳ they have not all obeyed the gospel. For Esaias saith, ˢ Lord, who hath believed † our ‖ report?

17 So then faith *cometh* by hearing, and hearing by the word of God.

18 But I say, Have they not heard? Yes, verily, ᵗ their sound went into all the earth, ᵘ and their words unto the ends of the world.

---

17. "The word of God." So A., K., L., P., most Cursives, Syriac; but ℵ, B., C., D., E., several Cursives (6, 9, 23, 47, 49, 57, 67**), d, e, Vulg., Goth., Sah., Copt., Arm., read "the word of Christ."

will come when preaching or heralding God's truth will be an ordinance of God, but also witness borne to the glory and excellency of that ordinance. The very feet of those who carry on their lips such a message of redemption are beautiful.

16. "But they have not all obeyed the gospel. For Esaias saith," &c. How was it, then, seeing that whosoever calleth upon the Name of the Lord shall be saved—seeing that the feet of those who publish peace were actively going to and fro in their midst, that they were not all saved? Because they did not all believe. The same prophet who foretold the blessedness and extent of the preaching proclaimed its rejection by the vast majority, so that he commenced the most evangelical message which he was commissioned to deliver with the words, "Who hath believed our report?" as if few, very few, had accepted the message of salvation.

17. "So then faith cometh by hearing, and hearing by the word of God." The "hearing" of this verse is the same as the "report" of the last. "Who hath believed our hearing, that is, the thing uttered by us with the intent that it should pierce men's ears?"

18. "But I say, Have they not heard? Yes, verily, their sound went into all," &c. This is a quotation from Psalm xix., and is spoken by David of the glories of the material heaven, which preach to all men, if they will hear it, of the power and greatness of God. But the Apostle here seems to use the words by accommodation. "We may," he seems to say, "describe the almost universal preaching of the Gospel in the words of the Psalmist,

CHAP. X.]   ESAIAS IS VERY BOLD.   237

19 But I say, Did not Israel know? First Moses saith, ˣ I will provoke you to jealousy by *them that are* no people, *and* by a ʸ foolish nation I will anger you.

ˣ Deut. xxxii. 21. ch. xi. 11.
ʸ Tit. iii. 3.

20 But Esaias is very bold, and saith, ᶻ I was found of them that sought me not; I was made manifest unto them that asked not after me.

ᶻ Isa. lxv. 1. ch. ix. 30.

---

speaking of the witness of the heavens to the glory of God, 'Their sound is gone out into all lands, and their words unto the ends of the world.'"

19. "But I say, Did not Israel know? First Moses saith, I will provoke," &c. If any Israelite had carefully, and in a believing spirit, considered the words of Moses thus quoted by the Apostle, he would have assuredly gathered from them that God intended to withdraw His favour from those who had hitherto been His people, and to give it to those who had hitherto been not His people—as Hosea expresses it (chap. ii.) a no-people. Now this exactly described the state of things then existing. Thus Acts xiii. 44, 45, "And the next sabbath day came almost the whole city together to hear the Word of God. But when the Jews saw the multitudes, they were filled with envy," &c. So that the Jews had then before their eyes the fulfilment of one of their most ancient prophecies—the Jews shutting their ears to the message of salvation; the Gentiles, till then no-people, listening and believing, and the Jews full of envy and jealousy, enraged at the reception, on the Gentiles' part, of the very Gospel which they rejected.

Some of our leading critics are pronouncing the Apostle's citations inapposite; on the contrary, no quotations could be more apposite. The preaching in every city and its consequences bore testimony to their truth. A foolish nation signifies, of course, an idolatrous one, for what can exceed the folly of degrading the Deity to the likeness of one of His creatures?

20, 21. "But Esaias is very bold, and saith, . . . a disobedient and gainsaying people." The words of Isaiah express the same truth as those of Moses. They first assert the acceptance of the Gentiles, who had not sought God, and had not asked after Him, because they had had no law from God—no prophetical messengers; no

21 But to Israel he saith, ^a All day long I have stretched forth my hands unto a disobedient and gainsaying people.

^a Is. lxv. 2.

appointed shrine or ordained ritual, in the due use of which they might find God. Whereas the Jews had the law, the prophets, the Temple, the ritual, by all which God, as it were, stretched out His hands to them, inviting them to come back to His Bosom.

CHAP. XI.

I SAY then, ^a Hath God cast away his people? God forbid. For ^b I also am an Israelite, of the seed of Abraham, of the tribe of Benjamin.

2 God hath not cast away his people which

^a 1 Sam. xii. 22.
Jer. xxxi. 37.
^b 2 Cor. xi. 22.
Phil. iii. 5.

1. "I say then, Hath God cast away his people? . . . Benjamin." What the Apostle had been laying down seemed to lead to this one conclusion, that Israel was finally cast away.

"No," the Apostle answers, "such a thing cannot be. I myself am, in my own person, a proof to the contrary. I, who am a Christian, separated to the Gospel of God, am also an Israelite of the seed of Abraham and of the tribe of Benjamin. I belong to one of the two tribes that continued, in a manner, faithful to God, and to the house of David."

To this it might be replied, "You are but one." "No," the Apostle, in effect, answers, "I am one of a vast number who keep up the true continuity of the people of God."

2. "God hath not cast away his people which he foreknew," &c. (or rather preordained). There is a difference of opinion amongst expositors as to whom the Apostle alludes in the words, "his people which he foreknew." Some suppose that he means the elect remnant, the comparatively small minority who had accepted Jesus of Nazareth; others, that he means the foreordained or elect nation ("Israel, mine elect"), but, after all, both

CHAP. XI.]   THE ELECTION OF GRACE.   239

ᵉ he foreknew. Wot ye not what the scripture saith † of Elias? how he maketh intercession to God against Israel, saying,

3 ᵈ Lord, they have killed thy prophets, and digged down thine altars; and I am left alone, and they seek my life.

4 But what saith the answer of God unto him? ᵉ I have reserved to myself seven thousand men, who have not bowed the knee to *the image of* Baal.

5 ᶠ Even so then at this present time also there is a remnant according to the election of grace.

ᶜ ch. viii. 29.
† Gr. *in Elias?*
ᵈ 1 Kin. xix. 10, 14.
ᵉ 1 Kin. xix. 18.
ᶠ ch. ix. 27.

---

amount to the same, for the nation, as a nation, was elected, but God continued the election through the remnant.

The argument throughout this eleventh chapter is clearly in favour of the nation being the elect. Their casting away was but temporary, and their final reinstatement sure and certain.

"Wot ye not what the Scripture saith of Elias? . . . they seek my life." Elias, or Elijah, supposed that he was the only servant of God in apostate Israel, but God assured him that there were no less than seven thousand who, like himself, had not bowed the knee to Baal.

And the Apostle's inference from what he knew of the state of the chosen people, was

5. " Even so then at this present time also there is a remnant," &c. This may mean that the Jews or Israelites who believe in Christ, do so because, through God's grace, they are chosen individually out of the mass of unbelieving ones; or it may mean that the election of Israel to be the people of God, is continued, not through the unbelieving mass, but through the believing remnant. Both these meanings, as I have shown, come to the same thing in the end. But we will now take it as if the first hypothesis were the right one, that the election is of individuals selected each one by himself out of the mass. On account of what were they selected? On what principle? if it may be lawful, even for a moment, to entertain the question. On what principle did God elect one Jew and not another? There must have been some reason, and that reason

6 And ^g if by grace, then *is it* no more of works: otherwise grace is no more grace. But if *it be* of works, then is it no more grace: otherwise work is no more work.

7 What then? ^h Israel hath not obtained that which he seeketh for; but the election hath obtained it, and the rest were || blinded.

<small>g ch. iv. 4, 5. Gal. v. 4. See Deut. ix. 4, 5.</small>

<small>h ch. ix. 31, & x. 3.</small>

<small>|| Or, *hardened*. 2 Cor. iii. 14.</small>

---

6. "But if it be of works, then it is no more grace: otherwise work is no more work." This half of the verse omitted by ℵ, A., C., D., E., F., G., P., 47 text, d, e, f, g, Vulg., Sah., Copt., Arm.; but retained by B., partially L., almost all Cursives, and Syriacs.

something in the man chosen, for it is not possible to imagine that God chose them, as it were, at random; or as men chose others, by drawing lots. Now the Apostle tells us that it was by grace; but this, by the surest implication, demands that it should be through faith, for faith is, with St. Paul, the means by which grace reaches the soul. The remnant in the Apostle's days entirely consisted of those who believed in Christ, and by this submitted themselves to the righteousness of God (x. 3). It was not of works—that is, of the works of the law, or any other works, otherwise it would not have been free and unmerited. It was of faith that it might be by grace.

7. "What then? Israel hath not obtained that which he seeketh for," &c. What was it that Israel sought? It may have been the righteousness of God—*i.e.*, justification, or it may have been the Messiah; but these may be reckoned the same, for they received the righteousness of God only through the reception of the Messiah. It was the same evil frame of mind which made them reject the Messiah, and reject the righteousness of God. They rejected the Messiah because they rejected with their whole souls the sort of righteousness with which He desired to endow them—a righteousness of poverty of spirit, of mourning for sin, of meekness, of earnest craving for righteousness. All these the grace of the Son of God would work in them, but they sought it not. They sought a worldly Messiah, and they sought an outside righteousness, and so they obtained not that which God designed for them.

"The election hath obtained it." The election, as we gather from some passages in the Acts of the Apostles, though by far the minority, seems to have been considerable in numbers. Thus St.

CHAP. XI.]   THE SPIRIT OF SLUMBER.   241

8 (According as it is written, ¹God hath given them the spirit of ‖ slumber, ᵏ eyes that they should not see, and ears that they should not hear;) unto this day.

9 And David saith, ¹ Let their table be made a snare, and a trap, and a stumblingblock, and a recompence unto them:

ⁱ Is. xxix. 10.
‖ Or, *remorse.*
ᵏ Deut. xxix. 4. Isa. vi. 9. Jer. v. 21. Ezek. xii. 2. Matt. xiii. 14. John xii. 40. Acts xxviii. 26, 27.
¹ Ps. lxix. 22.

---

9. " A trap." Properly a net.

James says to St. Paul (Acts xxi. 20) : " Thou seest, brother, how many myriads (μυριάδες) of Jews there are which believe." "A great company of the priests were obedient to the faith" (Acts vi. 7).

" And the rest were blinded."

8-10. " According as it is written, God hath given them the spirit of slumber .... bow down their back alway." The two verses with the quotations they contain are proofs or illustrations of the words, " The rest were hardened." Would God harden the hearts of His people? The Apostle cites the Jewish Scriptures to show that such hardening had taken place in former times; and, if so, it was not contrary to God's justice or mercy, and might take place now.

The first clause of verse 8 is from Isaiah xxix. 10, " The Lord hath poured out upon you the spirit of deep sleep," and the latter clauses from Deut. xxix. 4. It may be well to give some of the context: " Moses called unto all Israel, and said unto them, Ye have seen all that the Lord did before your eyes in the land of Egypt unto Pharaoh, and unto all his servants, and unto all his land; the great temptations which thine eyes have seen, the signs, and those great miracles. Yet the Lord hath not given you an heart to perceive, and eyes to see, and ears to hear, unto this day."

The ninth and tenth verses are taken from Psalm lxix.: " Let their table be made a snare and a trap (or net) and a stumblingblock, and a recompence unto them. Let their eyes be darkened, that they may not see, and bow down their back alway." This is quoted from the Septuagint, and is in the Psalm, which is a Messianic one, put into the lips of the Messiah Himself. For the verse before these two is, " They gave me also gall for my meat, and in my thirst they gave me vinegar to drink." Our Lord Jesus Christ speaks in the Scriptures in two capacities: most frequently He

R

10 ᵐ Let their eyes be darkened, that they may not see,
and bow down their back alway.

ᵐ Ps. lxix. 23.

---

speaks as the Mediator, drawing all men to God through the accents of tender invitation, but sometimes He speaks as the just and severe Judge, and He does so in this Psalm. The people of God had committed a fearful crime in rejecting and crucifying Him, and though a door of repentance was opened very wide to receive them back, yet it was a very few who availed themselves of it, and the rest were reprobated, and the Messiah here, from His very Cross of Mercy, pronounces their doom.

Now these three verses contain a very fearful truth, which is, that certain states of soul in which men are unable to receive the plainest truths, or to receive the lessons of the plainest providential dispensations, are penal. The key to this is in certain well-known words of our Lord, three times, at least, repeated by Him: "Whosoever hath, to him shall be given, but whosoever hath not, from him shall be taken away, even that he hath" [or seemeth to have, or thinks that he has—Luke]. (Matth. xiii. 12; Mark iv. 25; Luke viii. 18.)

What is it which the disciples—representing the elect remnant of the Jews—had, and which the body of the nation had not? Evidently this one thing, sincere, humble, childlike faith. God gave to the Jews the Scriptures, which testified to two things in particular —to the holy, righteous, and just character of God, and to the Messiah, Whom He was about to send.

But these Scriptures were to the people to whom they were given according to what the people were in themselves. Those who had anything of God in them heard in these Scriptures the message of a holy, pure, loving God, and they accepted the words of Scripture as designed to lead them to Him, and conform them to His character, and so, being thus prepared, they heard, in the accents of Christ, the voice of One sent from God, and accepted Him. This is the account or solution which our Lord gives of the difference between Jew and Jew, why one accepted Him and another rejected Him. (John viii. 47.) We cannot go deeper than this. We cannot penetrate further into the secrets of God on the one hand, and of the soul on the other. If we attempt to go further back and say that God has made one soul to be of Himself, and another not, then still the question remains, what induced God to make so exceedingly awful a difference in souls fresh from His hand, that one should be for eternal life, and another for eternal death? and if we say that the difference is in the soul itself, the answer is, that the soul did not make itself—and so we must be content to treat the mystery as unthinkable.

But the teaching of these verses is something above and beyond this. It is that not the future, but the present state of the souls who abide in impenitence and unbelief, is penal. The present state is the consequence of the past. In the past history of the soul it has accepted or rejected some action of God upon it, and its present state is turned Godwards, or turned from God, accordingly. But this is not owing to the past actions of the soul alone. It is in a measure owing to God, for the seventh verse says, "The rest were hardened;" and the eighth, "God hath given to them the spirit of slumber;" and the ninth, that their table, *i.e.*, their means of sustenance, is a snare; and the tenth, that their eyes are darkened. So that here is the direct action of God in the matter of their continuance in unbelief. Now I humbly conceive that the following—though I would not put it forth for a moment as the solution of the mystery—may in some way serve to mitigate its severity. Men receive illumination from God in two ways. They receive it as they receive other mental light or knowledge, as we say, intellectually, and they receive it morally. If they receive it intellectually only, it has still a marvellous effect upon them; for a new world—the unseen and supernatural world—is opened out to them. They have new views respecting the greatest things which can occupy the human mind. But this accession of illumination has to be received morally. It has all to be acted upon in the heart or will, and it *may* not be, in numberless instances it *is* not, thus acted upon. But the moment the truth, whatever it be, is revealed to the mind or understanding, the moral reception of it is bound to follow. If it does not—as in vast numbers of cases it does not —the man is in a worse condition. He has, to use the words of one Apostle, "known the way of righteousness, and yet turned from the holy commandment given to him;" to use the words of another, "He holds the truth in unrighteousness."

Now our Lord had regard to this in this matter of hardening the hearts of the Jews, and closing their eyes; and I believe that this hardening on God's part was done, not in judgment merely, but in judgment tempered with mercy. If the normal typical Jew of our

Lord's day had accepted Jesus as the Messiah, he would assuredly have accepted Him wrongly and perversely. In his then state of heart, without repentance, without any true faith in God as hating sin and loving righteousness, without a particle of real spiritual perception, he would have accepted Him, if he accepted Him in His sacrificial aspect, as a mere substitute—the Messiah atoning for his sins, whilst he continued in them; if he accepted Christ as a King it would be as a Jewish king, upholding the national carnal ascendency, and with it the national pride and exclusiveness. What is the significance of the ministry of St. John the Baptist ? It is that the way of Christ has to be prepared, and that by repentance; or otherwise, Christ may be received to men's injury, because received carnally. So that it was not only in judgment, but in some degree of mercy that God poured upon the unhumbled, self-sufficient, carping, questioning Jews the spirit of slumber, and gave them darkened eyes, and backs bowed down as in crouching mental slavery. I have noticed (on p. 182) that the election of God, as set forth in the Apostolical Epistles, was not so much to a place in heaven, as to a place in His Church here, which Church was to be the means whereby His manifold wisdom was to be made known to the angelic world. Now nothing, humanly speaking, could have been more disastrous than the admission of the Jewish nation as such, in its then carnal state, into the mystical body; to say the least, it would have destroyed the catholicity of the Church from the very first. Even the remnant of believing Jews seem never to have taken cordially to the unreserved acceptance of the Gentiles; and so, what difficulties would there have been if the power of the whole nation had been thrown into the scale of exclusiveness !

With respect to the future state of those thus hardened, we must remember that if the Scriptures teach us one thing more than another respecting the character of Almighty God, it is that He is just, and so we may trust with the utmost confidence that no action of His upon the soul, apart from its own action upon itself, will in the least degree add to the severity with which its final impenitence will be visited.

Such is the great argument respecting God's election and reprobation, but it is by no means concluded, for he proceeds:

11. "I say then, Have they stumbled that they should fall?" *i.e.*, that they should fall finally as a nation from the favour of God.

CHAP. XI.] THROUGH THEIR FALL. 245

11 I say then, Have they stumbled that they should fall? God forbid: but *rather* ⁿ through their fall salvation *is come* unto the Gentiles, for to provoke them to jealousy.

ⁿ Acts xiii. 46.
& xviii. 6. &
xxii. 18, 21.
& xxviii. 24,
28. ch. x. 19.

11. "Have they stumbled that they should fall?" "Did they stumble that they might fall?" Revisers.

"God forbid; but rather through their fall salvation is come unto the Gentiles," &c. The elect nation of Israel has not fallen irrevocably from grace. This was far from God's intention in hardening the majority, and giving them the spirit of slumber; rather the restraining of His mercies to them was but for a season, and took place in order that He might enlarge His mercies by inviting the whole Gentile world to partake of them. It has been noticed how the opposition of the Jews to the Gospel was the occasion of its spreading the more widely. Thus on the persecution under the preaching of Stephen, they that were scattered abroad went everywhere preaching the word (Acts viii. 4). It was the opposition of the Jews to the preaching of St. Paul in Jerusalem which caused the Lord to send him at once to the Gentiles. It was the opposition of Elymas which confirmed Sergius Paulus in the faith. It was the jealousy and bitterness of the Jewish hatred which in Antioch of Pisidia caused the whole city to crowd to hear the Word of God (xiii. 44); but still all this does not meet the difficulty, which is, why was it necessary that the Jews should reject the truth before the Gentiles could be brought in to fill the places at the Gospel banquet, vacant through their rejection of it? Has God in each generation only a certain number of souls, and some must fall away before others can be brought in? Not so. The solution seems to be that the nation, as a nation, was not ripe for serving the purposes of God in His Church. That generation inherited the evil of all before it: they had rejected the prophets, they had rejected John and his preaching of repentance, which was to prepare them for Christ: they had rejected the life, the example, the patience, the meekness of Christ. If they had believed, after a fashion, in Him, so as to have crowded into the Church, they would have flooded it with their own pride and exclusiveness, and in all probability through adherence to their prejudices and false traditions, occasioned a schism in it from the very first.

12 Now if the fall of them *be* the riches of the world, and the ‖ diminishing of them the riches of the Gentiles; how much more their fulness?

‖ Or, *decay,* or, *loss.*

"To provoke them to jealousy." That is, to provoke the Jews themselves. The Jews can only be provoked to jealousy at the sight of Gentile Christians possessing their privileges. If those Christians by their life and conduct exhibit manifestly the grace of God which was forfeited by His ancient people, may not the conversion of the Jews be indefinitely retarded by the irreligion, the coldness, and the divisions of Christians?

12. "Now if the fall of them be the riches of the world, and the diminishing . . . . their fulness," &c. Various significations have been given to this verse according as commentators have understood the words "diminishing" and "fulness." It may mean with Olshausen: "If so small a number of Israelites has been able to effect so much in the Gentile world, what will Israel effect when the whole body comes to act?" Or it may be explained somewhat in this way, "When the whole world sees the prophecies respecting Israel fulfilled, and their pre-eminence restored to them, and the nation all righteous, inheriting the land of Abraham, will they not all be compelled to acknowledge the God of Israel and accept His Christ?"

Bishop Butler has a remarkable argument respecting the effect of the example of a perfectly righteous nation, in which virtue and wisdom rule all councils, and everyone, from the least to the greatest, works for the public good. He concludes with the words, "And thus, for instance, the wonderful prosperity promised to the Jewish nation in the Scriptures, would be, in a great measure, the consequence of what is predicted of them, that 'the people should be all righteous, and inherit the land for ever.' The predictions of this kind, for there are many of them, cannot come to pass in the present known course of nature; but suppose these come to pass, and then the prosperity promised must naturally follow, to a very considerable degree." ("Analogy," ch. iii.)

13, 14. "For I speak to you Gentiles, inasmuch as I am the apostle of the Gentiles, I magnify mine office: If by any means," &c. It is difficult to explain how St. Paul, by magnifying his office of Apostle of the Gentiles, could aim at provoking to jealousy some of his own countrymen, or, as he here more endearingly calls them,

CHAP. XI.] I MAGNIFY MINE OFFICE. 247

13 For I speak to you Gentiles, inasmuch as °I am the apostle of the Gentiles, I magnify mine office:

14 If by any means I may provoke to emulation *them which are* my flesh, and ᵖ might save some of them.

15 For if the casting away of them *be* the reconciling of the world, what *shall* the receiving *of them be,* but life from the dead?

° Acts ix. 15. & xiii. 2, & xxii. 21. ch. xv. 16. Gal. i. 16. & ii. 2, 7, 8, 9. Ephes. iii. 8. 1 Tim. ii. 7. 2 Tim. i. 11.
ᵖ 1 Cor. vii. 16. & ix. 22. 1 Tim. iv. 16. James v. 20.

---

13. "For I speak." So D., E., F., G., L., most Cursives, d, e, f, g, Vulg., Goth.; but א, A., B., P., four Cursives, 10, 31, 47, 73, Syr., Copt., Arm., read, "but I speak."
13. "The Apostle of the Gentiles." Revisers, "An Apostle of Gentiles."

his own flesh. In what way did he magnify his office or glorify his ministry? Some have explained it as if he magnified his office by not confining his ministrations to the Gentiles, but by extending it to the Jews, inasmuch as the Lord had sent him not only to Gentiles and kings, but also to the children of Israel. But may it not be somewhat in this way? When the Jews saw a man, who was in labours equal to or beyond the chiefest of the Apostles, laying himself out heart and soul for the conversion of the Gentiles, would they not be provoked to say within themselves, Why does this man lay himself out for the conversion of aliens? If he is from God, as his miracles seem to show, why does he not chiefly attach himself to us? And so this jealousy might lead to examination and so to faith, and so some of them, if not all, might be saved. That such was the effect of St. Paul's earnestness in asserting his mission to the Gentiles upon those of the Jews who were somewhat wavering, and inclined to believe, might surely have been the case.

15. "For if the casting away of them be the reconciling of the world," &c. It is impossible, here, to help reverting to Rom. v. 10: "If when we were enemies we were reconciled to God by the death of His Son, much more being reconciled we shall be saved by his life."

How was the casting away of the Jews the reconciling of the world? Somewhat in this way I conceive. The crucifixion of Christ by which the world was reconciled to God was a great national crime, and must be visited on the nation as such. It was so visited. They bore the punishment of it in their national rejection. God imputed to them the crime, but He imputed not

16 For if ᑫ the firstfruit *be* holy, the lump *is* also *holy:* and if the root *be* holy, so *are* the branches.

ᑫ Lev. xxiii. 10. Numb. xv. 16, 19, 20, 21.

the crime, but the atonement, to the Gentiles, and so the casting away of the Jews was the reconciling of the world; but when the crime is, in a sense, atoned for by the casting away of Israel as a people, and their subsequent miseries, then they are to be received back, and their ultimate reception will be the occasion of such overflowing mercies that it will be life to a dead world.

I do not think that either a mere spiritual revival, or the resurrection of the body, are alluded to in the terms "life from the dead." It is rather an immense extension of the same life as accrued to the world by the labours of the elect remnant, but commensurate with the vastly greater number of the restored nation.

16. "For if the firstfruit be holy, the lump is also holy: and if the root be holy," &c. We have in this verse, if rightly considered, a twofold reason for the restoration of Israel.

(1.) From the use of the firstfruits of the dough. Thus in Numbers xv. 20, "It shall be, that, when ye eat of the bread of the land, ye shall offer up an heave offering unto the Lord. Ye shall offer up a cake of the first of your dough for an heave offering: as ye do the heave offering of the threshingfloor so shall ye heave it." The heave offering they offered was assumed to consecrate the whole of the dough of the year to the Lord.

(2.) From the analogy of the root. The plant is what it is because of its root. The term holy, of course, does not mean moral or spiritual holiness, but dedication to God. Under the Jewish dispensation the altar, the vestments of the priest, the oil of anointing, were considered holy, because dedicated to the service of God. This signification of relative holiness survives in the New Testament. The Christians of any particular place were accounted holy people or saints, not because they were all pure in heart, but because they were dedicated or separated to God that they might be so.

And now what is the dough made into the offering of firstfruits, and what is the root? They cannot well be both the same (except in one way), for the cake made from the dough is the opposite of the root. It is the ultimate production of the root. The root is in the ground, and bears the stem, the branches, the flower, the fruit,

CHAP. XI.]   A WILD OLIVE TREE.   249

17 And if ʳ some of the branches be broken off,   ʳ Jer. xi. 16.
ˢ and thou, being a wild olive tree, wert graffed   ˢ Acts ii. 39. Ephes. ii. 12, 13.

---

and then the fruit by being made into dough becomes serviceable to man.

Now the dough, or heave offering, taken from it, seems to signify the elect remnant. Taken from the lump, or body of the people of Israel, they were taken by God as the firstfruits to Himself and to Christ; and if they were then taken and accepted by God, so will all Israel be when God's time comes; for these firstfruits, the Apostles, the first disciples, St. Paul, and the early converts, sanctified the nation, as the offering of the firstfruits of the dough sanctified all the bread of the year.

But what is the root? Evidently Abraham, Isaac, and Jacob, in whom God chose the Jewish race, and for whose sake and not their own they were accepted and loved. Now is it possible for these two things, so far apart, to coalesce? Yes. They coalesce in Christ. No Christian can so much as think of the Jewish remnant without thinking of Him Who called the Apostles His brethren. So far as His human nature was concerned He was the fruit of the Jewish system; His parentage, His education, His worship were Jewish, "Of whom, as concerning the flesh, Christ came."

And He is equally the root. If He was the root and the offspring of David, so was He of Abraham. From Him came the call, the election, the law, the Presence in the Temple, the promises. And yet not in an exclusive sense, for He was the firstfruits of Israel, but also the firstfruits of humanity. He was the Root of David and of Abraham, but also of all human nature, "He is before all things, and by Him all things consist." (Coloss. i. 17.)

17, 18. "And if some of the branches be broken off, and thou, being a wild olive tree, ... but the root thee." The Apostle here compares the Gentiles to a wild, uncultivated olive tree, *i.e.*, the oleaster, and the Jewish stock, derived from Christ, to a good olive tree, of which some of the branches were broken off, and branches of the wild olive grafted into their place, thus partaking of the richer sap and goodness of the cultivated tree.

Attention has been drawn to the fact that, in the process of grafting, the branch from the good stock, whatever it be, is always grafted on the wild stock; but sufficient evidence is produced from

in ‖ among them, and with them partakest of the root and
fatness of the olive tree;

‖ Or, *for them.*

---

early writers on husbandry to show that it was the practice to graft branches of the oleaster into the cultivated olive, though not for the sake of the engrafted branches, but for the original good tree which was supposed to benefit by it.[1] We need not, however, press this too closely. St. Paul has to do with the *fact* that branches from the wild tree were grafted into the cultivated tree, and this was enough for his purpose. The branches so engrafted did partake of the superior richness of the juices of the good olive. Augustine notices this seeming incongruity in the figure, and explains it by the term "contrary to nature," παρὰ φύσιν, "Quis inseret oleastrum in olivâ? Oliva solet in oleastro, oleastrum in olivâ nunquam vidimus. Quisquis fecerit non inveniet baccas nisi oleastri. Hoc ostendens Apostolus ad omnipotentiam Dei revocans. "Si tu . . . . *contra naturam.*" (Aug. on Psalm lxxii., quoted in Wordsworth.) It is clear, however, from the testimony of Columella and Palladius, that Augustine was mistaken in supposing that branches of the oleaster were never grafted into the olive. The figure is no doubt used by St. Paul after Jeremiah, "The Lord called thy name a green olive tree, fair and of goodly fruit: with the noise of a great tumult he hath kindled fire upon it, and the branches of it are broken." (Jer. xi. 16.)

And now what is this olive tree from which certain branches, the unbelieving Jews, were broken off, and into which certain believing Gentiles were inserted? It cannot, I think, be the family of Abraham, because the Gentiles, though made the children of Abraham by faith, were not grafted into Abraham. They could not be said, without something approaching to blasphemy, to receive of the root and fatness of Abraham. No, a Greater than Abraham is here. And yet we have a difficulty in saying that the olive tree is Christ Himself, inasmuch as the branches broken off were never in Him. May not the olive tree signify the Church of God? or rather,

---

[1] Thus Columella, "De Re Rusticâ," v. 9: "Solent etiam quamvis lætæ arbores fructum non afferre. Eas terebrari gallicâ terebrâ convenit, atque ita in foramen viridem taleam oleastri arcte demitti. Sic velut inita arbor fœcundo semine fertilior extat." So "Palladius de Insitione," xiv. 53, 54: "Fæcundat sterilis pingues oleaster olivas, et quæ non novit munera ferre docet," quoted in Philippi.

18 ᵗBoast not against the branches. But if thou boast, thou bearest not the root, but the root thee.   ᵗ 1 Cor. x. 12.

19 Thou wilt say then, The branches were broken off, that I might be graffed in.

---

perhaps, the body abiding in the favour of God which in a certain sense was one both in the times before and after Christ; though by the coming of Christ, He, rather than Abraham, became its centre or stem?

18. "Boast not against the branches .... but the root thee." Though boasting was usually the fault of the Jews, yet it is too probable that the Gentile believers would recriminate, and urge against the Jews their exclusion, brought about, according to this Epistle, that room might be made for the Gentiles. St. Paul meets this by a remarkable assertion of the supreme place of the Jew in the Divine Economy. We do not do justice to this place if we narrow it to the reception of the Gentiles among the spiritual seed of Abraham—it rather seems to mean that the whole Christian Economy has its root or foundation in the Jewish. Not only was Abraham the spiritual father of all the faithful; not only was the Redeemer a Jew, and all the Apostles and first teachers of Christianity, Jews, but every one of the books of Scripture, both of the Old and New Testament, was written by Jews. The book of Psalms was the Christian hymn-book for centuries before any Christian author, Greek or Latin, contributed a word to the devotional store. It seems as if for some mysterious reason it was given to the Jewish mind only to apprehend God, His unity, His will, His holiness.

19-23. We now come to the conclusion of the argument respecting the defection of Israel and the call of the Gentiles. It may be properly said to end with verses 23 or 24. For the remainder of the chapter is a prophecy of what was then in the very far future. These verses are of very great importance, as they teach us the profound differences between the views of the Apostle on this whole matter, and those which in modern times have been attributed to him. It is quite clear that the Apostle never could have written these verses if he had entertained the views of a modern Calvinist or Predestinarian who held that grace or saving faith is indefectible, for here we are taught that those who are taken out of the wild natural olive and are grafted into the good olive tree and "stand by faith," have to take warning by God's severity to the members of the older election who were broken off because of unbelief, and must take heed to continue in His goodness, otherwise the same severity will overtake them.

It is remarkable that the Apostle, who had hitherto been speaking respecting bodies of men, now for the first time begins to individualize: "Thou wert graffed in," "If thou boast," "Thou wilt say," "I might be graffed in," "Thou standest by faith," "Take heed lest he spare not thee," "Toward thee goodness," "If thou continue." The change is most marked: there has been as yet nothing like it throughout the Epistle, and as far as I can see, it can teach but one lesson, that however God may secretly foreknow or determine upon the salvation of individuals, that foreknowledge or predetermination is secret to us—we cannot rely upon it so as to say "I shall certainly be saved,"—so as to put aside fear and hearty endeavours to continue in His goodness. For, consider, how can you describe the safety of a particular Christian at any time in more distinct terms than that "he stands by faith," and that whilst God exhibits to certain other persons who have fallen away, severity, to him God exhibits goodness. Now in this goodness he has to continue, otherwise he will be cut off after the example of others who did not continue in God's goodness and were cut off. The Apostle here follows up the teaching of our Blessed Lord Himself in the parable of the vine and its branches. "I am the Vine, ye are the branches." "If a man abide not in me, he is cast forth as a branch and is withered."

Now from all this it seems to be abundantly manifest that the election which St. Paul has in view all through this long argument is not one which has for its chief element indefectible grace, or indefectible faith, just as we have shown that it cannot be an election in which God's will overpowers that of the individual, so that he should be in the position of mere lifeless clay, in which the exercise of will, or freedom, or acquiescence, or rejection, cannot be taken into account.

Again, according to St. Paul's view, there was a national election, which, as we shall see, was in a sense absolute as regards the nation or Church (which might be regarded as identical), but was consistent with the falling away of individuals, and in our Lord's time many did so fall—in fact, the great majority. By their fall a gap, as it were, was left in the sides of the goodly

CHAP. XI.] BE NOT HIGHMINDED. 253

20 Well; because of unbelief they were broken off, and thou standest by faith. ᵘBe not highminded, but ˣfear:

ᵘ ch. xii. 16.
ˣ Prov. xxviii. 14. Isai. lxvi. 2. Phil. ii. 12.

olive tree, which was filled up, not by a nation, but by individual believers, who accepted Christ, and so stood by faith. Now we should have supposed that such, having accepted Christ willingly, and *ex animo*, and in the face of very great danger to life and property, and very bitter persecutions from their heathen fellow-countrymen, would possess, if any did, indefectible faith; but, according to the Apostle, it was not so. He speaks to them words of serious warning, much more serious than we should have supposed they needed. We will now examine each of these verses singly.

19. "Thou wilt say then, the branches were broken off that I might be graffed in." This seemed to be the fact, but it was not so. The truth really was the branches were broken off, *and* they were graffed in. The branches were broken off for no other reason than their refusal to believe in Him Whom God sent, *and* the Gentiles were graffed in, in accordance with the Lord's saying, "Go out into the highways and hedges and compel them to come in, that my house may be filled."

20. "Well; because of unbelief they were broken off, and thou standest by faith," &c. "Thou standest by faith." Nothing stronger can be said of anyone's faith than that he stands by it; he stands justified. "We have access by faith unto this grace wherein we stand" (v. 2). "By faith ye stand" (2 Corinth. i. 24). Some, remarking on this passage, have said, that by faith the Apostle here means professed faith, and not real faith. But how can men stand by anything but real faith? Professed faith, if not sincere, must be hypocritical, or, at least, worthless; but the faith here is so availing, that because of it God exhibits His goodness to them, as distinguished from those to whom He exhibits severity.

"Be not highminded," &c. As if God had some personal preference for thee apart from thy love, or godly fear, or good works.

"But fear." The Lord, in the most solemn, earnest way, bids His own Apostles fear: "I say unto you, my friends, Be not afraid of them that kill the body—fear him which, after he hath killed, hath power to cast into hell; yea, I say unto you, fear him."

21 For if God spared not the natural branches, *take heed* lest he also spare not thee.

22 Behold therefore the goodness and severity of God: on them which fell, severity; but toward thee, goodness, ʸ if thou continue in *his* goodness: otherwise ᶻ thou also shalt be cut off.

ʸ 1 Cor. xv. 2. Hebr. iii. 6, 14.
ᶻ John xv. 2.

---

21. "Take heed lest he also spare not thee;" rather, "Neither will he spare thee," Revisers, after א, A., B., C., D., F., G., L., P., and many (seventy-five) Cursives.

22. "Toward thee, goodness." א, A., B., C., D., d, Vulg., Cop., Arm., read, "goodness of God;" but F., G., L., most Cursives, Goth., Syr., Æth., as in Rec. Text.

(Luke xii. 4, 6.) Again, "Work out your own salvation with fear." (Phil. ii. 12.) Again, "Pass the term of your sojourning here in fear." (1 Pet. i. 17.) And yet this fear is in no way inconsistent with rejoicing in God: "Serve the Lord with fear, and rejoice unto him with reverence," nor with the highest comforts of religion, for the primitive churches, "walking in the fear of the Lord, and in the comfort of the Holy Ghost, were multiplied" (Acts ix. 31).

21. "For if God spared not the natural branches, take heed," &c. The use of the word "natural" applied to the elder election is remarkable. The promises of God to Abraham and to his seed were all out of the usual course of nature, but the length of time which had elapsed since the original call, had made the reception of grace on the part of the Jews, in a measure, natural in the sense of according to the course of things. And if we believe in God as the Creator, so it is with all natural sequences. God first established them by His fiat, and it is only because of their long and uninterrupted continuance that they are now called natural.

"Take heed, lest he also spare not thee." The natural, *i.e.*, the older branches, might be supposed to have a sort of natural claim which the engrafted branches had not.

22. "Behold therefore the goodness and severity of God: on them which fell," &c. "On them which fell," *i.e.*, by not accepting Christ, which we have seen arose from the hard and impenitent state of their hearts.

"But toward thee, goodness," &c. In the gift of the Holy Spirit issuing in their conversion and continuance in the faith to that present time. Again I desire the reader to mark how he speaks of those who fell in the plural number, but to the Gentile singly, "toward thee, goodness."

CHAP. XI.] GOD IS ABLE. 255

23 And they also, ᵃ if they abide not still in unbelief, shall be graffed in: for God is able to graff them in again.   ᵃ 2 Cor. iii. 16.

24 For if thou wert cut out of the olive tree which is wild by nature, and wert graffed contrary to nature into a good olive tree: how much more shall these, which be the natural *branches*, be graffed into their own olive tree?

"If thou continue in his goodness," &c. If thou continue in faith— in *the* faith, in faith working by love. Rather, perhaps, in Christ, according to the Lord's words, "Abide in me and I in you," or those of His servant, "And now, little children, abide in him."

This, then, is the conclusion of this long and deep argument respecting the election and the casting away of God's ancient people. Not knowing the whole of the Apostle's mind upon this great mystery, inasmuch as in these chapters we have nothing like a set treatise upon it, conceived and planned to elucidate sixteenth or seventeenth century controversies, we can only say that the Apostle says nothing respecting indefectible grace or faith, that for some reason or other he seems carefully to exclude from his purview the final condition of individual souls, on or after the Day of Judgment, and that the acceptance or rejection of persons, so far as it is foreseen, is because of their character.

23. "And they also, if they abide not still in unbelief, shall be graffed in ... again." Notice here how the Apostle does not say, "they if they abide not in unbelief shall be received into heaven," but "shall be graffed in again," that is, into the olive-tree of God's favour, or family, or into His Church, if that is, as is most probable, the olive-tree of St. Paul corresponds to the Vine and the branches of his Divine Master.

"God is able to graff them in again." What is the meaning of this reference to God's power? We should rather have expected a reference to His willingness. It probably means "consistently with His justice." They have not so sinned, but that God can, consistently with His moral attributes, restore them.

24. "For if thou wert cut out of the olive tree ... graffed into their own olive tree?" Gentilism, as opposed to Judaism, is here called " wild by nature." The Jews, from the time of Abraham to that of Christ, had been well cared for by God. They were His

25 For I would not, brethren, that ye should be ignorant

vineyard (Isaiah v. 1-8; Matth. xxi. 33), His fig-tree (Luke xiii. 6), and so might be called a good olive tree, in the sense of a cultivated one. The Gentiles, on the contrary, had been left to themselves, having only to guide them that light of nature which, though it comes from God, is exceedingly deficient in the matter both of clearness and authority, as compared with the light of Revelation vouchsafed to the Jews through Moses and the prophets. Now, inasmuch as the Revelation of God in Moses and the prophets was to prepare the Jews for Christ, one may say that naturally, *i.e.*, according to the settled course of God's providential dealings, Christianity, or the Christian Church, belonged to Israel, as the olive tree tended by God, and those who were taken out of Gentilism, and grafted into the Church, were so treated παρὰ φύσιν, beside nature, out of the usual course of nature. Philippi's comment is excellent: "The Jews, as natural descendants of the patriarchs, have a prior right, confirmed by Divine choice and promise, to share in the Messianic kingdom and salvation, just because their forefathers received the promise on behalf of them—their posterity—as well as on their own account. If God in this way placed Himself in a closer relation to Israel, He will the more certainly maintain this relation, and make Israel partaker in the blessing pertaining to it, since He Himself endowed with this blessing the Gentiles, who are further removed from Him."

25. "For I would not, brethren, that ye should be ignorant of this mystery . . . fulness of the Gentiles be come in." What is the mystery? It is that blindness has (in part) happened unto Israel; in other words, that a nation whom God has chosen to be His own people are incapable of discerning as others may, and do, discern, truths of God which are by right peculiarly theirs, and that this blindness is not natural, but an infliction on God's part by way of penalty for their national rejection of His Son and His Spirit. This is, in itself, a most mysterious action on the part of God, and never can be understood by us in our present state, in which the mode and manner in which God enlightens the mind, or prevents it from receiving light, is wholly unknown to us, and is a very deep moral mystery, as well as a mental one.[1] It is expressed

[1] As this is the first instance of the occurrence of this word "mystery" in the Epistles,

CHAP. XI.]   WISE IN YOUR OWN CONCEITS.   257

of this mystery, lest ye should be ^b wise in your own
conceits; that ^c ‖ blindness in part is happened
to Israel, ^d until the fulness of the Gentiles be
come in.

b ch. xii. 16.
c ver. 7. 2
Cor. iii. 14.
‖ Or, *hardness*.
d Luke xxi.
24. Rev. vii. 9.

in different language in 2 Cor. iii. 15, " But even unto this day,
when Moses is read, the vail is upon their heart."

"Lest ye should be wise in your own conceits," *i.e.*, lest ye
should think that the deepest things of God are on a level with your
understandings. The Gentiles might say, "It is through our intellect, our wisdom " [1 Cor. i. 22, "The Greeks seek after wisdom"],
"that we have attained to the knowledge of Christ; and that these
stupid, besotted Jews have not, is through their dulness of comprehension." "No," the Apostle says, "what you have received is
through faith, a gift of God, and, for their sins blindness has
happened unto them. It is a judicial blindness, and is only for a
time."

"Until the fulness of the Gentiles be come in." Our Blessed
Lord is reported in St. Luke's Gospel to have thus expressed Himself: "And they [the Jews] shall fall by the edge of the sword, and

---

many commentators give a definition of it which goes far, if accepted, to remove all
mystery from the deepest truths of Christianity, and place them entirely within the reach
of the ordinary human intellect. Thus Philippi, " Paul uses the word 'mystery' to designate the fact he is about to announce. He does not mean by this, as might be thought
from the meaning this term has taken in ecclesiastical language, that this fact represents
something incomprehensible to reason. In the New Testament the word denotes a truth
or fact which can only be known by man through a communication from above, but
which, after this revelation has taken place, falls into the domain of the understanding."
But, we must ask, is it a fact that the truth or fact, after it is revealed, falls into the
domain of the understanding? Take what St. Paul calls the mystery of the Gospel. Is
it a fact that any one article of the great mystery of godliness is level with human comprehension? That the Word was made flesh—that after being so made He could say, " I and
my Father are one "—that His Death could atone for all sin—and that by His Resurrection
He could impart His own Life to all that receive Him—that His Body was so spiritualized
that it could pass through the closed door—that in this Body He ascended far above all
heavens—that in Him dwells the fulness of the Godhead bodily—that He has a knowledge
of mankind so infinite that He can understand and sympathize with all their wants, and
intercede with His Father for each one in particular—surely none of these revealed
facts can rightly be said to fall into the domain of the understanding. By being revealed
they lose none of their real inherent mystery. And so with the mystery that "blindness
in part has happened unto Israel." What the vail on their hearts really is, how God
draws it over their hearts, how God holds it over them, and how God removes it and
why He does all this, and does not take some other way of punishing them, is an amazing
mystery.

S

26 And so all Israel shall be saved: as it is written,
*There shall come out of Sion the Deliverer,
and shall turn away ungodliness from Jacob:

* Isai. lix. 20.
See Ps. xiv. 7.

---

shall be led away captive into all nations: and Jerusalem shall be trodden down of the Gentiles, until the times of the Gentiles be fulfilled." (Luke xxi. 24). Daniel also seems to prophesy the restoration of the Jews, both to spiritual belief and to temporal prosperity, in the words, " And at that time shall Michael stand up, the great prince which standeth for the children of thy people ; and there shall be a time of trouble, such as never was since there was a nation even to that same time: and at that time thy people shall be delivered, every one that shall be found written in the book "(xii. 1). All these three places, in St. Paul, in St. Luke, and in Daniel, seem to refer to the same time—a time which, perhaps, St. Paul deemed to be closer at hand than it really was.

The fulness of the Gentiles does not seem to refer to the whole body of the Gentile nations, but to the true elect people of God amongst them.

26. " And so all Israel shall be saved: as it is written, There shall come," &c. This verse, fairly interpreted, can, it seems to me, have but one meaning—that there will be a restoration of Israel, as a nation, to their lost privileges as the ancient people of God. Israel in this verse cannot possibly mean the whole Catholic Church, Jew and Gentile, considered as one body in Christ, in which there is neither Jew nor Greek, because the Apostle has been dwelling on the mystery of the acceptance of the elect Gentiles, and their being grafted into the Body, and then of the Jews or Israel as broken off, and now he predicts the restoration of those broken off, and prophesies that it will be national in contrast with the blindness, which has been only in part. There will thus be salvation, not of a mere remnant, but of the whole people ; and as the matter is clearly in the future, and so in its details known only to God, I do not see that we have any right to limit that to which God has set no limits.

There are several distinct prophecies that the conversion or regeneration of the nation will be of a kind such as the world has never seen before. Thus Isaiah lx. 21, " Thy people shall be all righteous: they shall inherit the land for ever, the branch of my planting, the work of my hands, that I may be glorified." And

CHAP. XI.]   THIS IS MY COVENANT.   259

27 'For this *is* my covenant unto them, when   f Isai. xxvii. 9.
I shall take away their sins.   Jer. xxxi. 31,
&c. Hebr.
viii. 8. & x. 16.

again Isaiah lxvi. 8, "Who hath heard such a thing? who hath seen such things? Shall the earth be made to bring forth in one day? or shall a nation be born at once? for as soon as Zion travailed, she brought forth her children." Again, in the last verses of several of the Minor Prophets, a restoration of Israel is foretold, compared to which the restoration after the Babylonish captivity seems as nothing. Thus the last verses of Hosea xiv. 4, " I will heal their backsliding, I will love them freely: for mine anger is turned away from him. I will be as the dew unto Israel: he shall grow as the lily, and cast forth his roots as Lebanon." And Joel iii. 21, "I will cleanse their blood that I have not cleansed: for the Lord dwelleth in Zion." So also with the last words in the prophecies of Amos, of Obadiah, of Micah, of Zephaniah, of Zechariah, and especially Hosea iii. 5, to which I have before referred.

There may be difficulties as to the time of this restoration and regeneration. Sometimes it seems connected with the Second Advent and the Judgment. Some have speculated wildly upon it and have pronounced it Pre-Millennial or Post-Millennial: some that it will take place in the present course of things, others, as Bishop Butler, that "These things cannot come to pass in the present known course of nature." But I cannot see that these difficulties, which are all in our own minds, and are entirely owing to our want of knowledge of the future, can affect declarations in Scripture very plain and very numerous.

"As it is written, There shall come out of Sion the Deliverer, and shall turn away ungodliness from Jacob." This quotation agrees more with the Septuagint than with the Hebrew. In the former it reads, "And the deliverer shall come for Zion's sake, and shall turn away ungodliness from Jacob." The Hebrew reads, "Thy Redeemer shall come to Zion, and unto them that turn from transgression in Jacob." Both renderings are alike in their spiritual meaning—the Redeemer comes to them that turn from transgression, and His spiritual approach to them is the cause of their turning from transgression. The Redeemer comes out of Zion and turns away ungodliness by His coming.

27. "For this is my covenant unto them, when I shall take away their sins." This is a very obscure place, and being such is passed

28 As concerning the gospel, *they are* enemies for your sakes: but as touching the election, *they are* ⁸ beloved for the fathers' sakes.

ᵍ Deut. vii. 8. & ix. 5. & x. 15.

---

over by several commentators. It seems to refer to the last verse and to the words "to turn away ungodliness from Jacob," and is thus a reproduction of the sense of the words of Jeremiah xxxi. 31: "Behold, the days come, saith the Lord, that I will make a new covenant with the house of Israel, and with the house of Judah. . . . . I will put my law in their inward parts, and write it in their hearts. . . . . I will forgive their iniquity and remember their sin no more." It seems simply to mean, "When I take away their sins I will remember the covenant made with their fathers, that they shall be all righteous and all My people." [1]

28. "As concerning the gospel, they are enemies for your sakes," &c. How can this be? I think in this way. The extension of the Gospel and the Church to the Gentiles more than all else hardened the Jews in unbelief, and made them reject the preaching of Christ, and so they continued in their national alienation from God. This was for your sakes, (δἰ ὑμᾶς,) because the Jews would, humanly speaking, have far more widely accepted Christ if the acceptance of Him had not been united with the acceptance of the equality of the Gentiles with them in Christ.

"But as touching the election, they are beloved for the fathers' sakes." We can find no better illustration of this than in Levit. xxvi. 41: "If their uncircumcised hearts be humbled, and they then accept of the punishment of their iniquity: then will I remember my covenant with Jacob, and also my covenant with Isaac, and also my covenant with Abraham will I remember." And again, "Only the Lord had a delight in thy fathers to love them, and he chose their seed after them, even you above all people, as it is this day." (Deut. x. 15.)

Notice here St. Paul's view of election. It is a body of people chosen in a particular man; first in Abraham, then in Isaac, then in Jacob. The history seems to tell us that in no particular generation did the mass of the people adhere to God, but God continued

---

[1] It has been supposed that the Apostle cites Isaiah xxvii. 9 in the Septuagint: "Therefore shall the iniquity of Jacob be taken away: and this is his blessing when I shall have taken away his sin;" but there is no mention of a covenant, as would seem necessary.

29 For the gifts and calling of God *are* ʰwith-   h Num. xxiii. 19.
out repentance.

---

the election through a small minority, so that there never failed to be a remnant in whom He made good His word and promises.

29. "For the gifts and calling of God are without repentance." The calling is, of course, the calling of the Israelites in Abraham to be the people of God. This is irrevocable. Even in their then state of unbelief and opposition to the Gospel, "God hath not cast away His people." There was even then, and has ever been since, a remnant according to the election of grace, and when the times of the Gentiles are fulfilled, the whole elect nation as one man will return. But what are the gifts which are irrevocable? Godet has a remarkable exposition, which is, that they are special gifts for making known the truth of God: "Who can fail to see that the people of Israel are really endowed with singular qualities for their mission as the Salvation-people? The Greeks, the Romans, the Phœnicians, had their special gifts in the different domains of science and art, law and politics, industry and commerce. Israel, without being destitute of the powers related to those spheres of mundane activity, have received a higher gift, the organ for the Divine, and the intuition of holiness. The calling of God is on the one hand the cause, on the other the effect of those gifts. It is because God called this people in His eternal counsel that He entrusted the gifts to them, and it is because He enriched them with these gifts that in the course of time He called on them to fulfil the task of initiating the world in the way of salvation, and of preparing salvation for the world. Of this august mission, they have been, for the time, deprived; instead of entering first, they will enter last. But their destination is, nevertheless, irrevocable; and through the overflowing of Divine mercy (ch. v. 20) it will be realized in them at the period announced by the Apostle, when saved themselves they will become a stream of life from above to flow into the hearts of Gentile Christendom."

With respect to the calling and gifts of individuals, it is impossible to speak so absolutely in the face of such passages as the 22nd verse of this very chapter, and in the face of such words as those of the Lord, "From him that hath not, shall be taken away even that which he hath," and "Take from him the pound, and give it to him that hath ten pounds." (Luke xix. 24.) Still, if God has given to

30 For as ye ¹in times past have not ‖ believed God, yet have now obtained mercy through their unbelief:

31 Even so have these also now not ‖ believed, that through your mercy they also may obtain mercy.

¹Ephes. ii. 2.
Col. iii. 7.
‖ Or, *obeyed.*
‖ Or, *obeyed.*

---

men repentance and faith, it is a plain proof of His desire that they should serve Him in this world, and enjoy the fruits of so doing in the next; and though we are utterly unable to make the indefectibility of grace a dogma, yet we can take abundant comfort from the assertion "He that hath begun a good work in you, will perform it until the day of Jesus Christ." (Phil. i. 6.)

30, 31. "For as ye in times past have not believed God, yet have now obtained mercy," &c. This may be rendered, "As ye have not obeyed God, and through their disobedience," &c. How was it that the Gentiles obtained mercy through the faithlessness or disobedience of the Jews? Supposing that the Jews had believed in, and, consequently, obeyed Christ, could not the Gentiles have been converted? Humanly speaking, they might, but it seems to have been required by the hidden wisdom and secret counsel of God that what is implied in the figure of the olive tree with its broken branches, and the wild branches filling up the vacancy, must take place. Godet throws out the hint "that time of disobedience has now taken end; the Gentiles have found grace. But at what price? By means of the disobedience of the Jews. We have seen this, indeed: God needed to make the temporary sacrifice of His elect people, in order to disentangle the Gospel from the legal forms in which they wished to keep it imprisoned." This is what I have said, that the influx of the majority of the Jewish people at the first, in their then state of indomitable prejudice, would have rendered the Catholicity of the Church impossible. But may it not be that it was Jewish unbelief which brought about the Crucifixion and Death of Christ, and through it, mercy to the world?

"Even so have these also now not believed [or obeyed], that through your mercy," &c. This seems to refer to the dispensation of God alluded to in the words of Moses, cited in x. 19, that the Jews should be provoked to jealousy by seeing the grace of God manifestly displayed in the conversion of the Gentiles.

32 For ᵏ God hath ‖ concluded them all in unbelief, that he might have mercy upon all.

ᵏ ch. iii. 9.
Gal. iii. 22.
‖ Or, *shut them all up together*

33 O the depth of the riches both of the wisdom and knowledge of God! ¹ how unsearchable *are* his judgments, and ᵐ his ways past finding out!

¹ Ps. xxxvi. 6.
ᵐ Job xi. 7.
Ps. xcii. 5.

---

32. "For God hath concluded them all in unbelief, that he might," &c. This seems to have somewhat of the same significance as Gal. iii. 22, 23, "The Scripture hath concluded all under sin, that the promise by faith of Jesus Christ might be given to them that believe. But before [the] faith came we were kept under the law, shut up unto the faith which should afterwards be revealed." It pleased God to account all as sinners, that all might be saved by grace, for the repentance, and the shame, and humbleness of mind which attend true conviction of sin, all which is of grace, is far more receptive of the righteousness of God than an inferior outside righteousness attained by mere human endeavour. Both Chrysostom and Theodoret understand the word concluded [συνέκλεισεν] in the sense of convicted or convinced. Chrysostom, "Hath concluded them all in unbelief, that is, hath convinced them, hath shown them disobedient; not that they may remain in disobedience, but that He may save the one by the captiousness of the other, these by those, and those by these. Now consider, ye were disobedient, and they were saved. Again, they have been disobedient, and ye have been saved. Yet ye have not been so saved, as to be put away again, as the Jews were, but so as to draw them over through jealousy, while ye abide."

And Theodoret, "He has put the word 'concluded' instead of 'convicted.'" This verse is not to be taken in an universalist sense, but with reference to Jews and Gentiles as bodies of men. He hath concluded all in unbelief; not that He might save all in impenitence, but that He might save all by grace—all, that is, who submit to be so saved.

33. "O the depth of the riches both of the wisdom and knowledge of God!" Most expositors make St. Paul's exclamation of wonder and admiration to apply to three things—not the riches of the wisdom and knowledge, but God's riches, and His wisdom and His knowledge. His riches being, as it were, the infinite variety of His resources, His wisdom "denotes the admirable skill with

34 ⁿFor who hath known the mind of the Lord? or °who hath been his counsellor?

35 Or ᵖwho hath first given to him, and it shall be recompensed unto him again?

ⁿ Job xv. 8. Isai. xl. 13. Jer. xxiii. 18. 1 Cor. ii. 16.
° Job xxxvi. 22.
ᵖ Job xxxv. 7. & xli. 11.

---

which God weaves into His plans the free actions of man, and transforms them into so many means for the accomplishment of the excellent end which He set originally before Him, whilst His knowledge refers especially to the Divine foreknowledge, which God has of the free determinations of men, whether as individuals or as nations." (Godet.)

"Judgments" seem to mean decisions or decrees, and taking into account the things which the Apostle has been considering in the three chapters, they must be judicial decisions or decrees. Take, for instance, the blinding or hardening of the Jews—here His decrees or decisions are unsearchable: it is infinitely above the human comprehension, and the way in which He accomplished it is untrackable, and yet we must rest in the goodness and justice of all He has decided or decreed, and believe that He has ordained all, both means and end, in the most far-seeing mercy.

St. Paul could not possibly have written this doxology if he desired to uphold the mere wilfulness for which Calvin contends. Mere wilfulness would cut short everything, whereas here St. Paul worships a will which takes everything into account, and whose end is, even when concluding all men in unbelief, to have mercy upon all.

34. "For who hath known the mind of the Lord? or who hath been his counsellor?" This seems to refer to Isaiah xl. 13, "Who hath directed the Spirit of the Lord, or being his counsellor hath taught him?" Or as it is in the Septuagint, "Who hath known the mind (νοῦν) of the Lord, and who has been his counsellor?" And yet there was one Who knew His Mind, and with Whom He took counsel, even that Word, Who was in the beginning with God, and Who was God, by Whom all things were made: and when that Word was made flesh and dwelt amongst us, He said, "The Father loveth the Son, and sheweth Him all things that Himself doeth."

35. "Or who hath first given to him, and it shall be recompensed," &c. This is taken from Job xli. 11, "Who hath prevented me,

36 For ^q of him, and through him, and to him, *are* all things: ^r to † whom *be* glory for ever. Amen.

^q 1 Cor. viii. 6. Col. i. 16.
^r Gal. i. 5.
1 Tim. i. 17.
2 Tim. iv. 18.
Hebr. xiii. 21.
1 Pet. v. 11.
2 Pet. iii. 18.
Jude xxv.
Rev. i. 6.
† Gr. *him.*

[that is, hath been beforehand with me, in a matter of bounty] that I should repay him? whatsoever is under the whole heaven is mine." It seems to mean, in accordance with the doctrine of the rest of this Epistle, Who can claim anything of God, in the way of merit, or as wages for work done?

36. "For of him, and through him, and to him, are all things," &c. "Of him," as their origin; "through him," inasmuch as He upholds them in existence; and "to him," inasmuch as all things subserve His purposes, and willingly or unwillingly contribute to His glory.

CHAP. XII.

I ^a BESEECH you therefore, brethren, by the ^a 2 Cor. x. 1.

1. "I beseech you, therefore, brethren, by the mercies of God," &c. The Apostle now turns from his deep argument respecting the casting away of God's ancient people, and the calling of the Gentiles, to the practical conclusion of it all. And this conclusion is one of mercy. In looking back on all that he has written, he sees not the assertion of mere will—of iron will, unbending, unalterable, unswervable—but of mercy. And so he beseeches them, not by the predestination, but by the mercies of God.

"I beseech you." This may mean either beseech (*obsecro*) or exhort. Chrysostom, Theodoret, the Vulgate, and Syriac, all render it by "beseech." Chrysostom applies this very beautifully: "And though he is so great and good a person, yet he does not decline beseeching them, and that not for any enjoyment he was likely to get himself, but for that *they* would have to gain. And why wonder that he does not decline beseeching, where he is even

^b 1 Pet. ii. 5.
^c Ps. l. 13, 14.
ch. vi. 13, 16,
19. 1 Cor. vi.
13, 20.

mercies of God, ^bthat ye ^cpresent your bodies

putting God's mercies before them? For since, he means, it is from this you have those numberless blessings, from the mercies of God, reverence them, be moved to compassion by them. For they themselves take the attitude of suppliants that you would show no conduct unworthy of them. 'I entreat you, then,' he means, 'by the very things through which you were saved.'"

"By the mercies of God." What were these mercies? Of course they were, first of all, the mercies which he had been describing. The mercy of having been engrafted into the good olive tree of God—into the Church of Abraham and the Patriarchs; above all, into the Church of Christ and His Apostles. Then following upon this the mercy of justification by faith, sealed in Baptism—the mercy of a new nature, and full and perfect forgiveness, not bestowed according to desert, in which case they would have been destitute of God's gifts, but solely through grace—that is, bestowed freely; and then the source of all this, God sending His own Son in the likeness of sinful flesh, this Son dying for our sins, and rising again for our Justification, and entering the most holy place as our forerunner, and sitting there as our Advocate. And for what purpose does the Apostle appeal to all this? he tells us, "That ye present your bodies a living sacrifice, holy, acceptable to God," in contrast with all known sacrifices, Jewish or heathen, which consisted in the offering of bodies from which the life blood had been drawn.

Some commentators, as Philippi, assert that "your bodies" means "yourselves," your entire personality as both soul and body. But the Apostle assumes that they had already presented their souls and spirits by their belief or acceptance of Christ. This offering of the soul, the will, the heart, was to be daily, constantly consummated by the presenting of their bodies, and was to be accomplished by the mortification of the corrupt desires which resided in their bodies.

It is what the Apostle had expressed a little before in the words, "Let not sin reign in your mortal body, that ye should obey it in the lusts thereof; neither yield ye your members as instruments of unrighteousness unto sin: but yield yourselves unto God, as those that are alive from the dead, and your members as instruments of righteousness unto God" (vi. 12, 13).

A LIVING SACRIFICE.

^d a living sacrifice, holy, acceptable unto God, *which is* your reasonable service.   d Hebr. x. 10.

"Present your bodies a living sacrifice." And how is the body, it may be said, to become a sacrifice? "Let thy eye look upon no evil thing, and it hath become a sacrifice; let thy tongue speak nothing filthy, and it hath become an offering; let thy hand do no lawless deed, and it hath become a whole burnt-offering. Or rather, this is not enough, but we must have good works also; let the hand do alms, the mouth bless them that cross one, and the hearing find leisure evermore for reading of Scripture. Again, [the Jews] presented the thing sacrificed dead, this maketh the thing sacrificed to be living. For when we have mortified our members then shall we be able to live. For the law of this sacrifice is new, and so the sort of fire is a marvellous one. For it needeth no wood or matter under it, but our fire liveth of itself, and doth not burn up the victim, but rather quickeneth it."

"Holy." Dedicated to God by being surrendered to His service, and sanctified by the constant indwelling of His Holy Spirit.

"Acceptable unto God." Because resting on and in connection with His Son's Sacrifice.

"Your reasonable service." This may be said in contrast with the Jewish and heathen sacrifices of irrational creatures, whose wills were of no account in the service, whereas the essence of the Christian's sacrifice of his body is in the will being subdued to God's will, prompting the offering. In the one case the thing offered was unreasoning, in the other the reason itself, the man's highest faculty, presents the offering. The reader will remember how we are privileged to offer this sacrifice in our highest service of praise and thanksgiving: "And here we offer and present unto Thee, O Lord, ourselves, our souls, and bodies, to be a reasonable, holy, and lively sacrifice unto Thee." They are the most difficult words of the service, because requiring the deepest spirit of self-surrender.

2. "And be not conformed to this world, but be ye transformed," &c. "This world" comprehended the whole course of the unregenerate society, heathen or Jewish, which was not ruled by the Spirit of God. The Christian was not to be fashioned in his life and conversation by this society. He must keep out of it as much as he could. If obliged to mix in it for a time, he must do so, as it were, under protest, for he would be liable to be led into com-

^a 1 Pet. i. 14.
1 John ii. 15.

2 And ^a be not conformed to this world: but

---

pliances which were idolatrous and sinful. The words of St. John were literally true, "The world lieth in wickedness," "the world lieth in the wicked one." Everything by which the world acted or showed itself—the concourse of men, their assemblies, their amusements—were all deeply tainted with evil. Architecture, painting, statuary, poetry, even philosophy, all were evil, all unregenerate, and must be shunned if men would maintain a consistent profession of Christ. But is it so now, now that the world is baptized, and nations profess Christianity? If all the baptized lived to the grace given to them and ever remembered their vows, the world would be Christian; but if the vast mass of the baptized live as if they were not members of Christ, and disregard their vows, then the world is as dangerous now as it was then, and all who would be true Christians must take heed lest they be conformed to it. There is the lust of the flesh, the lust of the eyes, the pride of life, as much in the Christian world as in the heathen, only under another form.

"The world without God, is false, impure, and turbulent, a mighty heaving confusion of fallen spirits, wrestling with each other and with God. As such, this world is in eternal opposition to Him. It can only be reconciled by passing out of itself into His kingdom; by receiving the laws of truth and obedience, of holiness and order, that is, in ceasing to be the world, and being taken into the will of God. Besides the grosser kinds of sensual and spiritual evil, this world has a multitude of refined and subtle powers of enmity against the Divine Will. There is, besides the lust of the flesh, also the lust of the eyes; the vain-glory, pomp, glitter, ostentation, of ease, luxury, and self-pleasing; and there is, moreover, the pride of life, the stately self-worship, the fastidious self-contemplation of intellectual or secular men. And with this comes also a throng of less elevated sins—levity, love of pleasure, full fare, a thirst for money, a hunger for popularity, and its debasing successes. These things steal away the heart, and make men false to their Heavenly Master. Their obedience becomes habitually double, vain-glorious, self-advancing, or heartless, hollow, and reluctant. If they do not by express acts betray Him, it is either because they are not tempted, or because they would lose in the scale of the world's esteem or their own." (Manning's "Sermons," vol. iii. p. 49.)

CHAP. XII.]   BE YE TRANSFORMED.   269

be ye transformed by the renewing of your mind,   f Ephes. i. 18. & iv. 23. Col. i. 21, 22. & iii. 10.

"But be ye transformed by the renewing of your mind." There is not the same relation between the words, "conformed," "transformed," in the Greek as there is in the English. The former word for conformed (συσχηματίζεσθε) would be best represented by the English word "fashion." "In the use of his consecrated body, the believer has first an everywhere-present model to be rejected, then a new type to be discerned and realized. The model to be rejected is that presented to him by the present world, or, as we should say, the reigning *fashion*, taking this word in its widest sense. The term σχῆμα denotes the manner of holding one's self, attitude, pose, and the verb σχηματίζεσθαι, derived from it, the adoption or imitation of this pose, or received mode of conduct. . . . It is this mode of living anterior to regeneration which the believer is not to imitate in the use which he makes of his body. And what is he to do? To seek a new model, a superior type, to be realized by means of a power acting within him. He is to be transformed, literally metamorphosed. The term μορφή, form, strictly denotes, not an external pose, suitable for imitation, like σχῆμα, attitude, but an organic form, the natural product of a principle of life which manifests itself thus. It is not by looking around him, to the right and left, that the believer is to learn to use his body, but by putting himself under the dominion of a new power, which will, by an inward necessity, transform this use." (Godet).

Chrysostom also, in plainer language, goes deeper, and is more practical. "He says not change the *fashion*, but be transformed, to show that the world's ways are a fashion, but virtue's not a fashion, but a real *form*, with a natural beauty of its own, lacking not the trickeries and fashions of outward things, which no sooner appear than they go to nought. For all these things, even before they come to light, are dissolving (*i.e.*, approaching dissolution). If then thou throwest the fashion aside, thou wilt speedily come to the form. For nothing is more strengthless than vice, nothing so easily wears old."

"By the renewing of your mind," *i.e.*, by the power of God's Holy Spirit, according to the words of the Apostle in Titus iii. 5: "By his mercy he saved us, by the washing of regeneration, and renewing of the Holy Ghost." For this we pray in the Collect for

| | 270 | GOOD, ACCEPTABLE, PERFECT. | [ROMANS. |

<small>g Ephes. v. 10, 17. 1 Thess. iv. 3.</small>
<small>h ch. i. 5. & xv. 15. 1 Cor. iii. 10. & xv. 10. Gal. ii. 9. Ephes. iii. 2, 7, 8.</small>
<small>i Prov. xxv. 27. Eccles. vii. 16. ch. xi. 20.</small>

that ye may ^g prove what *is* that good, and acceptable, and perfect, will of God.

3 For I say, ^h through the grace given unto me, to every man that is among you, ⁱ not to think *of himself* more highly than he ought to think; but

---

Christmas Day: "That we being regenerate, and made Thy children by adoption and grace, may daily be renewed by Thy Holy Spirit."

"That ye may prove what is that good, and acceptable, and perfect, will of God." "Prove," *i.e.*, appreciate, discern, with the view of fulfilling it.

"Good, and acceptable, and perfect will." Wesley has an admirable pithy note: "The will of God is here to be understood of all the preceptive part of Christianity, which is in itself so excellently good, so acceptable to God, and so perfective of our nature."

3. "For I say, through the grace given unto me, to every man that is among you." This grace can be no other than the grace of the Apostles. "By whom we have received grace and apostleship" (i. 5). It comprehended, of course, the oversight of all other ministries. The Apostle was, so far as any man could be, in the place of Christ.

"To every man that is among you." In this he claims the power of acting for Christ with respect to every member of the mystical body, even though he had never been in Rome, nor seen the Church there.

"Not to think of himself more highly than he ought to think, but to think soberly." The translation of the Revisers represents more closely the words of the original: "Not to think of himself more highly than he ought to think: but so to think as to think soberly." What a difference it would have made in Christendom, if the prelates of this very Church had acted on the Apostle's strongly expressed warning! With the history of the Papacy before us, it is impossible to shut our eyes to the fact that the tremendous pretensions were, in very many cases, the result of personal ambition and self-assertion.

Chrysostom draws a remarkable parallel between what the Lord in His Sermon on the Mount and the Apostle here put in the first

CHAP. XII.]   THE MEASURE OF FAITH.   271

to think † soberly, according as God hath dealt ᵏ to every man the measure of faith.

4 For ˡ as we have many members in one body,

† Gr. *to sobriety.*
ᵏ 1 Cor. xii.
7, 11. Ephes. iv. 7.
ˡ 1 Cor. xii. 12.
Ephes. iv. 16.

place. "Here he is bringing before us the mother of good deeds, which is lowliness of mind, in imitation of his own Master. For as He, when He went up into the mountain, and was going to give a tissue of moral precepts, took this for His first beginning, and made this the foundation in the words, 'Blessed are the poor in spirit,' so Paul, too . . . . began from lowliness of mind as from the head."

"According as God hath dealt to every man the measure of faith." This faith cannot well mean saving faith—the faith in the exercise of which each soul lays hold on Christ; but it must rather mean the faith in each one, qualifying him for receiving and using aright the gifts which God gave for the instruction, the rule, the confirmation, the direction, the extension of the Church. This faith was given in different measures or proportions, according to the wise, but secret determination of God. This is the faith to which our Lord alludes: "If ye had faith as a grain of mustard seed, ye would say to this mountain," &c. And St. Paul seems to allude to it rather than to sanctifying faith, when he says, "If I had faith so that I could remove mountains." (1 Cor. xiii.)

But what St. Paul seems here to call attention to is, not the nature or strength of this faith, but that it is, in all its degrees, a gift of God; and, being a Divine gift, no one can boast of it, as if it was one of the faculties of his own mind. Wordsworth has a good note: "The measure of faith which God has allotted to each man (and not the amount of mere unregenerate reason, or of pride and confidence which he has in his own intelligence) is to be the rule according to which he is to be minded."

4, 5. "For as we have many members in one body, and all members have not," &c. Here we have the special doctrine of this Apostle, which is that Christ is the Head of a Mystical Body, the Church, which consists of human beings who believe in Him, are baptized into His Death and Resurrection, put themselves under His guidance, so as to be led by His Spirit, and partake of that Body and Blood without which they can have no life.

I say that it is the special doctrine of this Apostle, for no other sacred writers of the New Testament have been led to express

and all members have not the same office:

---

themselves about it in the plain terms which he uses. Justification by Faith is in an important sense subordinate to it, for justification by Faith is a means to an end, and that end is participation in the Risen Life of the Son of God; and this Life we partake of because, and as long as, we are in Him as members of His Body.

"As we have many members in one body, and all members," &c. The idea of membership in the Body of the Son of God is so thoroughly worked out on its human side by this Apostle in the twelfth chapter of his first Epistle to the Corinthians, that a fuller doctrinal examination must be reserved to my notes on that Epistle, if God spares me to write them.

Its Divine side—that is, beginning with Christ as the Head, and then contemplating the members as one in Him, and receiving grace from Him—is the subject of two Epistles, those to the Ephesians and Colossians. It will be well, however, to notice here in passing that the Headship of the Lord Jesus to the Church, and the inherence of the various members in Him as one Body under one Head, is not an illustration of a fact, but the fact itself, so far as such a fact can be expressed in human language. For instance, heathen writers have described the social or political state of a nation under the same figures of a number of limbs or members united in a body, and so mutually dependent upon one another; but there is, in such a case, no mysterious and necessary relation to one head: if the head were removed, any head or another form of headship, *i.e.*, of government, might take its place, whereas the Pauline doctrine not only depends on One ever-living Christ, but on the Church being in Him. In Him it lives, and moves, and has its being. United to Him, a branch or a limb lives, and performs its functions; sundered from Him, it dies. The body politic or social is *like* an organism. The Church under Christ *is* an organism.

There is a real flowing of spiritual strength and grace from Christ the Head into each and every member. This is the New Life. This is the Life of Justification. This Life when it enters into each member produces spiritual power in two ways: firstly, that by which the man works out his own salvation; and, secondly, that by which he is enabled to perform aright his particular function in the Body.

"All members have not the same office." The thinking of him-

CHAP. XII.] ONE BODY IN CHRIST. 273

5 So ^m we, *being* many, are one body in Christ, and every one members one of another.

^m 1 Cor. x. 17.
& xii. 20, 27.
Ephes. i. 23.
& iv. 25.

---

self more highly than he ought to think is the evil disposition which would make a man think that he is able to perform all offices, and so intrude into all, and criticize freely, and most probably uncharitably, the action of all other members.

The best condition of any part of the Church is when it supplies spheres of action to all its members, and gives them free scope in their respective spheres, and yet holds all under discipline; but still we are to remember that a member of Christ may be useful and necessary though he holds no office whatsoever, not even that of a teacher—for influence for good by no means entirely depends upon office. It depends upon holiness and goodness, upon secret prayer, upon wisdom in advising, upon the power of sympathizing, upon liberality in the disposal of worldly goods, upon self-denial and humility, and self-control in the matter both of the tongue and the temper, upon the ruling of an household well, and a hundred other things, quite apart from office, diocesan or parochial.

5. " So we, being many, are one body in Christ, and every one members," &c. One body in Christ, *i.e.*, in mystical and spiritual union with Him in His Church, not working as if we were separate units, unconnected with the Body, for if so, our spiritual gifts will end in what our Lord prays against and all His Apostles reprobate, the division of the Church.

" Every one members one of another." Our hold on Christ—I mean our separate individual hold—is not to be considered as if it belonged to us apart from our fellows, and to be regarded as isolating us; but we are rather to realize that we partake of a common grace, that of the Holy Spirit, which all Scripture would lead us to believe to be widely, rather than sparsely diffused amongst professing Christians. (Titus iii. 6.)

If it be objected to this, that the Church now is so different as respects unity to what it was in Apostolic days, that such words of St. Paul as these respecting the Mystical Body, are not applicable to Christian practice now as then, we answer, that the Head is the same, and the Spirit is the same, and the Apostolic government is the same, and the faith is the same, and the hope the same, and the Sacraments of Baptism and the Eucharist are

T

the same, and the Scriptures the same. Why, then, should not the Mystical Body be the same, and what hinders our addressing the members of the Church in the same practical terms as the Apostle used? It would be a very serious thing if it be not in our power so to do; for if so, such a parable as that of the Vine and the Branches, and far above half the Apostolic Epistles would be rendered useless for practical purposes. Consider for what holy purposes St. Paul uses the fact that all the members of the visible Church are members of Christ. He uses it here for purposes of humility, that each one should think soberly, *i.e.*, humbly of himself. In 1 Cor. he uses it to show that each member should keep both body and spirit pure and holy (1 Cor. vi. 15-20). In another part of the same epistle he uses it to inculcate upon all of them mutual sympathy (1 Cor. xii. 12-27). In the Epistle to the Ephesians he tells his converts that they are to forbear one another in love, and to endeavour to keep the unity of the Spirit in the bond of peace, *because* there is one Body, one Spirit, one hope (Ephes. iv. 2, 3, 4), and we are to put away lying, not merely because it is mean and disgraceful, but because we are in Christ members one of another (iv. 25). Husbands are to love their wives, and wives to reverence their husbands, because Christ is the Head of the Church (v. 22-30). All the holy teaching of Coloss. iii. is grounded on the truth of there being a mysterious life from, or rather " in " Christ, which belongs to all the members of His Body.

So that it is a very serious thing if so sanctifying purifying and unifying a truth, though it be abundantly clear in the pages of the New Testament, is no longer to be a part of Christian teaching. Thanks be to God, this Apostolic teaching is so reproduced in the Prayer Book, that it cannot be ignored except by those who are wilfully unfaithful to their ordination vows. It forms a leading feature of the baptismal offices—"that he may be received into Christ's Holy Church"—"Seeing now, dearly beloved, that this child is regenerate, and grafted into the body of Christ's Church." It is the first teaching addressed to the Christian child in the Catechism ["wherein I was made a member of Christ"] to prepare him for Confirmation. It is the great benefit of the Eucharist ["Then we spiritually eat the flesh of Christ and drink His Blood; then we dwell in Christ and Christ in us; we are one with Christ and Christ with us."—"Grant us, therefore, gracious Lord, so to eat the Flesh of thy dear Son Jesus Christ, and to drink his Blood,

6 ⁿ Having then gifts differing ᵒ according to   ⁿ 1 Cor. xii. 4.
1 Pet. iv. 10,
11.
ᵒ ver. 3.

that . . . we may evermore dwell in Him, and He in us."—" Dost assure us thereby . . . that we are very members incorporate in the Mystical Body of Thy dear Son, which is the blessed company of all faithful people."] Again, in the Solemnization of Matrimony, "That such persons as have not the gift of continency, might marry, and keep themselves undefiled members of Christ's Body." And in the same office the Scripture portions read instead of a sermon are those which set forth the duties of husbands towards their wives, and wives towards their husbands, as following upon the mystical relations betwixt Christ the Head, and His Church the members. In the Visitation of the Sick the Priest prays: "Continue this sick member in the unity of the Church." It is recognized in the Ordination of Priests: "The Church and congregation whom you must serve is His Spouse and His Body."— "Wherefore consider with yourselves the end of your ministry toward the children of God, towards the Spouse and Body of Christ."

Such is the doctrine of the Head and the members. I have said that it is the special Pauline doctrine, and so without doubt it is, for in Ephes. iii. St. Paul speaks of it as the mystery of Christ, hidden from ages and generations, but now made known to the Holy Apostles and himself especially, and the mystery is "that the Gentiles should be fellow-heirs and *of the same body*, and partakers of his promise in Christ by the Gospel."

6. "Having then gifts differing according to the grace that is given to us," &c. The gifts differing according to the particular grace given to each one, are evidently analogous to the functions of the various members of the body. Each member of the body requires not only its particular life, but its ability to discharge its proper function; and so the various members of the mystical Body have gifts differing according to the differences in their respective duties or offices.

The first of these gifts mentioned is prophecy. It is the first mentioned because in the first age it was by far the most important, but its form then was temporary. It has since ceased, because we have a "more sure word of prophecy to which we must take heed."

p Acts xi. 27.
1 Cor. xii. 10,
28. & xiii. 2.
& xiv. 1, 6, 29,
31.

the grace that is given to us, whether p prophecy, *let us prophesy* according to the proportion of faith;

Prophecy, as far as we can gather from the few clear notices which have come down to us, was the inspired teaching of the first age. It answered to our preaching, but was, if the prophet submitted to the entire guidance of the Holy Spirit, more authoritative and came more directly from the Spirit. It was absolutely necessary before the various books of the New Testament were collected and distributed amongst the Churches, that in each local Church men should be raised up having a deeper insight than their fellows into the spiritual meaning of the facts of the Lord's Godhead, Incarnation, Life, Death, Resurrection, Ascension, Intercession, and Second Coming, and the place of the Holy Spirit in the Godhead, and in the Church. God, according to the needs of the then existing Church, raised up such men, till the Gospels and the letters of the Apostles were collected and diffused throughout the Church. When this took place, prophecy apparently ceased, and preaching took its place—preaching, that is, in the sense of explaining and practically enforcing upon Christians the truths contained in the Gospels and Epistles. It may be asked, then, How is it that none of these prophecies of these innumerable prophets have come down to us? We answer, Because we have in a permanent form the prophecies of the greatest and most inspired amongst them. The Epistles of Paul, Peter, John, and James, contain what they prophesied put into a permanent form; for it is not for a moment to be supposed that they preached anything whatsoever different from what they wrote in their letters.

St. Paul, in thus exhorting these prophets of local Churches to prophesy according to the analogy of the faith (not faith, but *the* faith) gave them a most necessary command; for, if there were any doctrines of the Gospel taught in the primitive Church, some must have been of primary or overwhelming importance compared with others.

Thus St. John evidently considers that no prophet is a true one who does not confess that "Jesus Christ is come in the flesh" (1 John iv. 1, 2); and all these prophetic utterances, according to him, must be tried—but according to what rule or standard? There must have been a common standard, and we have constant

CHAP. XII.] MINISTRY. 277

7 Or ministry, *let us wait* on *our* ministering: or q he that
teacheth, on teaching;
q Acts xiii. 1.
Gal. vi. 6.
Ephes. iv. 11
1 Tim. v. 17.

references to that standard. Thus St. Paul speaks of there being
" One Lord, *one faith*," *i.e.*, one faith or truth held throughout the
Church. St. John declares that *the* truth which he had seen and
heard, and which he declared in order that his converts might have
fellowship with the Apostles, and through them with the Father
and with His Son Jesus Christ, was that the Eternal Word was
so incarnate that men "saw with their eyes, looked upon, and
their hands had handled of the Word of Life." St. Jude bids
Christians contend earnestly for the faith once delivered to the
saints (Ephes. iv. 4; 1 John i. 1-3; Jude 3).

So that it is evident that the Apostle means that prophets should
prophesy, not according to the analogy of each one's particular
faith, which never could be separated from each one's private
idiosyncrasies, but according to the analogy of *the* faith, and if they
did this, the truths of the most overwhelming importance would
occupy their right position in the public teaching of the Church.

7. " Or ministry, let us wait on our ministering," &c. There is
some doubt as to the meaning of this word " ministry." Some
suppose it to mean any ministry, taking ministry to include all
Church working, as in 1 Corinth. xii. 5, " There are differences of
administrations (or ministries, or workings); but the same Lord."
But, probably, it is used here more technically, referring to the
office held by Stephen and his coadjutors, of superintending the
giving of alms, and other duties of a like nature.

The reader will remember that when the necessity for appointing
the Seven arose, the Apostles directed the multitude to look out
seven men " of honest report, full of the Holy Ghost and wisdom,"
and the distribution of alms, if it is not to be harmful, especially
requires insight into character, and discretion. Those who exercise
this ministry must wait on their ministering, must be *in* it, as the
original has it, *i.e.*, absorbed by it, and perform it most carefully
and conscientiously.

" Or he that teacheth, on teaching." Most probably this refers
to a teaching other than that in public, as the preparation of
catechumens for baptism. In 1 Cor. xii. 28, the office of teachers
is mentioned as third, " first Apostles, secondarily prophets,

278   EXHORTATION.   [ROMANS.

r Acts xv. 32.
1 Cor. xiv. 3.
s Matt. vi. 1, 2, 3.

8 Or ʳ he that exhorteth, on exhortation: ˢ he that || giveth, *let him do it* || with simplicity; ᵗ he

| Or, *imparteth.*
|| Or, *liberally.*
2 Cor. viii. 2.
t Acts xx. 28.
1 Tim. v. 17.
Hebr. xiii. 7, 24. 1 Pet. v. 2.

thirdly, teachers;" and after it come miracles, gifts of healing, &c. So that taking Apostles, prophets, and teachers to be all ministers of the word, the last has the more restricted office. Blunt supposes that he may bear the same office as the catechist of later times. Theodoret speaks of him as instructing in Divine dogmas (διδασκαλίαν, τῶν θείων δογμάτων τὴν μάθησιν).

"Or he that exhorteth, on exhortation." This seems to indicate what we now call preaching, and yet it succeeds teaching. It seems strange that one man should teach and another exhort. Should not the teacher exhort, and the exhorter teach? But here, probably, the Apostle ceases to refer to the offices and alludes rather to the gifts, and from our present experience of the ministration of the word in the Church, we see that the especial gift of some is to expound such doctrines as the Incarnation and the Atonement, and the New Life in Christ, so that the souls of the hearers may be raised up to God by these truths, and of others, the practical application of the Christian faith in the duties of every-day life. But we are to remember that exhorting may mean " comforting," and if any Christian had particular gifts for comforting those that mourned or were afflicted, this ministry would of necessity be exercised more in private, if it was to be effectual. So that the Apostle means, whatever gift a Christian has, let him look upon it as a gift, and so not to be boasted of, but to be carefully cultivated, ever realizing that he will have to give account for its use.

"He that giveth, let him do it with simplicity." It has been made a question whether the person here in the Apostle's mind be one that distributes the public alms of the Church, or gives out of his more ample private means. It seems to be the latter if we are to make any distinction between it and the exercise of the diaconia of verse seven. If a man gives out of his own store, let him do so with a single eye to the glory of God, and to the good of him to whom he giveth. "The man who gives with simplicity," says Anselm (quoted in Cornelius à Lapide), "is one who does not consider whether he to whom he gives be his friend or his familiar, or

that ruleth, with diligence; he that sheweth mercy, ^u with cheerfulness.

^u 2 Cor. ix. 7.

one who will be of advantage to him or useful, or whether he will be grateful, but whether he is in need."

"He that ruleth, with diligence." The word translated ruleth literally signifies one standing before others, or one who is set before them, and so one presiding. Chrysostom has a remarkable interpretation: "He that defendeth with diligence, for it is not enough to undertake the defence, unless he do it with diligence and zeal." Of course he derives this meaning of defending from the idea of standing before. A man stands before others both to preside over them and to defend them. I think in every case in which this word occurs its root idea is that of standing before or presiding, so that it might be rendered "leading." This, of course, implies the exercise of authority; but we must remember that another word ('εξουσία) is mostly used to express authority. I desire to bring the following considerations before the reader as tending to elucidate this matter. The Roman Church at this time probably consisted of several thousand persons, and these must have met both for instruction and worship in very many comparatively small rooms, or courts of private houses: for a large public building capable of containing one of our modern congregations, could not have been erected for very many years. Now Justin Martyr, about one hundred years after the writing of this Epistle, speaking of the Eucharist, describes it thus: "And on the day called Sunday all who live in cities, or in the country, gather together in one place, and the memoirs of the Apostles or the writings of the prophets are read, as long as time permits; then when the reader has ceased, the president verbally instructs .... bread and wine are brought in, and the president in like manner offers prayers," &c. &c. Now Justin here used the word προεστὼς, which is translated president; but, as in this place, it signifies rather standing before, or set before as leader. Now, seeing that there were very probably in Rome twenty or thirty of such congregations at the least, may not the Apostle mean, he that presideth over the congregation, or leads public worship?

Of course it is very probable that the leader or president (ὁ προϊστάμενος) presided in other ways, as, for instance, in exercising discipline; but it appears to me that if we are to adhere to the

9 ˣ *Let* love be without dissimulation. ʸ Abhor that which is evil; cleave to that which is good.

original idea of προϊστήμι, we must put presiding in or leading the Church in the first place. He is to do this with diligence, or rather with earnestness. He must throw himself with all his force into his Eucharistic ministrations.

"He that sheweth mercy with cheerfulness." If this refers to showing mercy in the shape of visiting, relieving, and consoling the sick, the wisdom of it is manifest. Cheerfulness in dispensing merciful assistance seems to double its value, and certainly tends to a far more ready reception of spiritual counsel and advice on the part of the succoured one.

9. "Let love be without dissimulation. Abhor [or abhorring] that which is evil; cleave [or cleaving] to that which is good." The three clauses are all to be connected. Let love be unfeigned, and it cannot be true Christian love except in one who abhors that which is evil, and cleaves to that which is good. By such an understanding of the verse, the force of the participles (ἀποστυγοῦντες, κολλώμενοι) is preserved. " Then since there is a love for evil things such as is that of the intemperate, that of those who are of one mind for money and for plunder's sake, and for revels and drinking clubs, he clears it of all these by saying, 'Abhor that which is evil.' And he does not speak of refraining from it, but of *abhorring* it, that is, hating it, and hating it exceedingly. For this word ἀπὸ is often of intensive force with him, as when he speaks of earnest expectation (ἀποκαραδοκία, Rom. viii. 19), looking out for (ἀπεκδεχόμενοι, Rom. viii. 23) (complete) redemption (ἀπολύτρωσις, Rom. viii. 24). For since many who do not evil things still have a desire after them, therefore he says *abhor*. But what he wants is to purify the thought, and that we should have a mighty enmity, hatred, and war, against vice. For do not fancy, he means, because I said *Love one another*, that I mean you to go so far as to co-operate even in bad actions with one another; for the law that I am laying down is just the reverse; since it would have you an alien, not from the action only, but even from the inclination towards vice; and not merely an alien from the same inclination, but to have an excessive aversion and hatred of it too." (Chrysostom).

CHAP. XII.]   BE KINDLY AFFECTIONED.   281

10 ᶻ *Be* **kindly** affectioned one to another ‖ with brotherly love; ᵃ in honour preferring one another;

ᶻ Heb. xiii. 1.
1 Pet. i. 22. &
ii. 17. & iii. 8.
2 Pet. i. 7.
‖ Or, *in the love of the brethren.*
ᵃ Phil. ii. 3.
1 Pet. v. 5.

"Cleave to that which is good." Be united to or one with it, as a man cleaves to his wife, as men should cleave unto the Lord. Cleave not to one form of goodness which may be in accordance with your natural disposition, but to all good. "Whatsoever things are true, whatsoever things are honest, whatsoever things are just, whatsoever things are pure, whatsoever things are lovely, whatsoever things are of good report, ... think on these things" (Phil. iv. 8), for the thinking on them is the first step to be joined in heart and will to them.

10. "Be kindly affectioned one to another with brotherly love." "Ye are brethren, he says, and have come of the same pangs. Do not wait to be loved by another, but leap at it thyself, and be the first to begin it. For so wilt thou reap the wages of his love also." (Chrysostom.) Love one another with a love not only sincere, but fraternal—as children of the same heavenly Father, as brethren of the same Son of God and Son of man.

"In honour preferring one another." "Which you will do if you habitually consider what is good in others and what is evil in yourself." (Wesley.) "For this is the way that affection is produced, and also when produced abideth. And there is nothing which makes friends so much as the earnest endeavour to overcome one's neighbour in honouring him." (Chrysostom.) "They ought to yield that respect and precedency to others which ambitious men claim to themselves; and readily honour, and induce others to honour, the estimable conduct of their brethren, who, on one account or another, were disregarded or discouraged." (Scott.)

11. "Not slothful in business." To render the word σπουδή by "business" might convey a false impression to the reader: the word rather means zeal or diligence, or earnestness—"In zeal, not backward or remiss." The Revisers translate it somewhat clumsily, "In diligence not slothful." "Not backward in zeal. For this also gendereth love, when with honour we also show a readiness to protect: as there is nothing that makes men beloved so much as honour and forethought. For to love is not enough, but there

11 Not slothful in business; fervent in spirit; serving the Lord;

must be this also; or rather this also comes of loving, as also loving has its warmth from this, and they are confirmative one of another." (Chrysostom.) "No reason exists for explaining σπουδή in any limited sense of zeal in preaching and disseminating the Gospel, or of zeal in Christian devotion. Rather it is zeal in the discharge of any Christian duty whatever." (Philippi.)

"Fervent in spirit." Literally, boiling up in spirit. God is not well served in a cold, calculating, measured way, but by enthusiasm. This only kindles warmth and zeal. The enthusiastic man may be rash, and make mistakes, but this is more than atoned for by the fire he kindles in many breasts. One is tempted to say that if there is true love there must be fervency.

"Serving the Lord." Let all your service, even if it be the service, *i.e.*, the lawful service of men, be "to the Lord." The Apostle, in another Epistle, shows how servants, or slaves, in serving their masters according to the flesh, may yet serve God, and be rewarded for so serving Him, in the eternal world. (See Ephes. vi. 5-8; Coloss. iii. 22-24.) And if it be so with the household duties of slaves, so also with all other work which men have to do. It must be sanctified with the definite intention of being done to God, as in His sight, and to be ordered by Him, so as to promote His glory.

A few MSS. read, serving the time, *i.e.*, the opportunity. Luther, for instance, translates after them, "accommodate yourselves to the time;" but it seems, beyond measure, unlikely that amongst such precepts Paul should have written one with this meaning. If a man is always thinking of accommodating himself to the times, he is not likely to be fervent in spirit, or as follows, "rejoicing in hope, continuing instant in prayer."

12. "Rejoicing in hope." That is, in the hope of a joyful resurrection. The sense of present sin, of a conflict between the flesh and spirit, is not to prevent us rejoicing if we have taken the side of Christ, and have surrendered ourselves to Him. But, of course, those who, if there was no resurrection of the dead, were of all men most miserable, must have had far brighter and more vivid hopes than we who have comparatively so few persecutions and distresses to remind us that this is not our rest; and so the Apostle in connection with hope makes mention of the tribulations which made

12 ᵇ Rejoicing in hope; ᶜ patient in tribulation; ᵈ continuing instant in prayer;

13 ᵉ Distributing to the necessity of saints; ᶠ given to hospitality.

ᵇ Luke x. 20. ch. v. 2. & xv. 13. Phil. iii. 1. & iv. 4. 1 Thess. v. 16. Heb. iii. 6. 1 Pet. iv. 13.
ᶜ Luke xxi. 19. 1 Tim. vi. 11. Heb. x. 36. & xii. 1. Jam. i. 4. & v. 7. 1 Pet. ii. 19, 20.
ᵈ Luke xviii. 1. Acts ii. 42. & xii. 5. Col. iv. 2. Eph. vi. 18. 1 Thess. v. 17.
ᵉ 1 Cor. xvi. 1. 2 Cor. ix. 1, 12. Heb. vi. 10. & xiii. 16. 1 John iii. 17.
ᶠ 1 Tim. iii. 2. Tit. i. 8. Heb. xiii. 2. 1 Pet. iv. 9.

men long so earnestly for the coming of the Lord, and writes,

"Patient in tribulation." "There should be no greater comfort to Christian persons than to be made like unto Christ, by suffering patiently adversities, troubles, and sicknesses. For He Himself went not up to joy, but first He suffered pain. He entered not into His glory before He was crucified. So truly our way to eternal joy is to suffer here with Christ." (Visitation of the Sick.)

"Continuing instant in prayer." Constant intercourse with God in prayer is the secret of the Christian life. By bringing before God all our wants, all our troubles, even our little troubles, all our secret sins and infirmities, all our worldly and spiritual concerns, we do as He desires us to do; we treat Him as our God, in Whose eyes nothing that concerns His children is of small account, and Whose providence rules the minutest matters that can befall them. Let us remember Nehemiah, who, when the heathen king asked him for what he made request, *first prayed to the God of heaven,* and then said, "If it please the king, send me unto the city of my fathers' sepulchres."

There was, nearly fifty years ago, a saintly priest of our Church, a fellow of St. John's College, Cambridge, who, when anyone sought an interview with him, retired to his bedroom for but a few moments, that he might commend the interview to God.

13. "Distributing to the necessity of saints." Literally, sharing in, and so, by an easy transition, making them partakers of your good things. "Saints" here means all bearing the Name of Christ, all Christians, as in Acts ix. 32 and 41. It was one of the great objects of St. Paul's ministry to make Christians in far distant churches assist one another in temporal things.

"Given to hospitality." Hospitality was especially needed in the first ages, when Christians were so bitterly persecuted, and had to flee from one city to another. In a strange city they must starve

14 ⁵ Bless them which persecute you: bless, and curse not.

⁵ Matt. v. 44.
Luke vi. 28.
& xxiii. 34.
Acts vii. 60.
1 Cor. iv. 12.
1 Pet. ii. 23.
& iii. 9.

---

with cold and hunger unless the Christians of the city opened their houses to them. The word "given" is not sufficiently strong. It is "pursuing" hospitality. Chrysostom remarks, "He does not say doing it, but given to it, so as to instruct us not to wait for those that shall ask it, and see when they will come to us, but to run to them, and be given to finding them."

14. "Bless them which persecute you: bless, and curse not." It has been made a question whether St. Paul here quotes Matthew v. 44, or Luke vi. 28. When he was dictating this part of his Epistle he certainly did not stop and refer to the passage and reproduce it verbatim. For in St. Matthew it appears as "Pray for them that (despitefully use you and) persecute you," and in St. Luke as "Bless them that curse you." No doubt the Apostle knew that the Lord had said these words, and he reproduced them freely. He first cited "Bless" (εὐλογεῖτε), but instead of following it up with "them that curse you," he changed this into "those that persecute," simply because his last word in the preceding verse was διώκοντας, the transition being most natural from *pursuing* hospitality to being *pursued* by evil-minded men. The word in one meaning suggesting the word in another. "He did not say, be not spiteful or revengeful, but required something far better. For *that* a man which was wise might do, but *this* is quite an angel's part. And after saying *bless*, he proceeds and "curse not," lest we should do both the one and the other, and not the former only. For they that persecute us are purveyors of a reward to us. But if thou art sober-minded, there will be another reward after that, one which thou wilt gain thyself. For he will yield thee that for persecution, but thou wilt yield thyself the one from the blessing of another, in that thou bringest forth a very great sign of love to Christ. For as he that curseth his persecutor showeth that he is not much pleased at suffering this for Christ, thus he that blesseth showeth a great love. Do not, then, abuse him, that thou thyself mayest gain the greater reward, and mayest teach him that the thing is matter of inclination, not of necessity, of holiday and feast, not of calamity or dejection." (Chrysostom.)

"Bless, and curse not." Here the Apostle turns the particular

15 ʰ Rejoice with them that do rejoice, and weep with them that weep.

16 ⁱ *Be* of the same mind one toward another.

ʰ 1 Cor. xii. 26.
ⁱ ch. xv. 5. 1 Cor. i. 10. Phil. ii. 2. & iii. 16. 1 Pet. iii. 8.

precept respecting not cursing, but blessing our persecutors, into a general one. The Christian is to wish for and to pray for good to everyone. He is never to wish for or to pray for evil to any.

15. "Rejoice with them that do rejoice, and weep with them that weep." Thus did the Lord at the grave of Lazarus. He wept with those that wept, out of mere sympathy, for He was about to raise him from the dead. And at the very commencement of His ministry He rejoiced with those at the marriage feast; nay, He added to their innocent joy by turning the water into wine.

Chrysostom illustrates well this sentiment. "Yes," it will be said, "but to join in the sorrows of mourners one can see why he ordered them, but why ever did he command them the other thing, when it is no such great matter? Aye, but that requires more of a high Christian temper, to rejoice with them that do rejoice, than to weep with them that weep. For this nature itself fulfils perfectly: and there is none so hard-hearted as not to weep over him that is in calamity: but the other requires a very noble soul, so as not only to keep from envying, but even to feel pleasure with the person that is in esteem."

16. "Be of the same mind one toward another." Various shades of meaning have been given to this place. Some, as Williams, take it, as enjoining on men sympathy not only in their joys and sorrows, but also in their affections and pursuits, and an endeavour to have a fellow feeling with others, as in another place, "Remember them that are in bonds, as bound with them." Others, as Philippi, see in it an inculcation of modesty: "Be so minded one towards another, that the one places himself on a level with the other, and ascribes no more to himself than to him." Jowett suggests a counsel not so much of humility as of unity, of which humility is also a part. Chrysostom, whose comments on the precepts in this chapter are unapproachable, writes: "Has a poor man come into thine house? Be like him in thy bearing. Do not put on any unusual pompous air on account of thy riches. There is no rich and poor in Christ. Be not thou ashamed of him because of his external dress, but receive him because of his inward faith."

MIND NOT HIGH THINGS. [ROMANS.

k Ps. cxxxi. 1, 2. Jer. xlv. 5.
‖ Or, *be contented with mean things.*
l Prov. iii. 7. & xxvi. 12. Isai. v. 21. ch. xi. 25.

k Mind not high things, but ‖ condescend to men of low estate. *l* Be not wise in your own conceits.

"Mind not high things, but condescend to men of low estate." High things are here taken to mean worldly honours and distinctions, and such things, and to mind them not, does not simply mean "do not desire them or pursue them," but "be not influenced by them." For instance, in a Church assembly, defer not in the least to the opinion of those who have worldly rank or influence, but look at everything simply in the light of God's truth.[1]

"Condescend to men of low estate." It is doubtful whether we should render it "to men of low estate," or to things of low condition. But the word ταπεινός is never in the New Testament applied to things. Chrysostom understands it of persons: "Bring thyself down to their humble condition, ride or walk with them, be not humbled in mind only, but help them also and reach forth thy hand to them, not by means of others, but in thine own person, as a father taking care of a child, as the head taking care of the body."

The word condescending means rather to be carried away with. "The reference is to the most indigent and ignorant, and least influential in the Church. It is to them the believer ought to feel most drawn. The antipathy felt by the Apostle to every sort of spiritual aristocracy, to every caste and distinction in the Church, breaks out again in the last words." (Godet.)

"Be not wise in your own conceits." "Especially they should avoid all conceit of their own wisdom, as if they were above ordinary rules, had no occasion to ask wisdom of God, or to regard the counsel of their brethren; or, as if they ought to be at the head of every business, and nothing could be well done if they were not consulted or employed about it." (T. Scott.)

---

1 Godet has an interesting illustration: "There frequently forms in the congregations of believers an aristocratic tendency, everyone striving, by means of the Christian brotherhood, to associate with those who by their gifts or fortune occupy a higher position. Hence small coteries, animated by a proud spirit, and having for their result chilling exclusiveness." The Apostle knows these littlenesses, and wishes to prevent them; he recommends the members of the Church to attach themselves to all alike.

CHAP. XII.] IF POSSIBLE LIVE PEACEABLY. 287

17 ᵐ Recompense to no man evil for evil. ⁿ Provide things honest in the sight of all men.

18 If it be possible, as much as lieth in you, ᵒ live peaceably with all men.

m Prov. xx. 22. Matt. v. 39. 1 Thess. v. 15. 1 Pet. iii. 9.
n ch. xiv. 16. 2 Cor. viii. 21.
o Mark ix. 50. ch. xiv. 19. Hebr. xii. 14.

17. "Recompense to no man evil for evil." This naturally follows upon precepts of humility. Pride and self-consequence lead to retaliation. The proud man is almost necessarily resentful. This word, "to no man," was evidently intended to embrace the heathen around them, to whom they were to commend practically the Gospel of God's forbearance and forgiveness, by being forbearing and forgiving themselves.

"Provide things honest in the sight of all men." Or, as the Revised Version has it, "Take thought for things honourable in the sight of all men." St. Paul set an example of this by not carrying up the contribution of the Gentiles to the Saints of Jerusalem by himself alone, but by associating others to travel with him with the money, so that no one should have the opportunity of saying that they took any of it for the supply of their private needs. "Avoiding this, that no man should blame us in this abundance which is administered by us: providing for honest things, not only in the sight of the Lord, but also in the sight of men " (2 Cor. viii. 20, 21).

The Apostle exhorts the Church to be mindful of what is good, *i.e.*, of an upright, honourable walk before the eyes, or in the opinion of all men—not merely before Christians, but also before Jews and Gentiles. Whilst he is so concerned for their own reputation, he is withal in the last resort equally concerned for the honour of their God, Who by the evil walk of His people is scandalized before unbelievers (Rom. ii. 24), and for their neighbours' salvation, which is furthered by the sight of their good walk (Matth. v. 16).

18. "If it be possible, as much as lieth in you, live peaceably with all men." It may not always be possible, for St. James says: "The wisdom that is from above is first pure, then peaceable" (James iii. 17). If then we assert heavenly wisdom in its purity, it may rouse up opposition, it may bring to pass the Lord's words, "I came not to send peace, but a sword." And yet the truth must be spoken in love, or we may lose our reward. It must be also spoken in meekness. "In meekness instructing those that oppose

19 Dearly beloved, ᵖ avenge not yourselves, but *rather* give place unto wrath: for it is written, ᑫ Vengeance *is* mine; I will repay, saith the Lord.

p Lev. xix. 18.
Prov. xxiv. 29.
ver. 17.
q Deut. xxxii. 35. Hebr. x. 30.

---

themselves, if God peradventure will give them repentance to the acknowledging of the truth " (2 Tim. ii. 25). " By the most harmless and forbearing conduct, and by every sacrifice and concession they ought, *if possible*, to avoid all quarrels and litigations, and to live at peace amongst their most unreasonable and injurious neighbours; avoiding all contention as the greatest evil to their own souls, and to the cause of true religion, except it were a meek but steadfast contention for the truth. (T. Scott.)

19. " Dearly beloved, avenge not yourselves, but rather give place unto wrath." " Dearly beloved." Notice the affection in the address. He had at the beginning merely called them "brethren." Now he uses a more endearing word, "beloved," as if he would press upon them the importance of what he was saying with all tenderness and earnestness. It was a matter of feeling, and he exhibits thus his deep feeling.

" But rather give place unto wrath: for it is written, Vengeance is mine," &c. This giving place unto wrath must be closely connected with what follows. Give place, "for it is written, Vengeance is mine," &c. The Apostle means to say, "Vengeance does not belong to man. It belongs to the Supreme Judge, and if a man avenges himself, he intrudes into the office of that Judge." But it does not follow from this that the Apostle desires the Christian to think and hope that God will avenge him. If so, why should he be bidden to pray for "those that despitefully use him and persecute him"? It rather means, give place to your enemies' wrath; allow it to run its course rather than avenge yourself, because, if so, you intrude into God's office and injure yourself in His sight. τῇ ὀργῇ then, does not mean primarily the wrath of God, though it has the article, "*the* wrath." You are to leave the matter to God, to give your enemy repentance, or to avenge you, as He pleases. Consciously to hope that God will avenge is hardly Christian. The quotation is taken freely from Deut. xxxii. 35, and is said there of God's avenging the people of Israel upon their enemies, "To me belongeth vengeance and recompense; their foot shall slide in due time," &c.

20 ʳTherefore if thine enemy hunger, feed him; if he thirst, give him drink: for in so doing thou shalt heap coals of fire on his head.

21 Be not overcome of evil, but overcome evil with good.

ʳ Exod. xxiii. 4, 5. Prov. xxv. 21, 22. Matt. v. 44.

20. "Therefore." "But" read by א, A., B., P., 5, 10, 23, 37, 57, 67**, 73, d*, Vulg., Cop., Arm.; "therefore" by E., L., most Cursives.

20. "Therefore if thine enemy hunger, feed him; if he thirst, give him drink," &c. This is taken from Proverbs xxv. 21. (Sept.) The heaping of coals of fire on the enemy's head cannot be in the way of punishment: such a meaning is directly contrary to all that the Apostle or his Master inculcates. The coals of fire are to be understood of shame, as we say, "burning shame." St. Augustine says, "You will melt your enemy by the fire of God's love, the coals from His altar, which we may consider to be the love of Christ crucified; you will bring down his proud head to repentance." "Such coals of fire were heaped on Saul's head by David (1 Sam. xxvi. 7-21). And they burned brightly for a time (verse 25), but were unhappily quenched at last. Such coals of fire the Son of David endeavoured to kindle on the head of Judas (John xiii. 26; Matth. xxvi. 50). But they were smothered by covetousness, and went out in smoke." (Wordsworth.)

21. "Be not overcome of evil, but overcome evil with good." Taken in connection with what has gone before, this means: If you allow the injury and malice of your adversary to work in you a feeling of hatred and a desire of vengeance, then you are overcome by his evil: instead of being brought nearer to God by resistance in spirit to an evil spirit of revenge, you yield to the spirit, and your enemy works a far greater spiritual injury upon you than any temporal evil he may have inflicted. But if when hated and injured by another you call on God's help to smother all desires of retaliation, if you force yourself to pray for him, and mortify your natural pride by doing him some kindness, then you overcome evil with good. He hates, and speaks evil words, and detracts and slanders, and, if he has opportunity, injures you in reputation or property; but if you, following the example of your forgiving Saviour, are led by His Spirit to be humble and peaceable, then "the Lord thy God will turn the curse into a blessing unto thee" (Deut. xxiii. 5).

U

But this precept is capable of the most general application. We are in an evil world, surrounded with evil, permeated as to our fleshly nature with evil, but God has given to us good whereby this evil may be overcome. He has given to us the faith, and the Scriptures, and the Church, and the Sacraments; by these we may drive away Satan, overcome the world, subdue the flesh, and, by acquitting ourselves well in the fight, gain a more abundant reward.

I cannot conclude this chapter without one remark. There is one day which, as a day of the month, occurs but once in four years—the 29th February. The Church of England, in accordance with her plan of the daily reading of Scripture, must choose some lesson out of the ordinary course for this day, and this only. She has fixed upon the seventh of St. Matthew for her morning second lesson, and this twelfth chapter of the Epistle to the Romans for her evening one. So that, according to her mind, this chapter out of all the chapters of the Apostolical Epistles is the one to be remembered. In addition to this, three Epistles—those for the first, second, and third Sunday after Epiphany—are taken from this chapter. The whole of it is thus embodied in the Eucharistic service of the Church.

CHAP. XIII.

^a Tit. iii. 1.
1 Pet. ii. 13.
^b Prov. viii. 15, 16. Dan. ii. 21. & iv. 32. John xix. 11.
‖ Or, *ordered*.

LET every soul ^a be subject unto the higher powers. For ^b there is no power but of God: the powers that be are ‖ ordained of God.

1-4. "Let every soul be subject unto the higher powers. For there is no power but of God . . . a revenger to execute wrath upon him that doeth evil." At first sight the Apostle seems to lay down the principle of passive obedience to the civil power, no matter who wields it, and no matter what it decrees. But this could not be, for he himself suffered martyrdom, because he persisted in spreading a religion whose first principle was that the gods of Cæsar and those under him were no gods, and that to

2 Whosoever therefore resisteth ᶜ the power, re- ᶜ Tit. iii. 1.

---

worship them was treason against the God of heaven. All difficulty vanishes if we consider that the Apostle, in these verses, asserts two things. First he asserts a great principle good for all time, and then he asserts how it is to be carried out at that particular time.

The principle is that civil government is ordained by God, and that it is necessary not only for the good, but for the existence, of mankind. Even under the worst forms of government, administered by the worst persons, the governor is to the vast mass of those under him "the minister of God for good." He can, ordinarily, only oppress or rob or tyrannize over a few, whereas he protects the vast body of his subjects from the greatest curse which can befall a state, and that is anarchy. Anarchy enables the worst and most unscrupulous of men to bear rule, to rob, to plunder, to massacre, at their will; whereas it was in the interest of such governors of men as then existed (and worse could hardly be conceived)—Tiberius, Claudius, Nero—to keep the peace between man and man, to restrain the violent, and to maintain some sort of order. Such was the principle, but the Apostle writes to show how it was then to be carried out by the Christians of Rome.

Now some, perhaps a considerable number, of these Christians were Jews, who, whilst living in their own country of Judæa and Galilee, were always permeated by a spirit of insubordination to the imperial power. They looked upon the great heathen monarchies which had succeeded one another in the government of the world as spiritually evil, and especially at that time, both in Palestine, and out of it, were they restless and insubordinate. "The spirit of rebellion, against which the Apostle is warning them, was not a mere misconception of the teaching of the Gospel; it lay deep in the circumstances of the age, and in the temper of the Jewish people. It is impossible to forget, however slight may be their historical groundwork, the well-known words of Suetonius (Claud. c. 25), 'Judæos impulsore Chresto assidue tumultuantes, Româ expulit.' The narration of Scripture itself affords indications of similar agitations, so far as they can be expected to cross the peaceful path of our Saviour and His disciples," &c. (Jowett.)

The Apostle, then, having regard to this spirit of rebellion, which might carry away with it the Christian Jews of Rome, and even

sisteth the ordinance of God: and they that resist shall receive to themselves damnation.

---

extend to their Gentile brethren when under persecution, warns them of the sin as well as futility of all attempts at resistance to the civil power. The time would come, if they were assiduous in spreading the Gospel, that the "powers that be" might become Christian, but armed resistance on their part might indefinitely postpone such an issue.

It should be said at the outset that nothing which the Apostle here writes can be quoted against needful or beneficial changes in the government of a Christian country. If a monarch does not observe the conditions under which he rules, there is nothing here to hinder the majority of his subjects compelling him to observe these conditions. If the "powers that be" take the republican shape, there is nothing to hinder the great body of the people changing this if they think well so to do. The Apostle here lays down no principle except this, that civil government is an institution of God, and in its worst forms is better than no government at all; and, subordinately to this, that for Christians to take part in tumults and rebellions is contrary to the will of God, and will bring discredit on the Gospel, and retard its progress.

Let us now consider each verse separately.

"Let every soul be subject to the higher powers." "Every soul," *i.e.*, every person, Jew, Christian, or heathen.

"To the higher powers." As expressed by the Apostle St. Peter, "Submit yourselves to every ordinance of man for the Lord's sake: whether it be to the king, as supreme; or unto governors, as unto them that are sent by him for the punishment of evildoers, and for the praise of them that do well." (1 Pet. ii. 13-14.)

"For the Lord's sake." That is, for the honour of the Name and of the Gospel of Jesus Christ, which would be seriously hindered in its progress by Christians taking part in civil tumults.

"There is no power but of God." If any supreme worldly power exists, carrying out the will of God in maintaining order and saving men from anarchy, it exists by the providence of God.

2. "Whosoever therefore resisteth the power, resisteth the ordinance of God,"—*i.e.*, the ordinance by which society is held together, and quiet, well-disposed men are protected from the tyranny of their evil neighbours.

CHAP. XIII.] DO THAT WHICH IS GOOD.

3 For rulers are not a terror to good works, but to the evil. Wilt thou then not be afraid of the power? ᵈ do that which is good, and thou shalt have praise of the same:

ᵈ 1 Pet. ii. 14. & iii. 13.

4 For he is the minister of God to thee for good. But

"And they that resist shall receive to themselves damnation." Not, of course, eternal condemnation in hell, but judgment in the sense of being punished by the infliction of the ruler's judgment, death by the sword, imprisonment, or banishment; but we are to remember that all wilful continued resistance to the declared will of God is rebellion against Him, and provokes Him to withdraw His Spirit from us.

3. "For rulers are not a terror to good works, but to the evil .... praise of the same." Civil governors exist to administer the laws of human society, and these laws almost universally tend to the protection of those who live in it. They consequently discourage all vices which tend to the disruption of society, and encourage such virtues as mutual forbearance, self-control, and care for one another's welfare, which tend to hold it together and to secure to men its advantages. The Apostle, be it remembered, is here not writing a treatise on politics, but asserting a principle which, as a rule, pervades all bodies politic, that they encourage what tends to their preservation and prosperity, and frown upon that which tends to their dissolution. "Whence, too, has he the name of *minister?* Consider this: I (Chrysostom, the preacher) give you counsel to be sober-minded, and he, by the laws, speaks the same language. I (the preacher) exhort you not to be rapacious and grasping. And he sits in judgment in such cases, and so is a worker together with us (preachers) and an assistant to us, and has been commissioned by God for this end." (Chrysostom.)

4. "He beareth not the sword in vain." It has been inferred from this place, and very rightly, that the civil magistrate may inflict death, and in cases where life has been taken away he seems bound to do so, for it is a primeval law: "Whoso sheddeth man's blood, by man shall his blood be shed: for in the image of God made he man." (Gen. ix. 6.)

"He is the minister of God .... a revenger," &c. So that the civil governor is a minister both of the mercy and the justice of God.

if thou do that which is evil, be afraid; for he beareth not the sword in vain: for he is the minister of God, a revenger to *execute* wrath upon him that doeth evil.

^e Eccles. viii. 2.
^f 1 Pet. ii. 19.

5 Wherefore ^e *ye* must needs be subject, not only for wrath, ^f but also for conscience sake.

6 For for this cause pay ye tribute also: for they are God's ministers, attending continually upon this very thing.

He is the minister of God's mercy, in that he preserves to man the inestimable blessing of well-ordered human society, and he is the minister of the justice of God, for the temporal punishment which he inflicts is the expression of the righteous anger of God against evil-doing.

5. "Wherefore ye must needs be subject, not only for wrath, but also for conscience sake." "Not only for wrath," *i.e.*, not only through fear of his wrath which he can give effect to by punishing you, but also for conscience sake. Mark these words of the Apostle. How often do men urge their conscientious convictions on the side of disobedience! He, on the contrary, cites conscience on the side of obedience to the rulers of this world. And yet this very man a few years after submitted to death rather than disobey the ruling of his conscience.

6. "For for this cause pay ye tribute also: for they are God's ministers," &c. This "pay" is by most expositors considered to be indicative, not imperative—"for this cause ye pay tribute," that is, to maintain them, and to furnish them with the means of repressing disorder and violence, and protecting the persons and property of quiet citizens.

"For they are God's ministers." "Note how constantly he repeats this, but here he employs a stronger word. In verse four he had used the word διάκονος, here λειτουργία a word pertaining to the service of God in His Sanctuary, as if such governors were to be looked upon by us as performing a divine service to Him, and to be honoured as such." (Williams.)

"Attending continually upon this very thing." Their whole business is to protect and take care of you in the place which God has assigned them.

7. "Render therefore to all their dues: tribute to whom tribute

CHAP. XIII.] RENDER TO ALL THEIR DUES. 295

7 ᵍ Render therefore to all their dues: tribute to whom tribute *is due;* custom to whom custom; fear to whom fear; honour to whom honour.

ᵍ Matt. xxii. 21. Mark xii. 17. Luke xx. 25.

8 Owe no man any thing, but to love one another: for ʰ he that loveth another hath fulfilled the law.

ʰ ver. 10. Gal. v. 14. Col. iii. 14. 1 Tim. i. 5. Jam. ii. 8.

9 For this, ⁱ Thou shalt not commit adultery, Thou shalt not kill, Thou shalt not steal, Thou shalt not bear false witness, Thou shalt not covet;

ⁱ Exod. xx. 13, &c. Deut. v. 17, &c. Matt. xix. 18.

---

7. " Render therefore." So E., F., G., L., P., almost all Cursives, d, e, f, g, Syriac, Arm., Goth.; but "therefore" omitted by ℵ, A., B., D., 67, Vulg. (Cod. Amiat.), Sah., Copt.

is due." "Tribute," any direct tax on person or real property. It refers to the annual capitations.

"Custom to whom custom." Any indirect tax or toll on goods. "Fear" expresses the feeling due to the highest authorities, to supreme magistrates before whom the lictors walk, and who are invested with the power of life and death.

"Honour" applies generally to all men in office. St. Peter makes the precept general, "Honour all men."

"Owe no man any thing." Keep out of debt.

"But to love one another." There is one debt, however, which you can never discharge, *i.e.*, the debt of love. You owe it to all who are created in the image of God; you owe it to all who are redeemed by the Blood of Christ, especially do you owe it to all who are fellow-members of Christ, that you should love them. This debt you can never discharge, so that you should be free from the obligation to love your brethren and your fellow-creatures.

"He that loveth another hath fulfilled the law." Notice how the Apostle, who has throughout all the Epistle rejected the law as a means of justification, here upholds it as a rule of sanctification.

" He that loveth another hath fulfilled the law," for he proceeds to say,

9. "For this, Thou shalt not commit adultery, Thou shalt not kill, Thou shalt not steal .... Thou shalt love thy neighbour as thyself." How is it that St. Paul draws attention to the commandments of the second table only? for it is these commandments which are covered by the more general precept, "Thou shalt love

and if *there be* any other commandment, it is briefly comprehended in this saying, namely,[k] Thou shalt love thy neighbour as thyself.

10 Love worketh no ill to his neighbour: therefore [l] love *is* the fulfilling of the law.

11 And that, knowing the time, that now *it is*

[k] Lev. xix. 18. Matt. xxii. 39. Mark xii. 31. Gal. v. 14. Jam. ii. 8.
[l] Matt. xxii. 40. ver. 8.

---

9. "Thou shalt not bear false witness." Omitted by A., B., D., E., F., G., L., thirty-five Cursives, Vulg. (Cod. Amiat.), d, e, f, g, Syriac (Schaaf), Sah.; but ℵ, P., most Cursives, Copt., Arm., Æth. retain.

thy neighbour as thyself." It might be sufficient to answer that his Lord had done precisely the same when he tried the young ruler by the commandments of the second table only (Matth. xix. 18); but is it not the fact that the real test is the second table? St. John seems to think so when he writes: "If a man say I love God and hateth his brother, he is a liar, for he that loveth not his brother whom he hath seen, how can he love God whom he hath not seen?" (1 John iv. 20.) The commandments of the second table are especially those which require self-command and self-restraint, and a conscience determined to be void of offence both towards God and towards men. Lively feelings may deceive a man as to his love to God; but there can be no self-deception in the matter of a man striving to avoid doing the very least harm to his neighbour, and doing him all the good he can.

11. "And that, knowing the time, that now it is high time to awake," &c. "And that" (καὶ τοῦτο), rather "and this"—this should we do, this mind of obedience should we have, since we know the time, that the end draws near. The day of Christ's appearing was at hand when we first heard the Gospel, for part of that Gospel was "The day of the Lord cometh as a thief in the night." "Take ye heed, watch and pray, for ye know not when the time cometh." If we were bound to look for it and live in expectation of it then, much more should we do so now.

But had not the Roman Christians been awakened out of sleep when they were converted and baptized? Yes; but as Godet says, the most awakened in the Church has still need of awakening, and hence the Apostle reminds his readers that there are degrees even in this. It was said of some leading Christian at the beginning of this century, that, looking at the state of things then existing, and the

high time ᵐ to awake out of sleep: for now *is* our salvation
nearer than when we believed.

12 The night is far spent, the day is at hand;

ᵐ 1 Cor. xv. 34. Eph. v. 14. 1 Thess. v. 5, 6.

---

comparative apathy even of such as himself, he said to one who knew him well, " Brother, brother, we are not half-awake." In accordance with this, the Apostle reminds the Ephesian Christians of the words, " Awake thou that sleepest, and arise from the dead, and Christ shall give thee light." (v. 14.)

" For now is our salvation nearer than when we believed," *i.e.*, our full salvation. This is never connected with any crisis of the spiritual life here, or with death, but with the Lord's second coming, and our resurrection in our spiritual bodies.

12. " The night is far spent, the day is at hand." The present time is called the night, and the coming of the Lord the day. Now this time, night though it is called, is a day of grace. It is a day of acceptance and salvation. " Now is the accepted time, now is the day of salvation." (2 Cor. vi. 2.) We have much light in this night. We have the light of God's truth, of the Scriptures, of the Church, of the Holy Spirit. Twilight though it be, compared to the blaze of day which will soon burst upon us, we have light enough whereby to do our work. And it is remarkable that our Lord calls the present time day, " I must work the works of him that sent me while it is day. The night cometh when no man can work" (John ix. 4.) Night though it be, there is work to be done in it which cannot be done when the eternal day has come. Why, then, does the Apostle call this time of probation night? Because it is the time in which deeds of darkness are done. It is the night of sin and evil to the inhabitants of the world, and many Christians walk in darkness because they walk more or less according to the world. And it is night when compared with the clearness and brightness of the future day. " Now we see through a glass darkly, but then face to face. Now I know in part, but then shall I know even as also I am known." (1 Cor. xiii. 12.)

" The day is at hand." " What wonderful things will the light of that day reveal, which we now only see darkly, or feel around! What a new world will burst upon us: what faces, what eyes, what companies, of which we can now form no idea, and ourselves also like to blind men seeing for the first time our own countenances in

n Eph. v. 11. Col. iii. 8.	ⁿ let us therefore cast off the works of darkness,
o Eph. vi. 13. 1 Thess. v. 8.	and ᵒ let us put on the armour of light.
p Phil. iv. 8. Thess. iv. 12. Pet. ii. 12.	13 ᵖ Let us walk ‖ honestly, as in the day; ᵠ not in rioting and drunkenness, ʳ not in chambering
‖ Or, *decently*. q Prov. xxiii. 20. Luke xxi. 34. 1 Pet. iv. 3.	and wantonness, ˢ not in strife and envying.
r 1 Cor. vi. 9. Eph. v. 5. s Jam. iii. 14.	a mirror." (Williams.) This state is ever nearer and nearer, is fast approaching, is just appearing. And here it is, as if there were signs of the coming dawn,

at least to some amongst us. As Chrysostom says: "The birds twittering under the roof, or such other tokens that the night is on the wane, and men awaking each other, and saying, 'It is now time to arise, it is time to put on our armour for the day.'"

"Let us therefore cast off the works of darkness." By repentance, by confession, by faith, by constant and unremitting watchfulness and prayer, by self-denial, by using every means of grace.

"And let us put on the armour of light." The arms or weapons of attack as well as armour merely defensive. St. Paul, in Ephesians vi., calls it the panoply of God, and he enumerates the various parts of it as truth, as righteousness, as the Gospel of peace, as faith, as salvation, as the word of God.

13. "Let us walk honestly, as in the day." "Honestly," rather becomingly, putting away everything indecent and out of keeping with the light in which Christians ought to live; avoiding every word or action even remotely tending to evil; doing our best to commend our faith to others by remembering such words as "Let your light so shine before men, that they may see your good works, and glorify your Father which is in heaven," or "Abstain from every appearance of evil," or "See that ye walk circumspectly."

"Not in rioting and drunkenness, not in chambering and wantonness," &c. The works of darkness are enumerated in pairs; first intemperance and excess in feasting and banqueting; then fornication and its attendant lasciviousness, and then what naturally would arise from such indulgences, strife and envying, or rather jealousies. This passage is remarkable in that it was the means used by God for converting St. Augustine. I give the full account in a note taken from his Confessions.[1]

---

[1] "I cast myself down I know not how, under a certain fig-tree, and gave run to my tears; and the floods of mine eyes broke for 'an acceptable sacrifice to thee' (Ps. li. 19).

CHAP. XIII.] PUT YE ON THE LORD JESUS.

14 But ^t put ye on the Lord Jesus Christ, and   ^t Gal. iii. 27.
Eph. iv. 24.
Col. iii. 10.

14. "But put ye on the Lord Jesus Christ." But have we not, according to the Apostle's own words, put Him on in baptism? (Gal. iii.) Yes, but He has to be put on not once, but constantly—once sacramentally at the font, but constantly by being conformed to the example of His most holy Life. So also it is with the evil things which the Apostle had but just mentioned. They have been once for all put off in baptism, or in conversion, and yet, if we are not watchful and prayerful, they may return and re-assert their dominion, and, in the Lord's own words, our last state may be worse than the first.

"Put ye on the Lord Jesus Christ." By daily setting before yourselves His holy example, and that example reflected in His saints. Wesley has a valuable note: "Herein is contained the whole of our salvation. It is a strong and beautiful expression for the most intimate union with Him, and being clothed with all the graces which were with Him. The Apostle does not say, 'put on purity and sobriety, peacefulness, and benevolence.' But he says, all this and a thousand times more at once in saying, 'Put on Christ.'"

And not, indeed, in these words, yet to this purpose, spake I much unto thee : ' And thou, O Lord, how long? how long wilt thou be angry for ever? O remember not against us former iniquities' (Ps. lxxix. 5, 8), for I felt that I was holden by them. I kept on uttering wretched exclamations: ' How long? how long? to-morrow and to-morrow? Why not now? why not this hour make an end of mine uncleanness?'

"Such words I spake the while I wept in most bitter contrition of my heart. And lo, from a neighbouring house, I heard a voice, as of a boy or girl, I know not, singing and oft repeating, ' Take, read; take, read.' Instantly with a changed countenance I began to think most intently, whether boys in any kind of game used to sing such a phrase; nor could I remember ever to have heard the like. So checking the torrent of my tears, I arose; interpreting it to be no other than a Divine command to open the book, and read the first chapter I should find. For I had heard of Antony, that he had happened to come in during the reading of the Gospel, and had taken the passage read as a warning spoken to himself, ' Go, sell all that thou hast, and give to the poor, and thou shalt have treasure in heaven, and come and follow me' (St. Matthew xix. 21), and by such oracle he was forthwith converted unto Thee. With such an inspiration then I returned to the place where Alypius was sitting; for there I had laid the volume of the Apostle, when I arose thence. I seized, opened, and in silence read the passage upon which my eyes first fell : ' Not in rioting and drunkenness, not in chambering and wantonness, not in strife and envying: but put ye on the Lord Jesus Christ, and make not provision for the flesh, to fulfil the lusts thereof.' No further would I read; nor was there need, for instantly, at the end of this sentence, as though my heart were flooded with a light of peace, all the shadows of doubt melted away."

> ^u Gal. v. 16.
> 1 Pet. ii. 11.
>
> ^u make not provision for the flesh, to *fulfil* the lusts *thereof*.

"And make not provision for the flesh, to fulfil the lusts thereof." This does not, of course, mean that we are not to be industrious and economical, that we may have wherewith to live, but it means that we are not to amass money or property, in order that we may have more to spend on bodily, sensual, animal gratifications. As Quesnel says, "To satisfy both reason and faith, by giving to the body what necessity requires, and refusing it what sensuality craves, is to obey God Himself; to make provision for the corrupt inclination which reigns in the body, is to make ourselves the slaves of sin." See my notes on Luke xii. 16, &c.

CHAP. XIV.

> ^a ch. xv. 1, 7.
> 1 Cor. viii. 9,
> 11. & ix. 22.
> ‖ Or, *not to judge* his *doubtful thoughts*.
>
> HIM that ^a is weak in the faith receive ye, *but* ‖ not to doubtful disputations.

The Apostle now enters upon a matter apparently new, and commentators have much difficulty in finding the link between what he has just written and what he is about to write. But why should there be any difficulty? The Apostle is about to conclude his letter; he knew from his experience in Corinth, from whence he was writing, that there was especial difficulty in maintaining the unity and peace of the Church in the matter of meats, and drinks, and holy days. He perhaps knew for certain, he certainly thought it most probable, that such difficulties were present in the Roman Church, and he gives such directions as would, on the one side, not press heavily on individual consciences, and on the other obviate schism.

The question has been much debated who the persons were who went to the extreme of abstinence or asceticism; some suppose that they were Jews with Ebionite tendencies, others that they had in their heathen state been Pythagoreans; others that the Dualistic errors and heresies, which soon occasioned such trouble, were be-

2 For one believeth that he ᵇmay eat all things: another, who is weak, eateth herbs.

ᵇ ver. 14.
1 Cor. x. 25.
1 Tim. iv. 4.
Tit. i. 15.

---

ginning to assert themselves amongst the converts. It seems to me that there can be no doubt but that the abstainers from meats were the same as regarded certain days, and if so they must have been Jews, for though the Apostle might deal tenderly with those who, in a mixed Church, still kept new moons and Sabbaths, he would not for a moment tolerate the keeping of days on purely heathen grounds. The Jews, when abroad, constantly abstained from all animal food, either because it was not killed according to their rules, or because it might contain elements of pollution. Thus Daniel and his three friends refused meat even from the king's table. Thus Tobit kept himself from eating the bread of the Gentiles. (i. 10, 11.) Thus also the Maccabees. (2 Macc. v. 27.) John the Baptist fed on locusts and wild honey. Clement of Alexandria speaks of the Apostle St. Matthew abstaining from all animal food.

1. " Him that is weak in the faith receive ye, but not to doubtful disputations." " Him that is weak in the faith," that is, one whose faith has not so grasped the great truths of the Catholic faith, that he is above having regard to distinctions of meats and drinks. Such persons would not be Jews only, but often religious proselytes who would cling to such distinctions more tenaciously than the born Jews.

"Receive ye." Admit him freely to your fellowship and good offices.

" But not to doubtful disputations." Some interpret, "not to discussions of doubts," others, "not to discussion of opinions." It requires to be paraphrased, " not so as to worry him and unsettle him in endeavouring to bring him over to your opinions, but leave his faith to work greater strength and decision in him."

2. " For one believeth that he may eat all things: another, who is weak," &c. One, in accepting Christ, has had faith to accept all His words, such, particularly, as "not that which entereth into a man defileth him." Another has not yet fully accepted Christ as his Deliverer from the burdensome yoke of the law, and is tormented with scruples about "meats and drinks, and divers washings."

"Another, who is weak, eateth herbs." It is remarkable that

3 Let not him that eateth despise him that eateth not;
and ^c let not him which eateth not judge him that eateth: for God hath received him.

4 ^d Who art thou that judgest another man's

c Col. ii. 16.

d Jam. iv. 12.

---

the Apostle here takes exactly opposite ground to what we in England in this century do. He looks upon the total abstainer as the weak man, and rightly so, because in this matter of meats the total abstainer was the over-scrupulous, indeed, the superstitiously scrupulous man. Because there was a danger that the beast in being killed might not have lost *all* its blood; because it might have been cooked with something from a forbidden creature, he abstains from all meats whatsoever. Now by this he showed that he was not strong in Christ, that faith in Christ as the only begotten Son had not taken such hold upon him that he looked upon old things as passed away, and all things as having become new in Christ. He had a lurking idea that the system of Moses was not superseded by that of Christ. Now the Apostle deals very tenderly with him, very differently from what he would have done with a convert from pure heathenism, for having commanded that the Church should receive him, and to receive him generously and freely ("not to doubtful disputation"), he bids them not even look down upon him.

3. "Let not him that eateth despise him that eateth not . . . . God hath received him." Notice the difference in the expressions. The strong despises the weak: the weak judges (in the sense of condemning) the strong. The strong, *i.e.*, the Christian firmly established in the Catholic faith, despises the man who is yet somewhat in bondage to a system which is decaying or vanishing away: the weak, *i.e.*, the abstainer, condemns the one who has no religious scruples about what he eats, as indifferent to certain plain Scripture precepts.

"God hath received him," by opening his eyes to receive the truth of the Gospel, and by receiving him into the Church by Baptism. The words must be taken to refer both to the man who eats all things, and to the abstainer; for God hath received both, so that neither must look down upon or condemn the other.

4. "Who art thou that judgest another man's servant? To his own master he standeth," &c. This must, of course, be taken

CHAP. XIV.] HE SHALL BE HOLDEN UP. 303

servant? to his own master he standeth or falleth. Yea, he shall be holden up: for God is able to make him stand.

5 [e] One man esteemeth one day above another; [e] Gal. iv. 10. Col. ii. 16.

---

4. "God is able." So D., E., F., G., L., far the most Cursives, d, e, f, g, Vulg.; but ℵ, A., B., C., P., Sah., Cop., Arm., Goth., Syr. read, " the Lord."

within the limitation of the things (or things of an exactly similar character), which are treated of in this chapter, *i.e.*, things indifferent in themselves. It cannot refer to open sins, which must be pronounced upon as wrong by all Christians who are cognizant of them, and by the Church, if they are within the range of Church censures.

Things upon which the Lord has not pronounced a decision, but manifestly left open, it is not for us to decide upon. All Christians are the servants of Christ. He has ministers under Him to rule His Church, of which ministers He has said, "Whatsoever ye shall bind on earth shall be bound in heaven, and whatsoever ye shall loose on earth shall be loosed in heaven;" but this subordination in the Church does not undo the fact that Christ is the Lord of each particular servant, and each individual soul has to stand in His grace, or fall from His grace. In indifferent matters Christ leaves His servants at liberty, and if any one of their fellow servants presumes to deprive them of this liberty, he puts himself between them and Christ, and this intrusion Christ will sooner or later resent. Jowett has an admirable note: "'It is no concern of yours: not to you, but to his own master, he is accountable, whether he stand or fall;' and then, as if it were a word of ill omen even to suggest that he should fall, he adds, 'But he shall stand, as we may in faith believe, for God is able to make him stand.' He is a weak brother, I speak as a man, therefore he is likely to fall. But believing in the omnipotence of God, I say he is so much more likely to stand also, for 'my strength is made perfect in weakness.'"

5. "One man esteemeth one day above another: another esteemeth every day alike." There is some difficulty respecting the translation of this verse. It is asserted that the words ἡμέραν παρ ἡμέραν, cannot mean one day above another, but rather mean alternate days; "one man judges or distinguishes alternate days, another every day." But neither of the Greek commentators Chrysostom or Theodoret take it in this way. They both seem to

another esteemeth every day *alike*. Let every man be ‖ fully
persuaded in his own mind.

6 He that ᶠ ‖ regardeth the day, regardeth *it*

‖ Or, *fully assured*.
ᶠ Gal. iv. 10.
‖ Or, *observeth*.

understand it as it is translated both in the Authorized and by the Revisers of 1881. Most of the earlier commentators, I know not for what reason, consider the days to be fasting days; but if the error or weakness be the same as that alluded to in Coloss. ii. 16, "Let no man judge you in meat or in drink, or in respect of an holy day, or of the new moon, or of the Sabbath days," then the term "day" covers all days of Jewish religious observance.

Among the converts from Judaism there would be great difficulty in believing that the obligation of the Saturday as a day of absolute cessation from all worldly employment had ceased, and so with the new moons, and the days of Atonement, Passover, and Pentecost. We are to remember that the principal Scripture of the Roman Christians at that time was the volume of the Old Testament. By no possibility could they have had more than one of our Gospels, and very probably not one of the Apostolical Epistles. Here, then, their only Scriptures were full of the sanctity of the Saturday, or seventh day. Surely, then, the Apostle was wise in vindicating the right of what was probably the minority to keep the day which their forefathers had been so long commanded to observe. With respect to the observance of Sunday, or the first day, that would be partly provided for by the weekly Eucharistic celebration, but as yet there was no Church law on the keeping of Sunday as a day of rest.

"Let every man be fully persuaded in his own mind." Because, if not, his conscience would be perpetually burdened with a sense of sin in the matter of the observance or non-observance of the day. This is well expressed by Philippi, "If the weaker one permits himself to be led away with a doubtful conscience to a freer mode of life, he commits sin (verses 20-23), and the same if the freer one is not confident as to the case in hand, before the Lord has set him free, but merely gives himself to a freer course of life from casual wantonness, and with a guilty conscience."

6. "He that regardeth the day, regardeth it unto the Lord," *i.e.*, he considers that it is the will of Christ that he should observe it.

CHAP. XIV.]   NONE LIVETH TO HIMSELF.   305

unto the Lord; and he that regardeth not the day, to the Lord he doth not regard *it*. He that eateth, eateth to the Lord, for ^g he giveth God thanks; and he that eateth not, to the Lord he eateth not, and giveth God thanks.

^g 1 Cor. x. 31.
1 Tim. iv. 3.

7 For ^h none of us liveth to himself, and no man dieth to himself.

^h 1 Cor. vi. 19, 20. Gal. ii. 20.
1 Thess. v. 10.
1 Pet. iv. 2.

6. "And he that regardeth not the day . . . regard it." This clause omitted by ℵ, A., B., C., E., F., G., d, e, f, g, Vulg., Copt., Æth.; but retained by L., P., most Cursives, Syriac, and Arm.

"And he that regardeth not the day, to the Lord he doth not regard it." The reader will see that the genuineness of this part of the verse is very doubtful. It is, however, the proper complement of the last clause. He that regardeth not some Jewish day of obligation, does so because he believes that Christ has delivered him from the yoke of a state of things of which it forms a part, and so he thinks that he most honours the authority of Christ by its non-observance.

"He that eateth, eateth to the Lord, for he giveth God thanks." Which he could not do unless he believed that he received his meat, whatever it was, from the hand of God. The giving thanks to God for our meat hallows it, and the sense of our receiving it from God, if we duly considered it, would keep us from all excess in things lawful. And so we should "eat to the Lord,"—as the Apostle elsewhere says: "Whether ye eat or drink, or whatsoever ye do, do all to the glory of God."

"And he that eateth not, to the Lord he eateth not, and giveth God thanks." He acknowledges, by his giving thanks, that he receives his herbs from God as much as if he had given thanks for animal food, and so his strictness must not be despised; the Lord, in due time, may lead him into a higher state of liberty.

7, 8. "For none of us liveth to himself, and no man dieth to himself . . . . we are the Lord's." This is to be understood in a Christian sense, *i.e.*, of a conscious living to Christ. It does not mean that all men are under the rule of Christ, though, of course, such is the fact, because all things are put under His feet, but it means that the universal Christian principle is that we have surrendered body, soul and spirit, life and death, into His hands, and so are not our own, but His.

x

8 For whether we live, we live unto the Lord; and whether we die, we die unto the Lord: whether we live therefore, or die, we are the Lord's.

¹ 2 Cor. v. 15.   9 For ¹ to this end Christ both died, and rose,
^k Acts x. 36.   and revived, that he might be ^k Lord both of the dead and living.

10 But why dost thou judge thy brother? or why dost

---

9. "Christ both died, and rose, and revived." ℵ, A., B., C., Copt., Arm., Æth. read, "died and lived." Considerable difference in ancient authorities; some Cursives, and Syriac (virtually) read as in Text. Rec.; but L., P., and most Cursives, "died, and rose again, and lived."

But what is the meaning of "whether we die, we die unto the Lord"? Does it mean that we so surrender ourselves to Him as joyfully to lay down our lives when and how He pleases, it may be by a natural death, it may be by martyrdom? I think from the next verse we should rather gather that it means that the state into which we shall be ushered by death is as much a part of His domain as is this present world, and so His Mastership over us will never cease.

9. "For to this end Christ both died, and rose, and revived, that," &c. He died to purchase us, and He rose again that He might rule over and mould to His purposes those whom He has purchased.

The true reading probably is, "To this end Christ died and lived—*i.e.*, after death—that he might," &c. But, though we are not to separate the two as if He died to rule over the dead, and lived to be Lord of the living, yet we should remember that between His Death and His Rising again He exercised Lordship in the realms of the departed, and that the new Life which He received at His Resurrection He imparts to us now, that we should serve Him in this our present life by walking in newness of Life.

19. "But why dost thou judge thy brother? or why dost thou set at nought," &c. We shall all of us stand at the judgment seat of Christ to receive the things done in the body. How foolish, then, for those who are in the position (for the time at least) of fellow-prisoners before the same tribunal to judge one another, or to despise one another, about things indifferent; for that this dis-

thou set at nought thy brother? for ¹we shall all stand before the judgment seat of Christ.

11 For it is written, ᵐ *As* I live, saith the Lord,

¹ Matt. xxv. 31, 32. Acts x. 42. & xvii. 31. 2 Cor. v. 10. Jude xiv. 15.

ᵐ Is. xlv. 24.

10. "Judgment seat of Christ." So L., P., all Cursives, Syriac, Arm., Goth.; but ℵ, A., B., C., D., E., F., G., d, e, f, g, Vulg. (Cod. Amiat.) read, " of God."

cussion is about things indifferent, and not about good and bad deeds, is clear from verse 14.

"For we shall all stand before the judgment seat of Christ." The difference of reading requires serious attention. The principal Uncials read "God;" the Cursives read "Christ." This is attempted to be accounted for by the supposition that the minds of the later scribes ran on 2 Corinth. v. 10; but is not the reading "Christ" in accordance with almost all the rest of the New Testament? The Father certainly does not judge visibly, for Christ says, "The Father judgeth no man, but hath committed all judgment to the Son" (John v. 22). Again, St. Paul says in this very Epistle, "In the day when God shall judge the secrets of men by Jesus Christ according to my Gospel" (ii. 16). The Son does nothing without the Father, and the Father does all things by the Son: but the Son as distinguished from the Father will sit on the throne of His Glory (Matth. xxv. 31). Again, all the context of this place is about the supreme Lordship of Christ, "Whether we live, we live unto the Lord .... He is the Lord of the dead, and therefore of those who will stand at the bar of judgment after death." Again, take the citation from Isaiah in the next verse, "As I live, saith the Lord, every knee shall bow to me, and every tongue shall confess to God!" This is specially applied to Christ in Phil. ii. 11. The fact is that the three greatest functions of Deity—those of Creation, Redemption, and Judgment—are applied to God and to Christ as the Son of God with absolute indifference, as if He possesses Divine power, knowledge, and omnipresence, as His Father does, which, of course, we confess in the creeds of the Catholic Church. The difference of reading, then, is remarkable as exhibiting the absolute indifference of Scripture language on this matter.

11. "For it is written, As I live, saith the Lord, every knee shall bow to me," &c. This is taken from Isaiah xlv. 23, but is quoted freely. The Septuagint is, "By myself I swear, righteousness shall

every knee shall bow to me, and every tongue shall confess to God.

ⁿ Matt. xii. 36. Gal. vi. 5. 1 Pet. iv. 5.

12 So then ⁿ every one of us shall give account of himself to God.

13 Let us not therefore judge one another any more: but judge this rather, that ^o no man put a stumblingblock or an occasion to fall in *his* brother's way.

^o 1 Cor. viii. 9, 13. & x. 32.

---

surely proceed out of my mouth, my words shall not be frustrated: That to me every knee shall bend, and every tongue shall swear by God." I have shown in the last verse that this is applied to our Lord Jesus Christ. He then, to Whom every knee shall bend, is the Son of God in human form, not apart from God, but acting in the place of God, the Judge of all.

12. "So then every one of us shall give account of himself to God." The stress is to be laid upon "of himself." We shall each one have to give account of ourselves, so that we must prepare ourselves, and attend to ourselves, and leave our brother to His own Master and Judge.

I would notice, in passing, that the Apostle is here writing of believers, of whom he is one, and when he writes to them "every one of us shall give account," he includes himself not only among believers, but amongst those believers that will be judged. How is it, then, that men have ventured to say that believers are raised into a sphere above judgment? (See my notes on John iii. 18, 19, p. 78, and on v. 24, p. 130.) The Apostle St. Paul not only here, but elsewhere, asserts that he shall be judged. "He that judgeth me is the Lord." "We must all appear before the judgment seat of Christ." "I keep under my body and bring it into subjection, lest that by any means having preached to others I myself should be a castaway." "A crown of righteousness which the Lord, the righteous judge, shall give me in that day."

It is to be remembered that the reward of the righteous is as much the issue of a just judgment as the condemnation of the wicked.

13. "Let us not therefore judge one another . . . . but judge this rather," &c. Notice the play on the word judge: the first means to pass a judicial judgment, the second to form a moral judgment against ourselves in the matter of our conduct with respect to our

CHAP. XIV.] NOTHING UNCLEAN OF ITSELF. 309

14 I know, and am persuaded by the Lord Jesus, [p] that *there is* nothing † unclean of itself: but [q] to him that esteemeth any thing to be † unclean, to him *it is* unclean.

[p] Acts x. 15.
ver. ii. 20.
1 Cor. x. 25.
1 Tim. iv. 4.
Tit. i. 15.
† Gr. *common*.
[q] 1 Cor. viii. 7, 10.
† Gr. *common*.

---

brethren. There is no perceptible difference between a stumbling-block, and the occasion to fall. They both signify something that incites to sin.

14. "I know, and am persuaded by (or in) the Lord Jesus, that there is nothing unclean of itself." Was this a spiritual revelation made to St. Paul's spirit owing to his union with Christ, or was it the Spirit bringing some external teaching of the Lord home to him? Undoubtedly the latter, for the Lord had said, "There is nothing from without a man that, entering into him, can defile him." This is the widest and most dogmatic assertion possible, and St. Paul, if he knew anything whatsoever respecting our Lord's life and words, must have known it, and here he reproduces its spirit and essence.

"To him that esteemeth any thing to be unclean, to him it is unclean." Is, then, each man's private conscience the sole judge of right and wrong? No, by no means. But we must remember that this matter of clean or unclean meats was then, before the Catholic Church was firmly established and had given her decisions, a matter of extreme difficulty. The only Scripture (except, perhaps, one Gospel) which the Roman Christians had, contained these distinctions of meats and of days. The New Testament was not then in its fulness side by side with the Old, and accepted by all as the necessary comment upon, and correction of, the Old. Let us remember that St. Paul, in the Epistle to the Galatians, in proving the inability of the law to justify, had to appeal not only to Scripture, but to his own Apostolical authority as proved by his miracles, "He therefore that ministereth to you the spirit, and worketh miracles among you, doeth he it by the works of the law, or by the hearing of faith?" (Gal. iii. 5.) This has passed away, and liberty and scrupulosity now appear under other forms.

15. "But if thy brother be grieved with thy meat, now," &c. Almost all Uncial MSS. read "for" (γὰρ), instead of "but" (δὲ).

15 But if thy brother be grieved with *thy* meat, now walkest thou not † charitably. ʳ Destroy not him with thy meat, for whom Christ died.

† Gr. *according to charity*.
ʳ 1 Cor. viii. 11.

---

15. "But if thy brother." So most Cursives, Syriac and Goth.; but ℵ, A., B., C., D., E., F., G., P., about ten Cursives, d, e, f, g, Vulg., Copt., Arm. read, "For if thy brother."

If "for" is read, we must suppose that the Apostle goes back to the thought at the end of verse 13, "Judge this, rather that no man put a stumblingblock," &c.

"Be grieved," &c. Not in the sense of pained, but of "hurt" or "injured."

"Now walkest thou not charitably" (*i.e.*, if thou eatest that which gives him offence). Does this mean that the bulk of the Roman Christians were to abstain from all animal food because a small minority, recently converted from Judaism, considered it unlawful? Impossible. It can only mean that the strong who have no scruples should not eat what the weak considered to be unlawful in their presence, or when sitting at meat in the house with them, or the strong should not press the weak to partake of what in their secret hearts they believed to be forbidden by God.

"Destroy him not with thy meat, for whom Christ died." Could then a soul be destroyed by another partaking of what was lawful or indifferent? Certainly; and in this way. Either the weak one would be made to regard the strong, who thus indulged in his presence, with aversion, and this might set him against the Christian faith altogether, or else the weak would be led by his example or importunity to partake of what his secret conscience forbade him to eat; and so, going constantly against his conscience, he would lose his religion, and so there might be the foundation laid for a serious declension from God. In 1 Corinth. viii. 10, the offence is supposed to be given, not in a private house, but in the idol's temple.

The precept "Destroy not him with thy meat for whom Christ died," is capable of a very wide application. It may be taken "Destroy not thy Christian brother's soul with thy self-indulgence, with thy going to the extremest verge of what is lawful, with thy doing what is equivocal or doubtful, or which thy brother is sure to misunderstand."

CHAP. XIV.]   THE KINGDOM OF GOD.   311

16 ˢ Let not then your good be evil spoken of: ˢ ch. xii. 17.

17 ᵗ For the kingdom of God is not meat and   ᵗ 1 Cor. viii. 8. drink; but righteousness, and peace, and joy in the Holy Ghost.

18 For he that in these things serveth Christ
ᵘ *is* acceptable to God, and approved of men.   ᵘ 2 Cor. viii. 21.

---

18. "In these things." So E., L., most Cursives, Goth., Syriac, Arm.; but ℵ, A., B., C., D., F., G., P., d, e, f, g, Vulg., Sah., Copt. read, "in this."

16. "Let not then your good be evil spoken of." Some understand by your (or our) "good" our Christian liberty. Let it not be so maintained as to occasion slander and reviling, and so bring discredit upon your profession, especially, of course, among the unconverted Jews.

Others understand it of the whole faith or profession of the Gospel. Let not the faith be evil spoken of owing to the divisions and unseemly contests amongst its professors respecting things indifferent.

17. "For the kingdom of God is not meat and drink; but righteousness," &c. "Meat and drink" should rather be translated, "eating and drinking."

This means that the essence of the kingdom of God can be nothing external, but only in that internal conformity to the will of God, which everything external in the kingdom—such as sacraments— is designed to bring about. The holiest of all eating, the reception of the consecrated Elements, is that Christ may dwell in us, and we in Him, and if He be within us then there is righteousness, then there is peace, then there is joy in the Holy Ghost. It has been made a question whether these three spiritual affections are towards our brethren or towards God; but the things cannot be separated. He that is righteous towards men in all his temporal and spiritual relations to them is also righteous towards God. He that is at peace towards his Christian brethren in the true sense of the word, must have the peace of God ruling within him. If anyone can have true Christian joy in converse or communion with his brethren, it must be joy in the Holy Ghost.

18. "For he that in these things serveth Christ is acceptable to God, and approved," &c. "In these things" (or in this), *i.e.*, in righteousness, peace, and joy.

ALL THINGS ARE PURE. [ROMANS.

^x Ps. xxxiv. 14. ch. xii. 18.
^y ch. xv. 2. 1 Cor. xiv. 12. 1 Thess. v. 11.
^z ver. 15.
^a Matt. xv. 11. Acts x. 15. ver. 14. Tit. i. 15.
^b 1 Cor. viii. 9, 10, 11, 12.
^c 1 Cor. viii. 13.

19 [x] Let us therefore follow after the things which make for peace, and things wherewith [y] one may edify another.

20 [z] For meat destroy not the work of God. [a] All things indeed *are* pure; [b] but *it is* evil for that man who eateth with offence.

21 *It is* good neither to eat [c] flesh, nor to drink

---

19. "Let us therefore follow after." So C., D., E., by far the most Cursives, d, e, f, g, Vulg.; but א, A., B., F., G., L., P., 39, 43, 73, 116, 238 read, "we follow."

"Serveth Christ." Notice here how men serve Christ in the highest spiritual graces, just as they serve God, and this, of course, is because Christ is God.

"Is acceptable to God, and approved of men," *i.e.*, of Christian good men. Thus our great Exemplar "increased in favour with God and man," Luke ii. 52.

19. "Let us therefore follow after the things which make for peace." This, of course, applies to both parties. "Let us follow after things which make for peace" by not obtruding our differences, by not blaming others for enjoying that which Christ has allowed, by not being censorious, and by not being regardless of wounding the religious feelings of others.

"And things wherewith one may edify another." If we abstain, in his presence, from what our weak brother considers unlawful, we assure him of our Christian love, and of our desire that he should look upon us as much more regardful of his feelings than of our own private gratification, and the consciousness of this edifies him, *i.e.*, builds him up in Christ, to whose fellowship we both belong.

20, 21. "For meat destroy not the work of God . . . made weak." A question arises upon the meaning of these verses which should be considered, though I do not see that any commentators notice it. The Apostle is here, as in verse 15, and the next chapter verse 1, taking the side of the weak. Now the "weak" eat only herbs; did he, then, mean to advise the whole Church to abstain from animal food in order not to give offence to these weak brethren? Impossible. In such a case he who of all men asserted the liberty of the Gentiles would go beyond the Jews themselves

wine, nor *any thing* whereby thy brother stumbleth, or is offended, or is made weak.

22 Hast thou faith? have *it* to thyself before God. ᵈ Happy *is* he that condemneth not himself in that thing which he alloweth.

ᵈ 1 John iii. 21.

---

21. "Or is offended, or is made weak." So B., D., E., F., G., L., P., most Cursives; but ℵ, A., C., Syr., Copt., Æth. omit.
22. "Hast thou faith?" So D., E., F., G., L., P., all Cursives, d, e, f, g, Vulg., Syr., Sah., Arm.; but ℵ, A., B., C., Copt. read, "The faith which thou hast, have it," &c.

(*i.e.*, most of them) in the matter of Judaizing. Where then is the limitation? I think we must take as our guide, as I have noticed a little before, 1 Cor. viii. 10, "If any man see thee which hast knowledge sitting at meat in the idol's temple, shall not the conscience of him that is weak be emboldened to eat those things which are offered to idols?" It is quite clear from this that the evil was in the seeing of the eating. Gentiles, for instance, might eat the flesh of swine when eating with one another; but if they invited a weak brother to a feast, and set before him what he considered to be unlawful food, and partook of it themselves, boasting of their greater liberty, they did what they could either to wound his feelings, or make him sin against his conscience.

If anyone reading this objects to the explanation given above, he is bound to say whether he believes that by what the Apostle writes here he means to ask the Gentile Roman Christians to take as their rule of meats Leviticus xi., for nothing short of this would satisfy the scrupulous Judaizer. If not, then the Apostle must refer to private meals to which weak brethren were invited.

22. "Hast thou faith? have it to thyself before God." Faith here means, of course, not the faith of the Gospel, but confidence that God in that Gospel has so made all things new that there is nothing now common or unclean, but all may be partaken of without scruple.

"Have it to thyself before God." Do not boast of thy liberty before the weak.

"Happy is he that condemneth not himself in that thing which he alloweth." The man who condemneth himself, and yet alloweth himself to eat, is the man of doubtful mind, the man who eats with misgivings. Such an one should earnestly pray that his doubts may be set perfectly at rest.

HE EATETH NOT OF FAITH. [ROMANS.

23 And he that || doubteth is damned if he eat, because *he eateth* not of faith: for ᵉ whatsoever *is* not of faith is sin.

| Or, *discerneth and putteth a difference between meats*.

ᵉ Tit. i. 15.

One or two Cursives, and some Greek Fathers, as Chrysostom and Theodoret, insert there the doxology of xvi. 25, &c. I shall examine this in its proper place.

23. "And he that doubteth is damned if he eat, because he eateth not of faith," *i.e.*, he eateth not with the full conviction that he is doing right.

"For whatsoever is not of faith is sin." Everything which is not done from a conviction that it is right, is sin (Vaughan). "When a person does not feel sure, nor believe that a thing is clean, how can he do else than sin (if he partake of it)? Now all these things have been spoken by Paul of the subject in hand, not of every thing." (Chrysostom.)

The reader should mark this last sentence out of Chrysostom, for another Father, of equal, if not greater eminence (Augustine), has, in his zeal for the faith of the Gospel, given so general an application of these words, and turned them into so absolute an aphorism, that he uses them to show that no heathen man, even one who is not within sound of the preaching of the Gospel, can do a good thing. Now, if by this it is meant that he cannot do a perfectly good thing, it may be true: but surely, if one heathen man tells an untruth, and another heathen man, his neighbour, adheres to the truth, even though he may have to suffer for it, the one is more acceptable to God than the other. What would Augustine have the heathen to do? It is not through their fault that they have not heard the Gospel. Through God's election they have not been chosen to hear it. Are they to do nothing? Are they to commit sin? Are they to put an end to themselves? If the reader chooses, he will see many pages devoted to the discussion of this question in the second book of Hooker's "Eccles. Polity." The question *seems* settled by our Apostle in chap. ii. 14, 15, and 27.

NOTE.

It is a wonderful fact, in the history of the world, that this matter of meats, clean and unclean, is as unsettled now as it was in the first century. There are two hundred and fifty millions of our fellow-subjects in Hindostan, to whom it is a subject of vital religious interest. The very last missionary that I conversed with told me that a Hindoo who desired baptism said to him, all in one breath, " Sir, I wish to become a Christian, but must I eat pork ? " We had visiting amongst us some twelve years ago, or perhaps a little more, a remarkable Hindoo, Chunder Sen, the founder of a new religion there, the Bramo Somaj. This new creed is simply a form of modern English Unitarianism, from which, to all appearance, every particle of distinctive Christianity has been eliminated. He rejects not only all human priesthood, but the priesthood of Christ Himself. He holds (or held) that all mediation, even that of the Son of God, is an intrusion between God and the soul. He rejects as superstition, every approach to sacrificial atonement. He was admitted freely into the highest society, secular and religious. After spending some time here, and learning all he could about our institutions, our education, and such things, he went back to India, and at his arrival in Bombay he made known his views respecting the English to a large meeting of his co-religionists. His account of us was anything but flattering to our vanity. But what was the chief offence of all ? Not our selfishness, not our party divisions, not our social estrangements, not the vast masses outside the pale of our own, or any Church, not our extravagance, our gambling, our horse-racing, our betting—but what does the Christian reader suppose ?—Why, the huge pieces of beef put upon our tables. He could endure everything but this. So that whilst he utterly rejected the holiness of Sacraments, Bible, Churches, and Creeds, he adhered firmly to the intrinsic holiness of the cow. All this is no exaggeration. Having known something of English Unitarianism in early years, I got to know all I could about the man and his opinions, and till I read the account of his description of ourselves, I never realized how deeply this doctrine of the distinctions of meats had struck its roots into a large portion of humanity.

Now, how is this to be met ? In writing on this chapter, I write without any idea of how it is practically met, or whether, amongst our missionaries, there is any uniform rule on the subject. But I have in my possession journals of missionaries of the seventeenth century—Roman Catholics, of course—who, when they went amongst the Hindoos to convert them, in order to meet their prejudices respecting meats and drinks, ate nothing but rice, and their preaching seems to have had astonishing success. It was no uncommon thing to make five hundred converts in one place in a year. I heard also from the best authority, that one belonging to the so-called salvation army, had adopted the same course of self-denial, and was similarly rewarded.

CHAP. XV.

^a Gal. vi. 1.
^b ch. xiv. 1.

WE ^a then that are strong ought to bear the ^b infirmities of the weak, and not to please ourselves.

^c 1 Cor. ix. 19, 22. & x. 24, 33. & xiii. 5. Phil. ii. 4, 5.
^d ch. xiv. 19.
^e Matt. xxvi. 39. John v. 30. & vi. 38.
^f Ps. lxix. 9.

2 ^c Let every one of us please *his* neighbour for *his* good ^d to edification.

3 ^e For even Christ pleased not himself; but, as it is written, ^f The reproaches of them that reproached thee fell on me.

1, 2. " We then that are strong ought to bear the infirmities," &c. The first seven verses of this chapter deal with the subjects treated of in chapter xiv., and ought to have been joined with it in one chapter.

The Apostle, in the first verses, adds another consideration to what has gone before. We ought not to be intent upon pleasing ourselves. We ought rather to aim at pleasing others, if, by so doing, we can build them up in the faith, and this after the example of Christ Himself.

3. "For even Christ pleased not himself . . . . fell on me." This passage is cited, not with reference to abstinence or liberty, but simply to bring the example of Christ to bear upon those to whom the Apostle is writing. So far from pleasing Himself, Christ did all things, and endured all things, for God's sake, even so far as receiving on Himself, in His own person, the reproaches aimed at God. But when and how did Christ thus receive the reproaches aimed at God? We answer that the hatred with which the unbelieving Jews pursued Christ, was because of their deep-seated alienation from God, as He says, "he that hateth me hateth my Father also." It was because He had exhibited, as no man ever

CHAP. XV.] PATIENCE AND COMFORT.

4 For ^g whatsover things were written aforetime were written for our learning, that we through patience and comfort of the scriptures might have hope.

5 ^h Now the God of patience and consolation grant you to be likeminded one toward another ‖ according to Christ Jesus:

^g ch. iv. 23, 24. 1 Cor. ix. 9, 10. & x. 11. 2 Tim. iii. 16, 17.
^h ch. xii. 16. 1 Cor. i. 10. Phil. iii. 16.
‖ Or, *after the example of.*

---

before had done, the holy character of God, that it could be said, "Now have they both seen and hated both me and my Father."

4. "For whatsoever things were written aforetime were written .... hope." "Whatsoever things," &c. Remember, "All Scripture is given by inspiration of God, and is profitable for doctrine, for reproof," &c.

But what is meant by patience and comfort of the Scriptures? It may be the patience and comfort of which the Scriptures are full. All the saints whose lives are given in Scripture—Abraham, Isaac, Jacob, Joseph, Moses, Job, David, Samuel—were at some time of their lives afflicted or persecuted persons, and so had need of patience, and after enduring patiently, were all comforted by God: or it may mean the patience and comfort with which the contemplation of these Scripture examples inspires us. The great lesson of the Scriptures is reflected in the progress towards perfection of the Christian soul. We glory in tribulations also (as Job and David did), knowing that tribulation worketh patience, and patience experience, and experience hope, &c. (ch. v. 3-4.)

5. "Now the God of patience and consolation grant you to be likeminded," &c. St. Paul had written "patience and comfort of the Scriptures," now he designates God, Whose gift the Scripture is, as the God of patience and consolation.

"Grant you to be likeminded one toward another." To be of the same mind, esteeming all alike. "God is characterized as the true source of these two graces, which are communicated to us through the channel of the Scriptures. To get them we must, therefore, go, not only to the Scriptures, but to Himself. There is a close relation in a Church between the consolation and the union of its members. When all are inwardly consoled from above, the way is paved for communion of hearts, all together aspiring vehemently after the same supreme good."

6 That ye may ¹with one mind *and* one mouth glorify God, even the Father of our Lord Jesus Christ.

7 Wherefore ᵏ receive ye one another, ¹ as Christ also received us to the glory of God.

8 Now I say that ᵐ Jesus Christ was a minister of the circumcision for the truth of God, ⁿ to confirm the promises *made* unto the fathers:

j Acts iv. 24, 32.
k ch. xiv. 1, 3.
l ch. v. 2.
m Matt. xv. 24. John i. 11. Acts iii. 25, 26. & xiii. 46.
n ch. iii. 3. 2 Cor. i. 20.

---

7. "Hath received us." So B., D., P., many Cursives; but ℵ, A., C., E., F., G., L., most Cursives, d, e, f, g, Vulg., Syriac, Copt., Goth., Arm., Æth. read, "you."

8. "Now I say." So L., most Cursives, Syriac, Arm.; but ℵ, A., B., C., D., E., F., G., P., 5, 6, 19, 73, d, e, f, g, Vulg., Copt., Goth. read, "For I say."

"According to Christ Jesus." According to His example, and by His Spirit.

6. "That ye may with one mind and one mouth glorify God." As if ye were also so one that one mind and one utterance were common to all.

"God, even the Father of our Lord Jesus Christ." This should be rendered "the God and Father of our Lord Jesus Christ." And this would be quite in accordance with the Catholic faith; for the Son of God, by taking upon Him our nature, became the creature of God His Father, as we are. He depended upon His Father, He prayed to Him. At death He committed His Spirit to His Father's safe keeping. One of His last words upon the cross was, "My God, my God, why hast thou forsaken me?" and one of His first words after His Resurrection was, "I ascend unto my Father and your Father, and to my God and your God." (John xx. 17.)

7. "Wherefore receive ye one another, as Christ also received us to the glory of God." Christ by the Redemption and the communication of His Life and Spirit to each one hath received us into one holy fellowship, and so we must receive one another, "forbearing one another, forgiving one another, helping, sympathizing with, consoling, edifying one another."

8. "Now I say that Jesus Christ was a minister of the circumcision," &c. That is, Jesus Christ first ministered as a Jew, as one circumcised, as one made under the law, as one Who kept the law, to confirm to His countrymen the promises made to the fathers, which He did by His Birth, Life, Death, and Resurrection, and the pouring out of the Holy Ghost: but, besides this, He came a "light to lighten the Gentiles," and so He came, as the next verse reads,

CHAP. XV.] A ROOT OF JESSE. 319

9 And °that the Gentiles might glorify God for *his* mercy; as it is written, ᵖFor this cause I will confess to thee among the Gentiles, and sing unto thy name.

° John x. 16.
ch. ix. 23.
ᵖ Ps. xviii. 49.

10 And again he saith, ᑫRejoice, ye Gentiles, with his people.

ᑫ Deut. xxxii.

11 And again, ʳPraise the Lord, all ye Gentiles; and laud him, all ye people.

ʳ Ps. cxvii. 1.

12 And again, Esaias saith, ˢThere shall be a root of Jesse, and he that shall rise to reign over the Gentiles; in him shall the Gentiles trust.

ˢ Isai. xi. 1, 10. Rev. v. 5. & xxii. 16.

13 Now the God of hope fill you with all ᵗjoy and peace in believing, that ye may abound in hope, through the power of the Holy Ghost.

ᵗ ch. xii. 12.
& xiv. 17.

9-12. "That the Gentiles might glorify God for his mercy; as it is written," &c. Here are four prophecies which cannot be true, unless the Gentiles are, through the Messiah, received into the favour of God. The first of these (in verse 9) implies that the Gentiles would be gathered together into a holy congregation, and that the Messiah or the Psalmist would lead this worship. In the second (verse 10), Moses calls upon the Gentiles, along with the people of Israel, to rejoice in God. In the third (verse 11) the Gentiles are similarly called to join in the worship of God, and in the fourth, if we read according to the Septuagint, we learn, "in him (the Messiah) shall the Gentiles hope or trust;" or if according to the Hebrew, "To it," *i.e.*, to the rod of Jesse, "shall the Gentiles seek."

These last words, in which the Gentiles are said to hope in the Messiah, give occasion to the Apostle to pray to God as the God of hope.

13. "Now the God of hope fill you with all joy and peace in believing, that ye," &c. God is emphatically a God of hope. He leads all His intelligent creatures, no matter what present blessings they may have, to hope for still greater blessings in the future.

"Joy and peace." These go together amongst the fruits of the Spirit—love, joy, peace.

"In believing." In believing what? Evidently in the Christ in

14 And ⁿI myself also am persuaded of you, my brethren, that ye also are full of goodness, ʷfilled with all knowledge, able also to admonish one another.

15 Nevertheless, brethren, I have written the more boldly unto you in some sort, as putting you in mind, ˣbecause of the grace that is given to me of God.

ⁿ 2 Pet. i. 12. 1 John ii. 21.
ʷ 1 Cor. viii. 1, 7, 10.
ˣ ch. i. 5. & xii. 3. Gal. i. 15. Ephes. iii. 7, 8.

---

15. "Brethren" omitted by ℵ, A., B., C., Cop., Æth.; but retained by D., E., F., G., L., P., almost all Cursives, d, e, f, g, Vulg., Syr., Arm.

Whom are contained and fulfilled all the promises of God, and in those promises themselves as belonging to them as Gentiles.

"That ye may abound in hope, through the power of the Holy Ghost." Hope was what they especially required, living in a city in which all the present powers and fascinations of this evil world were dominant: but hope "through the power of the Holy Ghost." This is the great proof of the Godhead of the Holy Spirit, in that everywhere throughout the world He works in the hearts of men such things as repentance, faith, hope, love, joy, peace; how omnipotent must He be thus to transform the hearts of men; how omnipresent to work in them wherever they are; how omniscient to know the secrets of all hearts.

14. "And I myself also am persuaded of you, my brethren, that ye also are," &c. This is not flattery or mere compliment. He had spoken in the beginning of the Epistle of their faith being spoken of throughout the whole world, and if they had such excellent faith, it was but likely that they would have the fruits of such faith, in goodness, in knowledge, and in ability to apply to one another the truths which they knew so well. He had little need to admonish them, seeing they had such excellent gifts of the Spirit.

15. "Nevertheless, brethren, I have written the more boldly unto you in some sort," &c. Notice the gentle, somewhat deprecating tone of this verse. "I have written the more boldly—not altogether, but in some sort—in part," that is, parts of this Epistle being more authoritative in the way of injunction than others. ἀπὸ μέρους is taken by Jowett as signifying in some degree, to a certain extent, as if he had *ventured* only to teach them.

CHAP. XV.] THE MINISTER OF CHRIST. 321

16 That ʸI should be the minister of Jesus Christ to the Gentiles, ministering the gospel of God, that the || ᶻoffering up of the Gentiles might be acceptable, being sanctified by the Holy Ghost.

ʸ ch. xi. 13.
Gal. ii. 7, 8, 9.
1 Tim. ii. 7.
2 Tim. i. 11.
|| Or, *sacrificing.*
ᶻ Isai. lxvi. 20. Phil. ii. 17.

16. "That I should be the minister of Jesus Christ to the Gentiles, ministering," &c. St. Paul here speaks sacerdotally in a very marked way. He considers himself to be a priest, and the Gentiles to be the victim, and by the Gospel he consecrates them to God, so that they should be an acceptable sacrifice to God; sanctified, not with material oil, but by the Holy Spirit, Who by the preaching and invocation of the Apostle was made to descend upon them. Upon this place the late Dean Alford writes: "The language is evidently figurative, and can by no possibility be taken as a sanction for any view of the Christian minister as a sacrificing priest, otherwise than according to that figure, viz., that he offers to God the acceptable sacrifice of those who by his means believe on Christ." We must ask, however, What is a sacrificing priest? Does any minister of Christ now offer bullocks or lambs to God, or does any minister of Christ who believes that the celebration of the Eucharist is a sacrificial action, believe that in it he repeats the Sacrifice of Christ in those things which constituted its atoning value—its bitter pain, and shame, and death? No, no one, no Romanist, believes that he repeats the Sacrifice, only that he represents it before God and the Church. But let the reader ask himself this, Is it possible to suppose that if the Apostle believed that the Lord's priesthood was such that all sacrificial or sacerdotal terms are to be confined solely to Him and to His Sacrifice. that he could have used such language as this respecting his Apostolical functions? For, consider, who can offer up the Gentiles to God as an acceptable sacrifice? Surely our Great High Priest alone can say that He can do such a thing, and yet the Apostle here ventures to say that he does it. How can He use such language? Simply because Christ said to His Apostles, "As my Father sent me, so send I you;" simply because the Apostle believed that Christ had no jealousy that sacerdotal functions ascribed to His minister could possibly trench upon the uniqueness of His all-prevailing atonement. Surely to offer up the Gentiles is an infinitely more sacerdotal thing than the representation of

Y

17 I have therefore whereof I may glory through Jesus Christ ᵃ in those things which pertain to God.

18 For I will not dare to speak of any of those things ᵇ which Christ hath not wrought by me, ᶜ to make the Gentiles obedient, by word and deed,

ᵃ Hebr. v. 1.
ᵇ Acts xxi. 19. Gal. ii. 8.
ᶜ ch. i. 5. & xvi. 26.

---

the sufferings of the Lord in the Eucharist. "Oh, but," it is answered, "the one is figurative." Yes, but it has an underlying reality, and so has the other—the Eucharistic Oblation.[1]

17. "I have therefore whereof I may glory through Jesus Christ in those things," &c. If Christ had appointed him priest to offer up the Gentiles, he had, indeed, something to glory in, but only in Christ. He usually, indeed almost always, sunk all considerations of his own credit, but at times he must assert himself, particularly when his Apostolate, which was not assumed by himself, but given him by Christ, was called in question. (1 Thess. ii. 6; 2 Cor. xi. 17, 18-29, xii. 1, &c.)

18. "For I will not dare to speak of any of those things which Christ hath not wrought," &c. The Apostle, as the Apostle of the Gentiles, might have reasonably spoken of the work which had been going on everywhere among the Gentiles by his subordinates and those under his direction; but he will not do this, he will only bring forward what has been actually wrought by himself, and this, humanly speaking, was more than enough, and so he proceeds

---

[1] The following extract from Godet, an Ultra-Protestant Swiss commentator, may be helpful.

"The grace of Apostleship had been given to Paul for the accomplishment of a sublime task. The word λειτουργός denotes a public functionary. In this case the function involved is nothing less than presenting to God the Gentile world as an offering which may be acceptable to Him. This world-wide service to which Christ Himself had called St. Paul, was not only that of a preacher, it had a priestly character. This is certainly what is expressed by the term ἱερουργεῖν (see Meyer): 'to offer sacerdotally:' not that the preacher of the Gospel is a Mediator who comes between God and the believer; but his function does not consist in simple teaching; each time it is an act of consecration whereby the messenger of salvation offers to God his own person, as well as the person of all his hearers. We know how Paul prayed constantly for the Churches which he had already founded (comp. i. 8-10 and the beginning of all the Epistles), and we can thus imagine what the work of thus founding was. Thus was his whole Apostolate a priestly function" (Godet *in loco*). This writer, however, appears not to remember that whilst priesthood wrongly used may come between Christ and the soul so as to intercept between it and God, priesthood rightly used may bring the soul nearer to God.

CHAP. XV.] BY THE POWER OF THE SPIRIT. 323

19 ^d Through mighty signs and wonders, by the power of the Spirit of God; so that from Jerusalem, and round about unto Illyricum, I have fully preached the gospel of Christ.

^d Acts xix. 11. 2 Cor. xii. 12.

20 Yea, so have I strived to preach the gospel, not where Christ was named, ^e lest I should build upon another man's foundation:

^e 2 Cor. x. 13, 15, 16.

21 But as it is written, ^f To whom he was not spoken of, they shall see: and they that have not heard shall understand.

^f Isai. lii. 15.

---

19. "Through mighty signs and wonders, by the power of the Spirit of God; so that," &c. When he spake of being Christ's ministering priest to offer up the Gentiles, he did not speak of what had been done by others, or of a thing of which the testimony was conversion only, but along with the preaching of the Gospel there were the miraculous attestations of the Spirit. So that if anyone objected that he took too much upon himself by assuming to be a priest offering up the whole Gentile Church, he would have answered, God has given to me to say this, and not unreasonably, for all the regions of the Roman world east of Italy, have been partly or wholly evangelized by me, and in the performance of this work I have the testimony of the Spirit in "mighty signs and wonders" far exceeding those of any other Evangelist, and abundantly proving that God is with me in my offering. Jerusalem and Illyricum are mentioned as the furthest points; but he had penetrated into the central regions of Asia Minor, and had established churches in Galatia and contiguous districts.

20, 21. "Yea, so have I strived to preach the gospel, not where Christ," &c. This is somewhat clearer if we adopt the Revisers' rendering, "Making it my aim to preach the gospel, or being ambitious to preach the gospel, not where Christ was already named, lest I should build," &c. No doubt he was over careful about this, so as to avoid all reproach and slander, and the accusation that he unduly interfered in the province of other men.

"But as it is written, To whom he was not spoken of, they shall see," &c. This is a literal translation from the Septuagint. The Hebrew has exactly the same meaning: "That which had not

22 For which cause also ⁵I have been ‖ much hindered from coming to you.

23 But now having no more place in these parts, and ʰhaving a great desire these many years to come unto you;

24 Whensoever I take my journey into Spain, I will come to you: for I trust to see you in my journey, ⁱand to be brought on my way thitherward by you, if first I be somewhat filled † with your *company*.

⁵ ch. i. 13.
1 Thess. ii. 17, 18.
‖ Or, *many ways*, or, *oftentimes*.
ʰ Acts xix. 21. ver. 32. ch. i. 11.
ⁱ Acts xv. 3.
† Gr. *with you* ver. 32.

---

24. "I will come to you" omitted by ℵ, A., B., C., D., E., F., G., P., d, e, f, g, Vulg., Syriac; retained by L., and most Cursives.

been told them shall they see, and that which they had not heard shall they consider." It is cited by St. Paul as illustrative of his course of action, not as a prophecy.

22. "For which cause also I have been much hindered from coming to you." So many places in which there has been no preaching of Christ require my labours, that I have been much, or oftentimes, delayed.

23, 24. "But now having no more place in these parts." Properly "room" in these parts. Churches are planted everywhere, so that there is no reason for him to delay his journey to Rome. There is no place or room for him if he has no special Apostolic work there.

"And having a great desire these many years to come unto you." This desire is expressed in Acts xix. 21, "Paul purposed in the spirit when he had passed through Macedonia and Achaia to go to Jerusalem, saying, After I have been there I must also see Rome."

He purposed to see the Church of Rome by the way, as it were, on his journey to the far west. But God, Who alone disposes, saw fit that he should arrive there after a sea voyage of extraordinary peril, and live with them two years as a prisoner.

"To be brought on my way thitherward by you." Thus to the Corinthians he writes: "And it may be that I will abide, yea, and winter with you, that ye may bring me on my journey whithersoever I go" (1 Cor. xvi. 6). "If first I be somewhat filled with your

CHAP. XV.] I GO UNTO JERUSALEM. 325

25 But now ^k I go unto Jerusalem to minister unto the saints.

26 For ^l it hath pleased them of Macedonia and Achaia to make a certain contribution for the poor saints which are at Jerusalem.

27 It hath pleased them verily; and their debtors they are. For ^m if the Gentiles have been made partakers of their spiritual things, ⁿ their duty is also to minister unto them in carnal things.

k Acts xix. 21.
& xx. 22. &
xxiv. 17.
l 1 Cor. xvi.
1, 2. 2 Cor.
viii. 1. & ix.
2, 12.

m ch. xi. 17.

n 1 Cor. ix.
11. Gal. vi. 6.

---

company." "This does not mean that he is doubtful whether he shall enjoy his Christian intercourse with them, but the contrary—he is sure he shall not be sufficiently able to enjoy it. By saying '*be filled*,' he shows that he was eager for their love, and not only was eager for it, but exceedingly so. And this is why he does not say 'be filled,' but be somewhat so. That is, no length of time can fill me, or create in me a satiety of your company." (Chrysostom.)

25, 26. "But now I go unto Jerusalem .... poor saints which are at Jerusalem." "To minister," rather "ministering,"—not to the wants of their souls as an Apostle, but to their bodily needs, for owing to the famine, they were in great distress, being a Church composed principally of poor members, and so the Christians of Macedonia and Achaia had made a contribution for their relief, which they sent by the hands of the Apostle himself.[1] The poor saints should properly be rendered the poor among the saints.

27. "It hath pleased them verily; and their debtors they are. For if the Gentiles," &c. The Apostle restates the fact that the Christians of Macedonia and Achaia had made this contribution, in order that he might further assert that it was only right and what was due from them, for they had, by becoming Christians, been made partakers of the spiritual blessings which of right and in the first place belonged to the Jews, and so their duty was to relieve their temporal wants. The Apostle here follows up the line which

---

[1] There is a very interesting examination and comparison of the passages in the Acts and Epistles to the Romans, Corinthians, and Galatians relating to this collection in Paley's "Horæ Paulinæ," proving beyond all doubt the genuineness of these Epistles.

28 When therefore I have performed this, and have sealed to them ° this fruit, I will come by you into Spain.

° Phil. iv. 17.

29 ᵖ And I am sure that, when I come unto you, I shall come in the fulness of the blessing of the Gospel of Christ.

ᵖ ch. i. 11.

30 Now I beseech you, brethren, for the Lord Jesus Christ's sake, and ᵠ for the love of the Spirit, ʳ that ye strive together with me in *your* prayers to God for me;

ᵠ Phil. ii. 1.
ʳ 2 Cor. i. 11. Col. iv. 12.

---

29. "Blessing of the Gospel." So L., almost all Cursives, Syriac; but "of the Gospel" omitted by א, A., B., C., D., E., F., G., P., 67**, 179, d, e, f, g, Vulg. (Cod. Amiat.), Copt., Arm., &c.

he had taken in Chap. xi., where he lays down that the Gentiles did not partake of their spiritual blessings independently, but, after some of the original branches had been broken off, had been grafted into their place in the olive tree of God's grace.

28. "When therefore I have performed this, and have sealed to them this fruit," *i.e.*, the fruit of the faith and love of the Gentile churches—"Sealed unto them." "That is, when I have laid it up, as it were, in the royal treasuries, as in a place secure from robbers and danger." (Chrysostom.)

Respecting the question whether he ever was able to accomplish his journey to Spain, see my excursus on the later years of St. Paul's life in notes on the Acts, p. 506.

29. "And I am sure that, when I come unto you, I shall come in the fulness," &c. This means not only with the fulness of spiritual comfort and edification, but with those miraculous gifts of the Spirit which an Apostle only could impart. It may also imply that he is confident that no conduct on their part will hinder the flow of all manner of gifts and graces into them and upon them.

30. "Now I beseech you, brethren, for the Lord Jesus Christ's sake," &c. "For the love of the Spirit." This is usually interpreted as the love shed abroad in their hearts by the Holy Spirit; but why may it not mean the love of the Third Person of the Trinity to them? Surely the Spirit must Himself love those in whom He works, and for whom He deigns to intercede " with groanings which cannot be uttered."

CHAP. XV.]   ACCEPTED OF THE SAINTS.   327

31 ˢThat I may be delivered from them that
‖ do not believe in Judæa; and that ᵗ my service
which *I have* for Jerusalem may be accepted of
the saints;

32 ᵘThat I may come unto you with joy ˣ by
the will of God, and may with you be ʸ refreshed.

* 2 Thess. iii. 2.
‖ Or, *are disobedient.*
† 2 Cor. viii. 4.
ᵘ ch. i. 10.
ˣ Acts xviii. 21. 1 Cor. iv. 19. Jam. iv. 15.
ʸ 1 Cor. xvi. 18. 2 Cor. vii. 13. 2 Tim. i. 16. Philem. vii. 20.

32. " By the will of God." So A., C., L., P., all Cursives, Vulg., Syriac; but B., D., E., F., G. read, " by the will of Jesus Christ," or " Christ Jesus," or the " Lord Jesus."
32. " And may with you be refreshed " omitted by B. only.

"That ye strive together with me in your prayers to God for me." How earnestly and how frequently does St. Paul ask the Christians to whom he writes to give him their prayers: "Brethren, pray for us." " Praying for me that utterance may be given to me." " I know that this shall turn to my salvation through your prayer." (2 Thess. iii. 1; Ephes. vi. 19; Phil. i. 19.)

And ought not, after his example, pastors to ask in their sermons the prayers of their people that the work of God may prosper in their hands?

31. " That I may be delivered from them that do not believe in Judæa." This prayer was answered, but how differently from what he expected! He was delivered from the hands of his unbelieving countrymen, by whom he would have been torn to pieces, by the intervention of the Roman power. By that power he was kept in safety for some time, and by that power he was brought to Rome, to the Church he had so longed to visit.

"And that my service which I have for Jerusalem may be accepted," &c. Such was the prejudice against him, because he asserted the freedom of the Gentiles from the yoke of the law, that he feared that even the alms and offerings which he brought would not assure him a welcome. He seems to have been doubtful whether they would be accepted.

32. " That I may come unto you with joy by the will of God," &c. " With joy." It would be a deep sorrow if he should come to Rome after his mission to the Church of Jerusalem had been rejected with scorn. This would be indeed to come under a cloud. But when he did at last come, it was with a certain holy joy. All his utterances to his fellow-voyagers during the many fearful days

328 THE GOD OF PEACE BE WITH YOU. [ROMANS.

^z ch. xvi. 20.
1 Cor. xiv. 33.
2 Cor. xiii. 11.
Phil. iv. 9.
1 Thess. v. 23.
2 Thess. iii. 16.
Heb. xiii. 20.

33 Now ^z the God of peace *be* with you all. Amen.

---

passed in the tempest-tossed ship, were the expressions of a cheerful spirit, and when he saw the brethren trooping to meet him at Appii Forum he "thanked God and took courage."

"And may with you be refreshed." By seeing your faith, and love, and unity.

33. "Now the God of peace be with you all." We are led to suppose that this is a closing salutation, and that the next chapter was added as a sort of postscript. Such benedictions, prompted by the overflowing of his heart at the moment, are common throughout the Epistles. Thus Rom. ix. 5, xi. 36; Ephes. iii. 20, 21.

CHAP. XVI.

I COMMEND unto you Phebe our sister, which is a servant of the church which is at ^a Cenchrea:

^a Acts xviii. 18.
^b Phil. ii. 29.
3 John 5, 6.

2 ^b That ye receive her in the Lord, as becometh saints, and that ye assist her in whatsoever business she hath need of you: for she hath been a succourer of many, and of myself also.

1-2. "I commend unto you Phebe our sister .... and of myself also." Phebe was probably the bearer of the letter.

"Servant," or "deaconess," an institution of the Church from its very beginning. Thus in the letter of Pliny to Trajan, we read: "Upon receiving this account, I judged it the more necessary to examine, and that by torture, two maid-servants who were called ministers."

"Church which is at Cenchrea" (or Kenchrëæ). The eastern port of Corinth, on the Saronic Gulf, about nine miles from the city.

"That ye receive her in the Lord, as becometh saints," *i.e.*, with the utmost Christian kindness and hospitality.

Objection has been raised that if Phebe went to Rome she

CHAP. XVI.] PRISCILLA AND AQUILA. 329

3 Greet ᶜ Priscilla and Aquila my helpers in Christ Jesus:
4 Who have for my life laid down their own ᶜ Acts xviii. 2, 18, 26. 2 Tim. iv. 19
necks: unto whom not only I give thanks, but
also all the churches of the Gentiles.

5 Likewise *greet* ᵈ the church that is in their ᵈ 1 Cor. xvi. 19. Col. iv. 15.
house. Salute my wellbeloved Epænetus, who is Philem. 2.
ᵉ the firstfruits of Achaia unto Christ. ᵉ 1 Cor. xvi. 15.

---

3. "Priscilla." So many Cursives, Syriac, Æth.; but ℵ, A., B., C., D., E., F., G., L., P., with the great majority of Cursives, Ital., Vulg., Copt., Arm. read, "Prisca."

5. "Firstfruits of Achaia." ℵ, A., B., C., D., F., G., 67**, d, e, f, g, Vulg., Copt., Arm., Æth. read, "of Asia;" but L., P., almost all Cursives, and Syriac read, "of Achaia.";

would not sail from Cenchrea, but it is not said that she did, but simply that she was a deaconess of that place; she would more probably have sailed from Lecheum, the port of Corinth on the other side of the isthmus.

3, 4. "Greet Priscilla (Prisca) and Aquila, my helpers in Jesus Christ . . . . also all the churches of the Gentiles." Priscilla and Aquila are first mentioned in Acts xviii. 2 as living then in Corinth, because Claudius had commanded all Jews to depart from Rome. He afterwards sailed in their company to Ephesus, and left them there, whilst he himself went up to Jerusalem. During the time of his absence they were instrumental in bringing Apollos to a more perfect knowledge of the Gospel. They now appear to have returned to Rome. It is impossible to say to what the Apostle alludes when he writes, "Who have for my life laid down their own necks." It is conjectured to be an allusion to something which occurred in the tumult at Ephesus.

5. "Likewise greet the church that is in their house." This was one of the many private dwellings in which the Christians of Rome assembled for worship before they were able to erect any public building. Alford quotes a passage from the Acta Martyrii S. Justini in Ruinart. "Being asked by the Prefect Rusticus 'Where do you assemble?' He answered, 'Where each one can and will. You believe, no doubt, that we all meet together in one place; but it is not so, for the God of the Christians is not shut up in a room, but, being invisible, He fills both heaven and earth, and is honoured everywhere by the faithful.'"

"Salute my well-beloved Epænetus, who is the firstfruits of

6 Greet Mary, who bestowed much labour on us.

7 Salute Andronicus and Junia, my kinsmen, and my fellowprisoners, who are of note among the apostles, who also ᶠwere in Christ before me.

ᶠ Gal. i. 22.

8 Greet Amplias my beloved in the Lord.

---

6. "On us." So L. and most Cursives; but ℵ, A., B., C., D., E., F., G., P., &c. read, "on you." See below.

8. "Amplias." So D., E., L., P., almost all Cursives, Syr., Arm.; but ℵ, A., B., F., G., d, e, f, g, Vulg., Cop., Æth. read, "Ampliatus."

Achaia [Asia] unto Christ." The great majority of the oldest authorities read, " of Asia." Probably Achaia was early substituted because of the mention of the house of Stephanas as "the firstfruits of Achaia" in 1 Cor. xvi. 15. Of this Epænetus nothing whatsoever is known.

6. "Greet Mary, who bestowed much labour on us." "Mary," from her name, no doubt, a Jewess by birth. There is some doubt whether we ought to read, " on us," or " on you." The latter has the most ancient Manuscript authority, but the former the most intrinsic probability. St. Paul would far more probably send a salutation to one who had laboured in Corinth for himself and the Church there, than for one who had laboured in Rome, of whose work he could not, probably, have had much knowledge.

7. "Salute Andronicus and Junia [or Junias, a man's name], my kinsmen, and my fellowprisoners." That is, on some occasion they had been immured in prison with the Apostle. This is not at all improbable: for twice (2 Cor. vi. 5, and xi. 23) he speaks of imprisonments as if they were a common thing with him. With respect to their being his kinsmen, he may use the word as embracing all his fellow countrymen, as in Rom. ix., "my brethren, my kinsmen according to the flesh;" but it is not improbable that persons related to the Apostle more or less distantly might have lived in Rome.

"Who are of note among the Apostles." This may mean "were" well-known to the Apostles, having been very early converts, for they were converted before St. Paul himself; or the word "Apostle" may be used in a very wide sense, as one sent by the Church for the conversion of the heathen.

8. "Greet Amplias my beloved in the Lord." A shortened form of Ampliatus.

CHAP. XVI.] URBANE. STACHYS. 331

9 Salute Urbane, our helper in Christ, and Stachys my beloved.

10 Salute Apelles approved in Christ. Salute them which are of Aristobulus' || *household*. ‖ Or, *friends*.

11 Salute Herodion my kinsman. Greet them that be of the || *household* of Narcissus, which are ‖ Or, *friends*. in the Lord.

12 Salute Tryphena and Tryphosa, who labour in the Lord. Salute the beloved Persis, which laboured much in the Lord.

---

9. "Salute Urbane, our helper in Christ, and Stachys my beloved." Archdeacon Gifford notices that Amplias and Urbane are found in juxta-position, as here, in a list of imperial freedmen on an inscription, A.D. 115.

10. "Salute Apelles approved in Christ," *i.e.*, a tried Christian, who to merit such a word of commendation had gone through persecution in the cause of Christ.

"Salute them which are of Aristobulus' household." Very probably his slaves or freedmen. It was a large house, Jewish, perhaps, to which the Gospel had found access. From the form of the salutation it was probable that Aristobulus himself was not a Christian, or he would have been saluted with his household.

11. "Salute Herodion my kinsman." Probably a Jew, and called by St. Paul "kinsman," in the sense of Rom. ix. 3, before alluded to.

"Greet them that be of the household of Narcissus, which are in the Lord." Narcissus is by many supposed to have been the wealthy freedman of Claudius, who was put to death in prison before the writing of this Epistle, in A.D. 55. Either by confiscation, or by the law of succession, the household of the freedman of Claudius would pass into the possession of Nero, retaining the name of their deceased owner under the form Narcissiani. (Gifford.)

12. "Salute Tryphena and Tryphosa, who labour in the Lord." These were probably sisters; their names come from the Greek τρυφᾶν, to live voluptuously. Paul evidently wishes to contrast this meaning of their name with that of the epithet κοπιώσας, who work laboriously. They are in Christ the very opposite of what their name expresses.

"Salute the beloved Persis, which laboured much in the Lord."

13 Salute Rufus ^s chosen in the Lord, and his mother and mine.

s 2 John 1.

14 Salute Asyncritus, Phlegon, Hermas, Patrobas, Hermes, and the brethren which are with them.

15 Salute Philologus, and Julia, Nereus, and his sister, and Olympas, and all the saints which are with them.

---

14. There is some confusion between the Hermas and Hermes of this verse. א, A., B., C., D., F., G., P., d, e, f, g, &c. reading, "Hermes, Patrobas, Hermas;" and E., L., most Cursives, and Syriac reading, "Hermas, Patrobas, Hermes."

That is, in past days, when she was able, in contrast with the other two women, who are now labouring.

13. "Salute Rufus chosen in the Lord." The elect of the Lord. He is supposed to have been the son of Simon of Cyrene, whom Mark, writing his Gospel in Rome, mentions as the father of Alexander and Rufus. If so, he was probably a leading Christian of the Church of Rome.

"And his mother and mine." The Apostle, perhaps, in early youth, had received much motherly care and kindness in the house of the mother of Rufus, and widow of Simon, the Lord's crossbearer.

14. "Salute Asyncritus, Phlegon, Hermas, Patrobas, Hermes, and the brethren which are with them." Nothing whatsoever is known of any of these Christians. Hermas is supposed by Origen to have been the author of "The Shepherd," a work looked upon by many in the early Church as an inspired writing. But it seems now to be established from the Canon of Muratori, that this writing is of much later date, and written by one Hermas, who was the brother of Pius the ninth Bishop of Rome.

"And the brethren which are with them." Are these the Christian persons who lived in their houses as relatives, or lodgers, or are these five brethren the heads or presidents of Churches, which met in their houses?

15. "Salute Philologus, and Julia, Nereus, and his sister, and Olympas," &c. Nothing is known of any one of these Christians except their names. Olympas is the name of a man, probably the shortened form of Olympiodorus.

16. "Salute one another with an holy kiss." Not a mere spiritual

CHAP. XVI.] DIVISIONS AND OFFENCES. 333

16 ʰSalute one another with an holy kiss. The churches of Christ salute you.

17 Now I beseech you, brethren, mark them ⁱwhich cause divisions and offences contrary to the doctrine which ye have learned; and ᵏavoid them.

18 For they that are such serve not our Lord Jesus Christ, but ˡtheir own belly; and ᵐby good words and fair speeches deceive the hearts of the simple.

h 1 Cor. xvi. 20. 2 Cor. xiii. 12. 1 Thess. v. 26. 1 Pet. v. 14.
i Acts xv. 1, 5, 24. 1 Tim. vi. 3.
k 1 Cor. v. 9, 11. 2 Thes. iii. 6, 14. 2 Tim. iii. 5. Tit. iii. 10. 2 John 10.
l Phil. iii. 19. 1 Tim. vi. 5.
m Cor. ii. 4. 2 Tim. iii. 6. Tit. i. 10. 2 Pet. ii. 3.

---

salutation, but an outward rite. Tertullian thus mentions it: "Another custom hath now gained strength. They that are fasting having prayed with their brethren, withdraw the kiss of peace, which is the seal of prayer . . . . What prayer is perfect when severed from the holy kiss?" ("De Orat." ch. xviii.)

17. "Now I beseech you, brethren, mark them which cause divisions," &c. There is some difference of opinion as to who these were, and what pernicious doctrines they taught. Now throughout this Epistle the Apostle had warned the Roman Christians against two sorts of false teachers, and two only, viz., those who taught Justification by the works of the law, and those who Judaized on the matter of clean and unclean meats; but the latter, as we have seen, he treats very tenderly—in fact, as if they were to be indulged rather than otherwise; so that these false teachers must, in all probability, have been the same as those who troubled the Christians of Galatia and Philippi. The words divisions and offences have both the article, so the Apostle seems to allude to well-known causes of schism.

18. "For they that are such serve not our Lord Jesus Christ, but their own belly." One of the most deplorable features of a schism is, that teachers who depend upon the offerings of those who belong to it, have an interest in keeping wide the rent by perpetuating the teaching of the false doctrine.

"By good words and fair speeches." Teachers of schism would not be believed unless they bid for the favour of their hearers by good words and fair speeches, which promise salvation upon easy terms.

334   TIMOTHEUS MY WORKFELLOW.   [ROMANS.

ⁿ ch. i. 8.
o Matt. x. 16.
1 Cor. xiv. 20.
‖ Or, *harmless*.
p ch. xv. 33.
q Gen. iii. 15.
‖ Or, *tread*.
r ver. 24.
1 Cor. xvi. 23.
2 Cor. xiii. 14.
Phil. iv. 23.
1 Thess. v. 28.
2 Thess. iii. 18.
Rev. xxii. 21.
s Acts xvi. 1.
Col. i. 1.
Phil. ii. 19.
1 Thess. iii. 2.
1 Tim. i. 2.
Heb. xiii. 23.
t Acts xiii. 1.

19 For ⁿ your obedience is come abroad unto all *men*. I am glad therefore on your behalf: but yet I would have you ^o wise unto that which is good, and ‖ simple concerning evil.

20 And ^p the God of peace ^q shall ‖ bruise Satan under your feet shortly. ^r The grace of our Lord Jesus Christ *be* with you. Amen.

21 ^s Timotheus my workfellow, and ^t Lucius,

---

20. "The grace of our Lord Jesus Christ be with you." So א, A., B., C., L., P., almost all Cursives, and Vulg.; but D., E., F., G., &c., omit. "Amen" omitted by א, A., B., C., L., P., most Cursives, d, e, f, g, Vulg., Copt., Syriac, &c.; and a few Cursives only retain it.

---

19. "For your obedience is come abroad unto all men." This is the third time he praises their faith and obedience, once, i. 8, then xv. 14, and now.

"I am glad therefore on your behalf," &c. Rather "I rejoice therefore over you."

20. "And the God of peace shall bruise Satan under your feet shortly." In evident allusion to the promise to our first parents, "He shall bruise thy head, and thou shalt bruise his heel."

Notice how here as elsewhere the Apostle looks upon all divisions in the Church as coming from beneath, and never from above.

"The grace of our Lord Jesus Christ be with you." This also is a direct testimony to the Godhead of the Lord: for He is invoked as the fountain of grace to His Church. How can His grace be invoked along with that of God, except He partakes fully of the Divine Nature?

21. "Timotheus my workfellow, and Lucius, and Jason," &c. It has been asked, if Timothy was with the Apostle when he wrote this letter, how is it that St. Paul does not associate him with himself in the address? The answer is that Timothy was not known to the Roman Christians as he was to the members of other Churches, and St. Paul ventured to write to them as having had the Apostolate of the Gentiles committed to him by Christ, which Timothy had not.

"Lucius." Not the Evangelist St. Luke, but, perhaps, as some suppose, the Lucius of Cyrene, of Acts xiii. 1.

and u Jason, and x Sosipater, my kinsmen, salute you.

u Acts xvii. 5.
x Acts xx. 4.

22 I Tertius, who wrote *this* epistle, salute you in the Lord.

23 y Gaius mine host, and of the whole church, saluteth you. z Erastus the chamberlain of the city saluteth you, and Quartus a brother.

y 1 Cor. i. 14.
z Acts xix. 22.
2 Tim. iv. 20.

"Jason." Supposed to be the same as the Jason of Acts xvii. 5.

"Sosipater." Perhaps the Sopater of Beræa. (Acts xx. 4.)

"My kinsmen." Most probably in the sense in which it is used in verses 7 and 11.

22. "I, Tertius, who wrote this epistle, salute you in the Lord." "There is nothing strange," says Alford, "in this salutation being inserted in the first person. It would be natural enough that Tertius, the amanuensis, instead of writing 'Tertius, the writer of this epistle, salutes you,' should change it into the first person. The words 'in the Lord' are to be connected with the immediately preceding words. The work of an amanuensis, as well as of an Apostle, may be done, and ought to be done, in the Lord, as a labour of love for the Lord, and for the Church.

23. "Gaius mine host, and of the whole church, saluteth you." The Apostle lodged at his house, in which, probably, one of the assemblies of the Corinthian Church was held, or it may be that he was ready to welcome and entertain all who visited the Apostle. Most probably he was the Christian mentioned in 1 Cor. i. 14 as one whom the Apostle baptized with his own hand.

"Erastus the chamberlain of the city saluteth you, and Quartus a brother." "The chamberlain," rather the steward or treasurer of the city. An Erastus is mentioned in Acts xix. 22 as one of those who ministered to St. Paul, but he could scarcely have travelled with the Apostle and at the same time filled the office of treasurer to the city of Corinth.

"Quartus a brother," *i.e.*, a brother in the Lord, a member of the Church.

24. "The grace of our Lord Jesus Christ be with you all." The genuineness of this second repetition of the "grace" is somewhat doubtful.

24 ªThe grace of our Lord Jesus Christ *be* with you all. Amen.

25 Now ᵇto him that is of power to stablish you ᶜaccording to my gospel, and the preaching of Jesus Christ, ᵈaccording to the revelation of the mystery, ᵉwhich was kept secret since the world began,

ª ver. 20.
1 Thess. v. 28.
ᵇ Eph. iii. 20.
1 Thess. iii. 13.
2 Thess. ii. 17.
& iii. 3. Jude 24.
ᶜ ch. ii. 16.
ᵈ Eph. i. 9.
& iii. 3, 4, 5.
Col. i. 27.
ᵉ 1 Cor. ii. 7.
Eph. iii. 5, 9.
Col. i. 26.

---

24. "The grace of our Lord Jesus Christ be with you all. Amen" omitted by ℵ, A., B., C., 5, 137, Vulg. (Cod. Amiat.), Copt., Æth.; but retained by D., E., F., G., L., most Cursives, d, e, f, g.

25. "Now to him that is of power to stablish you according to my gospel," &c. This doxology is the doctrine of this Epistle turned into a gloria to Him that is of power to stablish. Such is the weak nature of man, such is the subtlety of Satan, such is the contrariety between the Gospel of God and the natural pride of the human heart, that it requires a putting forth of God's ability or power to establish either a Church or a soul in the truth of God.

"My gospel." St. Paul's Gospel, as we have seen, is emphatically the Gospel of the Resurrection (Rom. i. 2, 3, 4; 2 Tim. ii. 8; 1 Corinth. xv. 1-10), and that Resurrection is in all senses the most establishing thing in the whole Revelation. It establishes the truth of all that Christ and His Apostles have taught.

"And the preaching of Jesus Christ." The preaching of Jesus Christ may mean the Holy Doctrine which He preached while on earth, or it may mean the whole body of Christian doctrine, beginning with His Incarnation, and going on to His Atoning Death and Life-imparting Resurrection, and His Ascension, and consequent Headship over the Church, and His return to judge. All these in their due proportion formed the subject matter of St. Paul's preaching.

"According to the revelation of the mystery, which was kept secret." This passage is reproduced in Ephes. iii. 4: "The mystery of Christ which in other ages was not made known unto the sons of men, as it is now revealed unto his holy apostles and prophets by the Spirit; that the Gentiles should be fellowheirs, and of

CHAP. XVI.] THE OBEDIENCE OF FAITH. 337

26 But 'now is made manifest, and by the scriptures of the prophets, according to the commandment of the everlasting God, made known to all nations for ᵍ the obedience of faith:

f Eph. i. 9.
2 Tim. i. 10.
Tit. i. 2, 3.
1 Pet. i. 20.

g Acts vi. 7.
ch. i. 5. & xv. 18.

---

the same body, and partakers of his promise in Christ by the gospel."

This was the mystery. It was kept secret. There were intimations of it, but these intimations were rather for us than for those of old, as St. Peter assures us when he says, "Unto whom it was revealed, that not unto themselves, but unto us they did minister the things which are now reported unto you by them that have preached the gospel unto you." (1 Pet. i. 12.)

This glorious truth, that all should be gathered together in one body in Christ, was a hidden mystery.

26. "But now is made manifest, and by the scriptures of the prophets," &c. If one thing more than another is characteristic of the Apostle's teaching it is that he finds the calling and election of the Gentiles everywhere in the Jewish prophets.

"According to the commandment of the everlasting God, made known to all nations." This commandment of the everlasting God was the command to carry out His eternal purpose in the word of His Son when He said, "Go ye and teach all nations."

"For the obedience of faith." Faith is not given to be buried or nursed in the soul, but to be manifested in the life, and every part of the faith has its particular obedience. The Son of God was Incarnate, made flesh—that He might hallow our very flesh; He lived amongst us that we might follow His example; He died, not only to atone, but that we might die to sin in ourselves—crucifying the flesh with its affections and lusts; He rose again that we might rise to righteousness; He ascended that, with Him, we might in heart and mind ascend; He comes to judge, and our lives are to be a preparation for that Judgment.

27. "To God only wise, be glory through Jesus Christ for ever." The translation of the verse is very difficult. Taken verbatim it runs, "To God only wise, through Jesus Christ, to whom (be) the glory for ages of ages." This would make the glory to be given to Christ, but in that case there would be no glory specifically given to God, and so we must consider "through Jesus Christ," as in a

z

27 To ʰGod only wise, *be* glory through Jesus Christ for ever. Amen.

ʰ 1 Tim. i. 17. & vi. 16. Jude 25.

¶ Written to the Romans from Corinthus, *and sent* by Phebe servant of the church at Cenchrea.

---

parenthesis, and so understand it, To God only wise, to Whom or to Him be the glory.

Grammarians see much difficulty in this doxology, and no doubt the Apostle, as is not unfrequently the case with him, does not adhere to the construction with which he began. I am writing for English readers, and so cannot examine the Greek construction. The Revisers of 1881 give almost exactly the same rendering as the Authorized.

This doxology (verses 25, 26, 27) is found in this place in א, B., C., D*, E., some Cursives (d, e, f), Vulg., Syriac (Schaaf), Copt., Æth. It is inserted at the end of chap. xiv. in L., in 200 Cursives and Lectionaries, whilst A., P., Cursives 5, 17, and some Armenian insert it in both places. Chrysostom and Theodoret comment upon it at the end of chap. xiv.

Much has been made of the doubtfulness of its position. It has even been used by some German unbelieving critics to discredit the last two chapters, though, if any part of the Apostle's writings bears the impress of St. Paul's idiosyncrasy, it is surely chap. xv. For what conceivable purpose would anyone have forged such a passage, so full of personality?

The following extract from Bishop Lightfoot's article in Smith's "Dictionary of the Bible," explains, in few words, the supposed state of the case:—"In the received text a doxology stands at the close of the Epistle. The preponderance of evidence is in favour of this position, but there is respectable authority for placing it at the end of chap. xiv. In some texts it is found in both places, while others omit it entirely. How can we account for this? It has been thought by some to discredit the genuineness of the doxology itself, but there is no sufficient ground for the view. The arguments against its genuineness on the ground of style, advanced by Reiske, are met and refuted by Fritzche (Rom. vol. i. p. xxxv). Baur goes further still, and rejects the two last chapters, but such an inference falls without the range of sober criticism. The phenomena of the MSS. seem best ex plained by supposing that the latter was circulated at an early date (whether during the Apostle's lifetime or not it is idle to inquire) in two forms, both with and without the two last chapters. In the shorter form it was divested as far as possible of its epistolary character by abstracting the personal matter addressed especially to the Romans, the doxology being retained at the close."

One very strong argument against this conjecture seems to me to be the fact that the two last chapters are in all known MSS. and versions. Whereas, if at an early date it had been published in the truncated form, some MSS. at least would, we should think, have been copied from this form and have come down to us.

Some have thought that the part of chap. xvi. which contains the salutations is not genuine, because they imagine that St. Paul, who had never been in Rome, could not have been acquainted with twenty-five or thirty persons in the imperial city: but they who urge this altogether forget the exceedingly personal character of St. Paul's ministry.

It was not a mere preaching to crowds in synagogues or places of public resort; this was followed up by personal acquaintance, as far as possible, with all the converts: so, at least, he intimates in Acts xx. 30, 31. Now, considering the constant intercourse between the large cities of the empire and the capital, in all probability he was personally known to far more than the few to whom he sends Christian greetings in this chapter.

EXCURSUS I.

ST. PAUL AND JUSTIFICATION.

In this excursus I shall consider, not the whole subject of Justification, but Justification as it appears in the Epistles of St. Paul.

In order to do this it is necessary to examine the question, Why could not men be justified by the law, for if the law was given to make men obey the holy and righteous will of God, why could it not justify? The Apostle himself answers this question, and yet his answer has been all but ignored by the bulk of divines who have written on this subject, and for a reason which we shall afterwards notice.

The answer which the Apostle gives to the question, "Why could not the law justify?" is to be found in Galatians iii. 21, "If there had been a law given which could have given life, verily righteousness should have been by the law."

The law, when it addressed itself to men, addressed itself to those who were virtually dead. Righteousness, *i.e.*, any righteousness which God could accept as men's justification in His sight, could not be by any mere law, or under the dispensation of the law, because the law (any mere law) was command or precept only, and did and could not, from its very nature, give power to men to fulfil its commands. Such a power must be more than mere command, it must be life. All life is power; the smallest animalcule exhibits a power of motion and volition which no lifeless thing possesses; and so in spiritual things the only real power is spiritual life.

Now in the Epistle to the Romans there is a declaration on the subject which reasserts the doctrine contained in the Epistle to the Galatians, and expands it. It is in Rom. viii. 1-4: "There is, therefore, now no condemnation to them which are in Christ Jesus . . . . For the law of the Spirit of Life in Christ Jesus hath made me free from the law of sin and death. For what the law could not do, in that it was weak through the flesh, God sending His own Son in the likeness of sinful flesh, and for sin, condemned sin in the flesh. That the righteousness of the law might be fulfilled in us who walk not after the flesh, but after the Spirit."

This declaration exactly corresponds to that in the Epistle to the Galatians. It identifies the doctrine of the two Epistles. It expands that contained in the short declaration of the first Epistle, so that it covers the whole Pauline doctrine.

The law could not justify, not because it was not a holy, perfect law, but because of the moral and spiritual weakness, through the fall, of the men to whom it came; it was weak through the flesh, it could not of itself give life to those who were dead in sins. The law was to them a mere letter, a dead letter, and to remedy this state of things God sent not a law, but a Person. He sent amongst us the New Man in Whom humanity could take a new start. This was His Son, His own Son, in the likeness of sinful flesh, Who for sin, that is, as a sin offering (by making Himself an offering for sin), condemned sin in the flesh—condemned it so that it should be mortified and cast out—that the righteousness of the law might be fulfilled in us, &c.

Such is the justification of this Epistle. It is the remedy for the weakness of the law by the Gift of One Who is the very Life and Power of God amongst us: so that the righteousness which the law could not impart to us, because of its want of life, might be imparted to us by our connection with Him Who is the Life, and so be fulfilled in us who walk not after the flesh, but after the Spirit.

Putting these two passages, Gal. iii. 21, and Rom. viii. 1-4, together, we should gather that the Justification of the Apostle is Justification of Life—not forensic Justification—not Justification of mere imputation, but that Justification which consists in the Life of Christ being imparted to us.

Now this is precisely what the Apostle says that justification is, when he writes: "Therefore as by the offence of one, judgment came upon all men to condemnation, even so by the righteousness of one the free gift came upon all men to justification of life"—" Unto Justification of Life" (εἰς δικαίωσιν ζωῆς); justification, not of the outward life, βίος, but justification which consists in ζωή, the principle, the power of a new life, even the life of Christ, the New Adam,

EXCURSUS ON JUSTIFICATION. 341

within us. Justification, then, so far, seems a matter of life imparted rather than of righteousness imputed, and the two are distinguished by the Apostle in chap. v. 10: "If, when we were enemies, we were reconciled to God by the death of his Son, much more, being reconciled, we shall be saved by his life." But it is to be remembered that we require two things, pardon and life; and so the Apostle had written in the previous verse: "Being now justified by his blood, we shall be saved from wrath through him." "Justified" here evidently means pardoned—pardoned because of the atonement wrought through the Blood of Christ shed in death. It was solely through the Death of Christ, in which He offered Himself a sacrifice to God, that He was enabled to impart to us of the Life of His Risen Body.

The Death and Resurrection of the Lord are, in point of fact, inseparable; indeed, it may be said that the Incarnation, the Death, and the Resurrection, constitute one redeeming act, the Death owing all its redeeming virtue to the Godhead of the Sufferer, Who by His Incarnation received a Body in which He could die; and the Resurrection was the Resurrection of One Who had Himself borne our sins in His own Body on the tree. The humiliation and Death of God's own Son were the necessary prelude to His imparting His Life to us after His Resurrection.

And now we have to consider another point. The gift of God's Son to be to us what the law could not be, owing to the weakness of our flesh, was a gift to the world. It was given before any human being could understand it or apprehend it. How was it, or rather, how was He to become the property of each one, so that each one who received Him should receive a benefit in Christ corresponding to his loss in Adam, so that Christ should be to each one who received Him "wisdom, and righteousness, and sanctification, and redemption" (1 Cor. i. 30)? Now the Apostle answers this question respecting how men are to receive Christ in one way only, they are to receive Him, and all which God has treasured up in Him for us, through faith—faith as opposed to, or rather as independent of, the works of the law, and by the law is meant, no doubt, the moral law, the Decalogue; and if St. Paul had had in view any claims in regard of virtue put forth by the Gentiles, he would have said "any law," any body of mere commands or mere precepts. Now the reason of this is obvious. The gift of Justification of Life in Christ is not a reward, but a capacity; not the reward of previous works done in the past, but the power to produce them in the future.

It is the intention of God in this dispensation to justify not the godly, but the ungodly (Matth. ix. 13); not, of course, those who determine to continue in their ungodliness, but those who desire to be free from it, and to be separated wholly and completely from their past evil lives. And it is in the nature of things most desirable that this should take place at once, on their first believing, so that they who turn away from ungodliness may at once commence afresh with all the life and power which they can have from the Second Adam. Now such in Apostolic times had not to wait till they had done such or so many good works, but they had at once to be joined to Christ, to be brought into Him as branches of the true Vine, or Olive-tree of grace, in order that they might bring forth fruit unto God.

If St. Paul be inspired by the Spirit of God to teach the Church the doctrine of Justification, we are justified by faith; but this does not mean that any or every faith justifies, as we shall see, but it must be a faith which has respect to the gift which God offers in Christ, which is not a gift of pardon merely, but of a renewed nature, of power through the gift of Christ to fulfil the holy Will of God. Now it stands to reason that this faith must proceed from a certain state of the soul. It cannot be the faith of a soul indifferent to good and evil. It cannot be the faith of a soul which desires merely to escape punishment in the world to come, though the fear of punishment may, through God's mercy, lead to a better state of the soul. It must be a faith which springs from repentance, because faith is the looking out of the soul for something which it needs, and repentance is a profound sense of the soul's utter destitution and the need of internal goodness and holiness; and the soul which has no such sense of need will not look out of itself for the supply of the need, whilst the soul which has this sense of need will.

Now this, I may say in passing, seems to me to be the reason why such multitudes of supposed conversions under the immense amount of the preaching of Christ in the present day are so abortive. It was said some time ago in my hearing—and I do not think that the state of the case has altered for the better—that revival preachers never expect more than one out of ten of their converts to persevere. May not this be because there is no foundation laid in repentance?

EXCURSUS ON JUSTIFICATION. 343

One proof of this which is particularly noticeable, is that vast numbers of their converts speak with no shame of past sin—in fact, in many cases, boast of it.

True saving faith, then, must spring from repentance, because repentance is the soul turning from sin to a just and holy God, Who, when He pardons the past, gives power and grace to do better in the future. But, then, what is faith? I mean the faith insisted on in the Epistle to the Romans. It is belief (iv. 24 ; x. 9). But then believing postulates something to be believed. What is faith to believe in order that it may justify ? " Believe in the Lord Jesus Christ ; " but what about Him ? Not surely that He was a good and holy man Who lived to set us a good example, and died to teach us patience. This is not that about Him which St. Paul insists on our believing in order to our justification ; no, nor does the Apostle insist specifically on our believing in His Incarnation, or in His Death—for death is the common lot of all men—or in His being a King, or even in His being a Person in the Trinity; but the fact respecting Christ which the Apostle at the conclusion of his argument respecting justification by faith, at the end of chap. iv., insists on, is, that our faith must fasten upon His Resurrection, *i.e.*, God raising Him from the dead. The words are : " If we believe on him that raised Jesus our Lord from the dead, who was delivered for our offences, and raised again for our justification." And this he says not once nor twice. " If thou shalt confess with thy mouth the Lord Jesus, and shalt believe in thine heart that God hath raised him from the dead, thou shalt be saved " (x. 9); and also in contrast with His Death, " It is Christ that died ; yea, rather, that is risen again " (Rom. viii. 34). " If Christ be not raised, your faith is vain ; ye are yet in your sins " (1 Cor. xv. 17); and, again, St. Paul's brother Apostle : " Who by him do believe in God, that raised him up from the dead, and gave him glory ; that your faith and hope might be in God " (1 Peter i. 21).

And now is it given to us to see why our faith is to fasten on the Resurrection rather than on the Death of the Lord ? Clearly, for the Resurrection of the Lord is the Restoration of the Lord to Life, and Justification is Justification of Life.

The Resurrection of Christ has a twofold significance. It assures us that the Death of the Lord is all-atoning, and it assures us that Christ rose to be our life. Without the Resurrection of the Lord, His promise could not come true, " Because I live, ye shall live also."

EXCURSUS ON JUSTIFICATION.

And now a further question. Is justifying faith supposed by the Apostle to be an act of God, in answer to our faith, entirely confined to the inmost recesses of our souls? Do we exercise faith, and does God, because of this our faith, justify us by an act taking place within us, and only within us; or do God's grace and our faith meet in some outward visible act or sign? Unquestionably the latter, and this outward sign is the reception of the Sacrament of Baptism, according to the words of the Lord, "He that believeth and is baptized shall be saved;" and other words of the Lord: "Go ye and disciple all nations, baptizing them;" and other words of the Lord: "Except a man be born of water and of the Spirit, he cannot enter into the kingdom of God." These words of the Lord are reproduced by His Apostle, St. Peter: "Repent, and be baptized every one of you in the Name of Jesus Christ, for the remission of sins, and ye shall receive the gift of the Holy Ghost" (Acts ii.); and in his Epistle: "Baptism doth also now save us (not the putting away of the filth of the flesh, but the answer of a good conscience toward God), by the Resurrection of Jesus Christ" (1 Peter iii. 21); and by St. Paul, when he writes: "According to his mercy he saved us by the bath of regeneration and renewing of the Holy Ghost" (Tit. iii. 5); and in several other places.

But St. Paul, in his Epistles to the Romans and the Colossians, in a very remarkable way connects both aspects of Justification, its pardon of past sin, and its new life from Christ, with Baptism as a sacramental Death and Resurrection with Christ. This is the subject of the first part of Romans vi.: "We died to sin in Christ, we were buried with Him in Baptism, and we rose again in union with His Resurrection, so that we received a new power of life from Him, on account of which we have power to walk in newness of life, and are to reckon ourselves dead to sin and alive unto God, and are partakers of the promise, 'Sin shall not have dominion over you, for ye are not under the law, but under grace.'"

Such is the connection of Baptism with Justification in the view of both SS. Peter and Paul. It was the consummation of faith in their eyes. Owing to very imperfect teaching respecting Baptism, even in our own Church, we are some of us apt to look upon faith and Baptism as in some degree opposed. We have been taught that Baptism is an outward rite, and therefore a work; but in the Epistle to the Galatians, St. Paul having proved that justification could only be by faith, not by works, proceeds to write: "Ye are all the children

EXCURSUS ON JUSTIFICATION.

of God by faith in Christ Jesus," and substantiates this by saying, " for as many of you as have been baptized into Christ have put on Christ." It is impossible to suppose that he could imagine any antagonism between faith and Baptism if he could write this; or much less if, after speaking of justifying faith, as he did in the first five chapters of the Epistle to the Romans, he should at the beginning of the sixth destroy what he had built up, which he would do if it was possible for him to suppose any incongruity between faith and Baptism as parts of one justifying act of God—I say "act of God," for Baptism in the New Testament is always assumed to be an instrument of God.

St. Paul, in fact, looks upon Circumcision and Baptism as respectively the outward and visible embodiments of two opposite systems—Circumcision that of works, and Baptism that of faith.

Such is the Apostolic doctrine of Justification—the Justification of the first century; but how about that of the nineteenth? For there is a great seeming change, both in the faith and in the Baptism. The faith which in the first century was a faith of choice discerning by itself, through the preaching of the Gospel, a particular Death, certified as to its atoning and reconciling power by the Resurrection of Him Who died, is now an historical faith, an hereditary faith. The appearance of Christ in the world, His Death, and the establishment of His religion by the proclamation of His Resurrection is the great event of history. It cuts the history of the world into two. Every event, every action, every fact is judged by it, or is supposed to judge it. As to the Baptism there is not so much difference as some suppose; the Baptism of infants certainly took place in Apostolic times, and as certainly was continued without a break from the first age to the present, and, what is more to the purpose, there never has been any difference made in the educational or disciplinary treatment of those baptized in infancy and those in riper years, for the grace accompanying Baptism has always been supposed to be the same.

Is there then any difference between the Justification of the first and that of the nineteenth century? None, unless such difference is perversely invented and taught. The child is born in a professedly Christian community, in the midst of surroundings more or less Christian. He is Baptized, not by his own choice, just as he was not born in a Christian land and in a professedly Christian family by his own choice. He receives baptism in infancy just as he received original sin, or his connection with the first Adam, in his infancy. It is the intention of God and of the Church that he should grow in the state into which he has been brought in Baptism by being brought up in the knowledge and admonition of the Lord. If he does, he continues in the grace of God, and that grace is added to and strengthened by the means of grace; but if he falls from grace and commits sin, just as a large number of those baptized in riper years in the Apostles' times did, as we learn from every page of the Apostolical Epistles, then he has to be restored—his faith, the faith of his childhood, has to be renewed; such passages as, "If any man sin, we have an advocate with the Father, Jesus Christ the righteous," or such parables as those of the Prodigal Son, or the Pharisee and the Publican, are to be inculcated into him; the discipline of the family or of the Church has to be brought to bear upon him. Christian pastors and Christian friends are bound to admonish him from those Scriptures which are profitable for doctrine, for reproof, for correction, for instruction in righteousness, and so, by God's mercy, he is, or may be, restored, just as very many of the Corinthian and Galatian Christians had to be restored. I hope I am not saying what is wrong, when I assert that there seems to have been, when one considers the respective numbers in the primitive Church and in the modern Churches of Christendom, as much falling away from the grace of Justification, or union with Christ, in the Churches of the first as in those of the nineteenth century.

And now a word respecting the preaching of the Lord's Resurrection at the present time. Might it not make a great difference both in faith and holiness if the doctrine of the Lord's Resurrection was far more insisted upon than it is? For the doctrine of the Resurrection is the doctrine of life. The doctrine of the Death of Christ, or the Atonement, may be so preached as to foster antinomianism; but the doctrine of the Resurrection cannot: it is the transfusion into us of the Life of Christ, and the assurance of our judgment at the seat of Christ for the deeds done in the body, and, besides this, it is the one assurance on God's part that the Sacrifice itself is all-sufficient for forgiveness. (Acts xiii.)

Such is the doctrine of St. Paul as contained in this and in his other Epistles. I have confined myself in this excursus exclusively to it, and so have not considered that of St. James, or the aspect under which union with Christ appears in St. John's Epistles. Nor have I

EXCURSUS ON ELECTION. 347

turned aside to consider St. Augustine's statements, or Luther's, or Calvin's, or those of the Council of Trent, or those in the Articles and Homilies of the Church of England, or Barrow's statements, or Bishop Bull's, or J. H. Newman's.

And I have given no time to the famous distinction between imputed and imparted righteousness (the righteousness of Justification perfect, but not inherent, and the righteousness of sanctification inherent, but not perfect), because the Apostle seems to know nothing whatever about such a mode of dividing the one righteousness of the Eternal Son of God. With respect to faith being imputed for righteousness, I desire to refer the reader to my notes on chap. iv. 22, pp. 86, 87, and with respect to "submission to the righteousness of God," to my notes on chap. x. 3. If anyone desires to see this subject of Justification more fully handled by me, I would direct him to a short treatise of mine, entitled "Justification of Life," now republished. He will find in it an examination of the various books of the New Testament as to their bearing on it; also chapters on Justification by faith only; on works done before Justification; on our Blessed Lord's Moral Teaching; on the Spiritual Status of the members of the Apostolic Churches; on the relations of Justification to Faith—to the Sacramental system, and to Final Judgment.

EXCURSUS II.

ON ELECTION.

The first thing which strikes us in reading what St. Paul has written on Predestination is the entire absence of any abstract view of this profound subject. He has no doctrine whatsoever upon it except, perhaps, this, that God's choice is not absolute or irreversible. This is certainly the inference which we cannot but gather from the whole argument contained in chaps. ix., x., and xi.

I say that there is an entire absence of any abstract view. Now I will bring this to a point by presenting the reader with an abstract view. It is one that must be very familiar to him if he is a clergyman. It is that of the seventeenth Article, and a more reverent and guarded enunciation of the doctrine of Predestination and Election—as it is commonly understood—cannot well be conceived. It runs thus: "Predestination to Life is the everlasting purpose of God, whereby (before the foundations of the world were laid) he hath constantly decreed by his counsel secret to us, to deliver from curse and damnation those whom he hath chosen in Christ out of mankind, and to bring them by Christ to everlasting salvation, as vessels made to honour. Wherefore, they which be endued with so excellent a benefit of God be called according to God's purpose by his Spirit working in due season: they through Grace obey the calling: they be justified freely: they be made sons of God by adoption: they be made like the image of his only begotten Son Jesus Christ: they walk religiously in good works, and at length, by God's mercy, they attain to everlasting felicity."

Now I say that it is impossible to suppose that the Apostle, in writing upon election, intended to set forth, or to prove, or to confirm any such a doctrinal statement as this. Not that there is anything wrong in this statement of our Article—I mean, anything unscriptural; for if the reader will look into so common a book as, say, Bailey's "Liturgy compared with the Bible," he will see a goodly array of Scripture texts placed side by side with each paragraph of the Article; but the Article is the abstract statement of the doctrine carefully worded, so as to take its place amongst nearly forty abstract statements of Christian doctrines. The purpose of the compilers of the Articles was to get the clergy to agree, or at least not openly to dispute, upon certain points of Theology, and so it was a necessity that they should have an Article upon Election. St. Augustine's view upon God's decrees had been accepted by the Church. All the great mediæval divines affirmed it, and so the doctrine generally received by the divines of the middle of the sixteenth century must be affirmed, and have a place in any book of outlines of Christian truth, such as the Articles were intended to be.

But nothing could be further from the mind of the Apostle than to insert any such a doctrinal statement in his Epistle to the Romans; for if the Apostle held the truth of Predestination as stated in Article xvii. (and a milder and more guarded account cannot be conceived), and desired to give it a place in his letter to the Roman Christians, then (I say it with all reverence) never was there an argument so beside the mark. Take the last and crown-

EXCURSUS ON ELECTION. 349

ing statement of that part of the Article which affirms Predestination. "They (the elect) walk religiously in good works, and at length, by God's mercy, they attain to everlasting felicity." Something in all respects answering to this must be the crowning statement in every account of "Predestination and Election" since the time of Augustine. Now what is the corresponding statement in the Epistle to the Romans? Not one which assumes that the elect must finally persevere, but one which assumes exactly the contrary, that they can fall away, and that they must by their prayers and exertions "continue in his goodness, otherwise they will be cut off." (Rom. xi. 22.)

Again, it is quite clear that if a writer wishes to give a clear account of personal election he will take care to avoid all extraneous considerations, which can only confuse: such, particularly, as national or Church election, and keep himself to the one point necessary —the final perseverance of all individuals once effectually called. But St. Paul, instead of doing this, occupies by far the greater part of his argument with the election of bodies of men—Jews and Gentiles—and never brings in individuals till the conclusion, when he speaks to individual persons, not in the way of assurance, but in the way of warning.

But we have now a far more difficult matter to face—one too, which cannot be declined, if the subject is to be honestly treated.

The doctrine of Election has a necessary counterpart in that of Reprobation or Rejection. If out of a certain number of human beings (all, it is assumed, having an equal claim to God's wrath) He chooses some to be delivered from His wrath, He must reject the rest.

Now the Article of the Church of England entirely ignores this necessary counterpart of Election to Life. It speaks of those who "be endued with so excellent a benefit," but it avoids all mention of those who are not "endued with so excellent a benefit." No doubt mankind are, in the Article, supposed to be under "curse and damnation," and the elect to be the ones delivered from it; but there is a marked avoidance of the execrable and blasphemous harshness with which most Predestinarians of that time expressed themselves. Now it is to be particularly remarked that St. Paul, so far from avoiding this harsher side, occupies the greater part of his argument with it, and it alone. The whole of the ninth, tenth, and eleventh chapters are upon Reprobation or Rejection, not upon Election to Life.

We have not the Election of Isaac, but the Rejection of Ishmael; not the Election of Jacob, but the Rejection of Esau; not the Election of Moses and the Israelites, but the Reprobation of Pharaoh.

But the Apostle takes a step far beyond this. The harshest Calvinists never think of making God the author of the hardness of men's hearts. They say that the wickedness of mankind universally is such that He can justly sentence all men to inexpressible torments, but He chooses some out of them to life, and leaves the rest to themselves. But St. Paul does not teach that God left either Pharaoh or the unbelieving Israelites to themselves. He hardens Pharaoh's heart, and He diffuses over reprobate Israel a spirit of slumber, and gives them "eyes that they should not see, and ears that they should not hear unto this day." If we do not decline the devout consideration of this part of the subject, but duly and reverently face it, we shall find that it gives us a far deeper, more merciful, and more consistent view of the whole matter than we get by ignoring it.

Some general remarks are now needful.

How is it that there is, humanly speaking, such a doctrine as that of Election? How is it possible that men can and must hold it? The necessity for holding it lies in the religious history of the race.

1. Whatever revelation of Himself or His law God gave to all men in their first parent, they corrupted it, and each nation took its own way of worshipping God. This we are told by the Apostle, when he said to the idolators of Lystra, "The living God, who made heaven and earth and the sea, and all things that are therein . . . . in time past suffered all nations to walk in their own ways" (Acts xiv. 16).

2. But God had determined from all eternity to send a deliverer from sin and all its consequences in the Person of His Son. This Son of God was the Elect of God. All Election to Life centres in Him, all casting away or rejection is the rejection of Him.

3. Humanly speaking the Omnipotent Ruler of all events might have sent Him into the world at any time, in any nation, under any circumstances; but, instead of this, God sent Him to redeem us at a particular time, a Member of a particular race, and under circumstances which had been foreappointed.

EXCURSUS ON ELECTION. 351

4. In order to this God prepared a nation to be a receptacle, as it were, fitted to furnish the surroundings under which he decreed that His Son should be born and brought up.

5. This nation He chose or elected in the election of their great forefather Abraham. If heads of races can impress their character on their descendants, then this man was eminently fitted to be the ancestor of the elect race. Thus God, speaking by Isaiah, in vindication of Himself against Israel, says, "He planted it" (His vineyard, at its very beginning) "with the choicest vine" (v. 2); and, by Jeremiah, "Yet I had planted thee a noble vine, wholly a right seed" (ii. 21).

6. All through the history of this people God took pains to assure them that He had chosen them in their great ancestor. And that if they departed from Him, yet, if they repented and returned, He would, for the sake of that ancestor, restore them.

7. But they were not only chosen to be the nation of the Messiah. It was God's intention that they should be witnesses to His truth, holding up the lamp of truth in a very dark world. To this end He gave them a country in the very centre of the world, just where the two great continents meet. Their shore was washed by the sea, which was a high road to all Europe. They were close to, and had close relations with Tyre, the great maritime city of antiquity. They had constant intercourse with Egypt. It was ordained by God that they should come in successive contact with the four great empires, Babylon, Persia, Greece, and Rome, in order that they might impart to them some of their spiritual blessings. This is very remarkably revealed with respect to Babylon. In Jeremiah li. 9, we read, "We would have healed Babylon, but she is not healed." How would God have healed Babylon? Evidently by the influence of such men as Daniel and the three holy children. Daniel was ruler over the whole province, and these three holy children were, under him, put over the affairs of the province of Babylon. (Daniel ii. 18, 49.)

Such is the election which St. Paul learnt from his childhood. He seems to me to add nothing to it; he looks upon it entirely as it appears in the writings of Moses and the prophets, and never bases it on any abstract philosophical grounds, such as necessity, as held by the Stoics, or that men being all equally wicked and deserving damnation, God had a right to select whom He would from the general doom.

EXCURSUS ON ELECTION.

But there are two considerations which we derive from what the Old Testament says of Election which we must now notice.

(*a.*) The first of these is this. From the beginning to the end of the Old Testament in all its various references to God's Predestination and Election, there is not one syllable respecting an Election to reward or punishment, to joy or misery, in a future world. There are places which seem to speak of future happiness or misery, such as, "Thou wilt show me the path of life, in thy presence is fulness of joy, at thy right hand there are pleasures for evermore." Again, "The patient abiding of the meek shall not perish for ever;" and on the other side, "The wicked shall be turned into hell [Sheöl, Hades], and all the nations that forget God." But no glimpse of the future state contains the slightest intimation that men are by a decree of God chosen to a place of happiness or misery in that state.

And this, as I have noticed, St. Paul carefully avoids. Not one word of a decree assigning some to eternal life irrespective of character, or foreseen faith, or obedience, is to be found in his writings.

(*b.*) But the second consideration respecting God's dealings which we gather from the Old Testament, is that God, in carrying out His purposes, reserves to Himself the right of making use of evil men, upholding them as He did Pharaoh, in their resistance to Him, or casting upon them, as He did upon the Israelites, "the spirit of slumber," so that they should receive the full punishment due to their rejection of Him. For the consideration of this latter I must refer my reader to my notes on Matthew xiii. 15, p. 180, and on the parallel places, Mark iv. 12, John xii. 39, 40, Acts xxviii. 27.

But on the former (as in the case of the hardening of Pharaoh) I must say a word or two. "Even for this same purpose," God said, "have I raised thee up, that I might show my power in thee, and that my name might be declared throughout all the earth." (Rom. ix. 17, quoting Exod. ix. 16.) Now what was the showing forth of God's power? It is conceivable that God might have exhibited Pharaoh as suffering the vengeance of eternal fire; but instead of this, God's power was exhibited in the destruction of Pharaoh and his host, so that all the neighbouring kingdoms rang with it, and we have its effect upon one at least of the Canaanites, in the example of Rahab, who said to the spies, "I know that the Lord

EXCURSUS ON ELECTION. 353

hath given you the land, and that your terror is fallen upon us, and that all the inhabitants of the land faint because of you, for we have heard how the Lord dried up the water of the Red Sea for you," &c. (Joshua ii. 9, 10.) Now this was forty years after the event, so that if we had the entire history of the neighbouring nations, we should find that many humble-minded persons among them began to fear the God of Israel.

But there is a well-known passage (1 Kings xxii. 1-36) which shows us how God reserves to Himself the right of choosing evil spirits as well as evil men to carry out His purposes, and not only does it with perfect justice, but allows us to see the equity of His dealings. It was the intention of Almighty God to visit Ahab's sin upon him by the hands of the Syrians. The prophets were all assembled, and with one voice proclaimed the success of Ahab's intended expedition. There was one, however, who had not come up. His absence was marked by Jehoshaphat, who asked that he might be sent for; and when he came, he related the vision of what he had seen in prophetic trance—how that the Lord sat on His throne with all the hosts of heaven surrounding Him, and that when one spirit offered to go and be a lying spirit in the mouths of the prophets, the Lord said, "Thou shalt persuade him and prevail also, go forth and do so." Now, if we may ask the question with the utmost reverence, has God justified this His action to us? Yes, He has, and abundantly, for when the messenger came to call Micaiah to the king's presence, he gave him what no doubt he thought at the time to be a little sound advice, "Behold now, the words of the prophets declare good unto the king with one mouth, let thy words, I pray thee, be like the word of one of them, and speak that which is good." This lets us into the secret of God's action in the matter. Ahab and reprobate Israel, whilst acknowledging that prophecy came from God, and was His institution, treated it as if it was mere fortune-telling. They played fast and loose, as it were, with the holiest of spiritual gifts, and God chose their delusions. His action towards them was one of the many ways in which He gave them over to a reprobate mind.

Now, as I have said before, we may be quite sure—indeed it is part of our faith in the justice of God that we should believe it—that God's action in thus hardening, or deluding, in no way increases the eternal misery of those whom God in such a way uses for His purposes, but that He reserves to Himself the right of thus dealing with

354   EXCURSUS ON ELECTION.

us is most clear. Thus St. Paul, in the Second Epistle to the Thessalonians, speaks of God sending upon those that receive not the love of the truth, "strong delusion that they should believe a lie, that they all might be damned who believed not the truth, but had pleasure in unrighteousness." (2 Thess. ii. 11.) And St. John speaks of many false prophets having gone out into the world, and our Lord speaks of false prophets who should deceive, if possible, the elect. (1 John v. 1; Matth. xxiv. 24.)

We thus find that St. Paul's view of Election and Reprobation is strictly that in which he was educated. He reproduces the Old Testament doctrine in all its features, particularly in these two:— (1) That God, in speaking of the Election of His ancient people, seems to keep out of sight any bearing of that Election on the destiny of particular persons in the unseen and eternal world; and (2) that God seems, throughout the Old Testament, to assert very strongly that He has a right over the spirits of men, if they have hardened themselves, to harden them still more or uphold them in resistance; if they have allowed themselves to be deceived, to keep them in self-deception;[1] if they deal frowardly, to show Himself froward as respects them.

Now the key to all this is that God, in the Election of Israel to be His people, had a twofold purpose:—To make the nation as such the instrument of His purpose in upholding His truth in the world, and preparing the world for the Messiah; and (2) to sanctify the hearts of as many of the Israelites as would submit to the converting power of His word, to be His true servants.

With respect to the former, God softens the hearts of good men, and hardens the hearts of bad men, *i.e.*, men who had already made themselves very bad, to be His instruments. He has a world-wide purpose, and He makes all sorts of instruments work together for its completion. With respect to the latter, the treatment of individuals, God declares Himself, over and over again, a righteous Judge, irrespective of persons, assigning to each one his portion in the strictest spirit of equity, ever respecting their free will, behaving to them exactly according as they behave to Him, and to one another.

Now in the application of the truth of Election and (we may add)

---

[1] See particularly Ezekiel xiv., especially verse 9, "I the Lord have deceived that prophet."

EXCURSUS ON ELECTION. 355

of Reprobation, to the state of things in his own time, and to the Christian Church, St. Paul works exactly on the principles of the Old Testament Election. Men are not elected to serve God as units more or less working apart from one another, but as soon as they believe they are gathered together into the Church. Now the purpose of the Church is twofold; it is not only that the various members of the Church may pray together, and assist and encourage one another; but God has a purpose in it as wide as the universe, as high as the instruction of the angelic world. This purpose, the Apostle declares in the words, "Unto me, who am less than the least of all saints, is this grace given, that I should preach among the Gentiles the unsearchable riches of Christ: and to make all men see what is the fellowship (or dispensation) of the mystery, which from the beginning of the world (or from all ages) hath been hid in God, who created all things by Jesus Christ: to the intent that now unto the principalities and powers in heavenly places might be known, by the Church, the manifold wisdom of God." (Ephes. iii. 8-10.) Just, then, as God had a plan, a design, a counsel, in the Election of Israel, so He has a plan, a design, a counsel, in the Election of the Catholic Church.

So that just as Israel was elected to keep alive among men some knowledge of the true God, so the Church has been elected, that its history should set forth the Wisdom of God to other worlds besides this, and to beings who are of a higher order than we are.

But with all this the Church also is designed to receive all the scattered children of God into one fold, so that in that fold they should be fed and tended by the Good Shepherd, and prepared to be judged by Him at His Second Coming.

God, then, as the Supreme Governor, acts in a twofold way. He rules the Church according to a mighty plan, so that it should exhibit His wisdom and grace to the world of angels, and He rules the same Church as a vast multitude of souls whom He is preparing for eternity, and whom He will judge according as they have made their calling and election sure or not, according as they have done good or evil, so that each should receive his own reward according to his own labour.

Now a moment's consideration will serve to show us that the first of these, God ruling so as to exhibit His Wisdom according to a preconceived and predetermined plan, requires an election very different from the other. The plan which extends over all countries, and through all the ages between the first and the second coming, requires that God should act through fitting instruments, and that He should know and choose these instruments beforehand, each and all of them, or His whole plan may be frustrated. So that each member of the whole mystical body must be known beforehand, and be put in his place in that body (1 Cor. xii. 12-30), so that all should work together for carrying out the great purpose of God. Election and Predestination, in this aspect, mean the choice of instruments long before and the fitting them for their place and work. But it is also clear that, in carrying out this plan, God must not only work with the good, but overrule the bad; and, in fact, not only overrule them, but work through them. To take an example from the Old Testament, not only did God work through David, but through Joab and Jeroboam. Jeroboam's schism was a most evil thing, but nevertheless we are expressly told that it was from God, and it affected the religion and fortunes of Israel for ages.

Now no man that ever lived so influenced the teaching of the Church as St. Augustine. His views upon grace were reproduced in the schoolmen all through the dark ages, as they are called. Thus, humanly speaking, he was the author of the doctrine of Anselm, Bernard, Aquinas, Peter Lombard, Bradwardine, and many others, all of whom followed him in their views of grace, original sin, election, &c. But if Augustine was an instrument in the hands of God, so must Pelagius have been, for Augustine would have been nothing like what he was without the existence and opinions of Donatus and Pelagius. Was, then, Pelagianism owing to God? No, certainly it was not owing to God, but to Pelagius himself; but his persistence in opinions so opposed to Divine grace may have been owing to God, in order to bring out more clearly the counter truth respecting the necessity of grace taught by Augustine. We know nothing of the internal history of Pelagius; but, if we did, we might find that he once believed the truth of God, but that he went wrong in matters of such importance as the doctrines of grace, through pride or self-conceit, through refusing to listen to all Scripture as given "for doctrine and reproof." He chose his favourite texts. He turned his ear and heart away when the Spirit of God was desirous to enlighten him; and in the end he so hardened himself against the truth that God withdrew His teaching Spirit, and not only allowed him to remain in darkness, but raised him up, as it were, so that in the teaching of the truth by

EXCURSUS ON ELECTION. 357

men like Augustine, His grace might be known and acknowledged. And so with Athanasius and Arius, and so with all teachers of truth and its opponents. God has, in all ages, made use of the opponents of the truth as instruments to bring out the truth more fully. All religious movements in the Church, or in bodies who have put themselves apart from the Church, God must, if He has any plan such as that described in Ephesians iii. 10, take into full account, as such not only affect the fortunes and the action of the Church, but their members, if truly religious, according to their light, are in a measure belonging to the Church.

Carrying our thoughts on the lines of all these considerations, we cannot but see that if God has any consistent purpose, any unity in His great plan and counsel, of making His wisdom known to the angelic natures through the Church, then there must be an election of His instruments, and His instruments must be chosen from elect and reprobate; and He must make use of good and bad now, as He unquestionably did in the times of the Old Covenant, and in the times of Christ.

But when we turn to contemplate the other side of God's just government of the world—that He is a righteous Judge; that He will reward every man according to his work; that He will, as He is bound to do, take into account every thought, every word, every deed; that every man shall receive his own reward, according to his own labour—then there seems to be no place whatsoever for the doctrine of Election as commonly held. For God as a just Judge cannot possibly decree beforehand that some persons should do good and other persons do evil, and then accept them to happiness or condemn them to inexpressible misery, for what He has decreed that they should do or leave undone.

We cannot bear to hear of a human judge judging according to what people have been compelled to do or to leave undone by himself; much more is it intolerable to think of God as acting so contrary to those principles of justice which He has infused into us, and which, if we are righteous persons, we invariably carry out in our dealings with one another.

The doctrine of Election, then, whilst it is demanded by the idea of God acting according to a plan or purpose, is utterly inconsistent with the idea of God acting as a judge, and so it is felt to be by all, or almost all, predestinarians. Thus, to refer again to the most guarded and devout statement that I have ever seen, that of our seventeenth Article, there ought to be between the clause "they walk religiously in good works," and the clause "at length, by God's mercy, they attain to everlasting felicity," some such clause as "they stand before the Lord, the righteous judge, and receive according to the deeds done in the body." For assuredly, whether all the Articles in the world deny it, or pass it over, they will have so to stand and receive.

Did not, then, the writer of this Article believe that Christ would judge him? No doubt he said to Christ, probably daily, "Judex crederis esse venturus," or, "From thence He shall come to judge the quick and the dead," or sometimes, "At Whose coming all men shall rise again in their bodies, and shall give account for their own works." Why, then, was no reference made to that which must come between "walking religiously in good works," and "attaining everlasting felicity"? Because it would have been utterly incongruous: because it would have introduced a consideration alien from the doctrine of Predestination.

May we then sign, or compel others to sign, such an Article?

Certainly, if we remember that no human statement of twenty-two short lines can contain a full account of such a truth. We are bound, if we are Christians, to read within the lines a reference to the Lord Jesus Christ as the Righteous Judge, Who will render to every man according as his work shall be: for there is no single truth of God so often insisted upon as this.

And now another matter with respect to Predestination must be considered. Someone may object to what I have written in this excursus, and ask, have you not undone what you have written on page 179? "These words (verses 28, 29, 30, 31), are no doubt Predestinarian words, and if we deprive them of their Predestinarian meaning, we deprive them of all the comfort which God, Who inspired them, designed holy souls to receive from them. They have been miserably, indeed, one may say, wickedly perverted, but they are in accordance with Catholic truth, and the greatest doctors of the Church—Augustine, Bernard, Anselm, Thomas Aquinas, and others—have used them as setting forth the security of true Christians, and the comfort and joy which such ought to have from the sense of that security."

If, then, these words are Predestinarian, do they set forth the indefectibility of God's grace? Do they assert that those in God's Election cannot fall away, and must, of necessity, persevere, and if they fall, no matter how grievously, must be restored at last? Are

EXCURSUS ON ELECTION. 359

they so elected that they need have no anxiety respecting whether they shall endure to the end?

Now it seems to me impossible to assert this, not from any considerations of abstract doctrine, but simply because of the enormous number of counter-statements, which not only imply, but assert that there is no grace from which men cannot fall. In order that the reader may, in some degree, realize this, I will put before him a table of Predestinarian and Anti-Predestinarian statements of Holy Writ, taken from a book I published many years ago, "The Second Adam and the New Birth." Few, I should think, who read this volume of notes on the Romans, are likely to be possessed of that book: if they are, I trust they will pardon the repetition.

TEXTS ASSERTING ELECTION TO GRACE.	TEXTS ASSERTING MAN'S LIABILITY TO FALL FROM GRACE.
The Strength of Israel will not lie NOR REPENT: FOR HE IS NOT A MAN THAT HE SHOULD REPENT. (1 Sam. xv. 29.)	THE LORD REPENTED that he had made Saul king over Israel. (1 Sam. xv. 35.)
I SAID, I WILL NEVER BREAK MY COVENANT WITH YOU [*i.e.* to give you the whole land of Palestine], and ye shall make no league, &c. (Judges ii. 1, 2.)	WHEREFORE I ALSO SAID, I WILL NOT DRIVE THEM OUT FROM BEFORE YOU. (Judges ii. 3.)
I am the Lord, I CHANGE NOT; therefore, ye sons of Jacob are not consumed. (Malachi iii. 6.)	As for you, your carcases, they shall fall in this wilderness. . . . YE SHALL KNOW MY BREACH OF PROMISE. (Numb. xiv. 32, 34.)
	Wherefore the Lord God of Israel saith, I SAID INDEED that thy house and the house of thy father should walk before me for ever, BUT NOW THE LORD SAITH, BE IT FAR FROM ME. (1 Sam. ii. 30.)
For the Lord will not forsake his people, for his great name's sake: because it hath pleased the Lord to make you his people. (1 Sam. xii. 22.)	But if ye shall still do wickedly, ye shall be consumed, both ye and your king. (1 Sam. xii. 25.)
And of all my sons (for the Lord hath given me many sons,) he hath chosen Solomon my son to sit upon the throne of the kingdom of the Lord over Israel. And he said unto me, Solomon thy son, he shall build my house and my courts: for I HAVE CHOSEN HIM TO BE MY SON, AND I WILL BE HIS FATHER. (1 Chron. xxviii. 5, 6.)	And thou, Solomon my son, know thou the God of thy father, and serve him . . . for if thou seek him he will be found of thee, BUT IF THOU FORSAKE HIM HE WILL CAST THEE OFF FOR EVER. (1 Chron. xxviii. 9.)
Then the word of the Lord came unto me, saying, BEFORE I FORMED THEE IN THE BELLY I KNEW THEE; and before thou camest forth out of the womb I sanctified thee, and I ORDAINED THEE A PROPHET UNTO THE NATIONS. (Jer. i. 4, 5.)	

I have hallowed this house, which thou hast built, TO PUT MY NAME THERE FOR EVER. (1 Kings ix. 3.)

The steps of a *good* man are ordered by the Lord: and he delighteth in his way. THOUGH HE FALL, HE SHALL NOT BE UTTERLY CAST DOWN: FOR THE LORD UPHOLDETH HIM WITH HIS HAND. I have been young, and *now* am old; yet have I not seen the righteous forsaken, nor his seed begging bread. *He is* ever merciful, and lendeth; and his seed *is* blessed. Depart from evil, and do good; and dwell for evermore. For the LORD loveth judgment, AND FORSAKETH NOT HIS SAINTS; THEY ARE PRESERVED FOR EVER: but the seed of the wicked shall be cut off. The righteous shall inherit the land, and dwell therein for ever. The mouth of the righteous speaketh wisdom, and his tongue talketh of judgment. THE LAW OF HIS GOD IS IN HIS HEART: NONE OF HIS STEPS SHALL SLIDE. (Ps. xxxvii. 23-31.)

And the vessel that he made of clay was marred in the hands of the potter: SO HE MADE IT AGAIN ANOTHER VESSEL, AS SEEMED GOOD UNTO THE POTTER TO MAKE IT. O house of Israel, cannot I do with you as this potter? (Jer. xviii. 4, 6.)

In that day, saith the Lord of hosts, will I take thee, O Zerubbabel, my servant, the son of Shealtiel, saith the LORD, AND WILL MAKE THEE AS A SIGNET: FOR I HAVE CHOSEN THEE, SAITH THE LORD OF HOSTS. (Hag. ii. 23.)

BUT IF YE SHALL AT ALL TURN FROM FOLLOWING ME, ye or your children, then . . . this house, which I have hallowed for my name, I WILL CAST OUT OF MY SIGHT. (1 Kings ix. 6, 7.)

BUT WHEN THE RIGHTEOUS TURNETH AWAY FROM HIS RIGHTEOUSNESS, and committeth iniquity, *and* doeth according to all the abominations that the wicked *man* doeth, shall he live? ALL HIS RIGHTEOUSNESS THAT HE HATH DONE SHALL NOT BE MENTIONED: in his trespass that he hath trespassed, and in his sin that he hath sinned, IN THEM SHALL HE DIE. Yet ye say, The way of the Lord is not equal. Hear now, O house of Israel; Is not my way equal? are not your ways unequal? When a righteous *man* TURNETH AWAY FROM HIS RIGHTEOUSNESS, and committeth iniquity, and DIETH IN THEM; for his iniquity that he hath done shall he die. AGAIN, WHEN THE WICKED MAN TURNETH AWAY FROM HIS WICKEDNESS THAT HE HATH COMMITTED, AND DOETH THAT WHICH IS LAWFUL AND RIGHT, he shall save his soul alive. Because he considereth, and turneth away from all his transgressions that he hath committed, he shall surely live, he shall not die. (Ezek. xviii. 24-28.)

And at what instant I shall speak concerning a nation, and concerning a kingdom, to build and to plant it; IF IT DO EVIL IN MY SIGHT, THAT IT OBEY NOT MY VOICE, THEN I WILL REPENT OF THE GOOD, WHEREWITH I SAID I WOULD BENEFIT THEM. (Jer. xviii. 9, 10.)

As I live, saith the Lord, though Coniah the son of Jehoiakim king of Judah were the SIGNET UPON MY RIGHT HAND, YET WOULD I PLUCK THEE THENCE. (Jer. xxii. 24.)

EXCURSUS ON ELECTION.

NEW TESTAMENT.

* MY SHEEP HEAR MY VOICE, AND I KNOW THEM, AND THEY FOLLOW ME: AND I GIVE UNTO THEM ETERNAL LIFE; AND THEY SHALL NEVER PERISH, NEITHER SHALL ANY MAN PLUCK THEM OUT OF MY HAND. My Father, which gave *them* me, is greater than all; and·no *man* is able to pluck *them* out of my Father's hand. (John x. 27-29.)

* Now before the feast of the passover, when Jesus knew that his hour was come that he should depart out of this world unto the Father, HAVING LOVED HIS OWN WHICH WERE IN THE WORLD, HE LOVED THEM UNTO THE END. (John xiii. 1.)

* YE HAVE NOT CHOSEN ME, BUT I HAVE CHOSEN YOU, AND ORDAINED YOU, THAT YE SHOULD GO AND BRING FORTH FRUIT, AND THAT YOUR FRUIT SHOULD REMAIN: that whatsoever ye shall ask of the Father in my name, he may give it you. (John xv. 16.)

* And we know that all things work together for good to them that love God, TO THEM WHO ARE THE CALLED ACCORDING TO HIS PURPOSE. FOR WHOM HE DID FOREKNOW, HE ALSO DID PREDESTINATE TO BE CONFORMED TO THE IMAGE OF HIS SON, THAT HE MIGHT BE THE FIRST-BORN AMONG MANY BRETHREN. MOREOVER WHOM HE DID PREDESTINATE, THEM HE ALSO CALLED: AND WHOM HE CALLED, THEM HE ALSO JUSTIFIED: AND WHOM HE JUSTIFIED, THEM HE ALSO GLORIFIED. What shall we then say to these things? If God *be* for us, who *can be* against us? (Rom. viii. 28-31.)

* Peter, an apostle of Jesus Christ, to the strangers scattered throughout Pontus, Galatia, Cappadocia, Asia, and Bithynia,

How think ye? IF A MAN HAVE AN HUNDRED SHEEP, AND ONE OF THEM BE GONE ASTRAY, doth he not leave the ninety and nine, and goeth into the mountains, and seeketh that which is gone astray? AND IF SO BE THAT HE FIND IT, verily I say unto you, he rejoiceth more of that *sheep*, than of the ninety and nine which went not astray. (Matt. xviii. 12, 13.)

* I am the true vine, and my Father is the husbandman. EVERY BRANCH IN ME THAT BEARETH NOT FRUIT HE TAKETH AWAY: and every *branch* that beareth fruit, he purgeth it, that it may bring forth more fruit. IF A MAN ABIDE NOT IN ME, HE IS CAST FORTH AS A BRANCH, AND IS WITHERED; and men gather them, and cast *them* into the fire, AND THEY ARE BURNED. As the Father hath loved me, so have I loved you: CONTINUE YE IN MY LOVE. IF YE KEEP MY COMMANDMENTS, YE SHALL ABIDE IN MY LOVE; even as I have kept my Father's commandments, and abide in his love. (John xv. 1, 2, 6, 9, 10.)

* Well; because of unbelief they were broken off, and THOU STANDEST BY FAITH. Be not highminded, but fear: for if God spared not the natural branches, TAKE HEED LEST HE ALSO SPARE NOT THEE. Behold therefore the goodness and severity of God: on them which fell, severity; but toward thee, goodness, IF THOU CONTINUE IN HIS GOODNESS: otherwise thou also shalt be cut off. (Rom. xi. 20-22.)

* But he that lacketh these things is blind, and cannot see afar off, AND HATH FORGOTTEN THAT HE WAS PURGED FROM

---

* Let the reader particularly notice that the texts in the parallel columns which have an asterisk before them are spoken to the same persons. This applies in a measure to all the texts taken from the Apostolical Epistles, for all the Churches to whom these were addressed were in the same ecclesiastical and spiritual state.

ELECT ACCORDING TO THE FOREKNOWLEDGE OF GOD THE FATHER, THROUGH SANCTIFICATION OF THE SPIRIT, UNTO OBEDIENCE AND SPRINKLING OF THE BLOOD OF JESUS CHRIST: Grace unto you, and peace, be multiplied. Blessed *be* the God and Father of our Lord Jesus Christ, which according to his abundant mercy hath begotten us again unto a lively hope by the resurrection of Jesus Christ from the dead, to an inheritance incorruptible, and undefiled, and that fadeth not away, RESERVED IN HEAVEN FOR YOU, WHO ARE KEPT BY THE POWER OF GOD THROUGH FAITH UNTO SALVATION READY TO BE REVEALED IN THE LAST TIME. (1 Peter i. 1-5.)

* Jude, the servant of Jesus Christ, and brother of James, TO THEM THAT ARE SANCTIFIED BY GOD THE FATHER, AND PRESERVED IN JESUS CHRIST, *and* called. (Jude 1.)

They went out from us, but they were not of us; FOR IF THEY HAD BEEN OF US, THEY WOULD (*no doubt*) HAVE CONTINUED WITH US: but *they went out*, that they might be made manifest that they were not all of us. (1 John ii. 19.)

FEAR NOT, LITTLE FLOCK; FOR IT IS YOUR FATHER'S GOOD PLEASURE TO GIVE YOU THE KINGDOM. Sell that ye have, and give arms; PROVIDE YOURSELVES bags which wax not old, A TREASURE IN THE HEAVENS THAT FAILETH NOT, where no thief approacheth, neither moth corrupteth. (Luke xii. 32, 33.)

For there shall arise false Christs, and false prophets, and shall shew great signs and wonders; insomuch that, if (*it were*) POSSIBLE, THEY SHALL DECEIVE THE VERY ELECT. (Matt. xxiv. 24.)

HIS OLD SINS. WHEREFORE THE RATHER, BRETHREN, GIVE DILIGENCE TO MAKE YOUR CALLING AND ELECTION SURE: FOR IF YE DO THESE THINGS, YE SHALL NEVER FALL: for so an entrance shall be ministered unto you abundantly into the everlasting kingdom of our Lord and Saviour Jesus Christ. (2 Peter i. 9-11.)

* I will therefore put you in remembrance, though ye once knew this, how that the Lord, HAVING SAVED the people out of the land of Egypt, AFTERWARDS DESTROYED them that believed not. And the ANGELS WHICH KEPT NOT THEIR FIRST ESTATE, but left their own habitation, he hath reserved in everlasting chains under darkness unto the judgment of the great day. (Jude 5, 6.)

These are spots in your feasts of charity, when they feast with you, feeding themselves without fear: clouds *they are* without water, carried about of winds; trees whose fruit withereth, without fruit, TWICE DEAD, plucked up by the roots. (Jude 12.)

Wherefore WE RECEIVING A KINGDOM WHICH CANNOT BE MOVED, LET US HAVE GRACE, whereby we may serve God acceptably with reverence and GODLY FEAR: FOR OUR GOD IS A CONSUMING FIRE. (Heb. xii. 28, 29.)

Take heed therefore unto yourselves, and to ALL THE FLOCK, OVER THE WHICH THE HOLY GHOST HATH MADE YOU OVERSEERS, TO FEED THE CHURCH OF GOD, WHICH HE HATH PURCHASED WITH HIS OWN BLOOD. For I know this, that after my departing shall grievous wolves enter in among you, NOT SPARING THE FLOCK. Also OF YOUR OWN SELVES shall men arise, speaking perverse things, to draw away disciples after them. Therefore watch, and remember, that by the space of three

EXCURSUS ON ELECTION. 363

Being born again, NOT OF CORRUPTIBLE SEED, BUT OF INCORRUPTIBLE, by the word of God, which liveth and abideth for ever. For all flesh *is* as grass, and all the glory of man as the flower of grass. The grass withereth, and the flower thereof falleth away : but the word of the Lord endureth for ever. And this is the word which by the gospel is preached unto you. (1 Peter i. 23-25.)

For God hath not appointed us to wrath, BUT TO OBTAIN SALVATION BY OUR LORD JESUS CHRIST, who died for us, that, whether we wake or sleep, we should live together with him. (1 Thess. v. 9, 10.)

* But we are bound to give thanks alway to God for you, brethren beloved of the LORD, because GOD HATH FROM THE BEGINNING CHOSEN YOU TO SALVATION THROUGH SANCTIFICATION OF THE SPIRIT AND BELIEF OF THE TRUTH : whereunto he called you by our gospel, to the obtaining of the glory of our Lord Jesus Christ. (2 Thess. ii. 13, 14.)

The Lord is faithful, WHO SHALL STABLISH (στηρίξει) YOU, and keep you from evil. (2 Thess. iii. 3.)

And the very God of peace sanctify you wholly ; and *I pray God* your whole spirit and soul and body be preserved blameless UNTO THE COMING OF OUR LORD JESUS CHRIST. FAITHFUL IS HE THAT CALLETH YOU, WHO ALSO WILL DO IT. (1 Thess. v. 23, 24.)

years I ceased not to warn EVERY ONE night and day, with tears. (Acts xx. 28-31.)

This thou knowest, that ALL THEY WHICH ARE IN ASIA BE TURNED AWAY FROM ME ; of whom are Phygellus and Hermogenes. (2 Tim. i. 15.)

[" All they of Asia," that is, Proconsular Asia, including Ephesus, the Church in which city the Apostle addresses as " elect in Christ " and " predestinated."]

Now the parable is this : THE SEED IS THE WORD OF GOD. And some fell upon a rock ; and AS SOON AS IT WAS SPRUNG UP, IT WITHERED AWAY, because it lacked moisture. And some fell among thorns ; and the thorns sprang up with it, and choked it. (Luke viii. 11, 6, 7.)

Let us labour therefore to enter into that rest, LEST ANY MAN FALL AFTER THE SAME EXAMPLE OF UNBELIEF. (Heb. iv. 11.)

* QUENCH NOT THE SPIRIT. (1 Thess. v. 19.)

Now the Spirit speaketh expressly, that in the latter times some SHALL DEPART FROM THE FAITH, giving heed to seducing spirits, and doctrines of devils. Having damnation, because they have cast off THEIR FIRST FAITH. For SOME ARE ALREADY TURNED ASIDE AFTER SATAN. (1 Tim. iv. 1 ; v. 12-15.)

They that are unlearned and unstable wrest, as they do also the other scriptures, to their own destruction. YE THEREFORE, BELOVED, seeing ye know these things before, BEWARE LEST YE ALSO, being led away with the error of the wicked, FALL FROM YOUR OWN STEADFASTNESS (τοῦ ἰδίου στηριγμοῦ). (2 Peter iii. 16, 17.)

In the body of his flesh through death, to present you holy and unblameable and unreproveable in his sight : IF YE CONTINUE IN THE FAITH GROUNDED AND SETTLED, AND BE NOT MOVED AWAY FROM THE HOPE OF THE GOSPEL, which ye have heard, *and* which was preached to every creature which is under heaven ; whereof I Paul am made a minister. (Col. i. 22, 23.)

Hath not the potter power over the clay, of the same lump to make one vessel unto honour, and another unto dishonour? *What* if God, willing to shew *his* wrath, and to make his power known, endured with much longsuffering the vessels of wrath fitted to destruction: AND THAT HE MIGHT MAKE KNOWN THE RICHES OF HIS GLORY ON THE VESSELS OF MERCY, WHICH HE HAD AFORE PREPARED UNTO GLORY, even us, whom he hath called, not of the Jews only, but also of the Gentiles? As he saith also in Osee, I will call them my people, which were not my people; and her beloved, which was not beloved. (Rom. ix. 21-25.)

But in a great house there are not only vessels of gold and of silver, but also of wood and of earth; and some to honour, and some to dishonour. IF A MAN THEREFORE PURGE HIMSELF FROM THESE, HE SHALL BE A VESSEL UNTO HONOUR, sanctified, and meet for the master's use, *and* prepared unto every good work. (2 Tim. ii. 20, 21.)

Nevertheless the foundation of God standeth sure, having this seal, THE LORD KNOWETH THEM THAT ARE HIS. And, Let every one that nameth the name of Christ depart from iniquity. (2 Tim. ii. 19.)

These shall make war with the Lamb, and the Lamb shall overcome them: for he is Lord of lords, and King of kings; and they that are with him *are* called, and chosen, and FAITHFUL. (Rev. xvii. 14.)

[Not only called and chosen, but faithful —*i.e.* they endure to the end. "Be thou faithful unto death."]

* But we are bound to give thanks alway to God for you, brethren beloved of the Lord, because GOD HATH FROM THE BEGINNING CHOSEN YOU TO SALVATION THROUGH SANCTIFICATION OF THE SPIRIT AND BELIEF OF THE TRUTH: whereunto he called you by our gospel, to the obtaining of the glory of our Lord Jesus Christ. (2 Thess. ii. 13, 14.)

* WHEN HE SHALL COME TO BE GLORIFIED IN HIS SAINTS, and to be admired in all them that believe (because our testimony among you was believed) in that day. WHEREFORE ALSO WE PRAY ALWAYS FOR YOU, THAT OUR GOD WOULD COUNT YOU WORTHY OF THIS CALLING, and fulfil all the good pleasure of *his* goodness, and the work of faith with power: that the name of our Lord Jesus Christ may be glorified in you, and ye in him, according to the grace of our God and the Lord Jesus Christ. (2 Thess. i. 10-12.)

[Let the reader particularly notice that this place occurs in an epistle written to Christians, of whom the apostle says, "Knowing, brethren beloved, your election of God;" and respecting whom he gives thanks, "because God hath from the beginning chosen them to salvation through sanctification of the Spirit."

He deemed it right to pray for those thus "elect," that God would count them "worthy of this calling" of being glorified at Christ's coming.]

Wherein God, willing more abundantly to shew unto the heirs of promise the immutability of his counsel, CONFIRMED IT BY AN OATH: that by two immutable

Wherefore, HOLY BRETHREN, PARTAKERS OF THE HEAVENLY CALLING, consider the Apostle and High Priest of our profession, Christ Jesus. Wherefore

EXCURSUS ON ELECTION.

things, in which *it was* impossible for God to lie, WE MIGHT HAVE A STRONG CONSOLATION, who have fled for refuge to lay hold upon the hope set before us: which *hope* we have as an anchor of the soul, both sure and steadfast, and which entereth into that within the vail. (Heb. vi. 17-19.)

(as the Holy Ghost saith, To-day if ye will hear his voice, harden not your hearts, as in the provocation, in the day of temptation in the wilderness: when your fathers tempted me, proved me, and saw my works forty years. Wherefore I was grieved with that generation, and said, They do alway err in *their* heart; and they have not known my ways. So I SWARE IN MY WRATH, THEY SHALL NOT ENTER INTO MY REST.) TAKE HEED, BRETHREN, LEST THERE BE IN ANY OF YOU AN EVIL HEART OF UNBELIEF, IN DEPARTING FROM THE LIVING GOD. But exhort one another daily, while it is called To-day; lest any of you be hardened through the deceitfulness of sin. For we are made partakers of Christ, IF WE HOLD THE BEGINNING OF OUR CONFIDENCE STEADFAST UNTO THE END. (Heb. iii. 1, 7-14.)

* For by one offering HE HATH PERFECTED FOR EVER THEM THAT ARE SANCTIFIED. *Whereof* the Holy Ghost also is a witness to us: for after that he hath said before, This *is* the covenant that I will make with them after those days, saith the Lord, I will put my laws into their hearts, and in their minds will I write them; and their sins and iniquities will I remember no more. (Heb. x. 14-17.)

* He that despised Moses' law died without mercy under two or three witnesses: of how much sorer punishment, suppose ye, shall he be thought worthy, WHO HATH TRODDEN UNDER FOOT THE SON OF GOD, AND HATH COUNTED THE BLOOD OF THE COVENANT, WHEREWITH HE WAS SANCTIFIED, AN UNHOLY THING, AND HATH DONE DESPITE UNTO THE SPIRIT OF GRACE? For we know him that hath said, Vengeance *belongeth* unto me, I will recompense, saith the Lord. And again, THE LORD SHALL JUDGE HIS PEOPLE. *It is* a fearful thing to fall into the hands of the living God. (Heb. x. 28-31.)

Who shall separate us from the love of Christ? *shall* tribulation, or distress, or persecution, or famine, or nakedness, or peril, or sword? As it is written, For thy sake we are killed all the day long; we are accounted as sheep for the slaughter. Nay, in all these things we are more than conquerors through him that loved us. For I am persuaded, that neither death, nor life, nor angels, nor principalities, nor powers, nor things present, nor things to come, nor height, nor depth, nor any other creature, shall be able to separate us from the love of God, which is in Christ Jesus our Lord. (Rom. viii. 35-39.)

Who shall separate us from the love of Christ? *shall* tribulation, or distress, or persecution, or famine, or nakedness, or peril, or sword? As it is written, For thy sake we are killed all the day long; we are accounted as sheep for the slaughter. Nay, in all these things we are more than conquerors through him that loved us. For I am persuaded, that neither death, nor life, nor angels, nor principalities, nor powers, nor things present, nor things to come, nor height, nor depth, nor any other creature, shall be able to separate us from the love of God, which is in Christ Jesus our Lord. (Rom. viii. 35-39.)

[NOTE.—I have inserted this passage in both lists because of the fearfully significant omission of one word from the cata-

And the Lord shall deliver me from every evil work, and will preserve *me* unto his heavenly kingdom: to whom *be* glory for ever and ever. Amen. (2 Tim. iv. 18).

[NOTE.—I have inserted this text because I find it usually brought forward in lists of texts on final perseverance.

If the reader considers that the apostle wrote it on the eve of his martyrdom, when he had just written, "I am now ready to be offered, and the time of my departure is at hand. I have fought a good fight, I have finished my course, I have kept the faith:" I think he will agree with me that it is very perilous to quote it as decisive in favour of the necessary final perseverance of every one who has once begun the Christian race.]

In whom ye also *trusted*, after that ye heard the word of truth, the gospel of your salvation: in whom also after that ye believed, YE WERE SEALED WITH THAT HOLY SPIRIT OF PROMISE, WHICH IS THE EARNEST OF OUR INHERITANCE UNTIL THE REDEMPTION OF THE PURCHASED POSSESSION, unto the praise of his glory. (Ephes. i. 13, 14.)

logue of things here said to be unable to separate us from Christ. That word is "sin." If sin can be properly called "a creature," then this passage is decisive on the final perseverance of the apostle, and those whom he means by "we," "us." If the omission of the word is intentional, the passage is equally strong in the other direction.

St. Bernard, a strong predestinarian, in commenting on this passage, notices this omission. "He omits to add, 'nor our own selves,' because it must be with our own free will that we can alone forsake God. Excepting this free will of ours, there is nothing, absolutely nothing, for us to fear."]

For *it is* impossible for those who were ONCE ENLIGHTENED, AND HAVE TASTED OF THE HEAVENLY GIFT, AND WERE MADE PARTAKERS OF THE HOLY GHOST, AND HAVE TASTED THE GOOD WORD OF GOD, AND THE POWERS OF THE WORLD TO COME, IF THEY SHALL FALL AWAY, to renew them again unto repentance; seeing they crucify to themselves the Son of God afresh, and put *him* to an open shame. For THE EARTH WHICH DRINKETH IN THE RAIN THAT COMETH OFT UPON IT, and bringeth forth herbs meet for them by whom it is dressed, receiveth blessing from God: BUT THAT WHICH BEARETH THORNS AND BRIARS IS REJECTED, and *is* nigh unto cursing; whose end *is* to be burned. (Heb. vi. 4-8.)

EXCURSUS ON ELECTION.

Blessed *be* the God and Father of our Lord Jesus Christ, who hath blessed us with all SPIRITUAL BLESSINGS IN HEAVENLY PLACES IN CHRIST: ACCORDING AS HE HATH CHOSEN US IN HIM BEFORE THE FOUNDATION OF THE WORLD, that we should be holy and without blame before him in love: having PREDESTINATED US UNTO THE ADOPTION OF CHILDREN BY JESUS CHRIST TO HIMSELF, according to the good pleasure of his will, to the praise of the glory of his grace, wherein he hath made us accepted in the beloved. In whom we have redemption through his blood, the forgiveness of sins, according to the riches of his grace; wherein he hath abounded toward us in all wisdom and prudence; having made known unto us the mystery of his will, according to his good pleasure which he hath purposed in himself: that in the dispensation of the fulness of times he might gather together in one all things in Christ, both which are in heaven, and which are on earth; *even* in him; IN WHOM ALSO WE HAVE OBTAINED AN INHERITANCE, BEING PREDESTINATED ACCORDING TO THE PURPOSE OF HIM WHO WORKETH ALL THINGS AFTER THE COUNSEL OF HIS OWN WILL: THAT WE SHOULD BE TO THE PRAISE OF HIS GLORY, WHO FIRST TRUSTED IN CHRIST. (Eph. i. 3-12.)

Follow peace with all *men*, and holiness, without which no man shall see the Lord: LOOKING DILIGENTLY LEST ANY MAN FAIL OF THE GRACE OF GOD; lest any root of bitterness springing up trouble *you*, and thereby many be defiled; lest there *be* any fornicator or profane person, as Esau, WHO FOR ONE MORSEL OF MEAT SOLD HIS BIRTHRIGHT. For ye know how that afterward, when he would have inherited the blessing, he was rejected; for he found no place of repentance, though he sought it carefully with tears. (Heb. xii. 14-17.)

But YE ARE COME UNTO MOUNT SION, and unto the city of the living God, the heavenly Jerusalem, and to an innumerable company of angels, to the general assembly and church of the firstborn, which are written in heaven, and to God the Judge of all, and to the spirits of just men made perfect, AND TO JESUS THE MEDIATOR OF THE NEW COVENANT, AND TO THE BLOOD OF SPRINKLING, THAT SPEAKETH BETTER THINGS THAN THAT OF ABEL. SEE THAT YE REFUSE NOT HIM THAT SPEAKETH. For if they escaped not who refused him that spake on earth, much more *shall not* we *escape*, if we turn away from him that *speaketh* from heaven. (Heb. xii. 22-25).

But there were false prophets also among the people, even as there shall be false teachers among you, who privily shall bring in damnable heresies, even DENYING THE LORD THAT BOUGHT THEM, and bring upon themselves swift destruction. And many shall follow their pernicious ways; by reason of whom the way of truth shall be evil spoken of. FOR IF GOD SPARED NOT THE ANGELS THAT SINNED, but cast *them* down to hell, and delivered *them* into chains of darkness, to be reserved unto judgment. (2 Pet. ii. 1, 2, 4.)

CAST NOT AWAY THEREFORE YOUR CONFIDENCE, which hath great recompence of reward. For ye have need of patience, that, after ye have done the will of God, ye might receive the promise. For yet a little while, and he that shall come will come, and will not tarry. Now THE JUST SHALL LIVE BY FAITH: BUT IF

EXCURSUS ON ELECTION.

Be not thou therefore ashamed of the testimony of our Lord, nor of me his prisoner: but be thou partaker of the afflictions of the gospel according to the power of God; WHO HATH SAVED US, AND CALLED US WITH AN HOLY CALLING, NOT ACCORDING TO OUR WORKS, BUT ACCORDING TO HIS OWN PURPOSE AND GRACE, WHICH WAS GIVEN US IN CHRIST JESUS BEFORE THE WORLD BEGAN, but is now made manifest by the appearing of our Saviour Jesus Christ, who hath abolished death, and hath brought life and immortality to light through the gospel: whereunto I am appointed a preacher, and an apostle, and a teacher of the Gentiles. For the which cause I also suffer these things: nevertheless I am not ashamed: FOR I KNOW WHOM I HAVE BELIEVED, AND AM PERSUADED THAT HE IS ABLE TO KEEP THAT WHICH I HAVE COMMITTED UNTO HIM AGAINST THAT DAY. (2 Tim. i. 8-12.)

AND THE GLORY WHICH THOU GAVEST ME I HAVE GIVEN THEM; that they may be one, even as we are one: I in them, and thou in me, that they may be made perfect in one; and that the world may know that thou hast sent me, AND HAST LOVED THEM, AS THOU HAST LOVED ME.

[ANY MAN] DRAW BACK, MY SOUL SHALL HAVE NO PLEASURE IN HIM. (Heb. x. 35-38.)

[NOTE.—Much of the force of the original is lost by our translators having inserted the words "any man," in italics, in the last verse. In reality, the verse runs: " Now the just shall live by faith : but if he (*i.e.* ὁ δίκαιος, the justified man) draw back, my soul shall have no pleasure in him."]

Take heed unto thyself, and unto the doctrine; CONTINUE IN THEM: FOR IN DOING THIS THOU SHALT BOTH SAVE THYSELF, and them that hear thee. (1 Tim. iv. 16.)

HOLD FAST THE FORM OF SOUND WORDS, which thou hast heard of me, in faith and love which is in Christ Jesus. THAT GOOD THING WHICH WAS COMMITTED UNTO THEE KEEP by the Holy Ghost which dwelleth in us. This thou knowest, that ALL THEY WHICH ARE IN ASIA BE TURNED AWAY FROM ME; of whom are Phygellus and Hermogenes. IF A MAN THEREFORE PURGE HIMSELF FROM THESE, HE SHALL BE A VESSEL UNTO HONOUR, sanctified, and meet for the master's use, *and* prepared unto every good work. FLEE ALSO YOUTHFUL LUSTS: but follow righteousness, faith, charity, peace, with them that call on the Lord out of a pure heart. But CONTINUE THOU in the things which thou hast learned and hast been assured of, knowing of whom thou hast learned *them*. (2 Tim. i. 13-15; ii. 21, 22; iii. 14.)

[Timothy was one of the first saints of the apostolic age, but in the epistles addressed to him there is not one word respecting his final triumph being absolutely assured to him, but many words to exhort him to hold fast, continue, &c. This may not imply any doubt of Timothy's perseverance, but it certainly does teach modern assertors of this doctrine a strong lesson.]

Having eyes full of adultery, and that cannot cease from sin; beguiling unstable souls: an heart they have exercised with covetous practices: cursed children; WHICH HAVE FORSAKEN THE RIGHT WAY, and are gone astray, following the way of Balaam *the son* of Bosor, who loved the wages

EXCURSUS ON ELECTION.

Father, I will that they also, whom thou hast given me, be with me where I am; that they may behold my glory, which thou hast given me: FOR THOU LOVEDST ME BEFORE THE FOUNDATION OF THE WORLD. (John xvii. 22-24.)

GOD HATH NOT CAST AWAY HIS PEOPLE WHICH HE FOREKNEW. Wot ye not what the scripture saith of Elias? how he maketh intercession to God against Israel, saying, Lord, they have killed thy prophets, and digged down thine altars; and I am left alone, and they seek my life. But what saith the answer of God unto him? I have reserved to myself seven thousand men, who have not bowed the knee to *the image* of Baal. EVEN SO THEN AT THIS PRESENT TIME ALSO THERE IS A REMNANT ACCORDING TO THE ELECTION OF GRACE. (Rom. xi. 2-5.)

And this is the Father's will which hath sent me, THAT OF ALL WHICH HE HATH GIVEN ME I SHOULD LOSE NOTHING, but should raise it up again at the last day. And this is the will of him that sent me, that EVERY ONE WHICH SEETH THE SON, AND BELIEVETH ON HIM, MAY HAVE EVERLASTING LIFE: AND I WILL RAISE HIM UP AT THE LAST DAY. (John vi. 39, 40.)

of unrighteousness. For when they speak great swelling *words* of vanity, THEY ALLURE THROUGH THE LUSTS OF THE FLESH, *through much* wantonness, THOSE THAT WERE CLEAN ESCAPED FROM THEM who live in error. While they promise them liberty, they themselves are the servants of corruption: for of whom a man is overcome, of the same is he brought in bondage. For IF AFTER THEY HAVE ESCAPED THE POLLUTIONS OF THE WORLD THROUGH THE KNOWLEDGE OF THE LORD AND SAVIOUR JESUS CHRIST, THEY ARE AGAIN ENTANGLED THEREIN, AND OVERCOME, THE LATTER END IS WORSE WITH THEM THAN THE BEGINNING. For it had been better for them not to have known the way of righteousness, than, AFTER THEY HAVE KNOWN IT, TO TURN FROM THE holy commandment delivered unto them. But it is happened unto them according to the true proverb, The dog *is* turned to his own vomit again: and THE SOW THAT WAS WASHED to her wallowing in the mire. (2 Peter ii. 14, 15, 18-22.)

Ye are the salt of the earth: BUT IF THE SALT HAVE LOST HIS SAVOUR, wherewith shall it be salted? it is thenceforth good for nothing, but to BE CAST OUT, and to be trodden under foot of men. (Matt. v. 13.)

Salt *is* good: but IF THE SALT HAVE LOST HIS SAVOUR, wherewith shall it be seasoned? It is neither fit for the land, nor yet for the dunghill; *but* MEN CAST IT OUT. He that hath ears to hear, let him hear. (Luke xiv. 34, 35.)

But the CHILDREN OF THE KINGDOM SHALL BE CAST OUT INTO OUTER DARKNESS: there shall be weeping and gnashing of teeth. (Matt. viii. 12.)

And ye shall be hated of all *men* for my name's sake: but HE THAT ENDURETH TO THE END SHALL BE SAVED. (Matt. x. 22.)

Then his lord, after that he had called him, said unto him, O thou wicked servant, I FORGAVE THEE ALL THAT DEBT, because thou desiredst me: shouldest not thou also have had compassion on thy fellow-servant, even as I had pity on thee? And his lord was wroth, and delivered him to the tormentors, till he should pay all that was due unto him. So LIKEWISE SHALL MY HEAVENLY FATHER DO ALSO UNTO YOU, IF YE FROM YOUR HEARTS FORGIVE NOT EVERY ONE HIS BROTHER THEIR TRESPASSES. (Matt. xviii. 32-35.)

For *the kingdom of heaven is* as a man travelling into a far country, *who* called HIS OWN SERVANTS, and delivered unto them his goods. And unto one he gave five talents, to another two, and to ANOTHER one; to EVERY MAN according to his several ability; and straightway took his journey. . . . And CAST YE THE UNPROFITABLE SERVANT INTO OUTER DARKNESS: there shall be weeping and gnashing of teeth. (Matt. xxv. 14, 15, 30.)

And the Lord said, WHO THEN IS THAT FAITHFUL AND WISE STEWARD, whom *his* lord shall make ruler over his household, to give *them their* portion of meat in due season? BLESSED IS THAT SERVANT, whom his lord when he cometh shall find so doing. Of a truth I say unto you, that he will make him ruler over all that he hath. BUT AND IF THAT SERVANT say in his heart, My lord delayeth his coming; and shall begin to beat the men-servants and maidens, and to eat and drink, and to be drunken; the lord of that servant will come in a day when he looketh not for *him*, and at an hour when he is not aware, AND WILL CUT HIM IN SUNDER, AND WILL APPOINT HIM HIS PORTION WITH THE UNBELIEVERS. (Luke xii. 42-46.)

Now when the congregation was broken up, many of the Jews and religious proselytes followed Paul and Barnabas; who, speaking to them, persuaded them to CONTINUE IN THE GRACE OF GOD. (Acts xiii. 43.)

Confirming the souls of the disciples, *and* exhorting them to CONTINUE IN THE FAITH, and that we must through much tribulation enter into the kingdom of God. (Acts xiv. 22.)

For this cause, when I could no longer forbear, I SENT TO KNOW YOUR FAITH, LEST BY SOME MEANS THE TEMPTER HAVE TEMPTED YOU, AND OUR LABOUR BE IN VAIN. For now we live, IF ye stand fast in the Lord. (1 Thess. iii. 5, 8.)

BEING CONFIDENT OF THIS VERY THING, THAT HE WHICH HATH BEGUN

But if thy brother be grieved with *thy* meat, now walkest thou not charitably.

EXCURSUS ON ELECTION.

A GOOD WORK IN YOU WILL PERFORM IT UNTIL THE DAY OF JESUS CHRIST: even as it is meet for me to think this of you all. (Phil. i. 6, 7.)

[Do they who cite this text mean to assert that St. Paul predicates this perseverance of ALL his Philippian converts? for he distinctly says, "Even as it is meet for me to think this of you all." The Apostle cannot mean this: for, in the first place, he bids them "work out their salvation with fear and trembling;" then he tells them that he counts not himself to have "attained," or to have "apprehended." He bids them in this respect (iii. 15, 16) be like-minded with himself; and, above all, he warns them how many walked, of whom he had told them often that "their end was destruction:" and these could not have been the heathen.

Then, also, on this hypothesis, what an unaccountable difference there must have been between the Philippian and the Corinthian Churches. St. Paul's words of confidence respecting the Corinthians are as strong as those respecting the Philippians, when he says to the former, " Jesus Christ: WHO SHALL CONFIRM YOU TO THE END, that ye may be blameless in the day of our Lord Jesus Christ. GOD IS FAITHFUL, BY WHOM YE WERE CALLED unto the fellowship of His Son Jesus Christ our Lord" (1 Cor. i. 8, 9). And yet we see, by every chapter of this latter Epistle, that it was far indeed from his thoughts to assert the necessary and predestined completion of God's work in each of them.]

The elders which are among you I exhort, who am also an elder, and a witness of the sufferings of Christ, AND ALSO A PARTAKER OF THE GLORY THAT SHALL BE REVEALED. (1 Pet. v. 1.)

And all that dwell upon the earth shall worship him, WHOSE NAMES ARE NOT

DESTROY NOT HIM WITH THY MEAT, FOR WHOM CHRIST DIED. For meat DESTROY NOT THE WORK OF GOD. All things indeed *are* pure; but *it is* evil for that man who eateth with offence. (Rom. xiv. 15, 20.)

* And through thy knowledge shall the WEAK BROTHER PERISH, FOR WHOM CHRIST DIED? But when ye sin so against the brethren, and wound their weak conscience, YE SIN AGAINST CHRIST. (1 Cor. viii. 11, 12.)

KNOW YE NOT THAT YE ARE THE TEMPLE OF GOD, AND THAT THE SPIRIT OF GOD DWELLETH IN YOU? IF ANY MAN defile (or destroy, $\phi\theta\epsilon i\rho\epsilon\iota$) the temple of God, him will God destroy ($\phi\theta\epsilon\rho\epsilon\tilde{\iota}$); for the temple of God is holy, WHICH TEMPLE YE ARE. (1 Cor. iii. 16, 17.)

But I keep under my body, and bring *it* into subjection: LEST THAT BY ANY MEANS, WHEN I HAVE PREACHED TO OTHERS, I MYSELF SHOULD BE A CASTAWAY. (1 Cor. ix. 27.)

We then, *as* workers together *with him*, BESEECH YOU ALSO THAT YE RECEIVE NOT THE GRACE OF GOD IN VAIN. (2 Cor. vi. 1.)

Christ is become of no effect unto you, whosoever of you are justified by the law; YE ARE FALLEN FROM GRACE. (Gal. v. 4.)

If by any means I might attain unto the RESURRECTION OF THE DEAD. NOT AS THOUGH I HAD ALREADY ATTAINED, either were already perfect: but I follow after, if that I may apprehend that for which also I am apprehended of Christ Jesus. Brethren, I COUNT NOT MYSELF TO HAVE APPREHENDED: but *this* one thing *I do*, forgetting those things which are behind, and reaching forth unto those things which are before. (Philip. iii. 11-13.)

He that overcometh, the same shall be clothed in white raiment; AND I WILL

372 EXCURSUS ON ELECTION.

WRITTEN IN THE BOOK OF LIFE OF THE LAMB SLAIN FROM THE FOUNDATION OF THE WORLD. (Rev. xiii. 8.)

NOT BLOT OUT HIS NAME OUT OF THE BOOK OF LIFE, but I will confess his name before my Father, and before his angels. He that hath an ear, let him hear what the Spirit saith unto the churches. (Rev. iii. 5, 6.)

HE THAT OVERCOMETH shall inherit all things; and I will be his God, and he shall be my son. (Rev. xxi. 7.)

And if any man shall take away from the words of the book of this prophecy, GOD SHALL TAKE AWAY HIS PART OUT OF THE BOOK OF LIFE, AND OUT OF THE HOLY CITY, and *from* the things which are written in this book. (Rev. xxii. 19.)

[How can a man's name be blotted out of the book of life, unless it has been once written in that book? The Canon of the New Testament closes with a warning against Calvinistic perverseness.]

Now, in reading over these statements and counter-statements, it seems impossible to deny that God has called and chosen some persons, that they should, through His grace, serve Him as His children in this world, and enjoy His presence in the next, and yet it is equally impossible to deny that, no matter in what high terms this election is described, it is not absolutely indefectible. Are they sheep? they may wander from the fold, and in Matth. xviii. 13 it is implied that it is not absolutely certain that they will be brought back. Are they branches of the true vine? even that does not describe absolutely indefectible grace. They may be cast forth (John xv. 6). Are they the salt of the earth? it may lose its savour. Do they stand by faith? they must see that they continue in God's goodness (Rom. xi. 22). Do, then, these counter-statements rob the statements of God's Election of all their comfort? Only, we answer, in the case of those who have been brought up under, or have put their necks under, Calvinistic error. For the Calvinistic system makes God unreal. His proffers of mercy to all are unrealities, His cautions are unrealities. The very Judgment of God at the last day is an unreality.

The state of the case seems to be this. There is every reason for a devout and sincere Christian, who holds and realizes the Catholic faith, who looks to Christ as his only hope, and prays to God continually, who devoutly uses the means of grace, and is watchful over himself, and is careful to maintain good works; who, in the words of this very Apostle, " by patient continuance in well-doing, looks for glory, honour, and immortality,"—there is every reason for this man, in all humility, yet in all confidence, to regard himself as foreknown, predestinated, called, justified, and, with the adoption wherewith God has adopted him, glorified; but this cannot be held as a dogma, universally true, and that because the counter-statements are so very numerous, and so directly applied to each Christian as in a state of grace from which he may fall irrevocably.

EXCURSUS III.

CHRISTOLOGY OF ST. PAUL.

As the true interpretation of Romans ix. 5, is important, it may be well to examine, at some length, the Christology of St. Paul, with the view of ascertaining what his views of the Person of our Lord were—whether they were such as would naturally inspire him to ascribe divine blessedness to Christ as God, or whether they would rather lead him to withhold such a doxology as only due to His Father. A careful examination of all the places in his Epistles bearing on the Lord's Godhead, leads us to this conclusion, that he considers the Lord, Who appeared to him on his conversion, to be reigning side by side with God in heaven, the fountain and bestower of all spiritual grace, ruling and ordering all things, and, along with God, the object of all that faith, love, hope, obedience, and worship, which, in the Old Testament, are set forth as due only to the Supreme God. Moreover, He is all that to the Church of the New Testament which the Jehovah, or Lord of the Old Testament, was to the Church of the Patriarchs, and exercises all those functions of Supreme Godhead, such as Creation, Redemption, and final Judgment, which God had, in old times, most jealously reserved to Himself.

Let us take these points in the order in which we have mentioned them.

1. Christ is, along with God, the Fountain of all spiritual grace, and is constantly invoked as such, and grace is invoked, or called down, from Him, as being the very source and treasury of Divine grace.

Sometimes this invocation of grace is from Christ only. Thus, to the Galatians, "Brethren, the grace of our Lord Jesus Christ be with your spirit" (vi. 18). The same is found in Rom. xvi. 20 and 24; 1 Cor. i. 3; Phil. iv. 23; 1 Thess. v. 28; 2 Thess. iii. 18. In 2 Tim. iv. 22 it appears as "The Lord Jesus be with thy spirit." In Philemon 25, "The grace of our Lord Jesus Christ be with your spirit."

Sometimes it is from the Father and Christ. Thus, Rom. i. 7, "Grace to you, and peace from God our Father and the Lord Jesus Christ." Thus also 1 Cor. i. 3; 2 Cor. i. 2; Gal. i. 3; Ephes. i. 2, &c.

In the two Epistles to Timothy, and probably in that to Titus, it is "Grace, mercy, and peace." In Ephes. vi. 23, there is a striking difference: "Peace be to the brethren, and love with faith from God the Father and the Lord Jesus Christ."

Once it is from all the three Persons of the Trinity in the well-known words, "The grace of our Lord Jesus Christ and the love of God, and the communion of the Holy Ghost, be with you all,' 2 Cor. xiii. 14.

In accordance with this the kingdom of glory is called indifferently, "The kingdom of Christ and of God," Ephes. v. 5. Usually it is the kingdom of God; but in Coloss. i. 13 it is "The kingdom of his dear Son," and in 2 Tim. iv. 1, we have the explicit mention of God the Father, and yet the Kingdom is assigned to the Son. "I charge thee therefore before God, and the Lord Jesus Christ, who shall judge the quick and the dead at his appearing and his kingdom."

And again towards the conclusion of the same chapter: "The Lord shall deliver me from every evil work, and will preserve me unto his heavenly kingdom: to whom be glory for ever and ever." Here the Lord is unquestionably the same Lord Who is mentioned all through the chapter—in verse 8 as "The Lord, the righteous judge," assigning to St. Paul his Crown, and in verse 17 as the Lord Who stood with him at his trial.

Again, St. Paul accounts himself the servant or minister of this Christ as well as the minister of God. Thus, Rom. i. 1, he calls himself the slave of Christ, and so, Phil. i. 1; but in Titus he is the servant or slave of God, i. 1. In 1 Corinth. iv. 1, he asks men to account of him and his fellow-workers as "ministers of Christ, and stewards of the mysteries of God;" and he considers them all as deacons (or $\delta\iota\acute{\alpha}\kappa o\nu o\iota$) of God and Christ indifferently, thus, in 2 Cor.

CHRISTOLOGY OF ST. PAUL. 375

vi. 4: "In all things approving ourselves as the ministers of God," and in xi. 23, "Are they ministers of Christ? I am more."

Again, supreme power is said to reside sometimes in God, sometimes in Christ. Thus the Gospel is the power of God unto salvation, Rom. i. 16, and in the same chapter we have His (God's) "eternal power and Godhead." But in 2 Corinth. xii. we have the wonderful assertion of Christ, "My strength is made perfect in weakness," and St. Paul's conclusion from this truth, "Most gladly therefore will I rather glory in mine infirmities, that the power of Christ may rest upon me" (verse 9).

Again, Christ is, along with God, the object of faith, of love, of hope, of obedience, and of worship.

Of faith. "Abraham believed God" (Rom. iv. 3). "The Gentiles have not, in time past, believed God" (xi. 30). "They that have believed in God," Tit. iii. 8. But now Jesus Christ seems to have taken the place of God as the object of saving faith. The prophecy of Isaiah, "He that believeth in him shall not be confounded," is applied exclusively to Christ. By faith in him men are saved, justified, and made the children of God (Rom. iii. 22; Gal. ii. 20, iii. 26). By faith in Him men have the Spirit of God (Ephes. i. 13). One of the articles of the mystery of Godliness is that He was "believed on in the world" (1 Tim. iii. 16).

Then He is the object of supreme love as God is. "The love of God is shed abroad in our hearts." "All things work together for good to them that love God." But "The love of Christ constraineth us" (2 Cor. v. 14). "If any man love not the Lord Jesus Christ let him be Anathema" (1 Cor. xvi. 22).

Again, He is the object of hope, as God is. "We hope (trust, in A. V.) in the living God" (1 Tim. iv. 10). "She that is a widow, indeed, hopeth (trusteth, in A. V.) in God," but, "If in this life only we have hope in Christ" (1 Cor. xv. 19), and "Christ in you the hope of glory" (Coloss. i. 27).

And in one remarkable place Christ is said to share in the obedience of the spirit due to God, " Casting down imaginations and every high thing that exalteth itself against the knowledge of God, and bringing into captivity every thought to the obedience of Christ" (2 Cor. x. 5).

Again, all things are to be to the glory of Christ equally with God. Thus God is the God of glory, and Christ is "the Lord of glory" (1 Cor. ii. 8); and St. Paul will only glory in the Cross of Christ; and again, wicked men "shall be punished with everlasting destruction from the presence of the Lord, and from the glory of his power" (2 Thess. i. 9).

Following on this, His Name is honoured as if it was the Name of God, for men are besought by His Name as the highest of names (1 Cor. i. 10). In allusion to the greatness of His Name, St. Paul asks indignantly of some schismatical believers: "Were ye baptized in the name of Paul?" We are to do all in the name of Jesus (Coloss. iii. 17). For the honour of His Name the Gospel is to be preached among all nations (Rom. i. 5).

And so the preaching of salvation is the preaching of Him, even in the time of His utmost weakness, when He was crucified (1 Cor. i. 23).

Again, in the Old Testament, God claims for Himself exclusively the name of Saviour: "I, even I, am the Lord, and beside me there is no Saviour" (Isaiah xliii. 11); "I am the Holy One of Israel, thy Saviour" (xliii. 3); "A just God and a Saviour, there is none beside me" (xlv. 21).

Now in the Pauline Epistles this word Saviour is ascribed indifferently, as it were, to God and to Christ. Thus "the living God is the Saviour of all men, specially of those that believe" (1 Tim. iv. 10). St. Paul's apostleship is "by the commandment of God our Saviour, and Lord Jesus Christ" (1 Tim. i. 1). Prayers for all in authority are acceptable in the sight of God our Saviour, but it is Christ Who is the Saviour of the Body, the Church (Ephes. v. 23). From heaven we look for the Saviour, the Lord Jesus (Phil. iii. 20). Our Saviour Jesus Christ hath abolished death (2 Tim. i. 10). In the three chapters of the short Epistle to Titus the word Saviour is applied three times to God, three times to Christ: "God our Saviour, Christ our Saviour" (Titus i. 3, 4); "God our Saviour," "the great God and Saviour of us, Jesus Christ" (ii. 10, 13); "God our Saviour," "Jesus Christ our Saviour" (iii. 4, 6).

Again, in the Old Testament, God claims to be the husband of the Israelitish Church, the Old Mount Zion: "Thy maker is thine husband, the Lord of Hosts is His Name, and thy Redeemer the Holy One of Israel" (Isaiah liv. 5); but in the New Testament an infinitely greater and better Jerusalem is revealed, one compared to which the first was but a bondslave (Gal. iv. 26), and of this Jerusalem "from above" Jesus Christ is said to be the bridegroom and husband (Ephes. v. 22, 32). Also Romans vii. 4: "That ye should

CHRISTOLOGY OF ST. PAUL. 377

be married to another, even to him who is raised from the dead." This is the most suggestive argument respecting the Godhead and Incarnation of Christ that we have yet considered. It seems to imply—and indeed to necessitate—that those passages of the Old Testament in which God is said to be the husband of the Church (as Isaiah liv. 5, Jerem. iii. 14, xxxi. 32) in reality were spoken in anticipation of the Incarnation of the Second Person in the Trinity; He Who, having assumed our humanity, could more properly be said to be united to His Church in such a bond as Marriage.

Again, as I noticed on page 201, the three highest works of God—Creation, Redemption, and Final Judgment—are ascribed to Christ. Creation in Col. i. 16: "For by him were all things created, that are in heaven, and that are in earth, visible and invisible, whether they be thrones, or dominions, or principalities, or powers; all things were created by him and for him, and he is before all things, and by him all things consist." I may mention in passing respecting this place, that such a sublime description of creating glory is unrivalled in the sacred volume. We need cite no more places as to His function of Judgment. He is the Lord Who, at His coming, "will bring to light the hidden things of darkness, and make manifest the counsels of the hearts." "He will judge the quick and dead at his coming and his kingdom." He is "the Lord, the righteous judge," Who will give to Apostles the crown of righteousness at that day, the day of His appearing (1 Cor. iv. 5; 2 Tim. iv. 1, 8).

Lastly, He is said to bear that very peculiar relation to His people, which implies, if anything can, Divine and Spiritual Omnipresence. There are three Divine Persons *in* Whom Christians are said to be—God, Christ, and the Holy Ghost. For instance, the two letters to the Thessalonians are written to Christians who are *in* God the Father, and *in* the Lord Jesus Christ; and as regards the Holy Spirit, the Galatians are commanded to walk in the Spirit if they live *in* the Spirit.

But by far the most frequent application of this wonderful phrase is in connection with our relations to Christ. Take the two first chapters of the Epistle to the Ephesians. In these comparatively few verses Christians are said to be "blessed with all spiritual blessings in Christ," "chosen in Him," "accepted in Him as God's beloved." "In Him they have redemption through His blood," "In Him they have an inheritance," "In Christ they are raised up together and made to sit together in heavenly places," "In Christ they are made nigh by His blood," "In Christ they are builded together for an habitation of God."

Conversely, God, Christ, and the Holy Ghost are said to be " in " the Christian. "God is in you of a truth." " One God and Father of all, Who is . . . . 'in' you all" (1 Cor. xiv. 25 ; Ephes. iv. 6). " Christ is in you the hope of glory." "Know ye not that Jesus Christ is in you except ye be reprobates?" (Col. i. 27 ; 2 Cor. xiii. 5). "That good thing keep by the Holy Ghost that dwelleth in us " (2 Tim. i. 14).

Such then is St. Paul's conception of the Person of Christ. Side by side with God in heaven—working every work of God on earth—invoked as the Author and Giver of grace as His Father is —ordering all things in heaven and earth—in fact, directing the whole course of God's providence—the wisdom and power of God— the object of all faith, love, hope and obedience. All to the Church which God can be—its Head, Lord, Husband, Redeemer, Saviour— in Whom the Church *is* as it is in God and in the Spirit. Man, because incarnate, " the man Christ Jesus," and yet His Personality constantly contrasted with man's. Thus St. Paul is an Apostle, "not of men, neither by man, but by Jesus Christ, and God the Father, Who raised Him from the dead " (Gal i. 1).

What is the ground of such a conception ? What foundation has it in fact ? What is there in Christ that He should be capable of all this—that all this power and glory could be committed to Him ? Now the conception, the foundation, the underlying fact, is in a sense a natural one. He inherits all this. St. Paul's conception is not that God creates a being Whom He makes capable of receiving all the attributes of God, but that He has a Son Who naturally, as it were, receives them, just as a human son naturally receives the qualities with the nature of his father—thus Christ is the Son of God, the own (ἴδιος) Son, the Son in the proper sense of Sonship. Abraham, Moses, David are servants. He is the Son.

Now to what order of being as to His original or pre-existent nature could St. Paul have conceived that Christ belonged ? He tells us when He speaks of God giving His Son, His own proper Son (ἴδιος). To this Son He could naturally intrust, as He could to no angel, all the functions, prerogatives, powers, and relationships which He Himself exercised. This Son, in His pre-existent state, was in the form of God, which could only mean that He shared in the Divine Essence of His Father; and of the Person of this Son of God, St. Paul writes that "in Him dwelleth all the fulness of the Godhead bodily" (Col. ii. 9).

Now we must remember that St. Paul, in writing all this respecting the place of Christ in the universe, must have written with the full consciousness of what he was putting down or dictating. He could not have been unconscious that before his conversion he would have characterized these expressions respecting Christ as the veriest blasphemy, worthy of death, on hearing which devout Israelites should rend their garments. It is quite true that he does not express himself on this matter in Post-Nicene language, but his ideas of the Son of God are, if taken seriously, quite as irreconcilable with Socinianism or Rationalism as anything in the creeds of the Catholic Church.

Putting all these considerations together it seems incumbent upon us to translate Rom. ix. 5 as the Fathers, whose vernacular was Greek, translated it, "Of whom, as concerning the flesh, Christ came, Who is God over all, blessed for ever." He Who came in the flesh is God. In humbling Himself for us He parted with some manifestations of God, not with the Godhead, and He now abides for ever with the Father and the Holy Ghost in the blessedness of the One Supreme God.

THE END.

www.ingramcontent.com/pod-product-compliance
Lightning Source LLC
Chambersburg PA
CBHW071224230426
43668CB00011B/1297